Land for the People

Ohio University Research in International Studies

This series of publications on Africa, Latin America, Southeast Asia, and Global and Comparative Studies is designed to present significant research, translation, and opinion to area specialists and to a wide community of persons interested in world affairs. The editor seeks manuscripts of quality on any subject and can usually make a decision regarding publication within three months of receipt of the original work. Production methods generally permit a work to appear within one year of acceptance. The editor works closely with authors to produce a high-quality book. The series appears in a paperback format and is distributed worldwide. For more information, contact the executive editor at Ohio University Press, 19 Circle Drive, The Ridges, Athens, Ohio 45701.

Executive editor: Gillian Berchowitz
AREA CONSULTANTS
Africa: Gillian Berchowitz
Latin America: Brad Jokisch, Patrick Barr-Melej, and Rafael Obregon
Southeast Asia: Elizabeth Fuller Collins

The Ohio University Research in International Studies series is published for the Center for International Studies by Ohio University Press. The views expressed in individual volumes are those of the authors and should not be considered to represent the policies or beliefs of the Center for International Studies, Ohio University Press, or Ohio University.

Land for the People

The State and Agrarian Conflict in Indonesia

Edited by
Anton Lucas and Carol Warren

Ohio University Research in International Studies
Southeast Asia Series No. 126
Ohio University Press
Athens

© 2013 by the
Center for International Studies
Ohio University
All rights reserved

To obtain permission to quote, reprint, or otherwise reproduce or distribute material from Ohio University Press publications, please contact our rights and permissions department at (740) 593-1154 or (740) 593-4536 (fax).
www.ohioswallow.com

Printed in the United States of America
The books in the Ohio University Research in International Studies Series are printed on acid-free paper ∞ ™

20 19 18 17 16 15 14 13   5 4 3 2 1

Library of Congress Cataloging-in-Publication Data

Land for the people : the state and agrarian conflict in Indonesia / edited by Anton Lucas and Carol Warren.
    pages cm. — (Ohio University research in international studies. Southeast Asia series ; no. 126)
Includes bibliographical references and index.
Summary: "Half of Indonesia's massive population still lives on farms, and for these tens of millions of people the revolutionary promise of land reform remains largely unfulfilled. The Basic Agrarian Law, enacted in the wake of the Indonesian Revolution, was supposed to provide access to land and equitable returns for peasant farmers. But fifty years later, the law's objectives of social justice have not been achieved. Land for the People provides a comprehensive look at land conflict and agrarian reform throughout Indonesia's recent history, from the roots of land conflicts in the prerevolutionary period, and the Sukarno and Suharto regimes, to the present day, in which democratization is creating new contexts for peoples' claims to the land. Drawing on studies from across Indonesia's diverse landscape, the contributors examine some of the most significant issues and events affecting land rights, including shifts in policy from the early postrevolutionary period to the New Order; the Land Administration Project that formed the core of land policy during the late New Order period; a long-running and representative dispute over a golf course in West Java that pitted numerous indigenous farmers against the government and local elites; Suharto's notorious "million hectare" project that resulted in loss of access to land and resources for numerous indigenous farmers in Kalimantan; and the struggle by Bandung's urban poor to be treated equitably in the context of commercial land development. Together, these essays provide a critical resource for understanding one of Indonesia's most pressing and most influential issues."— Provided by publisher.
    ISBN 978-0-89680-287-2 (pb : alk. paper) — ISBN 978-0-89680-485-2 (electronic)
 1. Land reform—Indonesia. 2. Land tenure—Indonesia. 3. Land use—Indonesia. 4. Agriculture and state—Indonesia. 5. Indonesia—Rural conditions. I. Lucas, Anton E., editor of compilation. II. Warren, Carol, editor of compilation. III. Lucas, Anton E. Land, the law, and the people.
    HD1333.I5L35 2013
    333.3'1598—dc23
                                                2013005381

Tanah Untuk Rakyat (Land for the People), 1991 calendar-poster by political artist Yayak Yatmaka

About the Cover Illustration

The 1991 calendar-poster *Tanah Untuk Rakyat* (Land for the People) played a prominent role in publicizing the increasing conflict over land in Indonesia. It was created by political artist Yayak Yatmaka, also known by his other pseudonym, Iskra Ismaya. Of Yogyakarta origin, he had been a social activist since his time as a student at the Bandung Institute of Technology (ITB) in the 1970s. The poster, sponsored by eight NGOs, graphically publicizes six land disputes current at that time, including the Cimacan golf dispute covered in this volume and the well-known Kedung Ombo dam dispute. The calendar aimed to publicize the plight of farmers forcibly evicted in these land disputes. Various scenes depict conflicts between peasant farmers, holding placards asking "Where is justice?" and "Give us back our land," facing off against developers and the state, represented by figures in military and civil service uniforms and carrying placards reading "Land for palm oil and rubber plantations." A large sitting figure (Suharto?) in a blue uniform holds a bag of money labeled "foreign debt" while Uncle Sam looks down with a smaller bag of money marked IGGI (Inter-Government Group on Indonesia)/World Bank. Peasant smallholders in the disputed areas are being prevented from cultivating their land by barbed wire fences and violence from the military. In early 1991 the Indonesian attorney general banned the calendar, accusing its creator and those involved in its distribution of subversion and inciting hatred under an old colonial law. Yayak Yatmaka went into hiding and later into political exile in Germany, where his work formed the basis of a study of Indonesian political cartoons edited by Ulrich Debes and Iskra Ismaya, *High-Tech, Generäle und ein Präsident: Politische Karikaturen aus Indonesien,* Göttinger kulturwissenschaftliche Schriften 8 (Münster: LIT Verlag, 1995). Two students from Satya Wacana Christian University (UKSW), were jailed for several months, and a Gadjah Mada University student had to go into hiding abroad. Wiji Thukul, whose poem about the need for peasants to join a land rights movement was printed on the calendar, disappeared during the 1998 *reformasi* movement. Yayak Yatmaka's drawings and Wiji Thukul's poem publicized the impact of forced evictions that were widespread under the New Order. The poem remains iconic in the history of the Indonesian movement against injustice.

About a Movement

I was going to say:
I need a house
But then I changed it to:
Everyone needs land
Note: everyone
I thought about
a protest movement
but how's that possible
on my own?
I'm not a holy man
who can live on a handful of rice
and a pitcher of water
I need a shirt and a pair of pants
to cover my nakedness
I thought about a protest movement
but how's that possible
if I don't speak out?

(Anonymous poem on the calendar-poster *Tanah Untuk Rakyat*. The author, Wiji Thukul, is still missing, assumed kidnapped and later killed by the military during the 1998 *reformasi* movement.)

*For those who suffered in the struggles
for social justice and democracy in Indonesia
and those who continue to work
for the promise of "Indonesia Tanah Air."*

Contents

	Acknowledgments	xi
	Glossary	xiii
	Abbreviations	xv
	Note on Legislative References	xxi
ONE	The Land, the Law, and the People ANTON LUCAS AND CAROL WARREN	1
TWO	Land Concentration and Land Reform in Indonesia *Interpreting Agricultural Census Data, 1963–2003* DIANTO BACHRIADI AND GUNAWAN WIRADI	42
THREE	Indonesia's Land Titling Program (LAP)— the Market Solution? CAROL WARREN AND ANTON LUCAS	93
FOUR	The Cimacan Golf Course Dispute since the New Order ANTON LUCAS	114
FIVE	Oil Palm Plantations, Customary Rights, and Local Protests *A West Sumatran Case Study* AFRIZAL	149
SIX	Tenure and Transformation in Central Kalimantan *After the "Million Hectare" Project* JOHN MCCARTHY	183
SEVEN	Land Disputes and the Church *Sobering Thoughts from Flores* JOHN MANSFORD PRIOR	215

EIGHT	Legal Certainty for Whom?	
	Land Contestation and Value Transformations at Gili Trawangan, Lombok	243
	CAROL WARREN	
NINE	Dealing with the Urban Poor	
	Changing Law and Practice of Commercial Land Clearance in Post–New Order Bandung	274
	GUSTAAF REERINK	
TEN	The Agrarian Movement, Civil Society, and Emerging Political Constellations	308
	DIANTO BACHRIADI, ANTON LUCAS, AND CAROL WARREN	
ELEVEN	Agrarian Resources and Conflict in the Twenty-First Century	372
	CAROL WARREN AND ANTON LUCAS	

List of Contributors	392
Index	395

Acknowledgments

The Indonesian economic crisis and the end of the New Order regime in 1998 made the prominent land conflicts of the 1990s an even more urgent political issue, as one of the key areas driving demands for reform and democratization, including new initiatives toward decentralization and regional autonomy in the *reformasi* period. The origins of this study, an Australian Research Council grant titled "Land Tenure and Law in Indonesia: Implications for Livelihood, Community, and Environment," coincided with the early *reformasi* period, which saw an extraordinary outpouring of popular protest over long-running land disputes, six of which are included as case studies in this book. The many Indonesian informants and NGOs who shared an interest in our early research began with the Consortium for Agrarian Reform (KPA), to which we are grateful for assistance on researching the 1960s land reform program in West Java, the campaign for law reform culminating in the passing of the Policy Decision of the People's Consultative Assembly (TapMPR XI) in 2001, and more recently the passing of the new law on land acquisition. We also thank Akatiga, LBH Bali, LBH Cianjur, YLBHI Bandung, YLBHI Jakarta, YLBHI Malang, YLBHI Surabaya, Yayasan Koslata, and Yayasan Wisnu for their assistance. Workshops and conferences at Atmajaya University, Diponegoro University, Bogor Agricultural Institute (IPB), and Percik Foundation international seminars in Yogyakarta, Pekanbaru, and Salatiga saw many of the issues in this book discussed for the first time since the end of the New Order.

Although individual contributors to this volume have acknowledged assistance in the research for their own chapters, we wish to mention the advice and assistance of a number of people over the many years it has taken to bring this work to fruition: Greg Accaiolli, George Aditjondro, Dianto Bachriadi, Yudi Bachrioktora, Adrian Bedner, Franz von Benda-Beckmann, Keebet von Benda-Beckmann, Arief Djati, Noer Fauzi, Daniel Fitzpatrick, Keith Foulcher, Andik Hardiyanto, Joan Hardjono, Hardoyo, Herlambang Perdana Wiratraman, Franz Hüsken, Irwan, Arief Jati, Yudi Junaidi, Iwan Nurdin, Jan-Michiel Otto, Nancy Peluso, Pratikno, Gatot Rianto, Maria Ruwiastuti, Hilma Savitri, Jim Schiller, Usep Setiawan, Mohamad Shohibuddin, Nyoman Sirtha, Endriatmo Soetarto, Indro Tjahyono, Sediono Tjondronegoro, Leontine Visser, Ben White, Gunawan Wiradi, Roger Wiseman, and Yando Zacharia. Thanks to Bec Donaldson for editorial assistance.

Special thanks to the Asia Research Centre at Murdoch University, which was home for the project, and the Van Vollenhoven Institute of Law, Governance and Development at Leiden University, which made available its excellent law library and hosted several of the contributors to the book.

The editors wish to thank the Cornell University Southeast Asia Program for permission to republish revised and updated material from the article coauthored by Anton Lucas and Carol Warren entitled "The State, the People, and Their Mediators: The Struggle over Agrarian Law Reform in Post–New Order Indonesia" from *Indonesia*, no. 76 (October 2003): 87–124, and the Institute of Southeast Asian Studies (ISEAS) for permission to republish materials from the chapter coauthored by Anton Lucas and Carol Warren entitled "Agrarian Reform in the Era of *Reformasi*" in *Indonesia in Transition: Social Aspects of Reformasi and Crisis,* edited by Chris Manning and Peter van Diermen (Singapore: ISEAS, 2000), 220–38, in chapters 1 and 10; reproduced here with kind permission of the publisher, Institute of Southeast Asian Studies, Singapore, <http://bookshop.iseas.esu.sg>.

The editors also wish to thank Leiden University Press for permission to reprint a revised version of chapter 7 of G. O. Reerink, *Tenure Security for Indonesia's Urban Poor: A Socio-Legal Study on Land Decentralisation and the Rule of Law in Bandung* (Leiden: Leiden University Press, 2011), 187–211, as chapter 9.

Glossary

adat—customary practice and law
bupati—head of district-level government (*kabupaten*)
caco—middleman, rent seeker
desa—administrative village
girik garapan—land tax assessment
ganti rugi—compensation for loss
hak milik—individual ownership, private title
hak pakai—use rights
hak ulayat—customary or communal rights
Hari Tani—Peasants' Day
izin lokasi—location permit
kampung—urban settlement
kecamatan—subdistrict
kelurahan—administrative unit
nagari—traditional administrative unit of Minangkabau (West Sumatran) society
ninik mamak—*adat* chief, clan leader
pasal—article (legal)
pelepasan hak—renunciation of (land) rights
pembebasan tanah—compulsory release of title or occupancy
petani gurem—small peasants
pilkades—*pihihan kepala desa,* village head elections
preman—hired thugs
rakyat—the common people
reformasi—post–Suharto era reform movement
ruilslag—land compensation swap or exchange

tanah adat—customary land

tanah negara—state land

tanah terlantar—neglected or abandoned land

transmigrasi—transmigration; shifting landless peasants from Java to Outer Island settlements

> *Except where otherwise indicated, translations from the Indonesian language are those of the author(s) of each chapter.*

Abbreviations

AJM—Asian Journal of Mining

AMAN—Aliansi Masyarakat Adat Nusantara (Alliance of Indigenous [Adat] Peoples of the Archipelago)

AMAN NTT—Alliance of Indigenous Peoples of East Nusa Tenggara Province (Flores)

AMDAL—Analisa Mengenai Dampak Lingkungan (Environmental Impact Analysis)

AMUK—Aliansi Masyarakat Untuk Keadilan (Community Alliance for Justice—Cimacan case)

API—Aliansi Petani Indonesia (Indonesian Peasants Alliance)

BAL—Basic Agrarian Law (also UUPA)

BKD—Badan Keuangan Daerah (Regional [District] Government Financial Agency)

BKN—Badan Keuangan Negara ([National] Government Financial Agency)

BKSDA—Badan Konservasi Sumber Daya Alam (Natural Resources Conservation Agency)

BMD—Badan Musyawarah Desa (Village Consultative Council)

BPD—Badan Perwakilan Desa (Village Representative Council in Reform Era); Badan Permusyawaratan Desa (Village Consultation Council) after 2004 revision of the UU 22/1999 Law on Local Government

BPN—Badan Pertanahan Nasional (National Land Agency)

BPS—Badan [previously Biro] Pusat Statistik (Indonesian Bureau of Statistics)

Brimob—Brigade-mobil (police mobile brigade)

CAPS—Centre for Agricultural Policy Studies

DPD—Dewan Pemerintah Daerah (Regional Government Assembly)

DPR—Dewan Perwakilan Rakyat (People's Representative Assembly [National Legislature])

DPRD—Dewan Perwakilan Rakyat Daerah (Regional People's Representative Assembly)

FMPS—Forum Mahasiswa Peduli Sosial (Socially Concerned University Students Forum)

FPPB—Forum Perjuangan Petani Batang (Batang Peasants' Advocacy Forum—Central Java)

FSPI—Federasi Serikat Petani Indonesia (Federation of Indonesian Peasants' Unions)

GBHN—Garis Besar Haluan Negara (Guidelines of State Policy)

GPI—Gerakan Pemuda Islam (Islamic Youth Movement)

HGB—Hak Guna Bangunan (Building Use Right)

HGU—Hak Guna Usaha (Commercial Use Right)

HKTI—Himpunan Kerukunan Tani Indonesia (Indonesian Harmonious Peasants' Union)

HPH—Hak Pengelolaan Hutan (Forest Concession Right)

HPHH—Hak Pemungutan Hasil Hutan (Forest Harvesting Right)

HPKH—Hak Pakai Kawasan Hutan (Forestry Use Right)

HPL—Hak Pakai Lahan (Land Use Right)

HTI—Hak Tanaman Industri (industrial timber plantation lease)

ICESC—International Covenant on Economic, Social, and Cultural Rights

ILAP—Indonesian Land Administration Project (see LAP)

IMB—Izin Mendirikan Bangunan (Building Permit)

IPEDA—Iuran Pembangunan Daerah (Regional Development Tax)

IPK—Indeks Prestasi Kumulatif (cumulative grade point average)

JAGAD NTT—Jaringan Antara Gerakan Adat Daerah (Network of Indigenous Peoples' Movements of East Nusa Tenggara Province)

JKPP—Jaringan Kerja Pemetaan Partisipatif (Participatory Mapping Network)

KAN—Kerapatan Adat Nagari (Nagari Adat Council–West Sumatra)

KARAM—Tanah Koalisi Rakyat Tolak Perampasan Tanah (People's Coalition against Land Grabbing)

KepMenag—Keputusan Menteri Agraria (Minister of Agrarian Affairs Decision)

KepPres—Keputusan Presiden (Presidential Decree)

KKPA—Kredit Koperasi Primer untuk Anggota (Credit for Primary Cooperative Members)

KomnasHAM—Komisi Nasional Hak Asasi Manusia (National Commission on Human Rights)

KON—Komisi Ombudsman Nasional (National Ombudsman Commission)

KPA—Konsorsium Pembaruan Agraria (Consortium for Agrarian Reform)

KSPA—Kelompok Studi Pembaruan Agraria (Agrarian Reform Study Group)

LAP—Land Administration Project (titling project funded by Indonesian government, World Bank, and AusAID)

LARASITA—Layanan Rakyat untuk Sertifikasi Tanah (Serving the People with Land Certification)

LASA—Land Administration System Australia

LBH—Lembaga Bantuan Hukum (Legal Aid Institute, later YLBHI)

LBHNT—Lembaga Bantuan Hukum Nusa Tenggara Timur (Legal Aid Institute of the Province of NTT–Flores)

LKMD—Lembaga Ketahanan Masyarakat Desa (village community resilience board)

LMD—Lembaga Musyawarah Desa (Village Consultative Board)

LMPDP—Land Management and Policy Development Project, successor to LAP

LPM—Lembaga Pengembangan Masyarakat (community development board)

LPMA—Lembaga Persekutuan Masyarakat Adat (Alliance of Indigenous Community Organizations–Flores)

LPPT—Lembaga Pengembangan dan Pendidikan Pedesaan (Institute for Village Development and Education)

LRA—Lembaga Riset dan Advokasi (Advocacy and Research Institute)

MP3EI—*Masterplan Percepatan dan Perluasan Pembangunan Ekonomi Indonesia* (Master Plan for Accelerating and Expanding Indonesia's Economic Development)

MPR—Majelis Permusyawaratan Rakyat (People's Consultative Assembly)

Muspida—Musyawarah pimpinan daerah (district-level executive consultation)

NTT—Nusa Tenggara Timur (East Nusatenggara Province)

P3 (PPP)—Partai Persatuan Pembangunan (Development Unity Party; Muslim party)

PAD—Pendapatan Asli Daerah (revenue generated at provincial or district levels)

PAN—Partai Amanat Nasional (National Mandate Party; Muslim party)

PAP—Proyek Administrasi Pertanahan (Land Administration Project—see LAP)

PBB—Pajak Bumi dan Bangunan (Land and Buildings Tax)

PBB—Persatuan Bangsa Bangsa (United Nations)

PDBI—Pusat Data Bisnis Indonesia (Indonesian Business Data Center)

PDI-P—Partai Demokrat Indonesia-Perjuangan (Indonesian Democratic Party-Struggle)

Pemda—Pemerintah Daerah—refers to the two levels of regional government—provincial (*propinsi/tingkat* I) and district (*kabupaten/tingkat* II). Since decentralization, it typically refers to district and municipal (*kabupaten/kota*) government

PerMenag—Peraturan Menteri Agraria (Agrarian Ministerial Regulation)

PerMendagri—Peraturan Menteri Dalam Negeri (Home Affairs Ministerial Regulation)

PHBK—Pengelolaan Hutan Berbasis Komunitas (community-based forest management)

PHBM—Pengelolaan Hutan Bersama Masyarakat (community-based forest management)

PIR-Bun—Perusahaan Inti Rakyat Perkebunan (nucleus estate and smallholder plantations)

PKB—Partai Kebangkitan Bangsa (National Awakening Party; Muslim party)

PKI—Partai Komunis Indonesia (Indonesian Communist Party)

PKK—Pembinaan Kesejahteraan Keluarga (Family Welfare Organization, a women's group; after 1999 Pemberdayaan Kesejahteraan Keluarga, Family Empowerment Organization)

PKS—Partai Keadilan Sosial (Social Justice Party; Islamic party)

PLG—Proyek [Pengembangan] Lahan Gambut (Peat Land Development Project)

PP—Peraturan Pemerintah (government regulation)

PPAN—Program Pembaruan Agraria Nasional (National Agrarian Reform Program)

PPP—public-private partnerships (Kerjasama Operasi)

PPR—Partai Perserikatan Rakyat (People's Confederation Party)

PRD—Partai Rakyat Demokrasi (People's Democratic Party)

PRONA—Proyek Operasi Nasional Agraria (Agrarian National Operation Project)

PSDA—pengelolaan sumber daya alam (natural resources management)

PT Diag—Perseroan Terbatas Dioses Agung Ende (Ende Archdiocese Pty. Ltd., diocesan plantation company, Flores)

PTUN—Pengadilan Tata Usaha Negeri (administrative courts)

PT-TUN—Pengadilan Tinggi Tata Usaha Negara (higher administrative courts)

REDD—Reducing Emissions from Deforestation and Forest Degradation

REDD+—national program to implement REDD

RK—Rukun Kampung (kampung association)

RT—Rukun Tetangga (neighborhood association)

RTK—Register Tanah Kehutanan (Forest Land Register)

RTRWK—Rencana Tata Ruang Wilayah Kabupaten (district spatial plan)

RW—Rukun Warga (also called RK; subhamlet association)

SAE—Survei Agro Ekonomika (Agro Economy Survey Foundation)

SBY—Susilo Bambang Yudoyono (Indonesian President)

SK—Surat Keterangan (also Surat Keputusan; letter of clarification, decision, decree)

SKD—Surat Keterangan Domisili (residential identification)

SKEPHI—Seketariat Kerjasama Pelestarian Hutan Indonesia (Secretariat for Forest Conservation in Indonesia)

SK Menteri Pertanian—Surat Keputusan Menteri Pertanian (Decree of Minister of Agriculture)

SPI—Serikat Petani Indonesia (Indonesian Peasants Union, formerly FSPI)

SPJB—Sarekat Petani Jawa Barat (West Java Peasants' Union)

SPP—Serikat Petani Pasundan (Sundanese Peasants' Union [West Java])

STaB—Serikat Tani Bengkulu (Bengkulu Peasants' Union [Sumatra])

STPN—Sekolah Tinggi Pertanahan Nasional (National Land College)

SUPENAS—*Survei Penduduk Antar Sensus* (Intercensus Population Survey)

TGHK—*Tata Guna Hutan Kesepakatan* (Agreement on Forest Use—maps showing forest functions)

TNGP—Taman Nasional Gde-Pangrango (Mount Gede-Pangrango National Park)

UU—Undang-Undang (law or act)

UUPA—Undang-Undang Pokok Agararia (Basic Agrarian Law [BAL] of 1960)

WALHI—Wahana Lingkungan Hidup Indonesia (Friends of the Earth Indonesia—Indonesian's peak environmental network)

YLBHI—Yayasan Lembaga Bantuan Hukum Indonesia (Indonesian Legal Aid Institute Foundation—formerly LBH)

Note on Legislative References

Agrarian and natural resource management laws and regulations cited in this book can be found at the Agrarian Resource Center (ARC), Jalan Ice Skating No. 33 Arcamanik, Bandung 40293 Indonesia (which also holds copies of the original calendar-poster "Tanah Untuk Rakyat"); in various editions of B. Harsono, *Hukum Agraria Indonesia: Himpunan Peraturan-Peraturan Hukum Tanah* (Jakarta: Penerbit Jambatan); in R. Soedargo, *Perundangan-Undangan Agraria Indonesia Djilid I* (Bandung: N.V Eresco, 1962); at http://www.hukumonline.com/ and on the website of KPA (Consortium for Agrarian Affairs), http://www.kpa.or.id/?page_id=408.

The following abbreviations for types of legislation are listed in order of importance in the Indonesian legislative hierarchy. The law or regulation number is followed by the year of promulgation; § indicates article and section. For example, UU 5/1979 §7(2) refers to Law number 5 of 1979, article (*pasal*) 7, section 2.

UU—Undang-Undang (National Law)

PP—Peraturan Pemerintah (Government Regulation)

KepPres—Keputusan Presiden (Presidential Decision/Decree)

PerMenag—Peraturan Menteri Agraria (Agrarian Ministerial Regulation)

PerMendagri—Peraturan Menteri Dalam Negeri (Home Affairs Ministerial Regulation)

SK Menteri Pertanian—Surat Keputusan Menteri Pertanian (Agriculture Ministerial Decree)

Chapter 1

THE LAND, THE LAW, AND THE PEOPLE

ANTON LUCAS AND CAROL WARREN

No one seems to realize that Indonesia is entering a period of social revolution. The signs are there. It can be seen in the farmers who, having had their land stolen from them during the New Order, are now taking it back by force. It can be seen in the protests by farmers outside regional assembly buildings. It can be seen in the attacks on hundreds of police and military posts. In the past, these very same people would have let themselves be robbed of their voices, but now they are fighting back. Whether they realize it or not, they are the vanguard of a social revolution.

—Pramoedya Ananta Toer[1]

When Sundanese villagers carved "*Tanah Rakyat*" (People's Land) onto the fairway of the Cimacan golf course in 1998, shortly after the official demise of the "New Order" regime of President Suharto, they staked a claim against an unredeemed promise of the Indonesian revolution. Land and the welfare of ordinary people have been intrinsic to popular understandings of Indonesian nationhood since the early years of the nationalist movement.

At every significant juncture in Indonesia's recent history, land issues have played a pivotal role. "Land for the People" was the catchphrase of the land reform movement and peasant actions supported by the Communist Party (PKI) in the postrevolutionary period. Land issues were at the heart of the intense political conflict that ended in the anticommunist massacres of 1965–66 and the takeover by army general Suharto. Three decades later, land conflicts contributed to the overwhelming popular animosity that eventually ended Suharto's authoritarian rule.

Land tenure and access issues embody powerful tensions between elites and popular forces, between regional interests and central government, and between Indonesian national and transnational capital. The foundational importance of the land question was expressed in the 1960 Basic Agrarian Law, arguably the most important piece of legislation after the Indonesian constitution. Paradoxically this same piece of legislation oversaw diametrically opposed policies of the Old Order Sukarno (1950–65) and New Order Suharto (1966–98) regimes, and remains today a contentious focal point in the struggle for social justice by marginalized sectors of Indonesia's population.

The Basic Agrarian Law under Old and New Orders

In the postrevolutionary period there were high expectations that the government of Indonesia's first president, Sukarno, would deliver to the predominantly rural and poor population the well-being (*kesejahteraan*) they had been promised. After a decade of debate and political struggle, the Basic Agrarian Law was finally promulgated on 24 September 1960,[2] as the centerpiece of Sukarno's efforts to fuse nationalist, socialist, and populist political commitments. It asserted the "social function" of land and other resources,[3] reiterated the state's responsibility for managing those resources in the interests of "the people," prohibited absentee and foreign ownership of land, and paved the way for the redistribution of land through subsequent land reform legislation.[4] The Basic Agrarian Law (BAL/UUPA 5/60) has been so intimately connected with the ideological formation of the Indonesian nation, that it acquired almost sacrosanct status from its inception. The date of its proclamation is still annually celebrated as "Hari Tani" (Peasants' Day),[5] accompanied by public awards, seminars, and editorials in the national newspapers. But its "social function" principle had contradictory interpretations under the Sukarno (Old Order) and Suharto (New Order) regimes, with different implications for land poor and landless laborers of "inner island" Indonesia and the indigenous minorities occupying customary lands, primarily in the forested "outer islands" of the country.

UUPA/BAL:
The "Social Function" of Land and Land Reform

The implementation of land reform, the popular socialist cornerstone of the Basic Agrarian Law, depended on complex enabling legislation that was intended to limit the size of land holdings by individuals and redistribute surplus agricultural lands. Law No. 56/1960 set the maximum ceiling for landholdings according to land use, varying from five hectares of riceland in very densely populated areas to fifteen hectares in sparsely populated areas, and six to twenty hectares respectively for drylands (UU56/1960, §1/2). The act also charged the government with efforts to provide every peasant family with a minimum of two hectares of arable land (§8), an "arithmetic impossibility" on crowded Java, according to Mortimer (1972, 16–17), who regarded this minimum land stipulation "as a symbolic display of goodwill rather than as something to be given practical effect." Subsequent implementing regulations explained what land could be redistributed, how owners were to be compensated (PP 224/1961), and provided for a minimum 50:50 division of harvest in sharecropping agreements (UU 2/1960).

The Sukarno government planned to implement the land reform program in two stages over a three- to five-year period.[6] However, the redistribution process was very slow and insufficient to deal with the problem.

Wolf Ladejinsky, an expert on land reform, made several visits in the early 1960s to assess Indonesia's land redistribution program. These were sponsored by the Ford Foundation and the Agricultural Development Council, which regarded agrarian reform as "a necessary anti-communist strategy" (Shohibuddin 2009, xiv). Ladejinsky had misgivings about the Indonesian program, concluding that there was not enough land in Java for a significant land redistribution progam even if the maximum five hectares holding were reduced. "So long as the rural population continues to grow at the current rate, competing for a virtually fixed area of nine million hectares of cultivated land, the attainment of better tenure conditions is a very difficult task. In short, though a confirmed land reformer, I am of the opinion that the real issue in Java (and Bali) is not land redistribution but population redistribution on the one hand and a breakthrough in agricultural productivity on the other" (Walinsky 1977, 349). Ladejinsky was also concerned that no thought had been given to the pricing and financing of land to be redistributed or to the difficulties that the district land reform committees faced in enforcing reform because of conflicts between landholders and landless farmers. He noted that "despite the stated and implied promises of land to the tiller, the [BAL] enabling document is shot through with conservative safeguards in order to prevent any significant redistribution of land" (Walinsky 1977, 298).[7]

The events of 1965 dramatically reversed the political fortunes of the forces supporting land reform. The massacres and mass arrests of the main advocates of land reform—the PKI and its affiliated organizations, in particular the peasant organization Barisan Tani Indonesia (BTI)—and the dismantling of the land reform administration practically stalled the implementation of the program,[8] although the land reform law itself was never formally repealed (Utrecht 1969, 86–88; Mortimer 1972, 63–68; Huizer 1980, 122–26).

A later study of the fate of land actually redistributed during the program in three regions (five villages) in West Java by Bachriadi and Lucas (2001b) highlights the extent of corruption and manipulation at the village level in the New Order period.[9] Outcomes varied significantly depending on the actions of the village headman, the survival of local BTI leaders who still had copies of land registers recording 1962–68 land redistributions, and attitudes of local officials. Many local officials stopped implementing the land reform program after Suharto came to power, and some were involved in the illegal selling of redistributed land during the 1970s. In one of the Garut district villages (Simpen) 88 percent (276 of the 313 landholders) who obtained blocks of redistributed land are still cultivating it, whereas in the neighboring village of Pangeureunan in the same subdistrict, only 7 percent (14 of the 206 original recipients) still control the land they received. In both south Cianjur villages, 80 percent of cultivators still control their redistributed land. In Indramayu, the 42 percent of peasants who received redistributed state land were disenfranchised by the village head who "borrowed" the land redistribution letters (referred to as SK Redis—*Surat Keterangan Redistribusi*) and sold the land off.[10] The land redistribution process in the five villages studied had specific conditions attached, the most important of which were that each recipient had to pay for the land plus interest in annual installments over fifteen years; that until the land had been paid off in full, rights to the redistributed land could not be transferred; and that the farmer who received redistributed land was obliged to "actively cultivate it himself" (Surat Keputusan 1966).

Despite its negative association with the PKI's dramatic growth in popularity, land reform remained a popular concept among ordinary people in rural Indonesia. For this reason, land reform continued to be given lip service over the decades since Suharto's take over in 1965. In practice, however, it was completely sidelined by large-scale transmigration programs, shifting landless peasants from Java to outer island settlements, and the intensification and commercialization of agriculture, which were much more compatible with the capital intensive development drive of the New Order period. Bachriadi and Wiranto trace the impacts of changing state agrarian policies through an analysis of the agricultural census data from 1963 through 2003 in chapter 2 of this volume.

UUPA/BAL:
The Social Function of Land and *ADAT* Communities

The Basic Agrarian Law is associated with progressive social policies of the postrevolutionary Sukarno era that were popularly perceived to advantage the land poor and landless farmers of the rice-growing heartland of Inner Indonesia, mainly on Java where the majority of Indonesia's population was concentrated. But it does not have the same meaning for customary (*adat*) landholding groups in the sparsely populated forested areas of the Outer Islands. These minority ethnic cultures traditionally depended on shifting cultivation, requiring extensive fallow areas for forest regeneration to maintain their livelihoods and traditional ways of life.

The agrarian law of the nation and particularly its "social function" principles were proclaimed to be based ultimately on *adat* (customary law) (BAL/UUPA 5/1960, §5. Elucidation A3/1). Indeed, the legal framework for land and natural resource management effectively takes the *adat* concept of customary territorial rights of avail (*hak ulayat*)[11] and converts it to a national principle: "The land, water and atmosphere, including natural resources within them are controlled by the State at its highest level, as the organizational authority of all the people" (BAL/UUPA 5/1960, §2.1). In appropriating the local principle of customary community rights of precedence to the higher scale of national governance, however, the ground was laid for the transgression of local indigenous rights whenever a wider "national interest" claim could be invoked. As a result, despite rhetorical recognition of *adat* values as the foundation of Indonesian land law, the subordination of local customary rights to national interest claims was ultimately rationalized by the same evolutionary developmentalist ethos that had previously underpinned colonial policy and law.[12] The explanatory notes to the legislation go into considerable detail to make clear that the "recognition" that *adat* peoples have the right to receive, "does not permit legal communities based on *adat*, for example, to reject out of hand the opening of forest on a large scale for regulated implementation of large projects for increasing food output or resettlement of populations." Thus the oft-invoked qualification that *hak ulayat* territorial rights of *adat* communities are acknowledged only so long as they are "in accord with the national and State interest" and do not "conflict with higher laws" (BAL/UUPA 5/60 §3 and Elucidation II/3) underscored what became the defining experience of outer island minority cultures. The populist-socialist construction of the BAL was easily transformed by a regime with a different agenda into policies that expropriated customary lands to become sites for the mining, timber, and plantation concessions liberally dispensed to Indonesian conglomerates and foreign investors under Suharto. The transmigration program enabled the New Order to circumvent genuine land reform, provide labor for outer island resource development, and impose national unity through demographic redistribution and neocolonial cultural policies.[13]

The Basic Agrarian Law itself contains fundamental ambiguities and contradictions that facilitated the subversion of its foundational social function principles. Its overriding emphasis on a nationalist construction of popular interests became the most often cited legal justification, but its evolutionary presuppositions are also an expression of those revolutionary times. Although the Basic Agrarian Law's social function principle—restricting accumulation, prohibiting foreign ownership, and providing for land redistribution—had been geared to constrain the unfettered transformation of land into a commodity where social functions would be subordinated to antisocial market forces,[14] paradoxically the BAL/UUPA privileges the Western evolutionary legal concept of private property (*hak milik*) as the "strongest and most complete form" of title, with full rights of alienation and inheritance (BAL/UUPA 5/60, §20).[15] In contrast, as Fitzpatrick (1997, 2007) emphasizes, the customary *"hak ulayat"* claims of *adat* communities are not granted full statutory legitimacy under the BAL. *Adat* forms of tenure were assumed to "evolve" over time into individualized property rights (Fitzpatrick 1997, 188). The state would now be proxy to the collective priority over individual interest that had been the underlying principle of *adat* regimes. This interpretation permitted a situation in which "the state regularly denies formal rights to occupiers of virgin or abandoned land on the basis that it holds a "state *hak ulayat*' (Fitzpatrick 1997, 207). None of the regulatory provisions pursuant to the BAL/UUPA included *"adat* communities" as legitimate title-holding entities (Fitzpatrick 1997, 187–88).[16]

When Suharto came to power in 1966, following the violent suppression of the Communist Party, the "national interest" principle of the Basic Agrarian Law became the Achilles heel in the battleground over agrarian resources that continues to plague the "Reform Era." The BAL/UUPA was reinterpreted, reorienting the national interest proviso of the law to equate the people's well-being with the state's capital-intensive developmentalist program. Perverting the basic intent of the law to serve the private interests of Suharto's cronies, the New Order's policy orientation has been well described by Campbell (1999) as "reverse land reform." Although Campbell was referring to the expropriation of forest land belonging to *adat* communities for timber concessions, it is an apt description of the broader range of policy changes that facilitated land concentration in the hands of elite political-business interests during the New Order period—a concentration of resources that the BAL explicitly describes as "harming the public interest" (§7 and Elucidation II/7).

Whenever the Basic Agrarian Law proved inconvenient for the New Order regime, it was reinterpreted or ignored. A body of sectoral legislation on natural resource extraction undermined the integral relationship of land and resources with the needs of the common person that the Basic Agrarian Law had been intended to convey.[17] Where the BAL at least acknowledged local rights based on *adat* so long as they did not conflict with national law and interest, New Order mining and forestry laws, introduced the year after Suharto took power, stripped even residual rights from *adat* communities. The Basic Forestry Law of 1967 excluded some 70 percent of Indonesia's land area classified as forest from the provisions of the Basic Agrarian Law, and facilitated legal disenfranchisement of whole populations from ancestral lands. In exercising the nation's claim over the then vast forested land mass, New Order legislation appropriated to the state the exclusive and unqualified right of management and allocation of resource extraction rights, with only negligible provision for compensation to the original inhabitants dependent on these resources (Fitzpatrick 2007, 133–39; Bedner and van Huis 2008, 181–84).[18]

Although state policy and practice on agrarian issues dramatically altered the relationship between the land, the law, and the people under the New Order, it is worthy of note that over the three decades of Suharto's authoritarian rule the Basic Agrarian Law was never repealed or revised. This might be surprising given its overtly socialist premises and the association of the land reform issue with the dramatic rise of the Communist Party of Indonesia (PKI) in the early 1960s. It is perhaps less so, considering that the socialist and populist causes it reflected have been so intimately identified with Indonesian nationalism from its inception, and proved at least rhetorically necessary to achieve a semblance of legitimacy for the Suharto government and its military power base.[19]

It was the remolding of the state's role and its revised construction of the "national interest" principle in the disposition of "state land" (*tanah negara*) that caused the most acute conflicts between the "People" and the "State" in the high developmentalist period of the Late New Order from 1988 to 1998. Lands claimed by the state as "*tanah negara*" comprised vast tracts of forest inhabited by indigenous minorities in outer Indonesia, as well as former colonial plantation estates that had been occupied for decades by peasant cultivators in Java and Sumatra. These became attractive and lucrative sites for the voracious capital intensive megadevelopment projects for which the last ten years of the Suharto Era became notorious.

Anatomy of Land Disputes in the Late New Order

By the 1990s the land issue had become the single most prominent cause of conflict between the government and the heavily repressed civil society under the New Order. Despite political impediments to resistance, open protest and official complaints rose steadily in the last decade of the regime. The National Land Agency (BPN) recorded

1,395 complaints submitted in the six-month period before the end of 1998 (BPN 1999a, 1999b).[20] Land disputes made up the largest number of cases dealt with by the newly established Administrative Courts (PTUN) and National Human Rights Commission (Komnas HAM) at that time (see table 1.1 in the chapter appendix).[21] Between July 1994 and September 1996, Komnas HAM (1997) recorded 891 incidents of human rights abuses involving land expropriation, collated from reports in twenty-eight regional newspapers.[22]

Annually published Human Rights Commission data on land cases handled since its establishment in 1994 give some indication of the escalation and growing visibility of the land issue. In 1994 the commission dealt with 101 official complaints involving land issues, rising to 351 complaints in 1997, a threefold increase over the final four years of the New Order. In all but one year since 1991, land disputes represented the largest single category of cases brought to the Jakarta Administrative Court.

The Consortium for Agrarian Reform (KPA), the umbrella nongovernment organization that coordinates 187 affiliated peoples' organizations and NGOs from twenty-three provinces concerned with agrarian issues, compiled an inventory of structural land conflicts since 1970.[23] As of 2001, they had documented 1,753 cases covering 10.8 million hectares of land and affecting more than a million people. These "structural" cases, which were a systematic consequence of state policy, involved disputes between local people and one or a combination of government (42 percent), private (45 percent), and state (10 percent) corporations, and the military (3 percent). Direct military involvement in these disputes is reported in 7 percent of the cases covered.[24]

Of the 553 land conflict cases with which Indonesia's Legal Aid Foundation (YLBHI) dealt in 1998, the year that brought the demise of the New Order, 26 percent were due to the establishment of large-scale plantations, 23 percent to land clearance for industrial, residential, and tourist projects, and 13 percent to forest, mining, and aquaculture developments (YLBHI 1998, 1–4). The remaining "nonstructural" cases included complaints about the issuance of false land certificates, road expansion, and misappropriation by government officials. The disputes dealt with by the Legal Aid Foundation in 1998 alone involved a total of 827,000 hectares of land, and affected the livelihoods of more than a million people (see table 1.2 in the chapter appendix).

The 1998 Legal Aid Foundation report (YLBHI 1998) also provides what little information is available on the regional distribution of land conflicts. It reveals that 58 percent of the 553 cases it dealt with across fourteen of Indonesia's then twenty-seven provinces were located outside Java. However, 99 percent of the total land area and 95 percent of the total households affected were in these Outer Island provinces (table 1.2). It is reasonable to assume that land issues were even more acute at the periphery than these already heavily skewed statistics suggest. There is little information on the other thirteen relatively remote provinces, where it was much less likely that cases would find their way to legal aid networks.

* * *

In the early 1990s, the land question was one of the key issues taken up by student activists and nongovernment organizations (NGOs) in Indonesia. The political response to the satiric "Land for the People" (*Tanah untuk Rakyat*) calendar (see Lucas 1992 and cover illustration to this book) drew attention to the plight of farmers forced off their land without meaningful compensation. In Java, most of the large-scale land clearances under the late New Order involved urban and industrial expansion at the expense of squatter settlements, or the resumption of lands (often former colonial plantations) occupied and in some cases redistributed to local farmers in the land reform period between 1961 and Suharto's takeover in 1966.[25] Large-scale land clearances were associated with capital-intensive developments such as golf course/resort complexes, infrastructure, industrial and residential estates, or reforestation and new plantation concessions. The principal issues in these cases were the unresolved tenure status of smallholders on former colonial plantations and the aborted land reform program after 1965 that left most farmers without legal title, the consequent weakness of their position in the negotiation process, and the inadequacy of compensation.

Government regulations theoretically gave farmers occupying plantation lands some basis for claims to occupied land as long as these rights did not conflict with land use regulations or national interest development projects.[26] Where (as in most cases) plantation workers and peasant farmers did not hold certificates of title, compensation claims were easily discounted, however. These regulations, all derived from the Basic Agrarian Law, should have given some legal protection to long-term occupants of plantation land. Particularly where those lands had been occupied since the revolution, the popular expectation had been that land reform would lead to recognition of smallholder title.[27] But by the Late New Order (1988–98) the demands of "development," equating the "national interest" with those of conglomerates and their political patrons, invariably meant that well-connected investors were privileged over "illegal" occupants. The number of disputes on former plantation lands that persist into the present is a legacy of this unfulfilled promise of agrarian reform, particularly with respect to the claims of smallholder peasants and farm laborers on former Dutch plantation lands, converted under the New Order to HGU commercial cultivation right concessions.[28]

By 1992 large plantation estate leases covered 3.8 million hectares,[29] held by 1,206 foreign and domestic companies with an average holding of more than 3,000 hectares each (Bachriadi 1997, 128). This compared with the average size family holding of less than 0.5 hectares of agricultural land (1993 Agricultural Census). This figure for land accumulation in the plantation sector rose to more than five million hectares with subsequent conversion of large tracts of forest especially to oil palm plantations.[30] According to Ministry of Forestry and Crop Estates statistics, between 1982 and 1999 permits were issued to twelve conglomerates for conversion of more than four million hectares of Indonesia's forests to plantations. The Salim conglomerate alone, with its close connections to Suharto, was able to obtain in-principle permits (*izin prinsip*) for conversion of 1.2 million hectares of forest to oil palm estates in this period (Casson 2000, 24–25). Even smallholder farmers outside the plantation sector with legally certified title were often unable to protect their tenure in the face of corrupt officials acting in the name of "development" and backed by the state security apparatus.

To give some indication of the scale of land speculation associated with plantation, industrial, and real estate development, and of the amount of land withdrawn from smallholder agriculture and other productive purposes over the late New Order period, National Land Board records show that between 1993 and 1998 it had issued location permits (*izin lokasi*)[31] for development projects over some three million hectares of land throughout Indonesia. Most of this (96 percent) was for plantation developments. By 1998, 62 percent of the land on which location permits had been issued had been acquired by big business interests, but only a quarter of that land had actually been developed, leaving large amounts of "sleeping lands" (*tanah tidur*) at the time of the collapse of the Suharto regime.[32] These were technically "neglected" (*terlantar*), and according to the Basic Agrarian Law, rights in such land whether cultivation use rights (HGU) or private freehold rights (*hak milik*) should be automatically canceled. The issue of neglected plantation land remained a festering sore throughout the New Order.[33] Thousands of hectares of these lands became objects of reclaiming actions when Suharto fell from power in 1998. Across Indonesia, plantation crops were removed and food crops planted during the euphoric first months of the reform (*reformasi*) movement. Formal resolution of these cases remains one of the most intractable issues facing the successive governments of the post-Suharto Reform Era.

Tables 1.3 and 1.4 (see chapter appendix) show the magnitude of the "sleeping land" problem. By 1998 the BPN had issued location permits (*izin lokasi*) over an area of over three million hectares for several different land uses. Of that three million hectares, only 481,558 hectares (16 percent) had actually been developed. It should be noted that much of the undeveloped land had been subject to the notorious New Order compulsory release of title (*pembebasan tanah*) procedure. The Basic Agrarian Law does not deal with the issue of acquisition of land by private commercial interests. According to its provisions, land could only be compulsorily acquired by government in the public interest by presidential decree (UUPA 5/1960; Harsono 1996, 11, 890). In practice, during the New Order private interests also acquired compulsorily resumed land, although they had to have a location permit before applying for formal rights (HGU, HGB, or HPL) on such land.[34]

The very low prices at which land could be extracted from cultivators encouraged speculation and profiteering by developers and their intermediaries. Before the financial crisis of 1998, large landholdings were a means of obtaining bank credit in Indonesia, and selling of rights to foreign investors was a lucrative avenue for wealth accumulation by Indonesian conglomerates and local "calo."[35] In order to solve the demand for land by private investors (both domestic and foreign), regulations on release of title procedures were promulgated in 1975 and 1993. Although theoretically based on the prevailing market price, in practice compensation was invariably much lower. Although people had the right to refuse sale of their land by law where the purpose of land acquisition had nothing to do with public interest, in practice landholders were accused of being "antidevelopment," "subversive," or "ex-communist" if they attempted to exercise that right. Most people surrendered their land rather than risk being subjected to intimidation or attack. The role of the military in securing the interests of business concerns, often allied with the Suharto family, by assisting the process of land acquisition is well documented.[36]

The years leading up to the dramatic and unpredicted collapse of the Suharto regime in 1998 were marked by increasing conflict over land in both rural and urban Indonesia. A wave of direct actions to reoccupy lands resumed for development projects and to reclaim resources allocated to conglomerate interests became a prominent part of the political reform movement. But the new democratically elected governments of the post-Suharto "Reform Era" have remained ambivalent on these highly sensitive issues of land reform and *adat* rights, with the partial exception of Presidents Wahid and Yudhoyono.[37]

Reformasi: Land Occupations and Other People's Actions

A dramatic resurgence of agrarian protest and direct actions swept Indonesia in the wake of Suharto's resignation. In actions reminiscent of the peasant unilateral occupations of the early 1960s, dispossessed farmers involved in land disputes, some running for decades, took direct action to rectify their grievances. These "reclaiming" actions included occupation of plantation estates,[38] golf courses,[39] and neglected "sleeping land" acquired by investors for speculative purposes.[40] In East Java alone, according to Legal Aid Foundation sources, there were more than fifty actions by dispossessed farmers, reclaiming disputed lands.[41] At Situbondo, thousands of coffee and cacao plantation crops were destroyed and replanted with corn and soy beans by local farmers on the land they said the state had seized from them.[42] At Jenggawah, where a former Dutch plantation covering more than three thousand hectares had been taken over by a state tobacco plantation company under commercial plantation (HGU) lease, local people occupied the estate after a decades-long struggle.[43] In North Sumatra two thousand farmers demanded the return of 100,000 hectares of plantation land controlled by a state company (Nuh 1995). Protests were often accompanied by looting or destruction of plantation crops. Looting of fourteen state-owned plantations whose operations covered some two million hectares of land caused losses totaling billions of rupiah.[44] These occupations and other protest actions were aimed at obtaining additional payments or retaliating for land and resources previously expropriated without compensation or at unjust rates. They were also related to meeting daily subsistence needs during the economic crisis.[45]

No longer did the press use carefully sanitized New Order language to mute the effects of these protests. Newspapers spoke, as in the 1960s, of attacks on landlords,[46] of protesting women taking off their clothes in front of bulldozers about to raze their homes,[47] and of demands for the return of land stolen by the Suharto family.[48] Authorities sometimes resorted to violence in response to incidents of direct popular action.[49] But in the new climate of political freedom, the sympathy of the media and the public was generally with the protestors. Although many occupations took place without interference from the state apparatus, developers frequently tried to prevent them by using hired henchman (*preman*).[50]

In the outer islands where customary *adat* lands had been taken without acknowledgment of traditional rights for timber and mining concessions, occupations, blockades, and destruction of company assets were widely reported local responses, with substantial impacts on the investment climate and on the relative negotiating position of local and regional interests. During the 1998–2000 period, twenty-eight mining companies suspended their activities because of political insecurity and the lack of legal certainty.[51] The Australian gold mining company Aurora pulled out of its Sulawesi operation in 2001, citing the impossibility of controlling the influx of "wild" miners who were panning on their lease.[52] In the forested areas of the outer islands, which had been declared "State lands" under the Forest Law, reclamation often took the form of intensified "illegal logging" (Angelsen and Resosudarmo 1999). Dozens of timber companies were reported to have stopped operations owing to conflicts with local communities.[53]

In some cases, compensation demands for land forcibly acquired by plantation, mining, and other companies, which were documented by nongovernment organizations, led to official responses proffering negotiations toward compensation, distribution of shares, and/or co-management of plantations, national parks, and production forest zones.[54] The state-owned Forestry Corporation, Perum Perhutani, was charged with the responsibility of including communities in the management and income benefits arising from logging the country's forests, and to pay compensation for damage to state-managed forests.[55] At the grassroots level where protest was fierce, officials were sometimes forced to revoke unpopular decisions or found themselves removed from office. In Babatan, an urban ward in Surabaya, one thousand residents forced the headman to revoke the sale of 12.6 hectares of former communal land (*tanah ganjaran*)[56] to a developer, and to issue a public apology "for lying, for giving up this land without the agreement of residents, and for forging signatures."[57]

The phenomenon of peasants reclaiming plantation land that had already begun during the New Order became widespread in the immediate post-Suharto period. The Bandung YLBHI office has data on forty-five land disputes involving peasant farmers reclaiming large plantations between 1981 and 2007 in ten districts in West Java. Over 28,000 households are recorded as being involved in these actions, reclaiming a total of 17,229 hectares. The peasant smallholders faced a combined opposition from a broad alliance of state and private business interests. In all but one of the reclaiming actions, however, the people still control occupied land despite the fact that its legal status in the majority of cases remains unresolved.

It is difficult to present a comprehensive picture of the contested land situation for Indonesia that would enable clear comparison of the situation in the New Order and Reform Eras. Data collection and classification systems in Komnas HAM and PTUN Administrative Courts have changed, and NGOs are less focused on particular cases since *reformasi*.[58] According to the National Land Agency (BPN) director, Joyo Winoto, 7,491 land cases have been recorded by the agency, of which 2,052 cases remain subject to litigation in the courts. Of the total number of cases, only 1,180 have been settled through legal processes.[59]

Some indication of the depth and continuity of the land problem in the post-Suharto period is revealed in statistics collected from the Indonesian Supreme Court website; the court hears appeals cases. Data presented in table 1.5 (see chapter appendix) cover only those cases actually adjudicated and do not provide an indication of the actual number of appeals brought to the Higher Administrative Courts (PT TUN, *Pengadilan Tinggi Tata Usaha Negara*), or to the PTUN lower courts.[60] Nonetheless, they show a steady pattern of growth in the number and proportion of land cases adjudicated by Indonesia's administrative courts of appeal. Land cases rose from 3 percent to 48 percent of the total adjudicated caseload between 2000 and 2008.[61]

What has been achieved by these popular actions over land and resource rights in the so-called *Era Reformasi*? In the highly publicized cases at Jenggawah and Cimacan, there have been some concrete results. Five thousand cultivators at Jenggawa finally obtained title to plantation lands covering 3,117 hectares in seven villages, ending a thirty-year struggle in the face of state repression. Only a fortnight after Suharto's resignation, on 8 June 1998, the Bupati of Jember endorsed the farmers' claim for land rights in a written recommendation to the National Land Agency. A subsequent agreement moderated by the East Java Brawijaya military chief of staff was signed by farmers' representatives with the government in a negotiated settlement on 1 October 1998. In Cimacan (discussed in detail in chapter 4), cultivators dispossessed by collusion between the village head and a developer eventually received compensation for lost rights to highly productive former colonial plantation land which they had been cultivating for generations. But the vast majority of successful occupations have not to date achieved any legal resolution in the form of negotiated compensation or the issuance of legal title. Of the 753 hectares at Tapos, claimants had only succeeded in occupying and cultivating 36 hectares at the time they joined the Jakarta student protests. Since then they have been attempting to get recognition from the National Land Board for the land they have occupied, while maintaining a claim on a further 73 hectares of land cultivated by villagers before it was seized by Suharto in 1973. In Batang district, Central Java, farmers occupied three plantations, with mixed results.[62] In North Sumatra, land-reclaiming actions have taken place with the collaboration of various NGO groups and local movements to regain rights to plantation land.[63] In Central Sulawesi local villagers took over five plantations, in all cases without legal resolution.[64] In Bali and Lombok, reclaiming actions took place in relation to several high-profile resort-development cases, leading to still inconclusive outcomes.[65] A KPA inventory shows that up to December 2001 out of 1,753 cases, 133 (7.6 percent) had gone to court, and only 50 (38 percent) of those had been resolved by court decision (Bachriadi 2004, 518). Because of the costs of litigation and past experience with the corruption of the judicial system, farmers and NGOs have called for a completely new legal body to deal with all land issues by arbitration (*Kompas,* 25 Sept. 2001; *Forum Keadilan,* 7 Oct. 2001).

Beyond a select few among the "big name" cases, protesting farmers have as yet no assurance of recognition of their land rights or fair compensation for land taken during the Suharto Era. Nor can it be assumed that the gains achieved by these "people's actions" of the post-Suharto period will translate into secure futures for themselves and their children.[66] The Legal Aid Foundation of Indonesia predicted that land conflicts would increase in number and intensity as post–New Order governments resorted to extractive economic policies to bolster foreign exchange in the wake of Indonesia's economic crisis (YLBHI 1998, 8). Certainly, there was reluctance about tackling the land crisis in the first decade of reform despite what might have been considered a mandate for radical change.

In the reform atmosphere that swept Indonesia in 1998, local communities, NGOs, student groups, and academics demanded decentralization of decision-making and fiscal powers, revision of land laws, and a new natural resource management regime that would provide for the people's welfare and a sustainable future. They called for new laws that would revitalize land reform, fully recognize *adat* institutions and customary land tenure, and facilitate community-based forest management. There were also calls for the cancellation of forest concessions (HPH) large-scale cultivation (HGU), and timber plantation leases (HTI), and an end to the transmigration program. Under intense pressure, the transitional government began introducing new legislation on land, forests, and the decentralization of political authority and economic decision making.[67] This legislation scrapped or altered the workings of some of the most important pieces of national legislation affecting the regions. The fact that much of the "reform" legislation, including draft revisions of the Basic Agrarian Law, was already being formulated in the last years of the Suharto regime suggests the intensity of the pressure that was building against government policies well before cracks in the facade of the New Order appeared to threaten its foundations. But the origins of the revised legislation suggest, too, the limited extent to which it was likely to bring about the real transformation expected by the public.

Case Studies

In the wake of the Indonesian revolution, the Basic Agrarian Law was intended to satisfy popular demands for social justice and equity by providing access to land and just returns to farmers. Fifty years later, the Basic Agrarian Law's objectives of social justice, legal certainty, and national unity for the Indonesian people have not been achieved. This introductory chapter has presented a historical overview outlining the very different roles played by the Indonesian state in the Old and New Orders, and continuing into the ensuing "reform" era in the intimate and fraught relationship between the land, the law, and the people. The case studies that follow present a detailed, grassroots picture of land conflicts affecting local communities in different parts of the Indonesian archipelago from the independence period to the present.

These studies trace the roots of contemporary land conflicts in traditional land tenure arrangements, through colonial and postcolonial Sukarno and Suharto regimes, into the present, when democratization of governance and significant changes in law and administration pursuant to new regional autonomy legislation have altered the context in which these peoples' claims are being pursued.

The studies, selected from across Indonesia's diverse cultural and ecological landscape, reflect the two critical dimensions of the land problem in Indonesia, which have deep roots in the national psyche and the policies inherited from former regimes: The first is the core question of equity and the redistributive objectives of land reform policy, where case studies are primarily focused on densely populated Java. The second concerns land tenure questions in "outer island" Indonesia where national law has been used to override traditional land rights in the customary (*adat*) domains of indigenous minority groups.

In chapter 2 Dianto Bachriadi and Gunawan Wiradi discuss what Indonesia's five agricultural censuses between 1963 and 2003 reveal about change and continuity in land tenure and land use patterns under contrasting Old and New Order agrarian policies. Whereas the social function of land was a core principle of the 1960 Basic Agrarian Law, under the New Order land became increasingly commodified, with significant implications for the landless and the smallholder agrarian sector generally. Their study analyzes the relatively limited impact of the land reform program of the early postrevolutionary period and the very different New Order approach to redistribution through the transmigration program. The authors discuss the available evidence on land tenure inequities over five census periods (1963–2003) and the reasons for persisting high levels of rural poverty and landlessness.

Chapter 3 by Carol Warren and Anton Lucas reviews the Land Administration Project (LAP), a World Bank–funded land-titling program, which became the centerpiece of land policy in the late New Order period. Influenced by neoliberal arguments that formalization of land tenure is the key to alleviating poverty, certification was intended to provide legal certainty and greater tenure security for landholders and better access to credit. It would also facilitate more efficient allocation in the land market for development purposes. This chapter considers these claims and NGO criticisms of formal titling as the primary means for dealing with Indonesia's acute land problems.

In chapter 4 Anton Lucas discusses the long-running Cimacan golf course dispute in the Puncak region of West Java from 1983 to 2007, where local government and developers' interests were pitted against peasant smallholder vegetable farmers who had leased the land from the village. Despite farmers' fierce resistance to the development, significant NGO involvement, widespread media coverage, and litigation in the district, provincial, and supreme courts, as well as support from the reform era Cimacan village council, in the end the farmers accepted compensation for the loss of their valuable cultivation rights. This chapter analyzes the stages of this struggle in Cimacan, including attempts by dispossessed landholders to gain power in recent village elections.

In chapter 5 Afrizal (himself from the region of West Sumatra) traces local struggles for recognition of traditional land rights in Nagari Kinali, West Sumatra, which has been transformed into an oil palm plantation economy in the past decade. As a result, demands for fair compensation and restoration of customary (*adat*) land rights for local farmers have dominated agrarian struggles. The chapter analyzes the nature of protests over customary land, how local communities acted to legitimize their claims, the roles of *adat* leaders, and responses from plantation corporations and the local state apparatus.

Chapter 6 by John McCarthy reviews the impact of President Suharto's notorious "million hectare" megaproject on local Dayak communities who lost access to resources, as peat swamps were drained, and forests and gardens devastated by the 1997 forest fires. This chapter shows how the Peat Land Development Project fits into the wider transformation of Central Kalimantan province, where development strategies, geared toward capital accumulation by politically well-connected corporate actors, redefined tenurial categories and undermined traditional resource use. The author shows how indigenous actors eventually became opportunistic players in the short-term extraction of local resources, and reflects on whether a pilot Reducing Emissions from Deforestation and Degradation (REDD) program may provide a solution to protecting remaining peat swamp forests.

In chapter 7, John Prior examines several land dispute cases in Flores between villages and the state, which highlight disparate interpretations of customary (*adat*) and national law. He also examines the relationship between indigenous communities and the Catholic Church, which has played an ambiguous role as landowner, on the one hand, and credible mediator, on the other.

In chapter 8 Carol Warren traces the three-decades-long land conflict on the island of Gili Trawangan, Lombok. This case evolved in the context of rapid value transformations in the local, national, and global economies, as smallholders competed for land with commercial plantations, resort development, and more recent incursions of the international real estate property market. The case study documents repeated government land clearance campaigns, the reclaiming actions of local landholders, and the ongoing struggle of smallholder farmers and businesses against eviction by a regional government openly allied with big capital interests. The chapter explores competing understandings of "public interest" and contested interpretations by state and local actors of the legal and social justice principles at stake in this long-running conflict.

Chapter 9 by Gustaaf Reerink discusses the impact of changing commercial land development laws on the urban poor of Bandung, the provincial capital of West Java. Under the New Order, commercial land development was one of Indonesia's prime investment sectors, and low-income urban dwellers were under constant pressure to give up their valuable land in inner city urban wards (*kampung*) to developers aided by government coercive force. Post-Suharto democratic reforms have failed to end such practices. The case study of Bandung's Paskal Hyper Square development highlights how decentralization and new deregulation policies have contributed to the commodification of urban land, on the one hand increasing the risks to low-income earners confronted by land hungry developers, but on the other hand offering them new opportunities for resistance.

In chapter 10, Dianto Bachriadi, Anton Lucas, and Carol Warren reflect on the impact of more than a decade of Reform Era struggles to redress the excesses of the New Order and the neoliberal challenge to the socialist premises of land policies of the postrevolutionary era. This chapter considers the fate of the Basic Agrarian Law and efforts to revive progressive agrarian policies, the role of civil society groups, and new political programs that claim to address the long-standing land conflicts described in this book.

The concluding chapter, by Carol Warren and Anton Lucas, considers whether current policies will increase land security for the general population or create new forms of land concentration, and what challenges the emerging issues of global food security and environmental degradation pose for land use and land rights in a rapidly changing world system.

The case studies in this book offer a locally grounded perspective on the factors intensifying conflict over land rights and land use during this period of dramatic political change in Indonesia, within the context of important global debates about sustainable development, food security, democratization, globalization, and human rights. These studies of the long history of land conflicts across the country provide important insights into the extent and limits of the reform process in Indonesia today, and highlight the complexities of building a responsive, participatory "civil society" in the face of severe economic and ecological crisis, entrenched political corruption, and contending global forces.

Appendix

TABLE 1.1
Land cases as a proportion of total cases submitted to the Administrative Court (PTUN) for Jakarta and the National Human Rights Commission (KomnasHAM) 1991–98

	1991	1992	1993	1994	1995	1996	1997	1998
PTUN Jakarta*	37/166	53/207	35/156	30/158	40/171	56/191	55/163	40/130
KomnasHAM**				101/572	178/867	327/1406	351/1093	339/1221

*Administrative courts (PTUN) were instituted in 1991 to hear cases involving administrative arms of government. These statistics represent new cases submitted only to the Administrative Court for Jakarta (one of the twenty-six regional PTUN branches). They do not include cases carried over from previous years, which typically represented half the annual caseload. There are twenty-four categories of human rights cases of which the category "land" (*pertanahan*) represented the largest number of cases in all but two years (1991 and 1994) when cases classified under "housing" and "civil service" outstripped it (Source: PTUN Jakarta 1991–98). The slight decline in the Jakarta Administrative Court and Human Rights Commission figures for 1998 reflects the turbulent political and economic crisis of that year.

**KomnasHAM, the National Human Rights Commission, was established in 1994. These figures represent completed cases dealing with land issues out of total completed cases for the six categories reported: "land," "labour," "official abuses," "housing," "religion," "other" (KomnasHAM 1996, 8; 1997, 29; 1998, 38). Approximately 30 percent of complaints submitted were unresolved and carried into the following year's caseload.

TABLE 1.2
Land cases handled by the Legal Aid Foundation for fourteen provinces in 1998

Province	Number of cases	Land area (hectares)	Households affected
West Java	28	3,422	2,887
DKI Jakarta	116	637	844
Central Java	23	1,083	1,241
D.I. Yogyakarta	4	1,057	572
East Java	60	1,050	5,632
Subtotal	231 (42%)	7,249 (1%)	11,176 (5%)
D.I. Aceh	7	59,985	4,254
North Sumatra	42	113,050	53,727
West Sumatra	12	15,483	1,612
South Sumatra	135	195,585	26,284
Bandar Lampung	73	253,122	98,846
Bali	9	285	684
South Sulawesi	12	13,110	2,382
North Sulawesi	15	32,285	6,593
Irian Jaya	17	137,197	8,798
Subtotal	322 (58%)	820,102 (99%)	203,180 (95%)
Total	553 (100%)	827,351 (100%)	214,356 (100%)

Source: Adapted from YLBHI 1998 (*Divisi Tanah dan Lingkungan*).

TABLE 1.3
Comparison of unreleased (neglected) and released land with location permits

Allocation	Land with location permits				Total area with location permits (ha)
	"Unreleased lands" (ha) (passively neglected)	%	"Released lands" (ha)	%	
Housing	29,157	39%	45,578	61%	74,735
Industry	6,685	22%	23,412	78%	29,999
Tourism	7,788	42%	10,794	58%	18,582
Plantation estate	1,103,137	38%	1,799,049	62%	2,902,186
Total	**1,146,767**	**38%**	**1,878,833**	**62%**	**3,025,502**
Average	286,692	35.3%	469,708	64.7%	756,375

Source: Pusat Data Bisnis Indonesia. 1998. "Kebijakan Pertanahan Order Reformasi." *Informasi* PDBI 18, no 224 (October): 4.

Notes: "Unreleased" or passively neglected land means that the land still has occupiers/landholders on it, although a location permit has been issued. The original occupiers have not yet been evicted, usually because compensation had not been paid, or investment for the project has not materialized. "Released land" means that the original occupiers/landholders have been evicted (*dibebaskan*).

TABLE 1.4
Comparison of released land (holding location permits) that is in use or remains undeveloped (neglected)

Allocation	Released land				
	In use/developed	%	Not used/undeveloped (actively neglected)	%	Total area (ha)
Housing	6,722	15%	38,856	85%	45,578
Industry	2,875	12%	20,537	88%	23,412
Tourism	1,528	14%	9,266	86%	10,794
Plantation estate	470,433	26%	1,328,616	74%	1,799,049
Total	**481,558**	**26%**	**1,397,275**	**74%**	**1,878,833**
Average	120,389	16.7%	349,319	83.3%	469,708

Source: Bachriadi (2000, 26), calculated from data provided in Pusat Data Bisnis Indonesia. 1998. *"Kebijakan Pertanahan Orde Reformasi." Informasi PDBI* 18, no. 224 (October): 4.

Note: "Actively neglected" land means that the developer has cleared the land but has not done anything further to develop it.

TABLE 1.5
Administrative High Court (PT-TUN) cases adjudicated 2001–2008

Year	Number of land cases adjudicated	Total number of cases adjudicated	Land cases as % of total cases adjudicated
Before 2000	17	N/A	
2000	18	626	3%
2001	23	512	4%
2002	29	482	6%
2003	30	545	6%
2004	82	527	16%
2005	120	609	20%
2006	169	505	33%
2007	184	508	36%
2008	190	397	48%
Total	**862**	**4,711**	**19%**

Source: Data from Indonesian Supreme Court on cases adjudicated by Administrative High Court at http://putusan.mahkamahagung.go.id/app-mari/putusan/. Accessed on 12 April and 25 May 2009 by Hilma Savitri.

Notes

1. Interview with Pramoedya Ananta Toer, *Time Magazine*, 6 August 2001.

2. Undang-Undang Pokok Agraria (UUPA) 5/1960 is referenced in Indonesian and English as UUPA and BAL (Basic Agrarian Law), respectively.

3. On the social functions of land, see BAL/UUPA §2 /1–3, 4/1, 7, 8, 11/2, 12 and 13/1.

4. Most important among the regulations implementing land reform are UU 56/1960 on the size of agricultural land holdings, PP 224/1961 on land redistribution and compensation, and KepPres 131/1961 on implementation of land reform. Texts of the most important legislation on agrarian law have been published in the regularly revised editions of Harsono. For a summary and analysis of the 1960s land reform legislation, see Harsono 1996, 771–880; 2007b, 364–413. See also Gautama 1993; Parlindungan 1989, 1993, 1994a, 1994b; and Wiradi 2000, 3–22. For the most recent legislation, see www.hukumonline.com and www.kpa.or.id.

5. The Indonesian word *tani* (*petani*) can be translated either as "peasant," implying traditional village ties and semisubsistence household-based economic orientation, or as a more commercially oriented "farmer." In the Sukarno era *tani* were still "peasants" (the PKI-affiliated Barisan Tani Indonesia involved in the land reform program was usually translated as the Indonesian Peasants' Front). Translations of *petani* as "farmer" reflect the greater market dependence brought about by the Green Revolution in the contemporary period. But activist agrarian reform organizations generally prefer the translation "peasant" to describe small farmer-producers despite increasing market dependence because of the political history of the term and its more radical connotations. Here we use both terms, recognizing the importance and ambiguity of their connotations for the peasant farmers of Indonesia.

6. Stage One included Java, Bali, and Lombok; Stage Two included the rest of Indonesia, but mainly affected Sumatra after 1965.

7. Other issues covered in his report were the practice of listing large landholdings under names of owners' relatives; large landholders identifying themselves as "cultivators" and their tenant farmers as "agricultural laborers" to evade redistribution; the lack of written agreements on sharecropping arrangements; manipulation of land prices; the poor performance of land reform committees; and the burden of negotiating land redistribution through fifteen different government authorities (Walinsky 1977, 343–49).

8. The Land Reform Committees were abolished by KepPres 55/1980 and the Land Courts by UU 7/1970 (see Harsono 1997, 365–69).

9. This study was based on interviews carried out between March and May 2000 in Garut, Indramayu, and Cianjur districts.

10. The landholders took their case to the Bandung Legal Aid Institute in 1998, but the latter could not seek judicial redress because the Indramayu Land Agency Office refused to release the land transfer records, which would have shown to whom and how much land was originally redistributed and to whom the village headman had sold it off after 1965.

11. The term *hak ulayat*, literally "territorial right," implies concepts of collective authority over sometimes loosely defined territorial areas. Individual rights are generally understood to derive directly or indirectly from these local ancestrally sanctioned authorities recognized in the BAL as belonging to "*adat* law communities" (UUPA5/60 §3).

12. Under the 1870 Agrarian Act, introduced by the Dutch colonial administration, land not legally recognized as privately owned (*eigendom*) was deemed to belong to the state. Although the colonial "domain" principle was rejected by the legal-political regime of the postcolonial Indonesian nation-state (UUPA 5/60, Elucidation II/2), the "social function" and

"national interest" principles came to perform the same function, legitimating the expropriation of millions of hectares of customary lands belonging to *adat* communities, now designated as "state land" (Slaats et al. 2009, 495).

13. Like the colonial domain principle, the successor Indonesian government treated uncultivated land as "unowned" state land (*tanah negara*). In fact, most land throughout the country fell under mutually recognized territorial domains of *adat* communities, known as *hak ulayat*. Haverfield, following the Van Vollenhoven interpretation of *adat* law, argues that there is therefore no "owner-less" land in Indonesia (1999, 45). For a critical analysis of the assertions of Van Vollenhoven's influential *adat* law school of thought, see Burns (1999, 2007). Although this concept of *hak ulayat* may be somewhat reified, it is certainly the case that land did not have to be currently occupied or exploited to fall under the authority of *adat* communities and their guardian spirits.

14. See in particular the elucidation (*penjelasan*) to the BAL/UUPA, which establishes its intent to prevent oppression of the weak by the powerful, and to produce a modern legal regime that is adapted to Indonesian socialism and overcomes the influence of both capitalism and feudalism (UUPA 5/1960, Elucidation II/7, III/1). But the tension between socialist "use value" and capitalist "exchange value" principles nonetheless pervades the BAL/UUPA as well as the policy commitments of independent Indonesia's first government. See Harsono 1997, 528–40.

15. The most significant forms of title provided by the BAL in addition to *hak milik* (freehold) are commercial use right (HGU), building use right (HGB), and land use right (HPL) (UUPA 5/60 §III–VI). It was these concession rights that the Indonesian state dispensed to resource developers, on what it claimed as state land (*tanah negara*), ignoring the customary *adat* rights of indigenous peoples and long-term claims of untitled peasant smallholders. Under the New Order, separate sectoral legislation—granting HPH (Forest Utilization Concession) and HTI (Industrial Timber Plantation) rights under the Forest Act UU 5/1967—established another basis for accumulation and exploitation of vast areas of land claimed by the state, and became vehicles for disenfranchising local people from their traditional lands.

16. See Fitzpatrick (2007, 132–34). The BAL also negatively associates *adat* with the "feudalism" of the traditional kingdoms of Indonesia (BAL/UUPA 5, 1960, Elucid. 3/1).

17. The most important were UU Pokok Kehutanan 5/1967 (Basic Forestry Law); UU Pokok Pertambangan 11/1967 (Basic Mining Law).

18. Where granted at all, compensation was only for destroyed buildings and crops.

19. Suharto rose to power on the back of an alleged communist coup. The countercoup he led wiped out the Communist Party (PKI), which had been rapidly growing in popularity, and resulted in the slaughter of an estimated 500,000 people associated with the PKI, or its mass organizations, in particular the Indonesian Peasants Union (BTI). Although much of the land reform legislation of the Sukarno Era was left in place under Suharto, the mechanisms for carrying it out—the land reform courts and committees—were dismantled under the New Order.

20. Most of the complaints concerned irregularities in the certification process carried out by the BPN, and claims of forced expropriation by government authorities, the military, or private companies.

21. See also *Kompas,* 21 October 1996.

22. This publication recorded only land disputes reported in the press that appeared to have a human rights dimension, but it has an advantage over other sources in that it includes information on cases that were not formally taken to the authorities (Dianto Bachriadi, pers. comm., October 1999).

23. The KPA Database on Agrarian Conflicts was initiated in collaboration with the authors as part of a research project funded by the Australian Research Council between 1998 and 2001. It utilizes reports from local member organizations and KPA investigators, as well as their own collection of clippings from major national and some regional papers dating back to 1972. The statistics it provides are inevitably biased by media interest and accessibility of activist organizations to conflict sites, and must be interpreted carefully for these reasons. The majority of cases recorded in the database are for provinces in Java (58 percent) and Sumatra (26 percent). This is partly accounted for by the intensity of investment pressure in these provinces. But the low visibility of conflicts in remote locations means that outer island conflicts are most certainly underrepresented in KPA as well as in other official statistics. This database has not been updated by KPA since 2002, when the organization became more focused on organizing and education, and less interested in individual case advocacy (Bachriadi, pers. comm. 25 August 2009).

24. Setiawan (2010, 355). KPA's most recent annual report (2011) notes 163 agrarian conflicts throughout Indonesia for that year (an increase of 53 percent since 2010), with 60 percent of cases from the plantation sector, followed by the sectors of forestry (22 percent), infrastructure (13 percent), mining (4 percent), and aquaculture (1 percent). Laporan Akhir Tahun KPA Tahun 2011 "Tahun Perampasan Tanah dan Kekerasan Terhadap Rakyat" at http://www.kpa.or.id/?p=646. Accessed 27 January 2012.

25. See Pelzer (1991); Bachriadi and Lucas (2001a).

26. UU 51/1960, prohibiting the use of land without legal permit or authority, provides that in resolving conflicts over illegal occupation of

plantation lands, the Minister of Agriculture should give attention to the needs of the people using the land. Explaining the law in a 1962 letter, the minister advised that state lands not used by government or other authorized interests should in principle become agricultural land and be redistributed to the people (Harsono 1997, 110–16). A decree issued by President Suharto (KepPres 32/1979) stated that "HGU lands converted from former Western [that is, the old colonial lease] rights that were occupied by the people and that from the perspective of land use and environmental protection are better used for residence or farming, will be given under new rights to the people occupying them." But this and similar government decisions indicated that such redistribution is only "so long as they are not needed for public interest projects," and do not provide for conversion to full private property title (*hak milik*) (KepPres 32/1979, §2/4 and PerMendagri 3/1979, §10). In reality, the above legislation proved a weak basis for claiming unused or neglected leasehold plantation land.

27. Emergency Law 8/1954 attempted to deal with what was then a widespread decolonization issue. In the elucidation to this law it is noted that out of 200,000 hectares of plantation land in Java at that time, approximately 80,000 hectares were occupied by cultivators; in East Sumatra a further 65,000 hectares of tobacco plantations and 60,000 hectares of rubber, coconut, and other plantations were under occupation (Soedargo 1962, 280; Bachriadi and Lucas 2001a, 48–49).

28. Nineteen of forty-five land conflict cases dealt with by the Legal Aid Institute (LBH) for West Java alone between1984 and 2008 concerned HGU cultivation use rights. See Hardiyanto (1998, 160–71).

29. As part of the New Order development model, plantations were initially rehabilitated to increase export earnings. Coffee, rubber, and palm oil were the most important plantation crops.

30. A notorious example, covered in chapter 6 of this volume, was the disastrous million-hectare peat swamp forest project in Central Kalimantan, approved by presidential fiat in 1996 initially for a transmigrant rice cultivation scheme, and later for oil palm.

31. Under PerMenag/BPN 2/1993, which regulated procedures for companies to obtain location permits and land for investors, the National Land Agency (BPN) was able to issue location permits to companies seeking land for development. The company with a location permit could then take direct steps to acquire the land from landholders, circumventing the usually drawn-out negotiations involving land procurement committees in order to determine compensation, as stipulated in KepPres 55/1993, which regulates the procurement of land for public projects by government in the public interest. In practical terms PerMenag 2/93 made it easier for private

investors to obtain land under "building use right" leases (HGB), because it allowed the company to negotiate directly with landholders once the location permits (*izin lokasi*) had been issued. This circumvented the process of having to work through cumbersome (for investors) land clearance committees, as required for both public and private projects under earlier legislation (PerMendagri 2/1976, see Suhendar and Kasim 1996, 58–59). However, coercion in private land release often occurred, and speculation was widespread. Gustaaf Reerink's chapter 9 in this volume deals with the legal and practical problems of urban land clearance policy.

32. "Kebijakan Pertanahan Orde Reformasi," *Informasi*, no. 224 Tahun XVIII, October 1998, p. 4.

33. The Basic Agrarian Law provides that HGU leases that are neglected shall be canceled (§34). SK Menteri Pertanian 167/1990, §§3, 4, and 5 also provide for cancellation if a lease is not used for its specified purpose. In the Gili Trawangan case (chapter 8) the neglected status of the HGU plantation was ignored in the case put to the courts by smallholder claimants, and only acted upon to enable transfer to more powerful political business interests.

34. Even under these repressive circumstances, farmers did not always acquiesce. One of the original landholders at Tanah Lot, Bali, resisted pressure to sell and continued to pay tax on the 0.41 hectares of rice land that now stands under the lobby of the Meridien Hotel in the controversial Bakrie-owned Nirwana Bali Resort complex (interview with NS, October 1999; see also Warren 1998).

35. The term *calo* refers to middleman, or agent, and usually has pejorative overtones of extortion.

36. See, for example, accounts of some of the more notorious land conflicts at Kedung Ombo (Stanley 1994; Aditjondro 1998); Tanah Lot in Bali (Warren 1998); Tubanan in Surabaya (Lucas 1997); Cimacan and Tapos (Bachriadi and Lucas 2001a); and Jenggawah in East Java (Hafid 2001). See also the publications of the Legal Aid Institute (YLBHI) (*Laporan Kasus* 1990, 1991) and the Consortium for Agrarian Reform (KPA—the nongovernment umbrella organization that brings together a large number of local organizations struggling for land reform and *adat* land rights); Bachriadi, Faryadi, and Setiawan (1997); Hardiyanto (1998); and the publications of the social research institute AKATIGA (Suhendar 1994; Suhendar and Winarni 1998).

37. See chapter 10 in this volume for a detailed discussion of President Yudhoyono's controversial National Agrarian Reform Program (PPAN).

38. For detailed references to protest actions in this period, see Lucas and Warren (2003, 87–94). For background to these reclaiming actions

and the strategies adopted from the point of view of Legal Aid and local activist groups involved, see Wijardjo and Perdana (2001). Among the best known of the reclaiming cases involving former Dutch plantation estates were those at Cimacan and Tapos. Cimacan was one of the six cases that achieved notoriety in the "Land for the People" calendar for which two student activists were jailed by the Suharto regime (Lucas 1992); the Cimacan case is the subject of chapter 4 in this volume.

39. A publication of the Indonesian Golf Association (PGI) shows a total of 119 golf courses located in twenty-two provinces in Indonesia. One course of eighteen holes in Citeureup in West Java occupies seven hundred hectares, compared with an eighteen-hole course at the hill resort of Kaliurang (Yogyakarta) that uses only sixty hectares (Indonesian Golf Association, *Golf Map,* Jakarta, 2000–2001). By 2007 there were still 104 golf courses in Indonesia (Indonesian Golf Association 2006–7). Despite recognizing that golf courses absorbed a large amount of space that was only "enjoyed by a small number of wealthy people," the governor of West Java, H. R. Nuriana, rejected the proposal to convert golf courses to food crop cultivation even in that time of food crisis (*Kompas On Line,* 24 June 1998).

40. See table 1.4 (chapter appendix). According to the Basic Agrarian Law, all property rights including private *hak milik* title are automatically canceled when land is abandoned (*terlantar*) (UUPA 5/60 §27). As described in the elucidation to the legislation, "Land is deemed 'neglected' if with intention it is not used properly in accord with its condition or character and in accord with the purpose of attached rights." On the "abandoned lands" regulation (PP 36/1998 and PP 11/2010) see Setiawan (2010, 348–49, 422).

41. Herlambang Perdana, pers. comm., 11 December 2001. Long-running disputes over lands leased to plantations in East Java include those at Malang, Ngawi, and Pasuruan (*Surabaya Post On Line,* 17 September 1996).

42. *Republika,* 12 December 1998.

43. *Tempo,* 12 June 2001. In 1995, long before there were any signs of an end to the Suharto regime, several hundred farmers in Jember showed their anger at the government decision to issue an HGU lease on land they had worked for twenty-five years to a state plantation company by setting fire to nineteen tobacco sheds, administrative offices, and company vehicles (*Kompas,* 25 September 2000; Hafid 2001). It would be a mistake, therefore, to assume, as Pramoedya's remarks introducing this chapter might suggest, that there was no popular resistance to dispossession under the New Order.

44. *Surya,* 9 September 1998; *Indonesian Observer,* 24 May 2000.

45. For further detail on direct action agrarian protests that accompanied the *reformasi* movement, see Lucas and Warren 2003, 87–94.

46. *Republika,* 12 December 1998.

47. *Kompas,* 22 April 1998. See also reference to similar gendered protest in the Gili Trawangan case in this volume (chapter 8).

48. *Merdeka,* 24 September 1998.

49. *Tempo Interaktif,* 23 November 2001; *Surya,* 1 September 1998; *Inside Indonesia,* January–March 2002, pp. 16–17; *Prisma,* August 2001, no. 7, 27–28. The West Java Peasants' Union (SPJB) claimed to have evidence of 660 cases of the use of force toward farmers since Suharto stepped down (*Republika,* 15 September 2001; *Kompas,* 25 September 2001).

50. *Waspada,* 7 July 1998. While at Gili Trawangan and Cimacan state security officers stood by without intervening in these reclaiming actions of the *reformasi* period, developers hired thugs in attempts to thwart local occupations (see chapters 4 and 8).

51. See *Republika,* 26 June 2000; *Suara Kaltim,* 2 July 2000; *Waspada,* 23 July 1998, *Banjarmasin Pos,* 28 October 1999; *Sriwijaya Pos,* 25 September 1999; Agence France Presse, 15 May 2000.

52. *Far Eastern Economic Review,* 13 July 2000 and 18 July 2002 ; *Indonesian Observer,* 17 February 2001; *Time,* 28 May 2001.

53. *Jakarta Post,* 4 March 2000; *Bali Post,* 8 February 2000; *Suara Kaltim,* 22 March 2000; *Suara Merdeka,* 2 May 2000.

54. *Indonesian Observer,* 24 May 2000.

55. *Suara Merdeka*, 2 May 2000.

56. *Tanah ganjaran* (from *ganjar* meaning reward), elsewhere in Java termed *tanah bengkok,* is land provided to officials in lieu of salary. Since headmen and officials of urban communities designated as *kelurahan* under the Village Government Law (UU 5/1979) are now civil servants, *kelurahan* have had to give up *tanah ganjaran* to the next level of local government, where it is commonly sold off to investors. In Surabaya, this has become a serious problem (Arief Djati, pers. comm. 17 February 2002). Although technically the subdistrict *(kecamatan)* is responsible for the sale of the land, without the headman's approval the transfer of rights cannot be completed. Residents of Babatan, therefore, assumed that the subdistrict was in collusion with the village head *(lurah)* in this instance.

57. *Surya,* 11 July 1998.

58. There are two reasons for this. First, since *reformasi,* external funding for NGO human rights programs, including land disputes advocacy, has been replaced by programs to strengthen governance and civil society. Second, farmers' organizations formed during the Reform Era do not have the resources to collect, record, and report data on land disputes, After 2000, the Dutch aid organization NOVIB, YLBHI's biggest donor for twenty years, stopped funding this umbrella legal aid organization, and several of

its branches no longer collect data on land disputes (Bachriadi, pers.comm. 19 September 2009).

59. See BPN Director Joyo Winoto's speech at http://www.brighten.or.id/brighten/index.php/opinion/joyo-winoto/64-mewujudkan-keadilan-dan-kesejahteraan. Accessed 5 December 2011.

60. For the geographic location of the PTUN administrative courts see http://www.mahkamahagung.go.id.

61. The administrative courts, however, have extremely limited jurisdiction, and have a ninety-day term of limitation (Bedner 2011).

62. The local NGO, the Batang Farmers Struggle Forum, supported the takeover of 187 hectares of rubber and clove plantations by 2,200 families and an unsuccessful application to the local Batang Land Office to issue ownership certificates. Farmers were not successful in reclaiming another 113 hectares leased since 1966 under HGU by a company (PT Pagilaran) run by a Gadjah Mada University–controlled foundation. After they reclaimed the just-mentioned land, protesters were physically beaten by a three-hundred-strong mobile police brigade (Brimob) trucked in from neighboring districts (interview by Dianto Bachriadi with FPPB activist, Garut 26 April 2002; Statement, BPN Propinsi Jawa Tengah, 3 July 2001).

63. The North Sumatran land conflicts (which began in the early 1990s) involved occupation of both state-owned (including military-owned) and privately owned palm oil plantations. These actions have been part of an ongoing agrarian reform campaign by the North Sumatra Farmers Union (SPSU), and the national Indonesian Federation of Farmers' Unions (FSPI).

64. The five plantations totaling 23,000 hectares in Banggai, Donggala, and Bual districts have been reclaimed by 7,900 families with support from the local Yayasan Tanah Merdeka, but NGO activists believed government recognition was unlikely (*Tempo,* 28 April 2002).

65. See chapter 8 on the Gili Trawangan case in Lombok. At Serangan, Sendang Pasir, and Sumber Kelampok in Bali, negotiations have taken place between district officials and villagers over occupied lands, but no final agreements have been struck. Regional governments continue to resist occupants' demands, since large-scale development for capital-intensive projects on the lands claimed is in officials' interest.

66. It should not be assumed that local people perceive retention of reclaimed lands as a priority in all cases. This has been the cause of tension between activists and the local groups they have supported. The NGO focus on sustainable outcomes has meant that where the return of land is feasible, this is their preferred option. Activists frequently commented on the difficulty of persuading recipients not to sell off their land. The point

that farmers involved in reclaiming actions often preferred fair compensation to the return of their lands is a common complaint of NGO supporters. The very low prices received for agricultural commodities and the poor bargaining position of smallholders in the global market need to be taken into account when assessing the implications of such choices.

67. UU 22/1999 concerning regional government (revised by UU 32/2004 on regional government) and UU25/1999 on revenue sharing.

References

Aditjondro, G. J. 1998. "Large Dam Victims and Their Defenders: The Emergence of an Anti-Dam Movement in Indonesia." In *The Politics of Environment in Southeast Asia,* ed. P. Hirsch and C. Warren, 29–54. London: Routledge.

Affif, S., N. Fauzi, G. Hart, I. Ntsebeza, and N. Peluso. 2005. *Redefining Agrarian Power: Resurgent Agrarian Movements in West Java, Indonesia.* Center for Southeast Asian Studies Working Paper No. 2–05, University of California at Berkeley, available at http://respositories.cdlib.org/cseas/CSEASWP2-05.

Angelsen, A., and D. Resosudarmo. 1999. *Krismon, Farmers and Forests: The Effects of the Economic Crisis on Farmers' Livelihood.* Bogor: Center for International Forestry.

Bachriadi, D. 1997. "Situasi Perkebunan di Indonesia Kontemporer." In *Reformasi Agraria: Perubahan Politik, Sengketa dan Agenda Pembaruan Agrarian di Indonesia,* ed. D. Bachriadi, E. Faryadi, and B. Setiawan, 123–48. Jakarta: Lembaga Penerbit Fakultas Ekonomi, Universitas Indonesia.

———. 2000. "Sengketa, Konflik, dan Ketimpangan Penguasaan Tanah di Indonesia: Argumen Pokok untuk Pembaruan Agraria *(Agrarian Reform)* yang Menyeluruh di Indonesia Saat Ini." Paper presented to the seminar to formulate the Partai Amanat Nasional (PAN) program, Jakarta, 21 January 2000.

———. 2004. "Tendensi dalam Penyelesaian Konflik Agraria di Indonesia: Menunggu Lahirnya Komisi Nasional untuk Penyelesaian Konflik Agraria (KNUPKA)." *Dinamika Masyarakat,* 3:497–521.

Bachriadi, D., and A. Lucas, 2001a. *Merampas Tanah Rakyat: Kasus Tapos dan Cimacan.* Jakarta: KPG (Kepustakaan Populer Gramedia).

———. 2001b. "Losing Rights to Land and the Fate of the Land Reform Program: Three West Java Case Studies." Paper presented to Gadjah Mada FISIPOL Seminar, July 2001.

Bachriadi, D., E. Faryadi, and B. Setiawan, eds. 1997. *Reformasi Agraria: Perubahan Politik, Sengketa, dan Agenda Pembaruan Agraria di Indonesia.* Jakarta: KPA and Lembaga Penerbit Fakultas Ekonomi Universitas Indonesia.

Bedner, A. 2011. "'Shopping Forums': Indonesia's Administrative Courts." In *New Courts in Asia,* ed. A. Harding and P. Nicholson, 209–31. London: Routledge.

Bedner, A., and S. van Huis. 2008. "The Return of the Native in Indonesian Law." *Bijdragen tot de taal-, land- en Volkenkunde* 164:165–93.

Benda-Beckmann, F. von. 1979. *Property in Social Continuity.* The Hague: Martinus Nijhoff.

Benda-Beckmann, F. von, and M. van der Velde, eds. 1992. *Law as a Resource in Agrarian Struggles.* Wageningen, The Netherlands: Wageningen University.

Burns, P. J. 1999. *The Leiden Legacy: Concepts of Law in Indonesia.* Jakarta: Pradnya Paramita.

———. 2007. "Custom that is before all Law." In *The Revival of Tradition in Indonesian Politics: The Deployment of Adat from Colonialism to Indigenism,* ed. D. Henley and J. Davidson, 68–86. London: Routledge.

Campbell, J. 1999. "Hutan Untuk Rakyat, Masyarakat Adat, atau Kooperasi? Plural Perspectives in the Policy Debate for Community Forestry in Indonesia." Paper presented to the Seminar on Legal Complexity, Natural Resource Management and Social (in)Security in Indonesia, Padang 6–9 September 1999.

Casson, A. 2000. *The Hesitant Boom: Indonesia's Oil Palm Sub-Sector in an Era of Economic and Political Change.* Center for International Forestry Research, Occasional Paper No. 29. Bogor, Indonesia: CIFOR.

Fauzi, N. 1998. "Sesat Pikir." Undang-Undang Pertanahan Nasional: Pandangan KPA atas draft Undang-Undang Pertanahan Nasional yang disusun oleh BPN for consultation with DPR-RI. Jakarta: October.

———. 1999. *Petani dan Penguasa: Dinamika Perjalanan Politik Agraria Indonesia.* Yogyakarta: Insist Press, KPA and Pustaka Pelajar.

Fitzpatrick, D. 1997. "Disputes and Pluralism in Modern Indonesian Land Law." *Yale Journal of International Law* 22:171–212.

———. 2007. "Land, Custom, and the State in Post-Suharto Indonesia: A Foreign Lawyer's Perspective." In *The Revival of Tradition in Indonesian Politics,* ed. J. Davidson and D. Henley, 130–48. London: Routledge.

Gautama, Sudargo. 1993. *Tafsiran Undang-Undang Pokok Agraria.* 9th ed. Bandung.

Hafid, J. O. S. 2001. *Perlawanan Petani: Kasus Tanah Jenggawah.* Bogor: Pustaka Latin.

Hardiyanto, A. 1998. "HGU Harus Dibatasi: Revisi Pasal-pasal Hak Guna Usaha dalam UUPA untuk Keadilan dan Kemakmuran Kaum

Tani Miskin." In *Usulan Revisi Undang-Undang Pokok Agraria: Menuju Penegakan Hak-Hak Rakyat Atas Sumber-Sumber Agraria*, 160–71. Bandung: Konsorsium Reformasi Hukum Nasional (KRHN) dan Konsorsium Pembaruan Agraria.

Harsono, B. 1996, 2000, and 2007a (13th, 14th, and 18th rev. ed.). *Hukum Agraria Indonesia: Himpunan Peraturan-Peraturan Hukum Tanah*. Jakarta: Penerbit Djambatan.

———. 1997 and 2007b (7th and 11th rev. ed.). *Hukum Agraria Indonesia: Sejarah Pembentukan Undang Undang Pokok Agraria, Isi dan Pelaksanaannya*. Jakarta: Penerbit Djambatan.

Haverfield, R. 1999. "*Hak Ulayat* and the State: Land Reform in Indonesia." In *Indonesian Law and Society*, ed. T. Lindsey, 42–73. Melbourne: Federation Press.

Huizer, G. 1980. *Peasant Movements and Their Counterforces in Southeast Asia*. New Delhi: Marwah Publications.

Indonesian Golf Association. 2000/1 and 2006/7. *Golf Map*, Jakarta: 4th and 10th editions.

KPA. 1995. *Wawasan Sengketa Tanah Nusantara: KPA's Memorandum on Land Disputes: The Necessity for a Just and Civilised Resolution*. Bandung: Konsorsium Pembaruan Agraria.

———. 1998. *Deklarasi Pembaruan Agraria 1998*. Bandung: Konsorsium Pembaruan Agraria

Laporan Kasus/Case Reports Cimerak, Badega, Pulau Panggung. 1990. Vol. 1. Jakarta: YLBHI and JARIM.

Laporan Kasus/Case Reports Kedung Ombo, Kasus Arso, Cimacan. 1991. Vol. 2. Jakarta: YLBHI and JARIM.

Lucas, A. 1992. "Land Disputes in Indonesia: Some Current Perspectives." *Indonesia* 53:79–92.

———. 1997. "Land Disputes, the Bureaucracy and Local Resistance in Indonesia." In *Re-imagining Indonesia: Cultural Politics and Political Culture*, ed. J. Schiller and B. Martin Schiller. Athens: Ohio University Press.

Lucas, A., and C. Warren. 2000. "Agrarian Reform in the Era of Reformasi." In *Social Dimensions of Reformasi and Crisis* [Indonesia Assessment 1999], ed. Chris Manning and Peter van Diermen. London: Zed Books.

———. 2003. "The State, the People, and Their Mediators: The Struggle over Agrarian Law Reform in Post-New Order Indonesia." *Indonesia* 76:87–126.

MacAndrews, C. 1986. *Land Policy in Modern Indonesia: A Study of Land Issues in the New Order Period*. Boston: Oelgeschlager, Gunn and Hain, for the Lincoln Institute of Land Policy.

Mortimer, R. 1972. *The Indonesian Communist Party and Land Reform 1959–1965*. Melbourne: Monash Papers on Southeast Asia (1).

Moyo, S., and P. Yeros, eds. 2005. *Reclaiming the Land: The Resurgence of Rural Movements in Africa, Asia and Latin America.* London: Zed Books.

Nuh, A. 1995. "Dari Petani Reba ke Petani Jaluran." In *Pembangunan Berbuah Sengketa: 29 Tulisan Pengalaman Advokasi Tanah,* ed. B. Fidro and N. Fauzi, 297–315. Kisaran: Yayasan Sintesa; Lampung: Pos Yayasan LBH Indonesia; Bandung: Lembaga Pendidikan dan Pengembangan Masyarakat (LPPP) and Lembaga Kajian Hak-Hak Masyarakat (LEKHAT).

Nusantara, A. H. G., and B. Tanuredjo. 1997. *Dua Kado Hakim Agung Buat Kedung Ombo: Tinjauan Putusan-putusan Mahkamah Agung Tentang Kasus Kedung Ombo.* Jakarta: Lembaga Studi dan Advokasi Masyarakat (ELSAM).

Otto, J. M. 1996. "Implementation of Environmental Law in Indonesia: Some Administrative and Judicial Challenges." *Indonesian Law and Administration Review* 2:32–71.

Parlindungan, A. 1989, 1994a, 1994b. *Bunga Rampai Hukum Agraria Serta Landreform,* Bagian I–III. Bandung: Penerbit Mandar Maju.

———. 1993. *Komentar atas Undang-Undang Pokok Agraria.* Bandung: Mandar Maju.

Pelzer, K. J. 1991. *Sengketa Agraria: Pengusaha Perkebunan Melawan Petani.* Jakarta: Pustaka Sinar Harapan.

"Pertanahan Untuk Rakyat! Bukan Omong Kosong." 2009. Poster advertisement, sponsored by KMI (Kaum Muda Indonesia), FORSAS (Forum Harmoni Nusantara), BARINDO (Barisan Indonesia), Gerakan Teruskan SBY (GETSBY), DPP Jaringan Nusantara and 174 SBY-Boediono original supporter groups on Facebook.

Pusat Data Bisnis Indonesia (PDBI). 1998. "Kebijakan Pertanahan Order Reformasi." *Informasi PDBI* 18, no. 224 (October): 4.

Roundtable Discussion, 13 July 1999, PerMenag 5/1999, ELSAM, PKPM Unika Atma Jaya, KPA, PKBI 13 July 1999. Transcript.

Ruwiastuti, M. R. 1999. "Pengakuan Hak Ulayat: antara harapan dan kenyataan." Unpublished manuscript presented at Roundtable Discussion on PerMenag, May 1999.

Setiawan, U. 2010. *Kembali ke Agraria.* Yogyakarta: STNP.

Shohibuddin, M., ed. 2009. *Ranah Studi Agraria: Penguasaan Tanah dan Hubungan Agraris.* Yogyakarta dan Bogor: Sekolah Tinggi Pertanahan Nasional, and the Sajogyo Institute.

Slaats, H., E. Rajaguguk, N. Elmihan, and A. Safik. 2009. "Land Law in Indonesia." In *Legalising Land Rights,* ed. J. Ubink, A. Hoekema, and W. Assies. Leiden: Leiden University Press.

Soedargo, R. 1962. *Perundang-undangan Agraria Indonesia,* Jilid I. Bandung: N.V. Eresco.
Stanley. 1994. *Seputar Kedung Ombo.* Jakarta: Elsam (Lembaga Studi dan Advokasi Masyarakat).
Suhendar, E. 1994. *Pemetaahan Pola-Pola Sengketa Tanah di Jawa Barat.* Bandung: Akatiga.
Suhendar, E., and I. Kasim. 1996. *Tanah Sebagai Komoditas: Kajian Kritis atas Kebijakan Pertanahan Orde Baru.* Jakarta: ELSAM.
Suhendar, E., and Y. B. Winarni. 1998. *Petani dan Konflik Agraria.* Bandung: Akatiga.
Surat Keputusan Kepala Inspeksi Agraria Jawa Barat No Lr.326/D/VIII/65/1966, 13 September 1966.
Tjondronegoro, S. M. P. 1991 "The Utilization and Management of Land Resources in Indonesia." In *Indonesia: Resources, Ecology and Environment,* ed. J. Hardjono, 17–35. Singapore: Oxford University Press.
Utrecht, E. 1969. "Land Reform in Indonesia." In *Bulletin of Indonesian Economic Studies* 5 (3): 71–88.
Walinsky, L. J., ed. 1977. *Agrarian Reform as Unfinished Business: The Selected Papers of Wolf Ladejinsky.* New York: Oxford University Press.
Warren, C. 1998. "Tanah Lot: The Cultural and Environmental Politics of Resort Development in Bali." In *The Politics of Environment in Southeast Asia,* ed. P. Hirsch and C. Warren, 229–61. London: Routledge.
Wijardjo B., and H. Perdana. 2001. *Reklaiming dan Kedaulatan Rakyat.* Jakarta: YLBHI and RACA (Rapid Agrarian Conflict Appraisal) Institute.
Wiradi, G. 2000. "Tonggak-tonggak perjalanan kebijaksanaan agraria di Indonesia." In *Prinsip-Prinsip Reforma Agraria: Jalan Penghidupan dan Kemakmuran Rakyat,* ed. Tim Lapera, 3–19. Yogyakarta, Lapera Pustaka Utama.

Newspapers

Bali Post
Banjarmasin Post
Indonesian Observer—Surya
Jakarta Post
Kompas
Republika
Suara Kaltim
Suara Merdeka
Surabaya Post On Line
Waspada

Chapter 2

LAND CONCENTRATION AND LAND REFORM IN INDONESIA

Interpreting Agricultural Census Data, 1963–2003

DIANTO BACHRIADI AND GUNAWAN WIRADI

Fifteen years after Indonesian independence, on 24 September 1960, the Basic Agrarian Law (BAL) was promulgated,[1] placing agrarian justice at the center of the nation's economic life[2] and reflecting a particular concern for the rights of marginal people.[3] Indonesia's first president, Sukarno, in his famous speech on "The Progress of Our Revolution" in 1960, declared that "the Indonesian revolution without Land Reform is like a building without foundation, like a tree without a trunk, like big talk which is empty. The implementation of Land Reform means the implementation of an absolutely essential part of the Indonesian Revolution. . . . Land is not for those who sit around and become fat and corpulent through exploiting the sweat of the people whom they order to till that soil" (Soekarno 1960, 34). The spirit of the law was to free the Indonesian people, the majority of whom were dependent for their livelihoods on land and other agrarian resources, from precolonial "feudal" bonds and from colonial exploitation. For this reason land reform, which was aimed at protecting the interests of peasants (whether small farmers, tenants, or agricultural laborers), became the key policy focus of newly independent Indonesia.

BAL principles can be summarized as follows: Land must be treated as a means of production to create social welfare, not for individual interests that can lead to concentration of ownership and exploitation "of the weak by the strong." Accordingly, although individual ownership (*hak milik*) is paradoxically privileged, the land should not be commoditized. The owners of the land and agrarian resources within the territory of the unitary State of Indonesia are the people of Indonesia. Foreigners are not allowed to own land in Indonesia but can be granted limited rights to utilize agrarian resources. As a manifestation of "collective ownership," the state holds a mandate to manage resources for the social welfare of the Indonesian population as a whole.[4] For this reason, the BAL prohibits the monopoly of agrarian resources, except by the state in its role as the representative of the people's interest.[5] Implementation of the BAL 1960 through regulations establishing ceilings on agricultural land holdings (UU56/1960), land redistribution and compensation procedures (PP 224/1961), Land Reform Committees (KepPres 131/1961) and Land Reform Courts (UU 21/1964), underpinned the land reform program that aimed to limit private land holdings,[6] abolish private absentee holdings, and redistribute land. The lands targeted for redistribution were state land (*tanah negara*), privately owned land in excess of the maximum ceiling, absentee land, and lands belonging to former autonomous *swapraja* principalities. Meanwhile, the Share Cropping Act (UU 2/1960) aimed to reform the tenancy systems in rural areas that were considered unfair by the state authority and legislators. Land reform legislation also aimed to protect tenants in a weak position vis-à-vis landowners and to encourage economic development in the agricultural sector (Soemardjan 1984, 110–11).

The state-led land reform program, originally formulated as the foundation for Indonesian development and based on the principle of "land for the tillers," faced strong obstacles when Suharto came to power after the 1965 countercoup. In fact, similar land reform programs were being implemented as the basis of postwar development in Japan, South Korea, Taiwan, India, and Iran (see, for instance, Inayatullah 1980 and Ghose 1983). In Indonesia, however, critics had argued that the amount of available land to redistribute to the large population of the landless and land-poor was insufficient. This position was put strongly by scholars such as Ladejinsky (1964, in Walinsky 1977, 342–43) and Morad (1970, 36), and repeated subsequently by scholars including Booth (1988, 137), Billah, Widjajanto, and Kristyanto (1984, 278). At issue was the question of whether demographic and economic impediments to the land redistribution program in the densely populated parts of "inner Indonesia" would inevitably undermine the social justice objectives of the program.

Based on data from the first official agricultural census carried out in Indonesia (table 2.1), the pattern of agricultural landholdings and control in 1963 was certainly unequal. Of 12,883,868 hectares of agricultural land held by 12,236,470 households, the Gini ratio of land control in this year was 0.55, which means that the degree of land concentration in this year was moderately high. The Gini ratio, or Gini coefficient, is a measure of statistical dispersion used to indicate the degree of inequality of income, wealth, or land distribution. It is defined as a ratio with values between 0 and 1. In any landholding structure, a low Gini ratio indicates a more equal land distribution, while a high Gini ratio indicates more unequal distribution with a high level of land concentration. A value of 0 in this ratio corresponds to perfect equality (everyone holding exactly the same amount of land); and a value of 1 corresponds to perfect inequality (where one person holds all the land, while everyone else is absolutely landless).

Table 2.1 shows that 70.1% of farm households held only 28.6% of agricultural land, but does not reveal the outcome of the land reform programs that began in 1961.[7] As these programs had been running for less than two years, very little of the targeted land had been distributed. After four years of implementation, the program indicated some success in prioritized areas, especially Java and Sumatra. Table 2.7 (below) shows some progress in reducing the degree of concentration in land ownership and the proportion of "landless tenants,"[8] which was gradually but systematically reversed when Suharto's New Order government came to power.[9]

TABLE 2.1
Patterns of agricultural land control, 1963

Size of landholding* (hectares)	% farm households**	% land holdings
0.10–0.25	18.8	3.0
0.25–0.50	24.8	8.3
0.50–1.00	26.5	17.3
1.00–2.00	18.2	22.8
2.00–5.00	9.2	24.8
> 5.00	2.5	23.8

Source: Based on data from the Agricultural Census 1963 (Biro Pusat Statistik 1963, table 2).

*These landholding statistics do not distinguish between intensive wet rice and extensive dry cropping patterns characteristic of "inner" and "outer" island Indonesia respectively. Consequently, considerable caution is necessary in interpreting the equity implications of these data. Levels of productivity, incomes, and scales of landholding required for provision of basic household needs differ for these forms of agriculture. See table 2.9 for an indication of the different scales of land use associated with the two forms of agriculture. Nonetheless, landholding data in the Agricultural Census are focused on lands not classified as forest, and therefore exclude much of the smallholder data for "outer island" Indonesia.

**Nonlandholding farm laborers are not included.

Land Policy and Land Disputes during the New Order

The New Order government of Suharto brought about a huge alteration in agrarian politics in Indonesia after 1965. Unlike the previous regime, which had a populist agrarian political orientation of "land for the people" implemented through the land reform programs, New Order agrarian politics did the opposite. Its orientation was supportive of big investment, providing land on a large scale for the needs of both foreign and domestic investors. In this context, land was treated as a commodity,[10] contradicting the BAL principle that land has a primarily social function.[11]

As a result of this change, land speculation activities have become an integral part of the provision of land for business activity. Commodification of land is contradictory to the essence, principle, and spirit of the BAL. Mohammad Hatta, one of Indonesia's founding fathers, promoter of the concept that "land is not for sale," argued in 1946 that in order to prevent land from becoming an instrument of exploitative power, concentration of land ownership by private individuals and by business must be limited.[12]

In brief, the main characteristic of the New Order's agrarian policies was to treat land and other resources as commodities, to allow large enterprises to override the land needs of ordinary Indonesians in the name of development. The New Order focused on increasing agricultural productivity through technological improvement rather than land reform. When it abolished the land reform courts and land reform committees, systematic implementation of the program came to a halt. Since 1970–71, no allocation for land reform has appeared in the national budget (Himpunan Kerukunan Tani Indonesia 1979). Since then, land questions have been treated merely as routine administrative matters rather than as a foundation for the development of a people's economy (Sajogyo and Wiradi 1985).

Arguments that peasants' productivity could be facilitated by population redistribution through a transmigration (*transmigrasi*, shifting landless peasants from Java to Outer Island settlements) program and by breakthroughs in agricultural productivity with rice intensification were presented as early as 1963 when Wolf Ladejinsky, an expert with an international reputation on land tenure and overseas development, assessed the implementation of land reform in Indonesia (see Ladejinsky 1964, 349–51).[13] His report argued that given the increasing agricultural population in Java, on the one hand, and the very limited availability of agricultural land, on the other, land tenure reform would have no significant impact on agricultural productivity, economic development, and food supply. He urged Indonesia to take into account the contribution of plantation agriculture and industrialization to resolve these problems (Ladejinsky 1964, 351–52).

Ladejinsky's view influenced the New Order administration's emphasis on systematic transmigration in its five-year development programs since 1969[14] (Tjondronegoro 1972; Hardjono 1977) and on the Green Revolution program since the late 1960s[15] (Franke 1972; Booth

1988; Hüsken and White 1989). Plantation agriculture was intensified through new investments and the extensive smallholder program (*PIR-Bun*) which was combined with the transmigration program in the 1970s (see Parlindungan 1994; Tabor 1992; and Booth 1988, 214–18). Although the New Order was less concerned to limit private landholdings and redistribute excess privately owned lands, the allocation and redistribution of claimed state lands to small peasants through the transmigration and smallholders plantation programs (*PIR-Bun*) was nevertheless declared to be a kind of continuation of land reform (see Parlindungan 1994, 1–29). In total during the New Order regime from 1969 to 1997, around 2.2 million hectares were redistributed to around 1.1 million families through various transmigration schemes, although this figure does not include land allocated for other public facilities provided in each transmigration site. According to official data from the Department of Transmigration (1987), to 1986, around 3.6 million hectares of land were allocated for transmigration projects. According to the same data, only 43 percent of that land was used effectively. Table 2.2 shows comparative figures of total families involved in the transmigration program in Old and New Order periods.

TABLE 2.2
Total number of families and redistributed land through the transmigration programs, 1950–1997

Period	Total families involved	Total land redistributed* (hectares)
Pre/Early New Order: 1950–1968	103,169	206,338
New Order: 1969–1997**	1,099,372	2,198,744
Total	**1,202,541**	**2,405,082**

Sources: Calculated from BPS (1964), table 15, p. 24; (1972), table II.1.10; (1974), table II.1.13, p. 56; (1976), table II.2.1, pp. 46–47; (1978), table IV.1.37, pp. 192–93; (1986), tables 3.3.2 and 3.3.3, pp. 89–90; (1990), table 3.3.2, p. 97; (1991), table 3.3.2, p. 78; (1993), table 3.1.8, p. 49; (1994e), table 3.1.8, p. 33; (1996), table 3.1.10, p. 44; (1997), table 3.1.10, p. 56; Swasono (1985), tables 5.3b and 5.3d, pp. 82–84; and Saleh (2005), table V.2, p. 131.

*Calculated roughly based on land allocation of two hectares for each participant-family, excluding land allocated for public facilities and reserved land.

**Calculated based on the five-year development programs, which began in 1969/1970.

However, this high figure for land redistributed to small peasants through the transmigration program does not significantly alter the general picture of unequal land distribution as reflected in the steady high values of Gini ratios for land distribution from 1963 to 2003 (as shown in table 2.3 and figure 2.1, to be discussed in more detail below). But these transmigration outcomes cannot be separated from the social conflicts they generated at project sites. The transmigration program had been implemented in areas claimed as state land (*tanah negara*), which were in fact the customary lands of indigenous people. Beside the problems of infertile soil and poor facilities provided in some project sites (see, for instance, Hardjono 1977, 46–91; Otten 1986, 114–17; Simpul Bengkulu 2006), the eviction and marginalization of indigenous people from their customary land sometimes resulted in open clashes between transmigrants and the dispossessed indigenous people. This was the dark side of this population/ land redistribution program (see, for instance, Hardjono 1977, 39–41; Colchester 1986; Skephi and Kiddell-Monroe 1993, 245–56). Population redistribution to outer island Indonesia was also meant to provide labor for the large-scale forestry and mining concessions that were part of the New Order's economic development strategy.[16] The huge scale of land provision either for investment or speculation purposes was the cause of violent conflicts. The state used the BAL concept of "State's right of control" over land and natural resources to justify its serious human rights abuses, involving eviction and resource expropriation.

Current Agrarian Structure: A General Overview

In Indonesia today unequal land distribution occurs within the agricultural sector and also as a consequence of inequality of land allocated for extractive business projects compared to land allocated for people-based agricultural activities. This inequality of land allocation is glaringly apparent in the official separation of "forestry" and "nonforest" lands. Almost all land classified as forest is claimed as "State-land," covering until recently almost 70 percent of total land in Indonesia.[17]

Lands for Large-Scale Extractive Forestry Industries

The forestry industry was one of the boom areas of investment in the first decade of the New Order (Robison 1986, 186), and it grew rapidly over the next two decades through government efforts to achieve high national economic growth rates (Ramli and Ahmad 1983; D. W. Brown 1999; T. H. Brown 2002). The control of huge areas of land is now in the hands of enterprises that obtained rights to manage and exploit forest resources under collusive forestry concessions. By 1991, 567 concession units, including Perhutani (the state-owned forestry corporation), controlled around 60.5 million hectares claimed as forest area (Asosiasi Pengusahaan Hutan Indonesia 2007, table 4.1.1). Each unit controlled an average of 107,000 hectares of forest land.

Although the forestry industry has entered the sunset era, with the total number of concessions in decline since the end of the 1990s, the scale of its control over huge areas of land remains significant. In 1999, 420 forestry concessions still controlled around 51.6 million hectares.[18] Despite lease expiry and revocations, in 2005 the total area of forestry concessions remains around twenty-eight million hectares, controlled by 285 concessionaires holding an average of 98,000 hectares of land each (Asosiasi Pengusahaan Hutan Indonesia 2007, table 4.1.2). Where in previous decades forestry exploitation concentrated on timber extraction from natural forests, since 2000 an increasing number of concessions have been issued for forestry plantations (HTI), especially to produce raw materials for the pulp and paper industry. Between 2001 and 2005, the total area of forestry plantations increased tenfold from 67,000 hectares to 606,000 hectares (Asosiasi Pengusahaan Hutan Indonesia 2007, table 4.1.5).

Land for Large-Scale Mining Projects

As of 1999, the Department of Mining had allocated around 264.7 million hectares of land to 555 domestic (both private and state-owned) and foreign mining companies for exploration and exploitation. On average each company controlled around 0.5 million hectares.[19] Many of these concessions overlap, and only parts are in practice utilized by the concession holders, although mining regulations give them priority to use land within designated concession areas (Thalib 1971). The total concession area of big mining operations in Indonesia is today likely to grow further, since the post–New Order Megawati government provided permits in 2004 for thirteen mining companies to operate inside Protection/Protected Forest, over an area totaling 1.1 million hectares of forestland previously designated for ecological functions only.[20]

Land for Large-Scale Plantation Projects

The allocation of commercial use rights (HGU) for large-scale plantation projects continues to involve a massive concentration of agricultural land. In 2000, 2,178 enterprises, both private and state-owned plantation companies, controlled over 3.52 million hectares of plantation estates, on average 1.6 thousand hectares each.[21] High international demand for agro-fuel has driven increased land allocation and conversion for large-scale oil palm plantations. The Indonesian government plans to clear around 20 million hectares of land for palm oil commodity production in Sumatra, Kalimantan, Sulawesi, and Papua. In 2002, 50 percent of the 6 million hectares of oil palm plantations were controlled by private (both domestic and foreign) corporations (Colchester et al. 2006, 22–26).

Land for Residential, Tourism, and Industrial Estate Projects

Enterprises controlling land for new towns and tourism and industrial estate projects are also high on the list of large landholders in the overall agrarian structure in Indonesia. By 1996, in the vast semiurban sprawl that is Jabodetabek (Jakarta-Bogor-Depok-Tangerang-Bekasi) alone, ten conglomerates controlled 65,434 hectares of land for luxury real estate development.[22] Up to 1998 the National Land Agency

(BPN) issued location permits for housing projects throughout Indonesia on around 74,735 hectares of land. In 1994-95, the national association of developers recorded that 418 developers were involved in building new housing estates and settlements on 1.3 million hectares of land across Indonesia.[23] By 1995, thirty-two golf courses, mostly attached to real estate developments, used no less than 11,200 hectares of land in the Jabotabek (Jakarta-Bogor-Tanggerang-Bekasi) region; each project typically absorbing 350 hectares. By 2000, there were 119 country club and golf courses throughout the country.[24] Land allocated for industrial estates has also been highly concentrated. In 1998, forty-six major industrial estates were operating on around 17,470 hectares, averaging 379.8 hectares each. In addition, seventy-four other planned industrial estate sites (including fourteen state-owned) remained undeveloped; comprising around 25,254 hectares that had already been expropriated (Lerche 1999, 16, 28, 41-43, 66-67).

Land for People-Based Agricultural Activities

Land available for people-based agricultural activities is squeezed from remnants of these land allocations for capital-intensive developments. Based on the 1973 agricultural census, Kano estimated there were approximately 21.6 million farm households,[25] including both landholders and farmworkers (Kano 1994).[26] This meant around 84 percent of the population in Indonesia was involved in the peasant-based economy, cultivating around 14.2 million hectares of agricultural land (see table 2.3). Among these households, he estimated around 7.21 million (33.4 percent) were landless (Kano 1994, 47), referred to as "absolute landless" in this chapter. A further 14.4 million households with control over some agricultural land (hereafter called "peasant landholders"),[27] had quite small holdings, averaging one hectare.

Based on the 1983 agricultural census, 16.8 million hectares of agricultural land had to support the livelihoods of 23.8 million farm households, or around 60 percent of the total households in Indonesia at that time.[28] This percentage of farm households had declined by 9 percent from 1973 to 1983,[29] but at the same time the total number

TABLE 2.3
Farm households and landholdings, 1973–2003

	\multicolumn{5}{c}{Census year}				
	1963	1973*	1983	1993	2003
Total number of farm households (millions)	n/a	21.6	23.8	30.2	37.7
Peasant landholders (million households)	12.2	14.4 (67%)	18.8 (79%)	21.1 (70%)	24.3 (64%)
"Absolute landless" (million households)	n/a	7.1 (33%)	5 (21%)	9.1 (30%)	13.4 (36%)
Total landholdings by peasant landholders (million ha)	12.9	14.2	16.8	17.1	21.5
Average landholding by peasant landholders (ha)	1.06	0.98	0.89	0.81	0.88
Gini ratio of landholdings	**n/a**	**0.70**	**0.64**	**0.67**	**0.72**

Sources: Calculated from the results of agricultural censuses of 1963, 1973, 1983, 1993 and 2003 (Badan Pusat Statistik 2004, tables 1.c and 3.c; BPS 1975, table 2.0; 1985a, table 2.0; 1985b, table 4; 1994a, tables 2, 4, 5, and 13.1; 1994b, tables 2, 3, and 4; 1995, table 05; and data of 2003 Agricultural Census accessed directly at the BPS Jakarta office, 30 January 2007), and Kano 1994.

Note: The number of farm households and "absolute landless" in 1973 are based on Kano's estimates (Kano 1994), while the number of peasant landholders is based on the 1973 Agricultural Census data as published by the Central Bureau of Statistics (BPS). We calculated the Gini ratio of this year based on the combination of these two sources. Data used in this calculation cover only farm households involved mainly in cropping activities. Peasant households that depend on cattle breeding, dairy farming, poultry, and fish breeding, as well as plantation workers, are not included.

of farming households increased by 2.2 million. These figures reflect both population growth and absorption of a proportion of the farm population into industrial and other nonagricultural employment. Within this total number of farm households, around 21 percent were classified as "absolute landless," representing a decline of 12 percent in this category during the period 1973–83. A further 18.8 million peasant landholders also had quite small holdings in 1983, on average 0.89 hectare. We will explain later these two phenomena of declining "absolute landless" and average landholdings during the period 1973–83 when we discuss the dynamics of landlessness and average landholdings by peasant households below.

When the fourth agricultural census was conducted in 1993, only 17.1 million hectares of agricultural land were available for 30.2 million farm households, or 70 percent of the total households in Indonesia at that time.[30] Within this total number of farm households (which had increased by 6.4 million since 1983), nearly a third fell into the category of "absolute landless" (an increase of 9 percent during the period 1983–93), while a further 21.1 million households with control over some agricultural land had quite small holdings, which had declined on average to 0.81 hectare. In the agricultural census of 2003, the total amount of land for people-based agricultural activities increased by approximately 26 percent from 17.1 million hectares in 1993 to 21.5 million hectares in 2003. This total amount of land must support the livelihoods of around 37.7 million farm households (around 69 percent of total Indonesian households at that time).[31] The "absolute landless" category increased to 36 percent of the total number of farming households, while the average landholding controlled by 24.3 million peasant landholders rose slightly to 0.88 hectare per household. Agricultural census data show that the number of farm households has increased steadily from 1973 to 2003, following the rate of population growth. Along with this trend is an increasing level of landlessness. The total numbers of "absolute landless" households declined only once, from 1973 to 1983, and then increased steadily through 2003 (for reasons to be discussed below).[32]

Unequal Land Distribution and Rural Poverty

Two conditions have contributed to widespread poverty in rural Indonesia. The first is a steady increase, between 1963 and 2003, in the already substantial proportion of the population that constitutes small peasant households (over 40 percent). The second is the growth of landlessness (see tables 2.3 and 2.5). In-depth studies of rural dynamics by Mintoro (1984) and Saleh (1984) concluded that poverty in rural areas occurs mainly in landless households. Arief (1977, 72–103), based on his analysis of the 1973 agricultural census compared with other findings of microstudies in rural Java, concluded that inequality of landholdings is the basis of rural poverty. White and Wiradi (1989), analyzing landholdings in nine villages in Java, also concluded that small and landless peasants have fewer opportunities to increase their agricultural income or invest in nonfarm activities.[33] Although the relative importance of the factors driving these processes is open to debate, we would argue that the increasing number of small peasants and the growth of landlessness reflect a process of polarization in landholdings and proletarianization in Indonesian rural communities since 1973. Using the agricultural census data to assess inequality of land distribution in Indonesia, Gini ratios were found to range between 0.64 and 0.72, as shown in table 2.3.[34] Compared to the results of several other microstudies, these Gini ratios are relatively low. For example, Kano's study of a South Malang village in 1976–77 reported a Gini ratio of landholding of 0.81 (Kano 1990, 31); and Siahaan's microstudy in a village of Klaten District in 1975 reported a Gini ratio of landholding of 0.9 (Siahaan 1977, 21). Another study, by the Bogor-based Agro Economy Survey Foundation (SAE) in fifteen villages in West, Central, and North Java and South Sulawesi in 1982, reported a Gini ratio of landholdings ranging between 0.54 and 0.91. In twelve villages studied in Java, only one village had a Gini ratio of less than 0.6 (Wiradi and H. Makali 1984, 52). Kano's most recent study on Indonesian agricultural change (2008, 391) shows that in six villages in northern Central Java in 1990, Gini ratios of landholdings ranged from 0.65 to 0.89.[35]

Microstudies carried out mostly in Java, where population density and total number of farm households are high, have high Gini ratios, compared to figures shown here that are based on national landholding data. Our calculation, based on the 2003 census indicates the Gini ratio for Java is 0.70.[36] Booth's calculations of Gini ratios for landholdings in Java for 1973 and 1983 (which excludes landless households) are 0.49 and 0.47 (Booth 1988, 52, table 2.16).[37] However, with the inclusion of figures for landless households, all Gini ratio figures from 1973 to 2003 lead us to conclude that the deep inequality of landholding structures in Indonesia, particularly in Java, has never been corrected.

The pattern of landholdings as shown above has resulted from a combination of population growth and agrarian policies during the New Order regime that prioritized making land available for large-scale investment and natural resources exploitation by the private sector, at smallholders' expense. In this respect the New Order's agrarian policies are reminiscent of the former colonial government's agrarian politics, especially during the Liberal period of the late nineteenth century.[38] That pattern of land allocation and holdings also reflected "landowner bias." In both periods concentration of landholdings was tolerated, while little attention was paid to the reality of peasants' small land holdings and landlessness.

Under the New Order, peasant agriculture has been given little attention by government, and any attention it does get is limited to guaranteeing food supply in anticipation of possible food crises and social unrest (Mears 1982, 437, 469). That is one reason why soon after coming to power, the New Order launched the Green Revolution program to increase food production. This was aimed primarily at making Indonesia self-sufficient in rice production, in line with international interests at that time (White 2005). To achieve this aim, the New Order regime calculated agricultural statistics to show the success of the Green Revolution through increasing agricultural productivity. It also became more difficult to obtain valid official statistics revealing land ownership and land control, and to relate these figures to rural poverty (Wiradi 1984, 290). Official statistics are based on household landholdings (operational holding) rather than individual ownership. Agricultural statistics predominantly show annual areas harvested, crop yields, type of technology used, and farm income in general, calculated from crop yields and the commodity sale price.[39]

Reflections on the Structure of Landholdings from Five Agricultural Censuses

Fundamental weaknesses in data collection for the Indonesian agricultural census after 1963 affect interpretation of landholding patterns.[40] The focus on landholding instead of ownership means the census cannot be used to show polarization of land ownership for the later period, and it thus obscures the insecurity of tenure and poor terms

TABLE 2.4
Changing dynamics of peasant landholders, 1963–2003

Year of census	Total number of peasant landholders (millions)	Total landholdings (million ha)	Average landholdings (ha)	% of "small peasants" (holding land < 0.5 ha)	% Increase of peasant landholders between two censuses	% Increase of total landholdings between two censuses*
1963	12.2	12.9	1.06	44		
1973	14.4	14.2	0.98	46	1963–1973 = 18	1963–1973 = 10
1983	18.8	16.8	0.89	45	1973–1983 = 31	1973–1983 = 18
1993	21.1	17.1	0.81	49	1983–1993 = 12	1983–1993 = 2
2003	24.3	21.5	0.88	51	1993–2003 = 15	1993–2003 = 26

Sources: Calculated from the agricultural censuses of 1963, 1973, 1983, 1993, and 2003 (BPS 1963, table 2; 1975, table 2.0; 1985a, table 2.0; 1985b, table 4; 1994a, tables 2, 4, 5, and 13.1; BPS 1994b, tables 2, 3 and 4; BPS 1995, table 05; and data of 2003 agricultural census accessed directly at the BPS Jakarta office, 30 January 2007)

Note: All figures in this table have been rounded.

of employment of tenant farmers. Nor can data on large-scale land ownership, by rural or urban-based absentee landholders who invest in agricultural land, be obtained from these agricultural censuses. Another important weakness of the censuses is that landholdings of shifting cultivators in outer island areas are underreported. The census only assesses actual landholdings at the time the census was conducted, while shifting cultivation creates more complex and extensive landholding patterns and use over a longer period. Consequently, we can use the census data to obtain only a rough picture of the changing dynamics of the landholdings of shifting cultiavtors.

The five agricultural censuses (1963 to 2003) show that the increasing number of peasant landholders was not matched by a corresponding increase in the availability of land (see last two columns of table 2.4). Although the average landholding per household has been relatively stable (around one hectare), the percentage of "small peasants" (or farm households holding land less than 0.5 hectare) has increased in each census. Table 2.4 shows a relatively steady rise in the total amount of land controlled by peasant landholders over forty years, almost doubling between 1963 and 2003, but average landholdings per household were never above one hectare after 1963 because the total number of peasant landholders also nearly doubled in this period.

Between the 1973 and 1993 censuses there are two interesting phenomena occurring. First, even though the absolute number of landholders and land held by this group of peasants has increased, there is a significant drop in the percentage increase for both intervals 1973–83 and 1983–93. Second, there is a large gap between the percentage increase in the number of peasant landholders and the total increase in the amount of land available for peasant agricultural activity during the period 1983–93 (12 percent compared with 2 percent). We believe these two phenomena relate to the conversion of agricultural land for nonagricultural purposes, as well as to unbalanced rural-urban economic growth, which left less developed rural areas behind, forcing villagers to leave their communities and the agricultural sector. A massive process of land conversion (from agricultural to nonagricultural uses) was occurring in this period, and will be discussed below. However, the financial crisis of the late 1990s made the rural population fall back on agriculture for their livelihoods, increasing the total number of peasant landholders significantly at the last census (2003). We would argue that forest encroachment and occupation of state land have accounted for the significant increase in the amount of land held by peasant landholders in the 2003 census (although the census does not officially recognize these phenomena).

"Small Peasants" and Average Landholdings Controlled by Peasant Landholders

From 1963 to 2003, the average quantity of land held by peasant landholders remained relatively small, between 0.81 hectares and 1.06 hectares.[41] In densely populated Java, the average peasant landholding was only around 0.45 hectares over this forty-year period. Table 2.4 also shows that land-poor peasants holding less than 0.5 hectares across the country is increasing; they now constitute the majority of peasant households according to the 2003 census (see also table 2.8 below). Peasant landholdings have never met the minimum requirement of two hectares for optimum family farm productivity, as mandated by the Basic Agrarian

Law and supporting legislation. The BAL (§17) and UU 56/1960 (§8) stipulated that the state had a duty to fulfill this requirement for peasant households. Redistribution of land through a reform program was the Sukarno government's solution to overcoming both the imbalance of landholdings among farm households and the imbalance between land used for people-based agriculture and other (nonagricultural) purposes.

But Suharto's New Order focused on transmigration in lieu of land reform. Despite this, the average peasant holding during the New Order period was lower than the period before. During the New Order the average landholding by peasant landholders was never above one hectare, while the number of landless and agricultural laborers continued to grow. The massive systematic land reform program initiated by the BAL and land reform legislation in 1961 ceased under the New Order regime's administration; while large-scale land control by private business was aggressively facilitated.

In general, the average size of land controlled after independence did not change significantly from conditions during colonial times. Tauchid showed that the average land controlled by peasant households in Java, East Sumatra, and Bali in 1938 was 0.84 hectare (calculated from Tauchid 1952, 174–76). Land occupations that occurred in the ex-foreign plantation sector during the revolution and early 1950s, followed later by Sukarno's land reform program, led to only small changes in the average size of landholdings. Sizes increased to 1.05 hectares per household for peasant landholders by 1963, but the increase did not continue in subsequent years, with the exception of a small rise following the land occupations that accompanied the fall of Suharto, as suggested by the 2003 agricultural census data (table 2.4).

Indonesia's average holdings by peasant landholder have tended to decrease, unlike the trend in postwar Japan. The number of small peasants in Japan increased after implementation of the postwar land reform, but this occurred within a relatively equal land distribution structure. Between 1950 and 1980 the postwar Japanese land distribution structure, characterized by large numbers of small peasants, remained unchanged (Nozomu 1984). Instead, it was the pattern of income sources that changed, with the proportion of full-time peasants declining from 50 percent in 1950 to 13 percent in 1980, while part-time peasants, with different kinds of off-farm income, increased from 50 percent to 87 percent (Nozomu 1984).

Peasant Landholders' Income Sources

Unlike the Japanese situation, the increasing number of "small peasants' in Indonesia since 1963 was not followed by a dramatic change in sources of income. As shown in table 2.6 below, after the 1960 land reform program was replaced by the transmigration and Green Revolution programs, the 1983 agricultural census did not show an increase in off-farm incomes of peasant landholders, especially for "small peasants." In the 1995 intercensus population survey (Supas), only 46 percent of households located in rural areas gave agriculture as their sole

TABLE 2.5
Composition of peasant landholders based on landholdings and main income sources, 1983–1993

Size of landholdings (hectares)	% Peasant landholders by main income sources			
	1983		1993	
	Agricultural sector	*Nonagricultural sector*	*Agricultural sector*	*Nonagricultural sector*
< 0.1	74.6	25.4	62.4	37.6
0.10–0.19	86.9	13.1	73.7	26.3
2.00–0.49	92.2	7.8	82.7	17.3
0.50–0.99	94.9	5.1	89.1	10.9
1.00–1.99	95.6	4.4	91.6	8.4
2.00–5.00	95.8	4.2	92.3	7.7
> 5.00	95.5	4.5	90.8	9.2
Average	90.8	9.2	83.2	16.8
Total peasant landholders				
(million households)	17.1	1.7	17.6	3.5

Sources: Calculated from the agricultural censuses of 1983 and 1993 (BPS 1985b, table 12; and 1995, table 13).

income source in 1995 (Booth 2002, 179–80). But the 1993 agricultural census reported 83 percent of the total number of peasant landholders (70 percent of total farm households; see table 2.3) were still dependent on agriculture as their main income source. This represents only a small decline from the 1983 agricultural census, which reported that around 90 percent of landholders' main income was from the agricultural sector (table 2.6 below). Thus Booth was correct when she said, "Clearly it would be wrong to argue that the agricultural sector, even before the crisis of 1997, was not an important source of income for the great majority of rural households in Indonesia" (Booth 2002, 180).

From the 2003 agricultural census data made available to us at the Jakarta BPS, it was not possible to calculate how many peasant landholders were still dependent on agriculture as their main source of income. However, in table 2.6 we have made a comparison of available data from 1983 and 2003 to provide some indication of the composition of landholders' incomes.

An interesting question is raised by the relatively small difference in total incomes in the 2003 census, between the category of landholders who have less than 0.1 hectare and those who have holdings of 1–2 and 2–5 hectares. These larger landholding groups have total incomes only 27 percent and 72 percent higher respectively than the most landpoor category, despite landholdings 10–20 and 20–50 times greater. This is an indication of how much poorer the rewards are for labor in the agricultural sector. The proposition of a direct relationship between landholding and poverty is reflected in the 1983 statistics, but it is no longer apparent in 2003, after industrialization and diversification dramatically altered the rewards and opportunities for off-farm work. Microstudies are needed to examine the complexities of the picture suggested by these data. The 1983 data on the composition of peasant landholders' monthly household income showed that, on average, their income from farm and off-farm sectors was relatively equal. But in 2003, "small peasants" (holding below 0.5 hectares) had more income from the off-farm sector, while the percentage of income from farming activities for landholders holding more than one hectare was substantially greater than in the 1983 census. Meanwhile, peasant

TABLE 2.6

Composition of peasant landholders based on landholdings and main income sources, 1983 and 2003

Size of landholdings (hectares)	1983*						2003					
	# of landholder households (millions)	Source of income (monthly)					# of landholder households (millions)	Source of income (monthly)				
		Farm sector		Off-farm sector				Farm sector		Off-farm sector		
		%	Average amount (000s rupiah)	%	Average amount (000s rupiah)			%	Average amount (000s rupiah)	%	Average amount (000s rupiah)	
< 0.1	1.4	50.0	13.1	50.0	13.1		2.6	24.3	198.1	75.7	617.9	
0.10–0.19	2.0	49.8	22.6	50.2	22.8		3.0	31.7	221.7	68.3	477.3	
0.20–0.49	5.0	49.9	27.5	50.1	27.5		6.8	41.3	313.2	58.7	445.8	
0.50–0.99	4.4	50.1	79.7	49.9	79.4		4.8	51.8	440.1	48.2	409.9	
1.00–1.99	3.5	50.1	147.5	49.9	146.7		3.9	61.2	633.4	38.8	401.6	
2.00–5.00	2.1	49.2	284.6	50.8	293.9		2.8	70.0	978.5	30.0	418.5	
> 5.00	0.4						0.4	73.2	1,770.1	26.8	646.9	
Total	18.8	49.6	63.9	50.4	64.8		24.3	50.6	464.9	49.4	454.1	

Sources: Calculated from the results of agricultural censuses of 1983 and 2003 (BPS 1985b, tables 10 and 112; and the 2003 agricultural census data accessed directly at the BPS Jakarta office, 30 January 2007).

*The 1983 census data did not provide a breakdown of income sources for any landholder/farmer with more than two hectares. In this table all data of the landholders' income sources who hold between two and five hectares are combined for that year.

The 1993 agricultural census data could not be disaggregated in a way that can be used in this table. For a comparison of other data from the 1983 and 1993 agricultural censuses see Booth (2002, 183, table 4).

landholders who held between half and one hectare had similar incomes from both farm and off-farm sources.

From table 2.6 we can assume that from 1983 to 2003, the growth of job opportunities outside the agriculture sector has contributed to changes in income composition for small peasants, so they are no longer dependent on agriculture as their main source of income. However, aside from the growth of off-farm job opportunities, we can add that the low wages in the agricultural sector and the low profit margins of agricultural products have pushed small peasants to seek alternative sources of income. Their situation is different from that of largest-scale landholders (more than five hectares), whose landholdings enable them to farm on a bigger scale, and who can invest the profits of their farming activities in other sectors, including education for their children. These largest landholders have an average monthly income from their farms which is substantially greater than that generated by smaller landholders, but their off-farm income is not significantly different from that of households with the smallest holdings (less than 0.1 hectares).

Our analysis suggests that it is necessary to qualify Booth's assessment of the data. She concludes that there is "a clear tendency for total income to increase with holding size.... It was still the case that agricultural households on larger holdings earned more on average from all sources, both on and off the holding, than households operating smaller holdings.... Control over assets, including educated labour, permits households to diversify successfully into non-agricultural activities, and is thus an important determinant of total household income" (Booth 2002, 185, 187). The data from 2003 (table 2.6) show that the proportion of off-farm income has not been proportionately incremental across the scale of peasant landholding categories.

Dynamics of Landlessness and Share Tenancy

Table 2.7 shows figures of another kind of landlessness, namely "landless tenants." This table indicates a down-up-down trend of "landless tenants" in Indonesia between 1963 and 2003, although it shows a trend of declining numbers of "landless tenants" since 1983. The term "landless tenants" refers to a farm household that controls land (peasant landholder) as a sharecropping tenant only, and does not own any additional land.

In 1963 the proportion of landless tenants was 6.8 percent, but by 1973 this had decreased to 3.2 percent. This was due partly to the land reform program carried out during 1961–65 in Java and until the early 1970s outside Java. The land reform program, based on the principle of "land to the tillers," made land distribution to sharecroppers the main priority[42] and brought about this decrease of more than 50 percent in landless tenants over the decade 1963–73. However, between 1973 and 1983 there was a sharp increase in the number of landless tenants and an increasing polarization among the landholding peasantry (tables 2.7 and 2.8). The number of peasant landholders

TABLE 2.7
Landholder status of peasant households, 1963–2003

Status of peasant landholders	1963 (%)	1973 (%)	1983 (%)	1993 (%)	2003 (%)
Owner-operators only	64.1	74.8	69.3	71.7	70.5
Owner operators who are also share croppers	29.1	22.1	25.3	24.6	26.1
"Landless-tenants"	6.8	3.2	5.4	3.8	3.4
All peasant landholders (excludes "absolute-landless" agricultural workers)	100	100	100	100	100
[Total number of farm households (millions)]	n.a.*	[21.6]	[23.8]	[30.2]	[37.7]
[Total number of "landless tenant" households) (million)]	[0.832]	[0.460]	[1.015]	[0.804]	[0.826]

Sources: Calculated from the results of agricultural censuses of 1963, 1973, 1983, 1993, and 2003 (BPS 1963, table 3; BPS 1975, table 7; BPS 1985b, table 15; BPS 1995, table 17; and data of 2003 agricultural census accessed directly at the BPS Jakarta office, 8 September 2008).

*The 1963 agricultural census only provides data on total peasant landholders, while data on absolute landless were not collected. Consequently the total number of farm households cannot be calculated.

in the less than 0.1 and 2–5 hectares classes of landholdings increased, while peasants with 0.5–0.99 hectares declined. This polarization in landholding patterns was undoubtedly due to a combination of factors with conflicting implications: the polarizing effects of the Green Revolution, fragmentation of landholdings due to population increase, and the increases resulting from two hectare allotments granted under the transmigration scheme. Table 2.8 shows this very mixed picture.

There is obviously a connection here with the "end" of the land reform program in the early 1970s. Under the New Order, the only national large-scale program that gave small farmers ownership rights to agricultural land and that made a significant impact on landholding structures was the transmigration program. Otherwise, acquisition of agricultural land was mostly based on "market forces," such as land trading transactions or mortgaging. In other words, the increase in the number of farm households holding one to five hectares in the 1983 census was at least partly caused by the growth of the land tenancy market, rather than an increase in land ownership.

The Green Revolution contributed to the concentration of landholdings in this period. The credit dependence it promoted forced some small landholders to dispose of their rights to land. The productivity of small landholders remained low, because they could not meet increasing costs of production, especially fertilizer and seeds to grow the Green Revolution varieties of crops.[43] Some marginal farmers were able to increase their incomes and holdings as a result of increased outputs, while others were forced to sell or pawn their land to pay debts. The Green Revolution pushed small sharecroppers into becoming wage laborers, both on and off-farm, as labor absorption per unit of land was reduced by mechanization (see also Hüsken and White 1989; Hüsken 1998; Collier et al. 1996).

The decrease in the number of landless tenants during the period 1963–73 (table 2.7) was indeed because of land redistribution under the land reform program, when "landless tenants" became "owner-operators"; while the decrease between 1983 and 2003 could mean some of these "landless tenants" became "absolute landless." Along with other processes that led to the loss of land, such as eviction, conversion, or other kinds of land transactions, this transformation from landless tenants to absolute landless is contributing to the deepening of unequal land distribution structures in Indonesia.

The proportion of absolute landless increased from 21 percent of total peasant households in 1983, to 30 percent in 1993, and 36 percent in 2003 (table 2.3). This increase may be owing partly to diminishing possibilities to control land, either as owners or tenants, and partly to the transformation of farming activities from share-tenancy to wage labor. While the number of landless tenants from 1963 to 2003 has fluctuated, the phenomenon of landlessness in Indonesia shows an increasing trend. Combining available data on absolute landless and landless tenants, as shown in tables 2.3 and 2.7, we can see a clear trend of increasing landlessness in Indonesia during the twenty years from 1983 to 2003: 25.3 percent in 1983, 32.7 percent in 1993, and 38.2 percent in 2003.[44]

The relationship between the increasing number of landless peasants, and the imbalance between growth of population (number of farm households) and accessible land available for cultivation (as shown in table 2.4) will be clearer if we compare them with two other phenomena: the small portion of total land in Indonesia that is accessible for people-based agricultural activities as opposed to other agricultural purposes and land allocation for various "development" projects, including conversion of agricultural land into land for non-agricultural purposes.

Land Distribution among Peasant Landholders

Table 2.8 gives landholdings by peasant landholders from four agricultural censuses, 1973 to 2003.[45] From these figures we can see how the situation has changed for different categories of peasant landholders. The most important trend is the increasing proportion of "small peasants" over thirty years, in particular a significant increase in the proportion of peasant landholders with very small landholdings (less than 0.1 hectare), the category of "near-to-(absolute) landless." Also within the category of land-poor peasants (*petani gurem*) are those who hold land between 0.1 and 0.49 hectares. Their proportion declined in the 1983 agricultural census, before increasing in 1993 and 2003. The rate of land lost to "small peasants" during the period 1973–83 is high among this group, causing many of them to fall into the category of "near-to-(absolute) landless," which means they only hold enough land for their house and a very small yard.

We believe that the insignificant decline in the number of small peasants (see tables 2.4 and 2.8), the substantial increase in the number of "landless tenants" (see table 2.7), an increase in the number of relatively large landholders (two to five hectares) and some increase in the concentration of holdings by middle peasants at the expense of the poorest in the period 1973–83, are due to two factors. The first is that the increase in available agricultural land was not sufficient to keep up with the increase in numbers of peasant housholds. The second is the transfer of land to peasants with relatively larger landholdings, as a result of the Green Revolution, as well as increasing farm production costs. Those in the "near-to-(absolute) landless" category of 1973 were likely to become members of a higher category of landholder in 1983, through the tenancy market. Other "near-to-(absolute) landless" households who could not enter the tenancy market ended up as full-time agricultural workers.

TABLE 2.8
Categories of peasant landholders, 1973–2003

Category of landholding (hectares)	1973 (%)	1983 (%)	1993 (%)	2003 (%)
< 0.10	3.4	7.3	8.1	10.9
0.10 – 0.19	12.5	10.4	12.3	12.4
0.20 – 0.49	29.8	26.8	28.2	27.9
0.50 – 0.99	24.7	23.4	22.2	19.7
1.00 – 1.99	18.1	18.6	16.8	16.1
2.00 – 5.00	9.4	11.2	11.0	11.4
> 5.00	2.1	2.3	1.4	1.6
Total (millions)	**14.4**	**18.8**	**21.2**	**24.3**

Sources: Calculated from the results of agricultural censuses of 1973, 1983, 1993, and 2003 (BPS 1975, table 2.0; BSP 1985a, table 2.0; BPS 1985b, table 4; BPS 1994a, tables 2, 4, 5, and 13.1; BSP 1994b, tables 2, 3, and 4; BSP 1995, table 05; and unpublished data of 2003 agricultural census accessed directly at the BPS Jakarta office, 30 January 2007).

Figure 2.1 shows quantitative changes in the distribution of land control among peasant households over forty years from 1963 to 2003, as has been shown separately in tables 2.1, 2.4, and 2.8. These data help us understand the phenomenon of long-lasting unequal land distribution structures within the group of peasant landholders. This is confirmed through the Gini ratios for each census, which are relatively consistent at above 0.5 (0.3 is considered a threshold point of relative equality of landholding structure). In the 1993 and 2003 censuses, these Gini ratios are near 0.6, which indicates a very uneven distribution of landholdings.

Dynamics of Land Conversion

Over the four decades 1963–2003, the land area for people-based agriculture has increased (table 2.4). However, the number of peasant households grew faster than the amount of accesible agricultural land, and this caused average agricultural landholdings controlled by peasant households to decrease. Alongside the impact of population growth, people's access to agricultural land has not increased at the same rate as

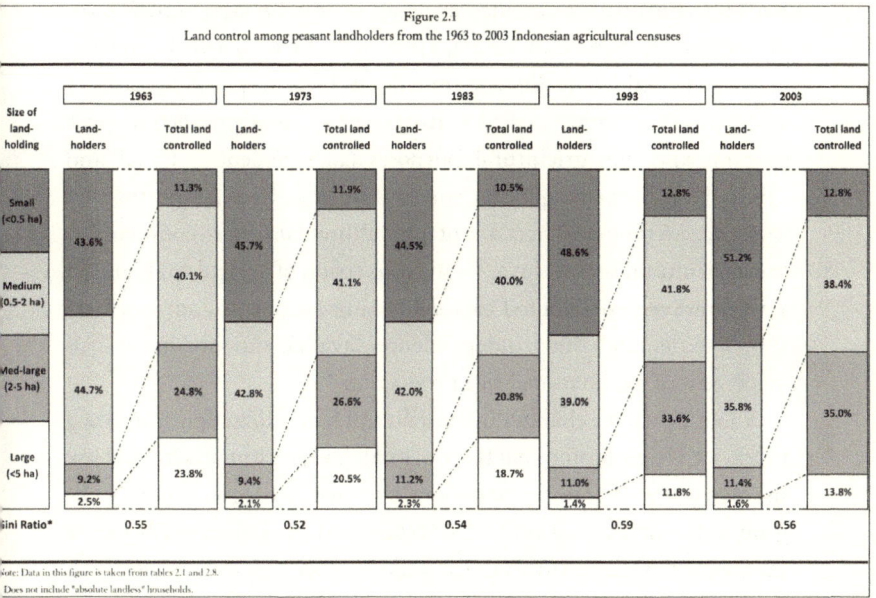

Figure 2.1
Land control among peasant landholders from the 1963 to 2003 Indonesian agricultural censuses

Land Concentration and Land Reform in Indonesia   65

the growth in the number of peasant households, because of the high rate of land conversion for many other (nonsmallholder) purposes.

It is not only peasants who require land for their livelihoods. Big commercial interests such as large-scale plantations, mining, forestry, manufacturing, housing, and tourism also require land. Economic growth and industrialization strategies of the New Order administration prioritized large-scale projects, which created the demand for land. Competition between these projects and the agricultural sector, especially people-based agricultural activities, created tension not only in Java, where the population density is already high, but also in regions outside Java. Ironically, much of the land acquired by speculators was misused or abandoned following the economic crisis. According to the National Land Agency (BPN), as of 1998 only 26 percent of the land for which "location permits" were issued was used in accordance with the conditions attached to these permits;[46] the rest was abandoned (or *tanah terlantar*)[47] (Pusat Data Bisnis Indonesia 1998, 4).

With the extensive growth of manufacturing, real estate, and development of new towns, the wet rice farming sector in Java faces strong competition for land. The result is the same: agricultural land has been converted for an increasing number of nonagricultural uses. According to Nasoetion (1991), from 1986 to 1989 rice harvesting areas decreased by 2.3 percent annually in Java: 2,242,000 hectares of rice fields were converted to non-rice agricultural production (55.8 percent) and nonagricultural purposes (44.2 percent).[48] Jamal and Djuhari (1998, 75–87) quoting Sumaryanto et al. (1995), reported that in 1995, 22.6 thousand hectares of agricultural land were converted to nonagricultural uses in Java.[49] This conversion of agricultural land in Java, however, contributed to a decreasing ratio of Indonesia's food supply to demand. Since independence, Java has supplied more than 50 percent of total national rice production.[50]

Table 2.9 shows changes in agricultural land utilization from 1963 to 2000. Even assuming that these are only rough estimates, they show the dynamics of transformation in land use, and give some background to our analysis of land structure and the imbalance between the amount of agricultural land and the number of peasant households

TABLE 2.9
Land utilization in Indonesia, 1963–2000[1]

	Java					Outside Java					Indonesia				
	1963	1973	1983	1993	2000	1963	1973	1983	1993	2000	1963	1973	1983	1993	2000
	(Percent)					(Percent)					(Percent)				
Nonforestland															
Rural settlements and urban areas[2]	4.0	3.4	12.2	13.0	13.9	0.1	0.3	2.0	1.9	7.7	0.4	0.5	2.7	2.7	2.7
People's agricultural land Wet rice (*sawah*)	19.1	19.9	26.5	26.0	26.5	0.9	1.2	2.5	2.8	2.5	2.1	2.5	4.1	4.4	4.1
Ladang and *kebun*[3]	19.2	16.7	24.7	24.4	25.7	2.9	2.7	5.8	5.1	5.8	4.0	3.6	7.1	6.4	7.1
Large-scale plantations	4.0	5.1	4.5	4.7	4.7	0.6	0.9	4.3	6.4	9.0	0.8	1.2	4.3	6.3	8.7
Bera[4] land & scrub (*Semak belukar*)	0.4	1.5	2.9	3.3	4.4	0.2	0.7	16.9	10.4	12.5	0.2	0.7	15.9	9.9	11.9
Grasslands (*padang rumput*)	0.1	0.1	0.5	0.3	0.3	0.0	0.0	2.2	1.1	1.2	0.0	0.0	2.1	1.0	1.1
Forestland[5]	22.6	21.9	18.1	22.8	24.3	67.0	67.3	61.9	71.5	65.3	63.9	64.2	58.9	68.2	62.6
Other[6]	30.7	31.4	10.5	5.6	0.4	28.3	26.9	4.5	0.7	-3.9	28.5	27.2	4.9	1.1	1.8
Total land	100.0	100.0	100.0	100.0	100.0	100.0	100.0	100.0	100.0	100.0	100.0	100.0	100.0	100.0	100.0

Sources: Badan Pusat Statistik (BPS) 2001b (tables 1, 2, 3, and 4); BPS 2001c (pages 4 and 200); BPS 1963 (tables 1, 7A, 8A, and 9.1.A); BPS 1964 (tables A.2 and H.1); BPS 1974 (tables I.1.2 and VII.3.1); BPS 1975 (tables 1 and 8); BPS 1983 (table I.1); BPS 1985c (tables 1 and 2); BPS 1985d (table V.3.3); BPS 1994c (tables 1 and 2); BPS 1994d (tables 1 and 2); BPS 1994e (tables 1.1 and 5.3.1)

Notes: There is a marked difference in the data on land utilized for dry land and gardens, small-scale plantation or *perkebunan rakyat*, swidden agriculture and scrublands, and grasslands categories recorded since 1983 and the data from previous years. This is because the 1983 and 1993 data are derived from the agricultural census, which collected more detailed data than yearly agricultural surveys, which were the main source before 1983.

[1] Land utilized for roads, water drainage, irrigation, sport facilities, graves, and other kinds of facilities was not included.

[2] Urban areas include residential and industrial uses.

[3] BPS data includes *tegalan*, *kebun*, *huma*, *ladang*, *kolam*, *tambak*, and *empang* agricultural land types (but not *pekarangan*, house gardens, which were included in the hamlets category).

[4] *Tanah bera* is land that is temporarily left to replenish its fertility, usually as part of a cycle of swidden agriculture.

[5] As defined by government regulation.

[6] Swamps and dams and so on are included in this category.

who require land. These macro figures also help to explain why land disputes have intensified between local communities and both the government and larger companies who accumulate land mainly for capital-intensive development.

The following trends can be interpreted from table 2.9.

1. Overall, the amount of peasant agricultural land (rice fields, gardens, and dry field land) increased from 6.1 percent of the total Indonesian land mass in 1963 to 11.2 percent at the beginning of the 1980s. But this growth in the amount of land accessible for peasant-based agriculture did not solve the problems of the decrease in the average amount of land under each peasant household's control, or the growth in the number of landless peasants.

2. The sharp increase in peasant-based agricultural land and land used for human settlement, particularly the expansion of cities from 1983, is owing to the conversion of forest and swamp areas to agricultural land use, at the same time as agricultural land is being converted to housing estates on the fringes of urban areas or to other nonagricultural (industrial and infrastructure) purposes.

3. By 1983 the area of forest both in Java and the outer islands decreased. The decrease in forest area outside Java has primarily been due to the conversion of forest to large-scale plantations and transmigration projects; in Java this expansion into forest is caused by the extension of people-based agricultural land, partially as a result of displacement from agricultural areas.

4. The loss of forestland during the period 1973–83 was "compensated" for by the increase in forestry land in 1993. The formal claim by government to almost all forestland as "state-forest" in accordance with the Forestry Law, and the formal delineation of land use classifications through government policy (TGHK),[51] implies the inclusion of small and people-based plantations, agro forest, *bera* (temporary fallow land),[52] scrub lands, and in some cases even land on which hamlets are located. This explains why in the period 1983–93, forestland increased significantly whereas *bera* land decreased. According to KPA's land disputes database, of the ten most common categories of conflict, cases of conflict related to the establishment of production forest areas ranked fourth, while cases relating to the establishment of conservation forest areas ranked tenth.[53] In the

outer islands, large areas of agricultural land belonging to local communities and individuals were claimed as state forest. In fact, local people have used these forests for swidden cultivation for many generations, and customary (*adat*) community rights of avail (*hak ulayat*) applied across the whole outer island landscape. The conservation forest program also converted large areas of people's land to protected forest status in Java.

5. The decline in the area designated as forest, particularly outside Java, from 71.5 percent (1993) to 65.3 percent (2003) indicates large areas of deforestation and conversion of forest to agricultural land use and/or settlements.

6. Between 1963 and 2000 the area of "large-scale plantations" outside Java increased from 0.6 percent to 9.0 percent of total land, with a sharp rise since 1973. This increase largely resulted from the reduction of both production forest and fallow (*bera*) land.

Absenteeism

Absenteeism[54] is the dark side of the land tenure picture in Indonesia. The high percentage of absenteeism reflects both the high degree of landholding inequality and the government's failure to deal with the problem of landlessness. Each local Land Office of the National Land Agency (BPN) at the district/municipal level is supposed to maintain data on land ownership and owner's residence. But these data are rarely kept up to date, and BPN officers tend to treat the data as exclusive information for official use only, which contributes to nontransparency of the true land ownership situation and the high incidence of land conflicts.

Despite the limited data on absentee land available from official records, it is widely considered that absenteeism is quite common in Java and well known to local villagers (see Sumardjono 1995). The head of the Bekasi District BPN is reported to have admitted that about 20 percent of land under his administration is absentee land (*Kompas*, 2 December 1996 and 9 December 1996). This is consistent with the results of local studies carried out by Collier and his colleagues in the

1990s in Java. They found that around 14 percent of agricultural land in the studied villages was owned by absentee landowners, and 48 percent of peasant households in the study areas were landless (Collier et al. 1996, 106–7, 121–26). Extrapolating from Collier's findings, we estimated that absentee wet rice (*sawah*) land is, on average, sixty hectares per village in the fourteen villages they surveyed (Collier et al. 1996, 121–26). If a land reform program were implemented in these villages, based on Collier's 1992–93 data no fewer than thirty landless peasant households (both landless tenants and absolute-landless) per village would have had the opportunity to improve their livelihood from a two hectare redistribution of *sawah* land at that time.

The Need for Reform

The growing imbalance between peasant households and available agricultural land has contributed to the agrarian conflicts over land access as described in this book. The Sukarno government tried to resolve agrarian inequities through the 1960 Basic Agrarian Law and subsequent land reform program. However, implementation problems and the events of 1965–66 left rural Indonesia still imprisoned in unequal agrarian structures, while population pressures and global capital-intensive development have increased this inequality. Instead of agrarian change becoming the foundation for social and economic development, it is obvious from the above data that no significant benefit has occurred in landholding structures over the forty years from 1963 to 2003. The Gini ratios of landholdings, both for peasant landholders and for total farm households, have never approached the 0.3 agreed-upon indicative value for a relatively equal landholding structure (see Booth 1988, 52). Further, the percentage of landlessness has increased over time. Landlessness is a key factor in vulnerability to exploitation and a threat to the basic needs of marginalized rural populations. It is also a major cause of social and political instability (Prosterman, Temple, and Hanstad 1990; Moyo and Yeros 2005).

Taking an economic perspective, widespread inequality and landlessness also contribute to the poor performance of a country's economy, particularly in countries whose economies are heavily dependent on agriculture. "Landlessness is a cause of low productivity on lands farmed by poorly compensated and poorly motivated tenants and laborers. Farmers with insecure tenure lack incentives to make capital improvements to the land or to invest the 'sweat equity' needed to produce high yields" (Prosterman, Temple, and Hanstad 1990, 1). Long-lasting poverty in rural areas pressures poor and landless peasants to migrate to cities or overseas to find jobs. If they are lucky in this struggle for livelihood, the formal sector will employ them. If not, they will add to the number of urban unemployed or underemployed in the informal sector. Indonesian workers who go abroad to find work and who come from rural areas are lowly paid and often treated unjustly.

Landlessness also contributes to deforestation and land erosion on a huge scale. Landless peasants attempt to cultivate forestland that should not be converted because of its valuable environmental functions, such as protection of water catchment areas and prevention of erosion.[55] The current environmental degradation of the Dieng Plateau and other regions of Wonosobo in Central Java, as well as Lore Lindu National Park in Central Sulawesi, illustrates how frequently farmers who need agricultural land for their livelihood have cultivated protected forest or conservation areas.[56] Inequitable agrarian policy contributes to sociopolitical instability. Russett (1964) examined international correlations between Gini ratios of land distribution, violent political death, and democracy, and concluded that levels of violence and political instability tend to be highest in the countries with the most inequitable landownership patterns. We believe his findings are relevant to Indonesia's current situation (Moyo and Yeros 2005).

Landholding inequality, landlessness, and long-lasting agrarian conflicts cannot, however, be resolved without a comprehensive approach to agrarian policy. As confirmed through various studies (Prosterman, Temple, and Hanstad 1990; Sobhan 1993; Borras Jr. 2007), land reform, conducted in the context of a broader overall development strategy, could contribute to a strong foundation for development and the national economy. Even though land reform will not succeed without financial and political costs, the human costs of inequality as argued by Eckholm are even higher: "Over time, severe inequality can take a direct human toll far greater than the more temporary costs of a successful land-reform effort" (1979, 35).

In this context, it is recognized that an effective land reform program will not achieve its aims without supporting programs, such as low-interest farm credit, improving the distribution of agricultural inputs, and reform in the agricultural marketing system. In this regard, we have to consider Morad's critical evaluation of the small impact of the original land reform program on the Indonesian national economy. He argues that this was because the government "gave more attention to the legal aspects of the program, and less or no attention . . . to the economic and technical aspects" (Morad 1970, 36). Conversely, a group of Indonesian agrarian scholars and activists in the Agrarian Reform Study Group argued:[57]

> However perfect rural development programs are, whether they be rural credit programs, the establishment of cooperatives, improving availability of seeds, fertilizer and water programs, the improvement of roads and other infrastructure, the development of small industry and so on, they will not be successful without the implementation of land reform. In this way land redistribution, which is the heart of land reform program, is the basic foundation for people-based national economic development. (KSPA 2001, 5)

Aside from its part in economic development, land reform in Indonesia must also aim to change power structures in agrarian relations. Land reform has the potential to empower the rural poor. Providing land to the poor is the only effective way to create a more balanced power structure, which in turn is the foundation for creating participatory sociopolitical institutions that will lead to strengthening democracy, at both the local and national levels (Prosterman, Temple, and Hanstad 1990, 2).

It is true that population growth has contributed significantly to the high person to land ratio in Indonesia, which has made it difficult to resolve the problems of landlessness and the small size of average peasant landholdings, particularly in densely populated areas such as Java, Bali, and Madura. However, we would argue that this deflects attention from the evidence of inequality of landholdings from the 1963–2003 agricultural censuses, as analyzed in this chapter, and the high concentration of land in the hands of large corporations, which resulted in the escalation in land conflicts in the late New Order. The neglect of the land poor and landless, on the one hand, and tolerance of land concentration, on the other, has intensified the agrarian problem, making it more difficult to resolve in conventional ways. That is why we argue for a fresh start to genuine agrarian reform to empower the rural poor.[58]

Ladejinsky and other critics of the limited potential of the early Indonesian land reform programs did not take account of state forestry lands and plantation estate lands on which commercial-use rights had expired or were abandoned. There has never been an accurate calculation of land available for redistribution. Accurate data on landholdings and ownership do not exist, because different government agencies (BPN, Department of Agriculture, Forestry, Bureau of Statistics) have different methods and criteria for measurement (Wiradi 2000, 181–82). BPN officers invariably reject requests for the data they have on commercial leases (HGU) and absentee landownership. There is a connection between the inadequacy and nondisclosure of these data and the lack of government interest in reducing land concentration.

In the current context, the calculation of potential objects of land reform must include: (1) abandoned land, especially inactive plantation and other designated land claimed for various "development" projects but actually used for speculation, most of which should legally be classified as *"terlantar"* (neglected/abandoned) and resumed by the state, to become the basis of a new land reform program as intended by the 1960s legislation; (2) many parcels of plantation estate and forestland, particularly those already occupied by landless peasants since the New Order period; (3) existing holdings above the maximum ceiling and absentee lands; and (4) the 1960s redistributed land that has been taken back from the beneficiaries.

Land reform must also take place in the context of a much broader approach to the smallholder agricultural sector. Improvements in farming technology, which have undoubtedly made it possible for farmers to improve their livelihoods on plots of less than two hectares of land,[59] should be implemented with serious attention paid to landholding structures. In this context small farmers have to be protected from the tendency to sell small plots of land, which occurs when they fail to obtain this improved technology and the credit needed for its implementation. In our view the failure of the Green Revolution program was that it did not protect small farmers from market volatility and other economic, social, and environmental pressures to sell off their land. It was the medium and large farmers, who could access subsidies, who gained most from the new technologies (Arief 1977, 99–103; Sinaga and White 1980, 150–51; Zacharias 1983). Government-subsidized credit, as Wiradi, Makali, and Mintoro proposed many years ago, should be provided only to small farmers, for at least ten years, to allow them to improve their productivity (Wiradi, Makali, and Mintoro 1979, 152).

The underlying argument in this chapter is that the post-1965 policies and agrarian politics, favoring large landholders and land concentration, closed off the possibility of seeing land reform.

Notes

The authors thank Hilma Safitri, Wisnu Adi (Timbul), and Nur Hidayat for their help in the collection and preliminary calculation of statistical data from the Indonesian Agricultural Censuses.

1. The BAL (UUPA 1960) was the culmination of a process of work by five committees initiated during the revolution.

2. The term "agrarian" in Indonesian law has meanings broader than those relating to agriculture. In the 1960 Basic Agrarian Law, the concept refers to rights over all natural resources (BAL/UUPA §1/2).

3. "It is necessary to provide protection for economically weak citizens against those who are economically strong ... to prevent overstepping the limits of domination of the life and work of others in agrarian activities, which is against social justice and humanity" (BAL/UUPA, Elucidation II [6]).

4. The BAL/UUPA explicitly reiterates the contents of article 33, paragraph 3 of the 1945 Constitution, which says: "The land, water and natural riches contained therein shall be controlled by the State and shall be exploited to the greatest benefit of the people." This article justified the principle of the "State Right of Control" (BAL/UUPA §2 [2]).

5. "The government shall prevent the private monopoly of agrarian activity, either by individuals or by organisations" (BAL/UUPA §13/2); "Government monopoly of agrarian activities can only be carried out by legislation" (BAL/UUPA §13/3).

6. Agricultural land ceiling regulations determined that no family can hold more than five hectares for *sawah* (irrigated rice land) and six hectares of dry fields in the more densely populated areas, and no family can hold more than fifteen hectares for *sawah* and twenty hectares of dry land in the less populated areas. For variations of these limitations on landholding, see UU 56/1960, §1 and Elucidation. For the implementation of these ceiling variations at provincial, district, and municipal levels throughout Indonesia's then twenty-two provinces, see Minister of Agrarian Affairs Decision (KepMenag) No. Sk. 978/Ka/1960 (Soedargo 1962, 107–17).

7. The program was launched in 1961 with Presidential Decree No. 131/1961 and Ministerial Decree No. 311/MP/1961 that regulate the formation, and duties of the Land Reform Committees from national to village level, and Government Regulation No. 224/1961 on the implementation of land redistribution (Soedargo 1962, 126–36). Before the redistribution processes could begin, the committees had to assess the total amount of land that would be redistributed and the number of beneficiaries in their areas of jurisdiction. The formal distribution processes began in the second year after the promulgation of the BAL 1960, on 24 September 1962 (Soedargo 1962, 91–105).

8. There are two categories of landless: "absolute landless" and "landless tenant" (*petani tak bertanah* or *tuna kisma*): "Absolute landless" refers to farm households who have no control over land, and are referred to as agricultural laborers in this chapter. "Landless tenants" refers to those who cultivate land owned by others under a share-cropping agreement.

9. In the 1969 report of the Directorate-General of Agrarian Affairs, 80.8 percent of available land, or an average of 0.5 hectares per beneficiary household, was distributed in Phase I of land reform program implementation (in Jakarta, Yogyakarta, West Java, Central, East Java, Madura, Bali, and Lombok); while in Phase II (which applied to the whole country) 72 percent of identified available land was distributed, with an average of 1.4 hectares per beneficiary household. The program nevertheless

remained concentrated in Java, Madura, and Bali and several regions in Sumatra (Morad 1970, 16).

10. In 1994 the Minister for Agrarian Affairs and Head of BPN (National Land Agency) explicitly stated that land in Indonesia is a strategic commodity. He argued that new regulations enabling the provision of land were needed to encourage large-scale investment to achieve economic growth of 7 percent (S. Harsono 1994).

11. The BAL 1960, article 6, says that "All land rights have a social function." Regarding this social function, the BAL/UUPA Elucidation II (4), states that "anyone holding individual title to land cannot use that land purely for their own purposes if this harms the interest of the community . . . but this doesn't mean that individual interests will be totally extinguished by the public interest."

12. Hatta said, in 1946, "Land shall not be used as an instrument for someone to exploit others, that's why large scale plantation lands cannot be owned by someone individually, but should be under the control of the government. . . . owned by the people . . . [and] must be managed and utilized by the State for social welfare purposes" (Hatta 1992, 8–11); although this does not mean that "the government itself becomes a business enterprize with all of its bureaucracy" (Hatta 1992, 150). In Hatta's opinion, all land used for large plantation estates is "state-land" that essentially belongs to the local communities. It means commercial plantations with abandoned or expired HGU leases must be returned to local people, or developed as a genuine cooperative enterprise (Hatta 1992).

13. This assessment about the importance of continuing a more systematic program of transmigration was reinforced by Morad, an FAO country representative and land reform adviser (1967–69). See his report to the Indonesian government on land reform (Morad 1970).

14. In fact, the transmigration *(transmigrasi)* program is an old program to move people from highly populated to less populated areas implemented since the early twentieth century, when it was called a colonization program (see Hardjosudarmo 1965, 100–118; Hardjono 1977, 16–21).

15. It should be kept in mind that attempts to provide credit and extension services to rice farmers and to stimulate the use of artificial fertilizers and improved seed varieties were already taking place during the Sukarno regime, which Franke (1972) identified as the "proto–Green Revolution" phase of Indonesia's agricultural development. However, the more systematic Green Revolution fully managed by the state-apparatuses in a "top-down" approach (Hardjono 1983), with large-scale subsidies, and supported by reorganization of rural politics and institutional life was implemented under the New Order.

16. Sectoral legislation, including the Basic Forestry Law (UU 5/1967) (later replaced by Law No. 41/1999, and further amended controversially by Law No. 1/2004 to include mining in Protection Forest), and the Mining Law (UU 11/1967), removed the management of these areas from provisions of the BAL/UUPA. For a critical overview of their impact on the human rights of local people, see Bachriadi (1998); Peluso (1992); Gunawan, Thamrin, and Suhendar (1999); and Brown (2002).

17. Based on government calculations in 2003, from around 190.5 million hectares of land in Indonesia, 67.4 percent have been declared "state-forest" areas (Departemen Kehutanan RI, 2003, 4–6, 13). The official figure is frequently 75.06 percent based on *Tata Guna Hutan Kesepakatan* tahun (Agreed Forest Land Use) 1983. See also Peluso (1990, 1992); Peluso and Vandergeest (2001).

18. Among these concession holders, twelve conglomerates controlled 16.7 million hectares of forest, or around 32 percent of all concession areas (*Warta Ekonomi* 1998, 12, cited in Bachriadi and Lucas 2001, 148n74).

19. These concessions range between 2,000 hectares and 100 million hectares. Data for these mining concession areas are calculated from a directory of mining companies operated in Indonesia (Gold Group et al. 1999).

20. Subsequent PP (Government Regulation) No. 1/2004 and UU 19/2004 permit mining operations in Protection Forests. This policy began under Megawati and continued under Yudhoyono.

21. Badan Pusat Statistik (2001c, tables 5.2.1 and 5.2.2).

22. See "Kebijakan Pertanahan Orde Reformasi," *Informasi* 18, no. 224 (1998): 9–10; and "Mati Karena Uang Receh," *Property Indonesia*, no. 58 (1998): 58–59.

23. Lukita (1996, 2).

24. This figure declined to 104 in 2006/2007, following the slow recovery from the 1997 economic crisis (*Golf Map, The Official Golf Map of Indonesia*).

25. Generally the Indonesian Central Bureau of Statistics (BPS) uses the terminology "*rumah tangga petani*" (here translated as "farm households") to indicate households that have at least one member whose source of income is agriculture. The term is not explained clearly in relation to peasant landholdings, i.e., it is not clear whether the BPS term covers both landholder and landless peasant households. But the data in the BPS ten-year agricultural censuses are mostly on farm households that hold land (*rumah tangga petani pengguna lahan*), in this chapter referred to as "peasant landholders." Like Kano (1994), we include "landless farm households" who did not control land, termed here "absolute landless," in our definition of "farm households." It was not possible to find the

number or percentage of farming households for 1963 from the 1963 agricultural census data.

26. The 1973 agricultural census did not provide data on the total number of farm households. For details on other estimates of the total number of farm huseholds, see Kano (1994, 45–47).

27. In Indonesia, *petani* are cultivators who have relatively small holdings of agricultural land, and whose socioeconomic and cultural life fit with the concept of "peasant" as developed by anthropologists such as Eric Wolf (1966).

28. The total number of households in Indonesia in 1983 was around 39.5 million (calculated from the total population in Indonesia in 1983, assuming that an average household consists of four members). See BPS, *Statistical Year Book of Indonesia 1983*, 34–35.

29. In 1973, the total number of households in Indonesia was around 31.5 million (see BPS, *Statistical Year Book of Indonesia 1974/1975*, 23). So 69 percent of total households were farm households in 1973.

30. The total number of households in Indonesia in 1993 was around 42.9 million households (see BPS, *Statistical Year Book of Indonesia 1993*, 29).

31. The total number of households in Indonesia in 2003 was around 54.5 million (see BPS, *Statistical Year Book of Indonesia 2004*, 64).

32. We can assume that the figure for "absolute landless" might also have dropped between 1963 and 1973 if data were available.

33. Macrostudies on the relationship between landholding structure and poverty also show that there is a strong relationship between unequal land distribution and rural poverty. See Griffin (1976) and Sobhan (1993).

34. For comparison with our Gini ratios on land distribution, see Rusastra, Lokollo, and Priyanto (2007, 12) showing the Gini ratio of landholding in Indonesia in the 1973–2003 period increasing from 0.5481 to 0.7171. Booth (1988, 57–58) gives Gini ratios for food-crop landholdings of 0.6 in 1973 and 0.5 in 1983.

35. In these Gini ratios, landless households were included in the calculation. Without including landless households, the Gini ratios in these six villages range from 0.45 to 0.57 (Kano 2008, 391, table 12–11).

36. Rusastra, Lokollo, and Priyatno (2007, 12) calculated a Gini ratio for Java of 0.7227 for 2003.

37. When they assessed the results of the 1973 agricultural census, Booth and Sundrum calculated the Gini ratio of land distribution in Indonesia as 0.556. However, landless households are excluded in their calculation. They conclude that "the degree of inequality in Indonesia is moderate compared with other countries for which data are available; only Taiwan and Japan show a lower degree of inequality" (Booth and Sundrum 1976, 95).

38. For an overview of agrarian politics in colonial Indonesia, see Booth (1988, 51–52); Tauchid (1952, 1953); Wiradi (2000). Such analyses of the impact of these colonial policies on peasants and plantation workers, as well as on land conflicts, remain relevant in the present. See also Stoler (1985); Agustono, Tanjung, and Suhartono (1997); and Hafid (2001).

39. Indonesian statistical data can be confusing. Figures on landlessness are often inconsistent because each agency develops its own classification categories. Officials also feel obligated to show an increase in agricultural productivity, which results in skewed statistics and biased decision making in the public sphere. See Geertz (1973) and T. H. Brown (2002) on the unreliability of Indonesian statistical data.

40. One should interpret national macrodata with caution, because the terms used, their definition, the criteria for classification of categories of data, and types and methods of data collection change from one census to the next. For example, before 1983 there was no "Agricultural Survey" (which from then on was conducted annually); previously there was only the "Agricultural Census." In order to provide an account of landholding structures among peasants, this section will be based on data from the agricultural censuses, which are conducted every ten years. Since independence the Indonesian government has conducted five agricultural censuses (1963, 1973, 1983, 1993 and 2003). The last census was conducted in the aftermath of the 1997–98 financial crisis and budgetary constraints, and the publication of the 2003 census results ran behind schedule. The authors are grateful for assistance received from the BPS office in Jakarta that provided access to 2003 census data, including information from the Province of Aceh.

41. In Indonesian, the term for peasants holding less than 0.5 hectare is *petani gurem* (see table 2.4).

42. See Government Regulation No. 224/1961, Article 8.

43. See Solon L. Baraclough (1969); Billah, Widjajanto, and Kristyanto (1984); Wiradi (1984, 291–311); and several Rural Dynamics Studies of the Agro Economic Survey Foundation (SDP-SAE) collected in Kasryno (1984). For the latter, see also White and Wiradi (1989).

44. For comparison, in 1995, the Inter-census Population Survey (Supas), as quoted by Booth (2002, 179), reported that slightly over 50 percent of all rural households either did not own agricultural land at all, or owned less than 0.25 hectares.

45. It is not possible to put 1963 census data in this table, because the presentation of the data on landholdings uses different categories from those used by later censuses. The categories of peasant-households in the 1963 census do not record the numbers of peasant households with less than

0.1 hectares or no holdings, those who can be categorized as near-to and absolute landless. For the data available for the 1963 census, see table 2.1

46. See chapter 9 by Reerink in this volume on the role of "location permits' with respect to land use.

47. See BAL §15 Elucidation II (4), which provides for cancellation of all kinds of property rights on land that is neglected, abandoned, or not used for its designated purpose. However, in practice abandoned land under private property rights (*hak milik*) is usually ignored by BPN officials.

48. Nasoetion's findings can only be explained by taking account of changes in forestland converted to agriculture, because the data in table 2.8 reveal an increase in the areas of both wet rice fields and dry agricultural land.

49. Even more disturbing figures are contained in a presentation of the national executive of the Association of Indonesian Developers (REI, Real Estate Indonesia) which indicates that in the last decade of the Suharto regime, one million hectares of agricultural land in Java were converted to industrial estates, housing estates, recreation, and other nonagricultural uses. See Lukita (1996, 3).

50. See the annual statistics on harvested areas and rice production in Indonesia in the Statistical Year Books of Indonesia published by BPS.

51. TGHK (Tata Guna Hutan Kesepakatan) is an agreement between the central government's Department of Forestry, local (provincial and district) government, and other related government agencies to designate (where and how much) forestland uses to be allocated based on forest functions. The TGHK is presented as maps of forest functions such as nature reserves, protection forest, production forest, and conversion forest. This process defines the resource base both for the timber industry and the national system of conservation areas. TGHK has been implemented since 1984.

52. *Bera* land is part of the swidden cultivation regime, where cultivated land is left fallow temporarily to allow natural ecological succession. Normally in this traditional regime, when the land has reverted to secondary forest, it can be recultivated.

53. KPA Agrarian Conflict Database, entries to 31 December 2001.

54. Absentee landholding refers to holders of land who do not live in the same location as their land. Such landholding is prohibited by law BAL/UUPA 1960, §§7, 10. Government Regulation 224/1961, §3 (1), §3 (5) stated that unless the absentee landlord moved to the subdistrict where his/her land was located, or transferred the landholding to a resident of that subdistrict within six months of issuance of the regulation, the land title would be revoked by the government and become the object of redistribution.

55. See also Barraclough and Ghimire (1995, 2000) who describe similar phenomena in Latin America, Africa, and other Asian countries.

56. See Bachriadi and Lucas (2002); Sangaji (2005); Acciaioli (2009).

57. For a brief discussion of this study group's role in agrarian policy reform in Indonesia, see Lucas and Warren (2003).

58. See chapter 10 of this volume, which critically discusses President Yudhoyono's National Program of Agrarian Reform (PPAN), announced at the beginning of 2007.

59. Several studies have shown that with technological improvements and diversification, it is possible to improve farmers' livelihood base on smaller landholdings. See Wiradi (2000, 110–11).

References

For a more complete bibliography to this chapter (including unpublished sources) see Bachriadi and Wiradi (2011, 63–82). Readers who require more information on the resources used in this chapter can contact Dianto Bachriadi at the Agrarian Resource Center in Bandung (Dianto.Bachriadi@gmail.com).

Acciaioli, G. 2009. "Conservation and Community in the Lore Lindu National Park (Sulawesi); Customary Custodianship, Multi-ethnic Participation, and Resource Entitlement." In *Community, Environment and Local Governance in Indonesia: Locating the Commonweal,* ed. C. Warren and J. McCarthy, 89–120. London: Routledge.

Agustono, B., M. O. Tanjung, and E. Suhartono. 1997. *Badan Perjuangan Rakyat Penunggu Indonesia vs PTPN II—Sengketa Tanah di Sumatera Utara.* Bandung: Yayasan Akatiga.

Ardhana, I. K. and R. H. Lubis. 2008. *Laporan Akhir Kajian Penguasaan Tanah Adat,* Land Management and Policy Development Project. Jakarta: Badan Perencanaan Pembangunan Nasional RI.

Arief, S. 1977. *Indonesia: Growth, Income Disparity and Mass Poverty,* Jakarta: SAA.

Asosiasi Pengusahaan Hutan Indonesia. 2007. "Various Data on Forestry." Available at www.aphi-net.com. Accessed 29 April 2009.

Bachriadi, D. 1998. *Merana di Tengah Kelimpahan: Pelanggaran-pelanggaran HAM pada Industri Pertambangan di Indonesia.* Jakarta: ELSAM.

———. 2004a. "Tendensi dalam Penyelesaian Konflik Agraria di Indonesia: Menunggu Lahirnya Komisi Nasional untuk Penyelesaian

Konflik Agraria (KNUPKA)." *Jurnal Dinamika Masyarakat* 3 (3): 497–521.

———. 2004b. "Mining in a Protected State Forest? This Is Indonesia! The Forestry Law Has Not Stopped Mining in Indonesia's State Forests." *Inside Indonesia*, no. 80:4–5.

Bachriadi, D., and A. Lucas. 2001. *Merampas Tanah Rakyat: Kasus Tapos dan Cimacan*. Jakarta: Kepustakaan Populer Gramedia.

———. 2002. "Hutan Milik Siapa? Upaya-upaya Mewujudkan Forestry Land Reform di Kabupaten Wonosobo, Jawa Tengah." In *Berebut Tanah: Beberapa Kajian Berperspektif Kampus dan Kampung*, ed. Anu Lounela and R. Yando Zakaria, 79–158. Yogyakarta: Insist Press.

Bachriadi, D., and G. Wiradi. 2011. *Enam Dekade Ketimpangan: Masalah Penguasaan Tanah di Indonesia/Six Decades of Inequality: Land Tenure Problems in Indonesia*. Bandung: Agrarian Resources Center (ARC) Bina Desa, and KPA.

Badan Pusat Statistik. 2000. *Statistik Perusahaan Hutan Tanaman Industri 1998*. Jakarta: Badan Pusat Statistik Indonesia.

———. 2001a. *Statistik Perusahaan Hak Pengusahaan Hutan 1999*. Jakarta: Badan Pusat Statistik Indonesia.

———. 2001b. *Agricultural Survey 2000: Land Area by Utilisation in Indonesia 2000*. Jakarta: Badan Pusat Statistik Indonesia.

———. 2001c. *Statistik Indonesia 2000*. Jakarta: Badan Pusat Statistik Indonesia.

———. 2004. *Sensus Pertanian 2003: Angka Nasional Hasil Pendaftaran Rumah Tangga*. Book A3. Jakarta: Badan Pusat Statistik Indonesia.

———. 2005. *Statistik Indonesia 2004*. Jakarta: Badan Pusat Statistik Indonesia.

Barraclough, S. L. 1969. "Criticism of the Green Revolution." *Ceres* (November–December).

Barraclough, S. L., and K. B. Ghimire. 1995. *Forests and Livelihoods: The Social Dynamic of Deforestation in Developing Countries*. New York: St. Martin's Press.

———. 2000. *Agricultural Expansion and Tropical Deforestation*. London: Earthscan.

Billah, M., M. L. Widjajanto, and A. Kristyanto. 1984. "Segi Penguasaan Tanah dan Dinamika Sosial di Pedesaan Jawa." In *Dua Abad Penguasaan Tanah: Pola Penguasaan Tanah Pertanian di Jawa dari Masa ke Masa*, ed. S. M. P Tjondronegoro and G. Wiradi, 250–85. Jakarta: Gramedia.

BPS. 1963. *Sensus Pertanian 1963 Republic of Indonesia: Final Report*. Jakarta: Biro Pusat Statistik Indonesia.

———. 1964, 1972, 1976. *Statistical Pocketbook of Indonesia 1963 (1970–71) (1974–75)*. Jakarta: Biro Pusat Statistik Indonesia.

———. 1974–97. *Statistical Year Book of Indonesia (1973–96)*. Jakarta: Biro Pusat Statistik Indonesia.

———. 1975. *Sensus Pertanian 1973*. Series 2A. Jakarta: Biro Pusat Statistik Indonesia.

———. 1985a. *Sensus Pertanian 1983: Hasil Pendaftaran Rumah Tangga Menurut Propinsi dan Kabupaten*. Series A2. Jakarta: Biro Pusat Statistik Indonesia.

———. 1985b. *Sensus Pertanian 1983: Hasil Sensus Sampel*. Series B. Jakarta: Biro Pusat Statistik Indonesia.

———. 1985c. *Sensus Pertanian 1983: Evaluasi Penggunaan Tanah Menurut Provinsi dan Kabupaten*. Series D. Jakarta: Biro Pusat Statistik Indonesia.

———. 1994a. *Sensus Pertanian 1993: Laporan Hasil Pendafataran Rumah Tangga, Sub Sektor Padi, Palawija dan Hortikultura*. Series A2. Jakarta: Biro Pusat Statistik Indonesia.

———. 1994b. *Sensus Pertanian 1993: Laporan Hasil Pendaftaran Rumah Tangga, Sub Sektor Perkebunan dan Kehutanan*. Series A3. Jakarta: Biro Pusat Statistik Indonesia.

———. 1994c. *Agricultural Survey: Land Area by Utilization for Outside Java 1993*. Jakarta: Biro Pusat Statistik Indonesia.

———. 1994d. *Agricultural Survey: Land Area by Utilization in Java 1993*. Jakarta: Biro Pusat Statistik Indonesia.

———. 1995. *Sensus Pertanian 1993: Sensus Sampel Rumah Tangga Pertanian Pengguna Lahan*. Series B1. Jakarta: Biro Pusat Statistik Indonesia.

———. 2005a. *Statistik Indonesia 2004*. Jakarta: Biro Pusat Statistik Indonesia.

———. 2005b. *Sensus Pertanian 2003: Hasil Pencacahan Survei Pendapatan Rumah Tangga Petani*, Book C. Jakarta: Biro Pusat Statistik.

Booth, A. 1988. *Agricultural Development in Indonesia*. Sydney: Allen and Unwin.

———. 2000. "Poverty and Inequality in the Soeharto Era: An Assessment." *Bulletin of Indonesian Economic Studies* 36 (1): 73–104.

———. 2002. "The Changing Role of Non-Farm Activities in Agricultural Households in Indonesia: Some Insights from the Agricultural Censuses." *Bulletin of Indonesian Economic Studies* 38 (2): 179–200.

Booth, A., and R. M. Sundrum. 1976. "The 1973 Agricultural Census." *Bulletin of Indonesian Economic Studies* 12 (2): 90–105.

Borras, S. M., Jr. 2007. *Pro-poor Land Reform: A Critique*. Ottawa: University of Ottawa Press.

Brown, D. W. 1999. *Addicted to Rent: Corporate and Spatial Distribution of Forest Resources in Indonesia: Implications for Forest Sustainability and Government Policy*. Jakarta: Indonesia-UK Tropical Forest Management Program.

Brown, T. H. 2002. "Whose 'Official' Data Should We Believe?" In *State of the Forest: Indonesia,* Annex 1, pp. 77–79. FWI (Forest Watch Indonesia)/GFW (Global Forest Watch), Bogor: Forest Watch Indonesia; and Washington, DC: Global Forest Watch,

Colchester, M. 1986. "The Struggle for Land: Tribal Peoples in the Face of the Transmigration Program." *Ecologist* 16 (2/3): 99–110.

Colchester, M., N. Jiwan, Andiko, M. Sirait, A. Y. Firdaus, A. Surambo, and H. Pane. 2006. *Promised Land: Palm Oil and Land Acquisition in Indonesia — Implications for Local Communities and Indigenous Peoples.* Bogor: Forest Peoples Programme, Sawit Watch, HuMA, ICRAF and the World Agroforestry Center.

Collier, W. L., K. Santoso, Soentoro, and R. Wibowo 1996. *Pendekatan Baru dalam Pembangunan Pedesaan di Jawa, Kajian Pedesaan selama Dua Puluh Lima Tahun.* Jakarta: Yayasan Obor Indonesia.

Departemen Kehutanan RI. 2004. *Forestry Statistics of Indonesia 2003.* Jakarta: Ministry of Forestry, Government of Indonesia.

Departemen Transmigrasi, Direktorat Jenderal Penyiapan Pemukiman. 1987. *Transmigrasi dalam Angka (Bidang Pankim),* microfiche document of Indonesian National Library, code I-91-944193.

Eckholm, E. 1979. *The Dispossessed of the Earth: Land Reform and Sustainable Development.* Worldwatch Paper 30, June 1979.

Fauzi, N., and D. Bachriadi. 1998. *Hak Menguasai dari Negara: Urusan Sejarah yang Belum Selesai,* Kertas Posisi KPA no. 04/1998. Bandung: Konsorsium Pembaruan Agraria.

Fidro, B., and N. Fauzi, eds. 1998. *Pembangunan Berbuah Sengketa: Kumpulan Kasus-kasus Sengketa Pertanahan Sepanjang Orde Baru.* Medan: Yayasan Sintesa and SPSU.

Fitzpatrick, D. 2007. "Land, Custom, and the State in Post-Sukarto Indonesia." In *The Revival of Tradition in Indonesian Politics: The Development of Adat from Colonialism to Indigenism,* ed. Jamie S. Davidson and David Henley 130–48. London: Routledge.

Franke, R. 1972. "The Green Revolution in a Javanese Village." Ph.D. diss., Harvard University, Cambridge, MA.

Geertz, C. 1973. "Comments on Benjamin White's 'Demand for Labor and Population Growth in Colonial Java.'" *Human Ecology* 1 (3): 237–39.

Ghose, A. K., ed. 1983. *Agrarian Reform in Contemporary Developing Countries.* London: Croom Helm.

Gibbons, D. S., R. de Koninck, and I. Hasan. 1980. *Agricultural Modernization, Poverty and Inequality: The Distributional Impact of the Green Revolution in Regions of Malaysia and Indonesia.* Farnborough: Gower.

Gold Group, Indonesian Directorate General of Mines and Energy, Australian Trade Commission, and Masindo. 1999. *AJM Indonesian Minerals Exploration and Mining Directory 1999/2000 edition.* Melbourne: Gold Group Operations (Gold Group Asia/Pacific Ltd).

Golf Map: The Official Golf Map of Indonesia. 4th ed. 2000–2001 and 10th ed. 2006–7. Jakarta: Indonesia Golf Course Association.

Griffin, K. 1976. *Land Concentration and Rural Poverty.* London: Macmillan.

Gunawan, R., J. Thamrin, and E. Suhendar. 1999. *After the Rain Falls: The Impact of the East Kalimantan Forestry Industry on Tribal Society.* Bandung: Akatiga.

Hafid, J. O. S. 2001. *Perlawanan Petani: Kasus Tanah Jenggawah.* Bogor: Pustaka Latin.

Hardjono, J. M. 1977. *Transmigration in Indonesia.* Kuala Lumpur: Oxford University Press.

———. 1983. "Rural Development in Indonesia: The Top-Down Approach." In *Rural Development and the State,* ed. D. A. M. Lea and D. Chaudhri, 38–65. London: Methuen.

Hardjosudarmo, S. 1965. *Kebidjaksanaan Transmigrasi dalam Rangka Pembangunan Masjarakat Desa di Indonesia.* Jakarta: Bhratara.

Harsono, B. 1995. *Hukum Agraria Indonesia: Sejarah Pembentukan Undang-undang Pokok Agraria, Isi dan Pelaksanaannya, Jilid I Hukum Tanah Nasional.* Rev. ed. Jakarta: Penerbit Djambatan.

Harsono, S. 1994. *Tanah sebagai Komoditi Strategis dalam Menghadapi Pembangunan Jangka Panjang II,* bahan pidato dalam Dies XIII Univ. Muhammadiyah Yogyakarta, 2 April 1994.

Hatta, M. 1992. *Beberapa Pokok Pikiran,* ed. Sri-Edi Swasono and Fauzie Ridjal. Jakarta: UI-Press.

Himpunan Kerukunan Tani Indonesia. 1979. "Pernyataan Musyawarah Nasional I Himpunan Kerukunan Tani Indonesia tentang Penyelesaian Masalah Pertanahan dan Pelaksanaan Landreform." In *Hasil-hasil Musyawarah Nasional I Himpunan Kerukunan Tani Indonesia (HKTI),* Jakarta, 13–16 February. Jakarta: HKTI.

Huizer, G. 1980. *Peasant Movements and Their Counterforces in South-East Asia.* New Delhi: Marwah Publications.

Huizer, Gerrit. 1999. *Peasant Mobilisation for Land Reform: Historical Case Studies and Theoretical Considerations.* Geneva: United Nations Research Institute for Social Development (UNRISD), Grassroots Initiatives for Land Reform Data Paper 103.

Hüsken, F. 1998. *Masyarakat Desa dalam Perubahan Zaman: Sejarah Diferensiasi Sosial di Jawa, 1830–1980.* Jakarta: Gramedia Widiasarana Indonesia.

Hüsken, F., and B. White. 1989. "Java: Social Differentiation, Food Production, and Agrarian Control." In *Agrarian Transformations: Local Processes and the State in Southeast Asia,* ed. Gillian Hart, Andrew Turton, and Benjamin White, 235–65. Berkeley: University of California Press.

Inayatullah, ed. 1980. *Land Reform: Some Asian Experiences.* Kuala Lumpur: Asia Pacific Development Administration Center.

Indonesia Golf Course Association. 2001–07. *Golf Map, the Official Golf Map of Indonesia, 4th edition—2000–2001 and 10th edition—2006/2007,* the Official Golf Maps of Indonesia.

Jamal, E., and A. Djauhari. 1998. "Kebijaksanaan Pengendalian Alih Fungsi Lahan Sawah." *Agro-Ekonomika* 28 (2): 75–87.

Kano, H. 1990. *Pagelaran: Anatomi Sosial Ekonomi Pelapisan Masyarakat Tani di Sebuah Desa Jawa Timur.* Yogyakarta: Gadjah Mada University Press.

———. 1994. "Landless Peasant Households in Indonesia." In *Approaching Suharto's Indonesia from the Margins,* ed. Takashi Shiraishi, 43–73. Translation of contemporary Japanese scholarship on Southeast Asia, Cornell University Southeast Asia Program Translation Series, vol. 4.

———. 2008. *Indonesian Exports, Peasant Agriculture and the World Economy, 1850–2000: Economic Structures in a Southeast Asian State.* Athens: Ohio University Press.

Kasryno, F., ed. 1984. *Prospek Pembangunan Ekonomi Pedesaan Indonesia.* Jakarta: Yayasan Obor Indonesia.

Konsorsium Pembaruan Agraria. 1996. *Our Land Is Not for Sale.* KPA second memorandum on LAP in Indonesia. Bandung: Consortium for Agrarian Reform.

KPA Agrarian Conflict Database. 1999–2002. Digital database of land conflicts occurring in Indonesia 1999–2002 (collection of D. Bachriadi).

KSPA. 2001. *Ketetapan MPR-RI Tentang Pembaruan Agraria sebagai Komitmen Negara Menggerakkan Perubahan Menuju Indonesia yang Lebih Baik.* Critical notes from the Kelompok Studi Pembaruan Agraria to PAH-II MPR-RI, 21 May.

Ladejinsky, W. 1961. "Land Reform in Indonesia." Memorandum, 24 January 1961. In *Agrarian Reform as Unfinished Business: The Selected Papers of Wolf Ladejinsky,* ed. Louis J. Walinsky, 297–99. New York: Oxford University Press.

———. 1964. "Land Reform in Indonesia." Memorandum, 27 February 1964. In *Agrarian Reform as Unfinished Business: The Selected Papers of Wolf Ladejinsky,* ed. Louis J. Walinsky, 340–52. New York: Oxford University Press.

Lerche, D. 1999. *Industrial Estates in Indonesia: A Guide for the Investor.* Jakarta: Dietrich Lerche Investment and Development Co.

LPPT. 1998a. "Kasus Tanah Cisewu—Garut." In *Pembangunan Berbuah Sengketa,* ed. B. Fidro and N. Fauzi, 127–52. Medan: SPSU and Yayasan Sintesa.

———. 1998b. "Kasus Cikalong Kulon—Cianjur." In *Pembangunan Berbuah Sengketa,* ed. Boy Fidro and Noer Fauzi, 153–62. Medan: SPSU and Yayasan Sintesa.

Lucas, A., and C. Warren. 2003. "The State, the People and Their Mediators: The Struggle over Agrarian Law Reform in Post–New Order Indonesia." *Indonesia* 76:87–126.

Lukita, E. 1996. "Pengadaan Tanah untuk Pemukiman." Paper presented at the national seminar on Land as Strategic Commodity: Its Impact to Peasant's Welfare and Food Self-Sufficiency National Executive of HKTI, Jakarta, 29 October 1966.

Lynch, O. J., and E. Harwell. 2002. *Whose Natural Resources? Whose Common Goods? Towards a New Paradigm of Environmental Justice and the National Interest In Indonesia.* Jakarta: ELSAM.

Mas'oed, M. 1989. *Ekonomi dan Struktur Politik Orde Baru, 1966–1971.* Jakarta: LP3ES.

McAuslan, P. 1986. *Tanah Perkotaan dan Perlindungan Rakyat Jelata.* Jakarta: Gramedia.

Mears, L. A. 1982. *Era Baru Ekonomi Perberasan Indonesia.* Yogyakarta: Gadjah Mada University Press.

Mintoro, A. 1984. "Distribusi Pendapatan." In *Prospek Pembangunan Ekonomi Pedesaan Indonesia,* ed. Faisal Kasryno, 263–301. Jakarta: Yayasan Obor Indonesia.

Morad, A. A. 1970. *Report to the Government of Indonesia on Land Reform.* Rome: Food and Agriculture Organization of the United Nations.

Moyo, S., and P. Yeros, eds. 2005. *Reclaiming the Land: The Resurgence of Rural Movements in Africa, Asia and Latin America.* London: Zed Books.

Nasoetion, L. I. 1991. "Beberapa Masalah Pertanahan Nasional dan Alternatif Kebijaksanaan untuk Menanggulanginya." *Analisis CSIS* 22:105–27.

Nozomu, K. 1984. "Fukutake Tadashi, Rural Sociologist of Post War Japan." *Bulletin of Concerned Asian Scholars* 16 (2): 12–22.

Otten, M. 1986. *Transmigrasi: Myths and Realities, Indonesian Resettlement Policy, 1965–1985.* IWGIA Document 57. Copenhagen: International Working Group for Indigenous Affairs.

Parlindungan, A. P. 1989. "Politik dan Hukum Agraria di Zaman Orde Baru." *Prisma* 18 (4): 3–14.

———. 1991. *Landreform di Indonesia: Suatu Studi Perbandingan.* Bandung: Penerbit Mandar Maju.

———. 1994. "Landreform Indonesia, Strategi dan Sasarannya Dikaitkan dengan Pelaksanaan Transmigrasi Menurut G.B.H.N./1978." In *Bunga Rampai Hukum Agraria Serta Landreform,* 3:1–29. Bandung: Mandar Maju.

Peluso, N. L. 1990. "A History of State Forest Management in Java." In *Keeper of the Forest: Land Management Alternatives in Southeast Asia,* ed. Mark Poffenberger, 27–55. Quezon City: Ateneo de Manila University Press.

———. 1992. *Rich Forests, Poor People: Resource Control and Resistance in Java.* Berkeley: University of California Press.

Peluso, N. L., and P. Vandergeest. 2001. "Genealogy of the Political Forest and Customary Rights in Indonesia, Malaysia, and Thailand." *Journal of Asian Studies* 60 (3): 761–814.

Prosterman, R L., M. N. Temple, and T. M. Hanstad, eds. 1990. *Agrarian Reform and Grassroots Development: Ten Case Studies.* Boulder, CO: Lynne Rienner.

Pusat Data Bisnis Indonesia. 1998. "Kebijakan Pertanahan Orde Reformasi." *Informasi PDBI* 18 (224) (October).

Ramli, R., and M. Ahmad. 1983. *Rente Ekonomi Pengusahaan Hutan Indonesia.* Jakarta: WALHI.

Robison, R. 1986. *Indonesia: The Rise of Capital.* Sydney: Allen and Unwin.

Rusastra, I. W., E. M. Lokollo, and S. Priyatno. 2007. "Land and Household Economy: Analysis of Agricultural Census 1983–2003." Presentation to national seminar "Land and Household Economy 1979–2005: Changing Roads for Poverty Reduction," ICASEPS and UN-CAPSA, Bogor, 25 June.

Russett, B. M. 1964. "Inequality and Instability: The Relation of Land Tenure to Politics." *World Politics* 16 (3): 442–54.

Ruwiastuti, M. R. 1998. *Menuju Pluralisme Hukum Agraria: Analisa dan Kritik terhadap Marjinalisasi Posisi Hukum-hukum dan Hak-hak Adat Penduduk Asli atas Tanah dan Sumber-sumber Agraria oleh Pembuat Undang-undang Pokok Agraria (UUPA 1960),* KPA Position Paper no. 006/1998. Bandung: Konsorsium Pembaruan Agraria.

———. 2000. *Sesat Pikir Politik Hukum Agraria: Membongkar Alas Penguasaan Negara atas Hak-hak Adat,* Yogyakarta: Insist Press-KPA-Pustaka Pelajar.

Ruwiastuti, M. R., N. Fauzi, and D. Bachriadi. 1998. *Penghancuran Hak Masyarakat Adat atas Tanah: Sistem Penguasaan Tanah Masyarakat Adat dan Hukum Agraria.* Bandung: KPA.

Sajogyo. 1993. "Agriculture and Industrialization in Rural Development." In *Development and Social Welfare: Indonesia's Experiences under the New Order*, ed. Jan-Paul Dirkse, Frans Hüsken, and Mario Rutten, 45–59. Leiden: KITLV Press.

Sajogyo, and G. Wiradi. 1985. *Rural Poverty and Efforts for Its Alleviation in Indonesia*. FAO In-depth Studies Series no. 18. Rome: Food and Agricultural Organization.

Saleh, C. 1984. "Pola Pengeluaran Rumah Tangga dan Penguasan Modal Bukan Tanah." In *Prospek Pembangunan Ekonomi Perdesaaan Indonesia*, ed. F. Kasryno, 357–85. Jakarta: Yayasan Obor Indonesia.

Sangaji, A. 2005. "National Park versus Farmers: The Experience of Conflict between Dongi-dongi Farmers and the Managers of Lore Lindu National Par." Paper presented to the workshop "Conservation for/by Whom? Social Controversies and Cultural Contestations Regarding National Parks and Reserves in the 'Malay Archipelago,'" at the 4th International Symposium of Jurnal Antropologi Indonesia, University of Indonesia, Depok, 16–18 May 2005.

Sinaga, R. S., and B. White. 1980. "Beberapa Aspek Kelembagaan di Pedesaan Jawa dalam Hubungannya dengan Kemiskinan Struktural." In *Kemiskinan Struktural: Suatu Bunga Rampai*, ed. A. M. G. Tan and S. Soemardjan, 139–58. Jakarta: Yayasan Ilmu-ilmu Sosial (YIS) and Himpunan Indonesia untuk Pengembangan Ilmu-ilmu Sosial (HIPIS).

Simpul Bengkulu, and the Inisiatif Perlawanan Lokal (IPL). 2006. "Tanah untuk Rakyat." In *Negara adalah Kita: Pengalaman Rakyat Melawan Penindasan*, ed. E. B. Subiyantoro, 135–51. Jakarta: FBB Prakarsa Rakyat and Perkumpulan Praxis.

Siahaan, H. 1977. *Pemilikan dan Penguasaan Tanah: Adopsi Teknologi Pertanian Modern dan Disparitas Pendapatan di Daerah Pedesaan*. Yogyakarta: Lembaga Studi Kawasan dan Pedesaan Universitas Gadjah Mada.

Skephi, and R. Kiddell-Monroe. 1993. "Indonesia: Land Rights and Development." In *The Struggle for Land and the Fate of the Forests*, ed. M. Colchester and L. Lohmann, 228–63. Penang: World Rainforest Movement, the Ecologist and Zed Books.

Sobhan, R. 1993. *Agrarian Reform and Social Transformation: Preconditions for Development*. London: Zed Books.

Soedargo, R. 1962. *Perundangan-Undangan Agraria Indonesia Djilid I*. Bandung: N. V. Eresco.

Soekarno. 1960. *Like an Angel That Strikes from the Skies: The March of Our Revolution*. A speech of the President of the Republic of Indonesia on the fifteenth anniversary of the founding of the Republic, 17 August 1960. Jakarta: Department of Information Republic of Indonesia.

Soemardjan, S. 1984. "Land Reform di Indonesia." In *Dua Abad Penguasaan Tanah: Pola Penguasaan Tanah Pertanian di Jawa dari Masa ke Masa*, ed. S. M. P. Tjondronegoro and G. Wiradi, 103–11. Jakarta: Gramedia.

Soetiknjo, I. 1987. *Proses Terjadinya UUPA: Peranserta Seksi Agraria Universitas Gadjah Mada*. Yogyakarta: Gadjah Mada University Press.

Soetrisno, L. 1995. "Tanah dan Masa Depan Rakyat Indonesia di Pedesaan." In *Tanah, Rakyat dan Demokrasi*, ed. U. Hadi and Masruchah. Yogyakarta: Forum LSM-LPSM DIY.

Stoler, A. L. 1985. *Capitalism and Confrontalism in Sumatra's Plantation Belt, 1870–1979.* New Haven: Yale University Press.

Suhendar, E. 1994. *Pemetaan Pola-pola Sengketa Tanah di Jawa Barat.* Bandung: Akatiga.

Sulaefi, A. S., and H. Yogaswara. 2008. *Draft Laporan Akhir Distribusi Tanah Negara.* Land Management and Policy Development Project. Jakarta: Badan Perencanaan Pembangunan Nasional RI.

Sumardjono, M. S. W. 1995. "Mengatasi Permasalahan Tanah Absente." *Kompas*, 13 February.

———. 1998. *Kewenangan Negara Untuk Mengatur dalam Konsep Penguasaan Tanah oleh Negara.* Pidato Pengukuhan Jabatan Guru Besar pada Fakultas Hukum Universitas Gadjah Mada. Yogyakarta, 14 February.

Sumaryanto, S. Friyatno, B. Irawan, et al. 1995. *Analisis Kebijaksanaan Konversi Lahan Sawah ke Penggunaan Non Pertanian.* 3rd Stage Report of the Center for Agricultural Socio-economy Research, Bogor Agricultural Institute.

Swasono, S.-E. 1985. "Kependudukan, Koloniasasi dan Transmigrasi." In *Sepuluh Windhu Transmigrasi di Indonesia, 1905–1985,* ed. Sri-Edi Swasono and Masri Singarimbun, 70–85. Jakarta: UI-Press.

Tabor, S. R. 1992. "Agriculture in Transition." In *The Oil Boom and After: Indonesian Economic Policy and Performance in the Soeharto Era,* ed. Anne Booth, 161–203. Singapore: Oxford University Press.

Tauchid, M. 1952. *Masalah Agraria sebagai Masalah Penghidupan dan Kemakmuran Rakjat Indonesia.* Djilid 1. Jakarta: Penerbit Tjakrawala.

———. 1953. *Masalah Agraria sebagai Masalah Penghidupan dan Kemakmuran Rakjat Indonesia.* Djilid 2. Jakarta: Penerbit Tjakrawala.

Thalib, S. 1971. *Hukum Pertambangan Indonesia.* Akademi Geologi dan Pertambangan.

Tjondronegoro, S. M. P. 1972. *Land Reform or Land Settlement: Shift in Indonesia's Land Policy, 1960–1970.* Land Tenure Center Working Paper no. 81. Madison: University of Wisconsin.

———. 2007. "A Brief Quarter Century Overview of Indonesia's Agrarian Policies." Paper presented at the national seminar titled

"Land and Households Economy 1979–2005: Changing Roads for Poverty Reduction." ICASEPS and UNESCAP-CAPSA, Bogor, 25 June 2007.

Utrecht, E. 1969. "Land Reform." *Bulletin of Indonesian Economic Studies* 5 (3): 5–13.

Walinsky, L. J., ed. 1977. *Agrarian Reform as Unfinished Business: The Selected Papers of Wolf Ladejinsky.* New York: Oxford University Press.

Warta Ekonomi. 1998. "Hutan Bukan Lagi Milik Raja-raja Kayu." No. 12, Tahun X, 10 August.

White, B. 2005. "Between Apologia and Critical Discourse: Agrarian Transitions and Scholarly Engagement in Indonesia." In *Social Science and Power in Indonesia,* ed. V. R. Hadiz and D. Dhakidae, 107–41. Singapore: Equinox.

White, B., and G. Wiradi. 1989. "Agrarian and Non-agrarian Bases of Inequality in Nine Javanese Villages.," In *Agrarian Transformation: Local Processes and the States in Southeast Asia,* ed. Gillian Hart, Andrew Turton, and Benjamin White, 266–302. Berkeley: University of California Press.

Wiradi, G. 1984. "Pola Penguasaan Tanah dan Reforma Agraria." In *Dua Abad Penguasaan Tanah: Pola Penguasaan Tanah Pertanian di Jawa dari Masa ke Masa,* ed. S. M. P. Tjondronegoro and G. Wiradi, 286–328. Jakarta: Yayasan Obor Indonesia.

———. 2000. *Reforma Agraria: Perjalanan yang Belum Berakhir.* Yogyakarta: KPA-Insist Press- Pustaka Pelajar.

Wiradi, G., and H. Makali. 1984. "Penguasaan Tanah dan Kelembagaan." In *Prospek Pembangunan Ekonomi Pedesaan Indonesia,* ed. F. Kasryno. Jakarta: Yayasan Obor Indonesia.

Wiradi, G., H. Makali, and A. Mintoro. 1979. *Aspek-aspek Kelembagaan dalam Pembangunan Pertanian: Studi Kasus DAS Cimanuk, Jawa Barat.* Rural Dynamics Study Project Research Report Phase-4, 1978/1979. Bogor: Agro-economy Survey and Planning Bureau of Ministry of Agriculture.

Wolf, E. R. 1966. *Peasants.* Englewood Cliffs, NJ: Prentice-Hall.

Yayasan, B. M. 1998. "Kasus Taman Nasional Kerinci Seblat." In *Pembangunan Berbuah Sengketa,* ed. B. Fidro and N. Fauzi, 61–68. Medan: SPSU and Yayasan Sintesa.

Zacharias, J. D. 1983. "A Lurah and His Dynasty: A Study of Village Officialdom in a Village of North Central Java Indonesia." MA thesis, Department of Politics, Monash University.

Zakaria, Y., and D. Suhendra. 1997. "Kemajemukan Hukum, Mengapa Tidak?" In *Reformasi Agraria: Perubahan Politik, Sengketa, dan Agenda*

Pembaruan Agraria di Indonesia, ed. D. Bachriadi, E. Faryadi, and B. Setiawan, 182–87. Jakarta: Faculty of Economy Press, University of Indonesia and KPA.

Newspaper

Kompas

Chapter 3

INDONESIA'S LAND TITLING PROGRAM (LAP)—THE MARKET SOLUTION?

CAROL WARREN AND ANTON LUCAS

While government policy in the early years after the Indonesian revolution was sensitive to populist and socialist demands for land redistribution and restrictions on the accumulation of land assets, land policy under the Suharto regime was thoroughly focused on market expansion and capital-intensive development. Although New Order rhetoric and even the law retained a veneer of earlier commitments to social justice and a people's economy, this could not be said of policy and practice. The New Order agenda fitted comfortably with the political and economic philosophy of the times, focusing on capital accumulation and technical and market-oriented development strategies. The Green Revolution stimulated the commercialization of production; transmigration redistributed landless persons from population-dense inner island Indonesia to "underpopulated" outer islands of the archipelago; and land-titling schemes were promoted in the name of legal certainty and economic development.

The World Bank Land Administration Project

By the 1990s the World Bank was playing an increasing role in funding Indonesian development programs and influencing policy directions toward greater economic liberalization. The Land Administration Project (LAP) began in 1994 as the first five-year phase of a twenty-five-year scheme that aimed at titling all nonforest lands, where it was estimated only 20 percent of land parcels had been registered (BPN 1993, 20). Its cost of US$135 million was funded jointly by the Indonesian government, a US$80 million World Bank loan and a US$15 million grant from the Australian Development Agency (World Bank/AIDAB 1993, 2). The LAP program was justified on grounds that land titling would bring about legal certainty and end the rising tide of land conflicts, which had become increasingly open, bitter, and protracted by the 1990s (CSIS 1991). The Indonesian people would benefit from a more comprehensive official land registration program that would provide greater security of tenure to landholders, greater access to credit, and protect their rights to compensation in cases of land resumption for development projects. At the same time, the titling program was also intended to create a more effective land market, reduce the cost of acquiring land by eliminating a range of costly inefficiencies in the process of certification and sale, and ultimately assure legal certainty to investors (BPN 1993, 18–20; World Bank 1994, 1995).

The conversion of traditional rights to private title (*hak milik*) was theoretically mandatory under the Basic Agrarian Law. But, despite the uncertain status of unregistered land, most Indonesians found it too expensive, cumbersome, and unnecessary to attempt certification. There had been earlier efforts by the Indonesian government to encourage systematic registration through the PRONA scheme, introduced in 1981, which offered streamlined block registration to selected communities deemed disadvantaged.[1] Despite some local response to the opportunity for low-cost certification, political manipulation and corruption plagued the scheme from the outset and restricted its effectiveness. Otherwise sporadic registration was the main mechanism for bringing unregistered land under the nationally recognized system. In practice, certification took place in order to sell land, mainly in urban areas or where development projects involving outside interests required "legal certainty." In most other situations land transfers took place under informal or customary regimes, sometimes involving letters of sale processed by notaries with varying degrees of official standing, and sometimes entirely based on verbal agreement and common knowledge (Soesangobeng 1996, 4–20).

The Land Administration Project was introduced in Indonesia in the context of worldwide pressure for the expansion, formalization, and privatization of property rights. Hernando de Soto was promoting an argument, later published in his influential book, *The Mystery of Capital* (2000), that the key to extending the benefits of capital to the poor and marginalized lay in legal recognition of their assets through formal titling. His thesis captured the imagination of policy makers for its apparent simplicity and compatibility with promarket approaches to development.[2] The poor had only to be brought into the fold through conversion of the extralegal status of their land and other resources. Adoption of the ambitious LAP program for nationwide registration and certification was late New Order Indonesia's response to pressures to improve governance and the rule of law and address the human rights of its poor while liberalizing market access.

The World Bank and Indonesian government presented the systematic conversion of people's land assets to formal private ownership status (*hak milik*) through the LAP as a win-win solution to Indonesia's land problems. It would facilitate investment, while landholders would benefit from a stronger legal negotiating position and greater access to credit (BPN 1993, 49–53; World Bank 1994, i–ii, 9ff., 28ff.). Critics in the NGO movement and academic circles, however, argued that the whole policy adopted a narrow and inappropriate approach to land as no more than a strategic commodity. The approach underpinning LAP undervalued the social security and environmental management functions as well as other nonmarket aspects of agrarian regimes operating in Indonesia.[3]

LAP Phase I (1994–1999)

The first phase of the Land Administration Project was primarily focused on Java where rapid industrial development, population growth, and urbanization were making the land problem acute. It was assumed that the high degree of de facto privatization of land in Java would ensure a smoother path for the conversion of holdings under traditional claims or long-term occupancy than was expected to be the case in the rest of the country, where various forms of customary (*adat*) tenure continued to prevail (LAP 1998, v; AusAID 2000a, 14).[4] A target of 1.2 million parcels were to be registered through streamlined processes carried out under special arrangements with the National Land Agency (BPN) in the initial five-year period of LAP.

The World Bank's commissioned evaluation of the Land Administration Project's first phase (Hardjono 1999) concluded that the certification program was well received by participants and did not significantly increase land alienation, although a long-term study remains to confirm this. Rates of turnover were largely a function of location in or near urban-industrial areas. Formal certification of land ownership (*hak milik*) was found to have raised market values by 10–25 percent in urban areas, but also the tax liability of registered owners, which reportedly rose by 50 to 100 percent in urban areas.[5] Evaluation studies showed increases in formal use of land titles as collateral for obtaining bank loans, but longer term implications for land alienation are difficult to ascertain. Increased access to credit is a double-edged sword: borrowing may increase risks alongside enhancing economic opportunities; although since bank loans are at considerably lower interest rates than private loans from money lenders, it is possible that better access to formal credit facilities would reduce the loss of land through default for some borrowers. This seems to have been one of the consequences of systematic titling which was introduced under a similar World Bank scheme in Thailand in 1987 (Slaats 1999, 104).

One concern raised by Hardjono's social assessment of the land certification program was its gender impacts (1999; see also SMERU 2002). There was an alarming tendency for lands purchased by married couples to be registered in the name of the husband alone, despite the fact that joint registration is possible under Indonesian law.[6] Women registered inherited property in their own names under the LAP, as did men. Nevertheless, when it came to registering purchased land acquired during marriage, women were not automatically registered as joint owners on the certificate, apparently because of the bureaucratic habit of dealing with the male "head of household" and the tendency for sale documents to be issued in the name of the husband.[7] A 1995 report by the team of legal advisors who researched customary legal practices associated with land registration in Depok, West Java, advises that inclusion of both names of husband and wife on a certificate is not deemed necessary to prove shared rights to land because generally, it is common knowledge that land is jointly owned by husband and wife under customary practice (Soesengobeng, Wright, and Harsono 1995, 76–78). Paradoxically, in the case of women, local knowledge and customary practice were regarded as sufficient to ensure their rights, although the thrust of the LAP is the contrary assumption that such rights are (or will become) insecure (see BPN 1993, 53).[8]

In direct opposition to the Indonesian government and World Bank positions, NGOs represented by the umbrella organization Consortium for Agrarian Reform (KPA) argued that land certification under LAP would accelerate dispossession through indebtedness and sale, disadvantage women and less powerful community or family members, and generally exacerbate inequality and land conflict (see KPA 1996a, 1996b, 1997a, n.d. [1997b?], 1998). KPA monitoring of LAP implementation in Depok, West Java (KPA 1997a), an area affected by heavy residential real estate development pressure, found accountability and public participation, which were among the LAP project objectives, to be inadequate. Complaints of bureaucratic discrepancies, unofficial payments, incorrect measurements recorded by surveyors, insufficient public information, and lack of a simple appeal procedure were widespread. These long-standing problems with the National Land Agency (BPN) tasked with carrying out the LAP project undermined proclaimed benefits in the view of KPA. Some of these criticisms of LAP implementation were confirmed by

World Bank consultants in informal discussions (pers. comm. 1996, 1999, 2000). But the general view was that the benefits of greater security of tenure through LAP certification far outweighed its failings, especially in urban areas where commercialization of land use was long-standing.[9]

Barraclough, Munggoro, and Chalid (1998, 33ff.) suggest that KPA opposition to land registration may be too ideologically driven and inflexible and that the organization needs to explore possibilities of democratically and locally defined forms of land registration and resource security systems.[10] To whatever extent specific criticisms of implementation may apply, the more fundamental critique from KPA and other activist NGOs is that the Land Administration Project is operating primarily to serve a liberalizing market model in which land and resources go to the highest bidders, irrespective of social need or productive use. The document setting out the rationale for Bank support of the LAP takes these market-oriented objectives as axiomatic: "Accelerated land registration, the major thrust of the project, would contribute significantly to the private sector development objective, by: (a) providing the basis for efficient and equitable land markets; (b) encouraging private investment by reducing investment risk; (c) mobilizing more financial resources by allowing land to be used as collateral" (World Bank 1994, 9). A USAID study similarly asserts: "Efficient and equitable land markets are a cornerstone of economic development.... [Their] absence ... has long been identified as one of the major sources of the difficulties and conflicts associated with land acquisition" (Thiesenhusen et al. 1997, 23).

A glaring gap in all of the official reviews of the land situation in Indonesia prepared for the Land Administration Project is the exclusion of any serious discussion of the issue of land concentration and redistribution, which was a significant factor in driving economic development in Japan, South Korea, and Taiwan (Moyo and Yeros 2005).[11] Nor was there substantive consideration in the otherwise extensive overviews of land law provided in materials prepared by the World Bank (1993, 1994, 1998), USAID (Thiesenhusen 1997), AusAID (2000) or the Indonesian Land Agency itself (BPN 1993) of the extensive body of existing laws and regulations on absentee ownership, maximum land holdings, and land redistribution,[12] despite strong representations on agrarian reform issues that came out of two high-level reports in 1978 and 1984 (Laporan 1978; White and Wiradi 1984) on land problems in Indonesia during the New Order period.

Whether the registration process increases the capacity of landholders to resist forced expropriation, or at least enhances their bargaining power in negotiations over compensation, as proponents asserted, will have as much to do with the accomplishment of more fundamental reform of the political and legal system as the systematic efficiency of official land title processing. Too many examples of duplicate or false titles being issued and of complete disregard of certificates by the courts can be recounted to place much store on titling as a resolution of the legal dimensions of this problem. Ultimately the worth of the title document depends on the political commitment of policy makers, law enforcement agencies, and civil society.[13]

The World Bank evaluation rues the continued reluctance of small landholders to register land through normal BPN procedures and the lack of "understanding of the real purpose and value of land registration" (Hardjono 1999, 6.2). Given the ordinary citizen's experience of the bureaucracy and legal system and widely circulated news reports of land cases where Indonesia's "little people" lose out regardless of the historical evidence or documentary validation of their claims, it is not surprising that those at the bottom of the socioeconomic hierarchy prefer to rely on local relationships and customary practice for what protection of their land rights these avail. The failure of the legal system in the Cimacan (chapter 4), Flores (chapter 7) Gili Trawangan (chapter 8) and Bandung (chapter 9) case studies in this volume indicate good grounds for general skepticism about judicial resort.[14]

Studies of the impact of systematic registration in Thailand indicate that title deeds were more often used as collateral, but at the price of heavier debt levels and increased land alienation. Follow-up studies indicated greater disparities across the socioeconomic spectrum, with a decline in informal lending and mutual assistance, and increased disputation over boundaries and inheritance associated with generally intensified social insecurity. Slaats (1999, 88–89, 104–6) concludes that the opposition between the social security orientation of communally based customary rights and the market orientation of the individually based statutory rights were exacerbated not resolved by the registration system.

Communal Lands and Nonmarket Values

Most contentious has been the question of implementing the LAP registration program in the "*adat* areas" outside Java, which was scheduled to take place in four phases between 1999 and 2019. The original World Bank and Indonesian government documents had left open the possibility that land registration as private property might be inappropriate where *adat* regimes "are not yet dead" (BPN 1993, 270). New regulations underpinning systematic registration were provided by a 1997 Government Regulation (PP 24/1997) on Land Registration, amending PP 10/1961. But like its predecessor, the 1997 regulation failed to acknowledge either communal land as an official category of land tenure equivalent to private *hak milik* rights or the *adat* community as a legal subject of registrable land rights (Atma Jaya and BPN 1998, xiv).[15] The presence of large migrant populations in outer island Indonesia further complicates the issue of indigenous rights, equitable distribution, and resource security, as illustrated in McCarthy's case study of the Central Kalimantan million hectare project in chapter 6 of this volume.[16]

The study of customary land rights commissioned under the Indonesian Land Administration Project, anticipating difficulties with registration of *adat* lands outside Java, decisively recommends against certification unless the request to do so comes from the community itself (Atma Jaya and BPN 1998, xvii–xviii). It argues that changing customary land access and use would erode local institutions and that communities would as a consequence lose the intimate social and cultural relationships that are tied to land. The critical implication of certification under the Basic Agrarian Law is its conversion to individual (*hak milik*) status and the consequent capacity to alienate land forever from clan or community control under state law. All four communities in Sumatra, Lombok, and Central Kalimantan studied by the Atma Jaya Research Team had *adat* prohibitions on the sale of land to outsiders, although various mechanisms for incorporating outsiders into the community and for internal land transfer among members existed in these villages (1998, v–xi).[17] In everyday practice, customary social and/or supernatural sanctions have been in varying degrees sufficient to maintain these norms, despite lack of recognition of registrable communal forms of property in state law. Although modernization and development have created pressures toward privatization of land in the study villages,[18] to date private right *hak milik* certificates had been sought in the Lombok and Minangkabau (Sumatra) study communities only by a few individuals, who took advantage of the opportunity to circumvent local *adat* land tenure arrangements by utilizing official registration procedures under state law (Atma Jaya and BPN 1998, xv).

The Atma Jaya/BPN report recommends registration without certification of the outer borders of communal land. This would permit official recognition of the community territory, without leaving it open to the potential for alienation implicit in the process of conversion to certified private property (*hak milik*) status. The study does not support the practice of registering communal land in the names of all right-holding members under the provisions of the current law. This is a recent practice adopted in some parts of Indonesia to deal with the lack of specification in the Basic Agrarian Law of the right of customary communities as corporate entities to hold a statutory *adat* title (Atma Jaya and BPN 1998, xvi). As Haverfield (1999, 57) points out, registration under the LAP presents a *Catch-22* situation in which "*adat* right holders lose both ways. If they convert their rights to rights acknowledged under the Agrarian Law and register their land on an individual basis, there is increasing prospect of monetarisation and dissolution of communities whose very existence integrally depends on communalism. If they do not register, they lose their land to the State, transmigrants or developers who will obtain superior title." (See also Evers 1995.)

Since the privileging of private rights in the Basic Agrarian Law implies a completely different (Western) philosophy and relationship toward land, the report urges caution and sensitivity to the broader cultural and social ties implicated in local constructions of land tenure (Atma Jaya and BPN 1998, xii, xvii). But despite the clear sympathy of the Atma Jaya research team with the autochthonous values and even "invented traditions" of *adat* community ties to land, they nevertheless indicate that the problem lies in the failure of the UUPA and government policy generally to provide for an "evolutionary" process "developing in stages" by which national law would be implemented (1998, vi, xix). Ultimately for these academic researchers too, legal pluralism appears to remain an interim accommodation (though with a self-determined time frame), not an end in itself.[19] Yet the character and directionality of change remains something of an open question. There is some evidence of reinstatement and reinforcement of community control of land disposition and resource use among *adat* communities in the post-Suharto Era (see Warren 2005; Acciaioli 2009).

Tenure Security, Local Practices, and the "Mystery of Capital"

The underlying question of the ultimate social and cultural embeddedness of economic interests embodied in the land question poses important questions for de Soto's (2000) influential thesis that formalization of property rights through legal registration is the single most important means of eliminating poverty in developing countries. Without registered title and the credit access this facilitates, he argues, the mysterious work of capital eludes those marginalized from involvement in the economic development that market forces make possible. But de Soto fails to address the critical issue of alienability, which allows him to evade the ultimate implications of market-oriented titling systems. Property has to be "freely" transferable to maximize its capital value on a "free" market. Both Marx and Weber recognized that without the capacity to separate property from its various social and cultural encumbrances, its "mysterious" role in the capitalist system is circumscribed. Lauding the advantages of fungible conversion of property assets permitted through formalized property systems (2000, 55–57), de Soto's path to reform through land commodification for a larger proportion of developing country populations disingenuously circumvents this paradox, since its parallel relation to proletarianization is not considered. The wider implication of selling land bound up with cultural and social ties to place is unexamined. Even in strictly commodified asset terms, the loss of this basic resource represents incalculable risk to the well-being of the next generation. The challenge de Soto has set "of making a transition to a market-based capitalist system" (which he considers "the only game in town") that "respects people's desires and beliefs" (2000, 242) founders on this crucial blind spot.

Notwithstanding de Soto's ambitious claims, formalized title does not necessarily guarantee access to capital for the marginalized because the small-scale, heavy transaction costs and difficulties of disposal make credit institutions reluctant to lend to smallholder farmers in remote areas with low value primary products. The ultimate possibility of land alienation leads to risk-averse tendencies among smallholders, and of course the landless do not benefit at all from the "market solution" unless land reform is part of the package. Nor do market mechanisms guarantee the most productive land use, as statistics on speculation and the huge scale of neglected "sleeping" lands discussed in the foregoing chapters suggest. Finally, where complex and overlapping property rights apply in noncapitalist land regimes, simplified land titling may permanently fix previously flexible arrangements and privilege some rights/claims holders (elites, males, the current generation) at the expense of others.

Hardjono (1999, 5.4) found that recipients of LAP certificates generally felt more secure in their rights since certification. But although some recipients of LAP certificates believed they had security from eviction, formal certification in law provides only "strong evidence" that the individual is the legitimate titleholder (Haverfield 1999, 68). Reerink (2011, 537ff.) found that the actual difference in degree of legal security experienced by urban poor dwellers who were formal titleholders and those who were not is much lower[20] than predicted so prominently in the recent work of de Soto (2000). In fact, Hardjono's study showed that LAP certificate holders were already reverting to informal processes of land transfer because this was deemed sufficient and less expensive than formal mechanisms. "Information from all nine study areas indicates that LAP beneficiaries have not been registering subsequent land transactions with BPN" (Hardjono 1999, 6.1). Barely half of Reerink's LAP participants indicated that they would do so (2011, 537).

The Atma Jaya research team, like the NGO movement, calls for significant revisions of the law to protect traditional land tenure and recognition of the de facto legal pluralism that prevails in rural Indonesia. Without these changes, the fundamental contradictions in the Constitution and Basic Agrarian Law, which acknowledge *adat* and other local tenure regimes in theory but do not accommodate them in practice, will continue to plague Reform Era politics and drive conflict. They argue that the focus of policy should be on local empowerment, including the right to reject development projects that may have detrimental social impacts (Atma Jaya and BPN 1998, xxiii). The legal scholar Daniel Fitzpatrick draws similar conclusions.

> Adat land law is cognizable only in the context of communal rights and obligations, which are underpinned by social processes of consensus, discussion, and deliberation. Individualizing and "freezing" tenure through a process of registering Western-style rights threatens to break down this subtle interaction between individuals and their community. In doing so, individual registration of land also threatens traditional village social structure itself, at least to the extent that this structure is based on communal and cooperative elements. As a result, rather than conferring legal unity and certainty, the registration of rights under the BAL is far more likely to lead to disputation, de facto pluralism, and ultimately the erosion of *adat* authority itself. Where the land law on which title registrations are based is inconsistent with social reality, the much-touted benefit of registration—increased certainty that leads to increased investment and access to formal credit—does not materialize. (Fitzpatrick 1997, 188–89)

The controversial LAP project was put on hold in the immediate aftermath of the 1997–98 political and economic crisis in Indonesia. But the emphasis on certification as the key agrarian policy framework has since reappeared in several recent programs implemented under the Yudohyono government. A low key phase of the LAP program now operates under the title Land Management and Policy Development Project (LMPDP 2005–2009) (World Bank 2004), focused on streamlining decentralized Land Agency procedures and accelerated land titling.[21] The current head of the National Land Agency, Joyo Winoto, an adherent of the de Soto policy line, has undertaken to accelerate the legalization of land assets dramatically.[22]

Politicians like to assume that formal certification of land rights is the solution to these land conflicts. That assumption is questioned by the head of the National Land College (STPN).

> Every time parliament holds hearings with BPN [the National Land Agency], the first thing they ask is "How many plots of land have been legalized?" ... They think that BPN can reduce the number of land disputes by legalising land [holdings] as quickly as possible. Their point of view is partly correct. But *adat* land can only be legalized if it is registered under individual names. This destroys the function of communal rights (*hak ulayat*) and will only cause more conflicts because *adat* land exists for collective welfare. (Interview with Endriatmo Sutatmo, Magelang, 12 December 2011)

The substantive critique of the Land Administration Project from NGO quarters remains: that the absence of genuine land reform and formal recognition of communal land rights protection in the systematic titling program, and in government legislative and policy revisions, would shift the balance further toward formal-legal processes for validating land tenure and legitimate or exacerbate existing injustices, including the illicit expropriations of the last decades (Suhendar and Winarni 1998; KPA 1996a, 1996b). As a case in point, KPA (1997a, 13) refers to the registration of land held by absentee landowners in Bekasi through the LAP project in violation of the Basic Agrarian Law. In this and similar cases, they argue, LAP became a tool for the "institutionalisation of existing unequal land distribution" (KPA 1997a, 12).

LAP documents give a great deal of attention to the questions of legal certainty and asset recognition; but there is little consideration given to questions of access for the land poor and landless and of limiting accumulation, once regarded as the pivotal issues in Indonesian land reform. This reflects both the political sensitivity of such policies as well as the tendency to regard them as out of date in an increasingly market liberal environment. The BPN/World Bank overview of the legal situation in Indonesia comments that the architects of the Basic Agrarian Law "were seeking to invoke a theory of socialist responsibility for land matters." It concludes that the disjunction between these "philosophical ideals" and "practical application . . . raises the general issue of the appropriateness of the UUPA and the legislation derived from it in assisting the nation as it seeks to integrate into the global economy" (BPN 1993, 269–70). The World Bank mission explicitly aimed to reverse this situation. "Initiatives such as ILAP have been designed and implemented to take Indonesia further down the path of development and toward globalisation (a free market)" (LAP 1998, 1).

Twenty-first-century economic and environmental crises, however, suggest that such strident faith in the market warrants reconsideration. Although the neoliberal hold on global institutions has to date been barely shaken by the world financial crisis, the new political climate at least presents the opportunity to reconsider alternative approaches that are genuinely pro-poor and less market driven.

Notes

1. Priority under the PRONA scheme was to be given to areas with development potential or that had been subject to land reform or transmigration schemes.

2. De Soto's influence on Indonesian policy makers is discussed in Fauzi (2009), and Fauzi in Setiawan (2010). For a critical discussion of the reasons for de Soto's appeal and the unrealistic assumptions behind some of his propositions, see Otto (2009).

3. On Indonesian debates about the transformation of land as a social good (as elaborated in the Basic Agrarian Law) to a strategic commodity, see Suhendar and Kasim (1996, 97).

4. Although spiritual and social *adat* ties to the land also exist in Java, it was generally held that agricultural property rights had over the centuries become individualized there and that *adat* bonds no longer directly defined the nature of land and resource claims to the extent that they did in the outer islands of Indonesia (Evers 1995, 8; Fitzpatrick 1997, 211).

5. An earlier World Bank preliminary report gives a range of 36 percent to 51 percent in Jakarta (1994, 3); see also Thiesenhusen et al. (1997, 41).

6. This is particularly ironic in that national law as well as Javanese customary law prescribes the equal division of property acquired during marriage in the event of divorce; similarly, equal property division between male and female heirs is customary in Javanese culture.

7. Thiesenhusen et al. (1997, 24). Another Land Administration Project study (Atma Jaya and BPN 1998, xxii) of land tenure practices in three regions outside Java (West Sumatra, Central Kalimantan, and Lombok) reports that in the matrilineal Minangkabau area, registration was known to have given the opportunity for the male clan leader (*mamak*) to alter matrilineal inheritance practices by registering clan land titles in his name. Taxation and banking institutions similarly privilege male heads of household in their documentary practices.

8. Land titling projects in Thailand and Laos have tried to resolve similar gender and customary land inheritance issues with varying degrees of success (Hall, Hirsch, and Li 2011, 42).

9. Slaats (1999, 100) reports a generally positive response to the early pilot project in suburban Jakarta, as does Hardjono in her 1999 evaluation report, at least with respect to the cost of the procedure and the sense of security it provided. Reerink (2011, 535) found that costs for participants in Bandung were much lower and waiting times shorter than reported for registration outside the LAP project.

10. In 1998 Solon Barraclough from the United Nations Research Institute for Social Development was invited to review agrarian reform in Indonesia and to evaluate KPA's activities on behalf of Oxfam (UK), which had been funding KPA since 1995.

11. The LAP Project Preparation Report, however, did include passing consideration of absentee landholders' rights and maximum holdings in urban land within new land legislation proposed under the terms of reference for the project (BPN 1993, 272).

12. See discussion of this legislation pursuant to the BAL/UUPA in chapters 1 and 2.

13. Hutchison (2008) argues that provision of legal security through titling is heavily contingent on other social structural considerations, an aspect underrecognized in the enthusiastic neoliberal promotion of its free-market potential.

14. The importance of certification for obtaining credit is also qualified by Ganie-Rochman's (1998, 7) evidence that banks did accept uncertified land as collateral in the sample communities she studied. She also notes that although the Village Government Law (UU 5/1979) effectively destroyed the *adat* governance system in Palembang, customary norms still operated in the disposition of land among community members there and at sites she studied in Java (Ganie-Rochman 1998, 12).

15. Registration is technically a separate process from issuance of certificates of title (UUPA 5/1960, §19), and it was proposed that the registration program could exploit this distinction in the absence of radical legal revisions (Atma Jaya and BPN 1998, xiii, xvii). But see KPA (n.d. [1997b], 17–18) objections to this option, as a step toward legitimating the separation of *adat* land from its social and cultural context, leading ultimately to its commodification. In 2009, the Indonesian Indigenous Peoples' Alliance (AMAN), the Indonesian Network for Community Mapping (JKPP), and Forest Watch Indonesia (FWI) initiated an Indigenous Peoples' Land Registration program, on the basis of which AMAN issues verification of maps and territorial claims to strengthen the basis for recognition of indigenous rights in the context of the UN program on Reducing Emissions from Deforestation and Forest Degradation (REDD) and other claims on their resources. In 2011, AMAN and BPN signed a memorandum of understanding to accommodate indigenous peoples' claims on land and territory (Nota Kesepahaman antara AMAN dan BPN-RI No. 05/MOU/PB-AMAN/IX/2011 and 11/SKB/IX/2011). Bachriadi (pers. comm. 28 January 2012) expressed concern that this initiative may nonetheless unintentionally contribute to privatization and alienation, since it represents a first step toward state-based and market-oriented formal titling. Others argue various forms of registration need not have this outcome. See, for example, Otto and Hoekema (2012).

16. For the ethnic minority *adat* communities throughout the rest of the country, the displacement wrought by late New Order development involved not only the loss of material resources of their customary domains but a threat to the cultural identities that were tied to them. During the last years of the New Order, some of Indonesia's minority indigenous communities began asserting their claims through identity movements, ultimately culminating in the formation of the Alliance of Indigenous (Adat) Peoples of the Archipelago (AMAN 1999a, 1999b). For an example of violence directed at in-migrant ethnic groups, see Henley and Davidson (2007).

17. See Warren (2005) for similar findings on *adat* land tenure in some parts of Bali.

18. The projects specifically referred to were a hydroelectric project in the Minangkabau area; an Asian Development Bank rubber plantation project in the Central Kalimantan community; and land speculation associated with West Lombok's tourism expansion (Atma Jaya and BPN 1998, xii–xv).

19. Soni Harsono, then State Minister of Agrarian Affairs and chairman of BPN, said in a public forum that preserving customary law regarding land ownership would be a "step backwards," since it would disappear as Indonesia develops: "With the trend toward individual land ownership, these customary laws would eventually die a natural death." He was also quoted as saying, "The government will continue to respect customary rights, but will not help preserve them" (*Jakarta Post,* 26 September 1996).

20. Zoning, building codes, and permit requirements mean most urban dwellers transgress one or more requirements for legal settlement beyond certification of their landholding.

21. The Land Management and Policy Development Project aims to accelerate and expand the land titling program, and build institutional capacity for consistent land legislation and management.

22. On government claims, the certification process has made significant inroads. An election poster advertisement for President Yudhoyono's land reform program claims an "astonishing" 13,158,816 certificates issued between 2005 and 2008 (Fauzi 2009), a figure later revised down to 4, 627,039 (Fauzi in Setiawan 2010, 20). Chapter 10 elaborates on the policy debates surrounding these Yudhoyono government initiatives in the post–New Order political context.

References

Acciaioli, G. 2009. "Conservation and Community in the Lore Lindu National Park (Sulawesi): Customary Custodianship, Multi-ethnic Participation and Resource Entitlement." In *Community, Environment and Local Governance in Indonesia: Locating the Commonweal,* ed. C. Warren and J. F. McCarthy, 89–120. London: Routledge.

AMAN. 1999a. "Catatan Hasil Kongres Masyarakat Adat Nusantara," 15–22 March 1999. Jakarta: Aliansi Masyarakat Adat Nusantara.

———. 1999b. Menggugat Posisi Masyarakat Adat terhadap Negara, Jakarta: Kongres Masyarakat Adat Nusantara and Lembaga Studi Pers & Pembangunan.

Atma Jaya and BPN (Pusat Kajian Pembangunan Masyarakat, Universitas Atma Jaya bekerja sama dengan Badan Pertanahan Nasional). 1998. Ringkasan Laporan Penelitian, Pola Penguasaan Tanah Masyarakat Tradisional dan Problema Pendaftaran Tanah: Studi Kasus di Sumatera Barat, Kalimantan Tengah dan Nusa Tenggara Barat. Laporan Penelitian Vol. I Indonesian Land Administration Project, Customary (Adat) Land Rights Studies.

AusAID. 2000a. Indonesian Land Administration Project LAP II. Draft Project Design Document (February 2000). Canberra: Australian Agency for International Development.

———. 2000b. *Improving Access to Land and Enhancing the Security of Land Rights: A Review of Land Titling and Land Administration Projects.* Quality Assurance Series no. 20 September 2000. Canberra: AusAid.

Bappenas and BPN. 1997. *Executive Summary of Final Report and Policy Matrix: Land Policy Reform in Indonesia.* A Topic Cycle 4 of LAP-Part C, Indonesian Land Administration Project.

Barraclough, S. 1998. "Land Reform in Developing Countries: The Role of the State and Other Actors." Unpublished Paper for UNRISD Project "Grassroots Initiatives and Knowledge Network for Land Reform and Tenurial Security in Developing Countries." Geneva: United Nations Research Institute for Social Development.

Barraclough, S., D. W. Munggoro, and Chalid. 1998. "Keeping Alive the Spirit of Agrarian Reform in Indonesia." Unpublished Assessment Report on KPA Programs 1996–98. Bandung: KPA.

BPN (Badan Pertanahan Nasional). 1993. *Project Preparation Report for Indonesian Land Administration Project.* Jakarta.

BPN and Bappenas. 1997 "Evolutionary Change in Indonesian Land Law: Traditional Law (Adat) Perspectives." Draft Final Report Topic Cycle 4, Land Administration Project (prepared by Arcadis Euroconsult in association with PT Pengembangan Agribisnis).

CSIS (Center for Strategic and International Studies). 1991. "Masalah Tanah Semakin Meningkat" (The Land Question as a Growing Problem). Special Issue, *Analisis* 20 (2).

De Soto, H. 2000. *The Mystery of Capitalism: Why Capitalism Triumphs in the West and Fails Everywhere Else.* New York: Basic Books

Evers, P. J. 1995. "Preliminary Policy and Legal Questions about Recognizing Traditional Land in Indonesia." *Ekonesia: A Journal of Indonesian Human Ecology* 3:1–24.

Fauzi, N. 2009. "Land Titles Do Not Equal Agrarian Reform." *Inside Indonesia* 47, available at www.Insideindonesia.org/edition-98-oct-dec-2009/land-titles-do-not-equal-agrarian-reform-18101247. Accessed 2 December 2011.

———. 2010. "Prolog." In Usep Setiawan, *Kembali ke Agraria*. Yogyakarta: STPN Press, KPA and Sajogyo Institute.
Fitzpatrick, D. 1997. "Disputes and Pluralism in Modern Indonesian Land Law." *Yale Journal of International Law* 22 (1): 171–212.
Ganie-Rochman, M. 1998. Indonesian Land Administration Project, Final Report, Community Development Adviser. Unpublished document. October.
Hall, D., P. Hirsch, and T. M. Li. 2011. *Powers of Exclusion: Land Dilemmas in Southeast Asia*. Honolulu: University of Hawai'i Press.
Hardjono, J. 1999. "A Social Assessment of the Land Certification Program, the Indonesian Land Administration Project." Unpublished report. Jakarta: World Bank Office.
Haverfield, R. 1999. "Hak Ulayat and the State: Land Reform in Indonesia." In *Indonesia: Law and Society,* ed. T. Lindsey, 42–73. Leichhardt, NSW: Federation Press.
Henley, D., and J. Davidson, eds. 2007. *The Revival of Tradition in Indonesian Politics: The Deployment of Adat from Colonialism to Indigenism*. London: Routledge.
Hutchison, J. 2008. "Land Titling and Poverty Reduction in Southeast Asia: Realising Markets or Realising Rights?" *Australian Journal of International Affairs* 62 (3): 332–34.
KPA. 1996a. *Land Disputes: Strawberries of Development: First KPA Memorandum on the Land Administration Project in Indonesia,* Bandung: Konsorsium Pembaruan Agraria.
———. 1996b. *Our Land Is Not for Sale: Second KPA Memorandum on the Land Administration Project in Indonesia*. Bandung: Konsorsium Pembaruan Agraria.
———. 1997a. *To Ignore or to Engage NGOs: Third KPA Memorandum on the Land Administration Project in Indonesia*. Bandung: Konsorsium Pembaruan Agraria.
———. n.d. [1997b?]. *Tidak! Untuk Pendaftaran Tanah Komunal [Fourth KPA Memorandum on the Land Administration Project]*. Bandung: Konsortium Pembaruan Agraria.
———. 1998. *Deklarasi Pembaruan Agraria 1998*. Bandung: Konsorsium Pembaruan Agraria
LAP. n.d. "Evolutionary Change in Indonesian Land Law: Traditional Law (Adat) Perspectives. Draft final report, Land Administration Project, Topic Cycle 4, prepared by Arcadis Euroconsult in association with PT Pusat Pengembangan Agribisnis for the National Development Planning Agency (BAPPENAS), funded by the Government of Indonesia and World Bank.

———. 1998. "Issues Relating to Strategic Planning and Institutional Restructuring in BPN." Unpublished paper in file: World Bank/ AusAID Supervision Mission #7, 14–25 September 1998. Jakarta: World Bank.

"Laporan Interim Masalah Pertanahan." 1978. Unpublished report to the President of Indonesia by the State Minister for Research, Sumitro Djojohadikusumo et al., Jakarta.

Moyo, S., and P. Yeros. 2005. *Reclaiming the Land: The Resurgence of Rural Movements in Africa, Asia and Latin America.* London: Zed Books.

Otto, J. M. 2009. "Rule of Law Promotion, Land Tenure and Poverty Alleviation: Questioning the Assumptions of Hernando de Soto." *Hague Journal on the Rule of Law* 1 (1): 173–94.

Otto, J. M., and A. Hoekema. 2012. *Fair Land Governance: How to Legalize Land Rights for Rural Development.* Leiden: Leiden University Press.

Reerink, G. 2011. "Land Registration Programmes for Indonesia's Urban Poor: Need, Reach and Effect in the *Kampongs* of Bandung." In *Legalising Land Rights: Local Practices, State Responses and Tenure Security in Africa, Asia and Latin America,* ed. J. Ubink, A. Hoekema, and W. Assies, 527–48. Leiden: Leiden University Press.

Setiawan, U. 2010. *Kembali ke Agraria.* Yogyakarta: STPN Press, KPA, and the Sajogyo Institute.

Slaats, H. 1999. "Land Titling and Customary Rights: Comparing Land Registration Projects in Thailand and Indonesia." In *Property Rights and Economic Development: Land and Natural Resources in Southeast Asia and Oceania,* ed. T. van Meijl and F. von Benda-Beckmann, 88–109. London: Kegan Paul International.

SMERU. 2002. *An Impact Evaluation of Systematic Land Titling under the Land Administration Project (LAP).* Jakarta: SMERU Research Report at http://www.smeru.or.id/report/research/lap/lap.htm.

Soesangobeng, H. 1996. "Implementation of Adjudication in PAP Project 1995/1996 Krawang." Jakarta: LASAILAP.

Soesangobeng, H., with W. Wright and B. Harsono. 1995. "Pengamatan atas Aspek Hukum dan Adat pada Proyek Uji Coba Pendaftaran Sistimatik di Kelurahan Depok, Bogor." Jakarta: LASA.

Suhendar, E., and I. Kasim. 1996. *Tanah Sebagai Komoditas: Kajian Kritis atas Kebijakan Pertanahan Orde Baru.* Jakarta: ELSAM.

Suhendar, E., and Y. B. Winarni. 1998. *Petani dan Konflik Agraria.* Bandung: Akatiga.

Thiesenhusen, W., T. Hanstad, R. Mitchell, and E. Rajagukguk. 1997. "Land Tenure Issues in Indonesia." Jakarta: AGRIDEC Inc. for USAID.

Warren, C. 2005. "Mapping Common Futures: Customary Communities, NGOs and the State in Indonesia's Reform Era." *Development and Change* 36 (1): 49–73.

White, B., and G. Wiradi, eds. 1984. *Agrarian Reform in Comparative Perspective: Policy Issues and Research Needs.* The Hague: Institute of Social Studies and Bogor: Agro Economic Survey Foundation.

World Bank. 1994. *Indonesia: Environment and Development: Challenges for the Future.* Report No. 12083-IND.

———. 1995. *Indonesia: Land Administration Project.* Unpublished internal document.

———. 2003. *Land Policies for Growth and Poverty Reduction.* Washington, DC: World Bank.

———. 2004, *Project Appraisal Document on a Proposed Loan to the Government of Republic of Indonesia for a Land Management and Policy Development Project,* 31 March. Report no. 28178-IND, Rural Development and Natural Resources Sector Unit East Asia and Pacific Region.

World Bank/AIDAB. 1993. *Proposed Indonesian Land Administration Project.* World Bank Appraisal Mission Aide Memoire 24 November to 18 December.

Wright, W. 1999. *Final Report on the Review of the Basic Agrarian Law 1960.* Unpublished report for the Indonesian Land Administration Project. Jakarta: BPN.

Chapter 4

THE CIMACAN GOLF COURSE DISPUTE SINCE THE NEW ORDER

ANTON LUCAS

> *A piece of land will be defended to death even if it is only the size of a finger.*
> —Javanese saying[1]

The Cimacan golf course dispute was one of a number of high-profile land disputes in Indonesia that erupted in the late 1980s as a result of the insatiable demand for land stimulated by New Order economic development policies. There were several reasons for the prominence of land cases, particularly in West Java. These included the advocacy of the West Java Peasants Union (SPJB, Sarekat Petani Jawa Barat) throughout the 1980s;[2] the location of student groups and NGOs supporting farmers in Bandung, the West Java provincial capital; the involvement of legal aid institutes in advocacy work for farmers involved in land disputes; the close proximity to the central government bureaucracy and the national parliament in Jakarta; and the reporting of land disputes in the national press mostly located in Jakarta and Bandung. Cimacan, sited in the Puncak resort region halfway between Bandung and Jakarta, was thus one of many cases that made headlines starting in the late 1980s (*Setiakawan* 1991; *Laporan Kasus/ Case Reports* 1991; Amir 1995a, 155–66).[3]

During the late New Order, huge tracts of land were being expropriated for industrial estates, agro-industrial plantations, aquaculture, commercial forestry leases, tourist resorts, golf courses, and land for public infrastructure projects, among which were several tollways, three national parks, and three dams (*Setiakawan* 1991;[4] Fidro and Fauzi 1995).

Developers used various forms of intimidation and subjugation, ranging from threats to physical violence, to obtain land from farmers (Fidro and Fauzi 1995, i–xv). Specific methods included delegitimizing proof of land rights, falsification of signatures, and labeling protesting farmers as "ex-PKI." Land dispute cases seldom went to court, and, if they did, developers influenced local district courts to obtain decisions in their favor through bribery and corruption.

This chapter is a case study of the Cibodas Golf Course Resort and Villas tourist development project in Cimacan village adjacent to the Cibodas botanical gardens and Mount Gede-Pangrango National Park (TNGP) in the Puncak resort region of West Java. It considers how farmers lost their land, and the impact this had on their livelihoods in the late 1980s. It then looks at the subsequent struggle for compensation during the early reform period, the efforts of the elected village representative council (BPD) to resolve the dispute, and what has happened since farmers received final compensation. Finally, we will look at how the dispute has affected village governance.

Background to the Dispute

Cimacan is a large and semi-urbanized village of 17,000 people located in the subdistrict of Pacet on the main road between Puncak Pass (Jakarta's closest hill resort) in the district of Cianjur, which produces 22 percent of West Java's total vegetable production,[5] in a productive market garden economy using an intercropping cultivation system, with an abundance of water during the dry season. As well as a highly profitable local vegetable sector (producing at least sixteen varieties of vegetables grown commercially and intensively), the village has an ornamental plant industry selling plants to many parts of Indonesia.

When 31.6 hectares of Cimacan Village land was leased to a Bandung property developer (PT BAM) for a golf course, club house, and luxury villas in 1987, without consultation with the cultivators, 287 farmers and 500 farm laborers lost the land they had been cultivating for many decades.

Loss of land without adequate compensation meant loss of livelihood and was a catastrophe for the Rarahan hamlet vegetable growers and their families. The Pacet subdistrict of Cianjur district contributed 60 percent of the locally raised part of the district budget. This income came from the Puncak accommodation and tourism industry, and levies on vehicles and the more than 100,000 annual visitors to the Cibodas botanical gardens and the national park, both located on the western boundary of the villagers' vegetable gardens, now the golf course. On the eastern side were the camping ground and guest bungalows of the Forestry Department. According to the village head, by 2002 these levies on visitors to Cimacan were raising Rp1.5 billion per annum for the district. But much to the frustration of both the village officials and the newly elected village council (BPD), the village got none of this income. The village head said that despite the decentralization laws of 1999 (UU 22/1999 and UU 25/1999), Cianjur district administration (Pemda) had not returned any of the levies collected in the village.[6] The other big issue was the long-running dispute over compensation for village land leased for the golf course in 1987 (Bachriadi and Lucas 2001).

Causes of the Land Dispute

The Cimacan farmers had cultivated the village land (*tanah kas desa*) for an annual rent since the early 1960s, and their forebears since colonial times. In 1983, to strengthen their case for gaining formal rights to this land, farmers had asked for *girik garapan,* the local term for land tax assessments (IPEDA).[7] After these were issued, they paid their IPEDA levy to the village, and received receipts for these payments, which they regarded as their only "proof" of occupancy rights to former plantation land that the village head said was now *tanah kas desa*.[8] Initially supporting their claim, when the developer appeared on the scene, the village head suddenly accused the leaders of the farmers who organized the request of being "communist troublemakers" (Bachriadi and Lucas 2001, 294–97).[9] Unexpectedly, without any consultation with the cultivators of the land, the village head and Cimacan Village Council (then known as LKMD),[10] leased out the land for thirty years to PT BAM (Bandung Asri Mulya), a Bandung developer, for a total payment of Rp 90 million (US$53,349) to build a golf course and resort.[11] When the farmers refused to give up their cultivation rights, PT BAM took them to court to force them off the land. From 1987 to 1991 the dispute was in and out of the district, provincial, and finally the Indonesian Supreme Court, with judgments upholding the validity of the developer's thirty-year leases (Bachriadi and Lucas 2001, 32–41).

Loss of Livelihood Caused by the Land Dispute

In the first case, brought against the twenty-eight farmers in the Cianjur district court by the developer in 1989, the farmers estimated lost income at Rp 4 million per year per household or an average monthly income of about Rp 335,000 (US$189.00). The figures for the second court case brought by Jakarta legal aid lawyers from YLBHI (Yayasan Bantuan Hukum Indonesia) in the Bandung high court are slightly higher (Rp 4.7 million annually or Rp 394,000 per month).[12]

With the loss of land came loss of livelihood for the Cimacan farmers and destruction of the environment.[13] The cases of the families of three cultivators, Emus Muhidin, Gogo Gojali, and Dja'i, illustrate the plight of these farmers and their families. At the time the land was leased to PT BAM, Emus Muhidin cultivated fifteen *patok*;[14] they had a sack of rice (twenty-five liters) and Rp 7 million in savings. When the PT BAM foreman (*mandor*) and his assistants subsequently bulldozed the vegetable plots, Emus had seven *patok* of carrots and onions ready to harvest. As a result of being evicted, two of his children dropped out of school, and it was difficult to afford to buy rice for the family. His wife tried to sell vegetables bought from other farmers from a stall outside the gates of the Cibodas botanical gardens (bordering on Rarahan hamlet) on weekends, not always profitably (interview in Cimacan, January 1999).

Gogo Gojali and his family were worse off. His onion crop was dug up and thrown away by PT BAM employees. Six of his children dropped out of school. He pawned his house for Rp 500,000 to rent land elsewhere. But after two harvests there, which paid off the pawn, the land was sold. So he became an agricultural laborer, and often sat at home in the mornings with nothing to do. "If I was still a vegetable farmer, my kids would be self-sufficient; maybe they could buy a car, or I could go on the pilgrimage to Mecca. It's hard for me to buy enough food for my family, let alone buy things for my kids" (interview in Cimacan, 20 March 1999).

In the third case, the seventy-year-old farmer Dja'i recalls:

Before I had 6 *patok* including broccoli, onions, green vegetables, orchids, roses, and garlic. I kept a place to grow strawberries. I could sell Rp 6,000 worth of strawberries per week. I could get Rp two million a year, sometimes even twelve million in a good year; [it was] enough for my kids and grandchildren. Why would I accept the consolation money [*uang pangjeujeuh*] they were offering us? It's crazy! Just imagine, only Rp 30 [per square meter]. Thirty rupiah wouldn't buy one cigarette. All I do now in the morning after I've had a bath is just sit in the sun.[15] Well, there is nothing else to do. At the most I go looking for jobs in Cibodas. I will do anything.[16] Two of my kids couldn't go on to junior high school. Even though all their older siblings completed senior high school. I feel a pain in my chest whenever I think of that damn golf course. My one hope is that I will be able to work the land again. Even if I have to start from scratch.[17] I don't want to get [compensation] money! (*DeTik*, 1993)[18]

These figures show the losses affecting these three families as representative of the twenty-eight farmers who had leased the village land since the early 1960s. Each family had been earning an average income of roughly Rp 4 million per year (US$2,285), so they understandably refused PT BAM's compensation offer of what the village administration and the developer called "consolation money," initially of Rp 30 per square meter (US$0.017) later raised to Rp 210 per square meter (US$0.12). This was nowhere near the market price of land in the village, and as the farmer just quoted remarked, was not enough to buy one cigarette.[19]

Legal Challenges

In order to remove the farmers from the land they were cultivating, the developer PT BAM randomly chose twenty-eight farmers from among those who had refused to accept the consolation payment, and took them to Cianjur district court in a civil action in late 1989 (Bachriadi and Lucas 2001, 32–41, 113, 313–17). PT BAM's lawyer R. D. Djuanda claimed that the company had sole rights to the land under the thirty-year lease agreement with the village and that farmers could not use land tax (IPEDA) payments as proof of cultivation rights to the land. Cimacan village argued that they had leased the land in order to increase village income.[20] But in order to "legally" rent out the land, the village had to apply for "use rights" (*hak pakai*) from higher authorities. In response, the governor of West Java in February 1998 issued a statement that the land had to be used for agriculture, which appeared to support the farmers. But in an about-face by the Bandung provincial government, use rights land certificates were hastily issued to the village one month later (Bachriadi and Lucas 2001, 261). As noted above, because the farmers were renting the land, the developer offered "consolation money." Farmers sent a letter of protest and then visited the office of Minister of Home Affairs, Rudini, who at first supported the farmers, but then changed his mind and supported the developer after meeting with the village headman and the governor of West Java.[21] Both these examples indicate that despite the usual pro-*rakyat* rhetoric in land disputes, vested interest practice tends to prevail.

The Indonesian Legal Aid Institute (YLBHI) lawyers from Jakarta defending the farmers responded by countersuing the developer in the Cianjur district court for compensation of Rp 112 million for loss of livelihood, including crops and land (Bachriadi and Lucas 2001, 34). They argued that under Indonesian laws the farmers who could prove they had cultivated the land since the early sixties (and who were descendants of cultivators going back to the colonial period)[22] had a prior claim of ownership rights to the land.[23] Furthermore, on the land use rights certificates issued to the village of Cimacan, it was stated that land was to be used for agriculture.[24] In September 1990, after the case had run for a year, the chief judge, Benjamin Mangkoedilaga, said interpretation of the validity of presidential decree (KepPres no. 32/1979) on giving new rights to expired leasehold land,[25] the legality of granting use rights by the governor of West Java, and the validity of using the land for a golf course and resort, was beyond the authority of the judges. According to the judges, the farmers had not been able to prove their rights to the disputed land. NGOs and legal aid people were disappointed in Mangkoedilaga, especially in the light of his record of defending rights to free speech in a celebrated case which successfully challenged the government's banning of *Tempo* magazine. In Cianjur he was considered to have been hand in glove with the Bupati of Cianjur who supported the golf course project and the developer who was reputed to have provided the company's lawyer (R. D. Djuanda) with large sums of money to bribe the court to get the decision they wanted (Bachriadi and Lucas 2001, 68, 113n91).[26]

The second case, also mounted by the YLBHI legal aid team, produced the same verdict against the farmers. This time representing 176 claimants in the Bandung High Court, the court deposition demanded compensation for destruction of their livelihood, specifically for forty-seven varieties of commercially grown vegetables. The judges were not impressed, saying that in their view "a golf course is part of the infrastructure of tourism which can increase local government revenue. Cooperation between the West Java provincial government and PT BAM to build a golf course is part of the tourism program" (Bachriadi and Lucas 2001, 41). They ruled in favor of the developer. The Indonesian Supreme Court rejected an appeal by the farmers in 1995 (Bachriadi and Lucas 2001, 279).

The Impact of Reformasi on the Cimacan Land Dispute

In 1998, in one of the iconic direct actions accompanying the overthrow of Suharto, the farmers of Rarahan hamlet in Cimacan village used their hoes to inscribe into one of the golf course greens "Land for the People" (*Tanah Untuk Rakyat*). In 2000, supported by the new political momentum of *reformasi,* the Community Alliance for Justice (Aliansi Masyarakat Untuk Keadilan, AMUK) was formed by a group of activists whose parents had lost their land twelve years earlier to the golf course developer. Their initial aim was to get the land back from the developer; and they almost succeeded. In July 2001 the village headman HM Dahlan signed a letter revoking the leases[27] after farmers demonstrated at the Cianjur district assembly (DPRD) (*Pikiran Rakyat,* 1 August 2000). The District Head of Cianjur, the Cianjur Land Office, and provincial Land Agency Office (BPN) and the National BPN also issued instructions canceling the leases (*Kompas,* 4 September 2000).[28] As part of the euphoric AMUK campaign, farmers occupied and began cultivating parts of the golf course. Undeterred, PT BAM evicted the farmers with hired thugs (*preman*) and immediately went to the Cianjur district court again, this time to get a ruling on the legality of the original 1987 leasing of village land to the developer, which still had nineteen years to run (interviews in Rarahan hamlet, July 2002).

The court confirmed that the leases were valid. It was then that Rarahan hamlet leaders, on the advice of SKEPHI (the Secretariat for Forest Conservation in Indonesia), decided that any further legal attempts to regain their land would be a waste of time. Nor was there any point in continuing to protest against the original developer, because PT BAM had illegally sold the leased land to another developer, PT Argo Pantas, whose subsidiary company PT Bukit Asri Padang Golf was now running the golf course.[29] Protest leaders decided they had no choice but to negotiate with the new developer. In order to do this they needed more political power, which they hoped to achieve by getting members of the families of the 287 farmers who had lost their livelihoods after the court cases of 1987–89 elected onto the newly created Cimacan Village Representative Council (BPD).

The Village Representative Council (BPD)

Under Suharto's New Order, most of Indonesia's 61,000 villages were part of the "floating mass" that had no effective political representation (political parties were not allowed to campaign at the village level). There was little space for change, innovation, or expression of grassroots political aspirations, and clients of the state tightly controlled political life. Two generations of ordinary Indonesians lost important political skills, without the opportunity to learn how to raise issues, lobby for their interests, or build constituencies (Antlöv 2000). The village headman directly appointed or influenced the election of members of the two village councils (LMD and LKMD), set up under the 1979 village government law (UU 5/1979) as vehicles for government development projects. The headman and the village secretary were ex officio chairman and secretary of both the LMD and LKMD. There was no separation of powers between legislature and executive at the village level (Antlöv 2000). District officials and the military monitored administration at all levels, and public displays of dissatisfaction were treated with suspicion, This all added up to thirty years of more or less unrepresentative village government during the New Order.

A comparison of the new and old village government laws (Regional Autonomy Law 22/1999 with the earlier New Order Village Government Law 5/1979), show how President Abulrachman Wahid and his reformist cabinet meant changes to work (Antlöv 2001). Under the new law, village heads had to share power with BPD: the village government was now responsible to these elected councils through an annual accountability report which the BPD could reject (at least in theory). Sharing authority was difficult for many heads, and its effectiveness tended to depend on whether a village head was elected before or after *reformasi* began. Village heads elected during *reformasi* put forward programs of government to appeal to local voters. In theory the directly elected headman was responsible to the BPD for a maximum of two five-year terms, but this depended on the implemented regulations issued by each district. BPDs had the power to draft village regulations (Perdes, *Peraturan Desa*). Villages could also bypass subdistricts (*kecamatan*), and deal directly with district governments (Antlöv 2000).

Elected BPDs were set up to promote more democratic village governance. The 1999 Regional Autonomy Law expanded public space at the village level with the intention that village society would be less likely to be "co-opted by outside interests" (Saragi 2000, 2002). Other issues have emerged from early research on BPDs reflecting what had happened in many villages, including the majority of those in the Cianjur district (Antlöv 2000; Christina 2001; Suwondo 2001; Supini 2001; Eko 2001). In general these early studies gave a pessimistic impression of how BPDs were operating; the new village representative councils were not functioning according to the intention of the new laws, because the implementing regulation of Ministry of Home Affairs Regulation (Kepmendagri 64/1999) had emasculated the law in order to preserve the power of the village headmen under the direct control of the districts, which in turn were circumscribed by the new Home Affairs Ministry decree no 64.[30]

These early studies also show that money politics was already establishing itself in the BPDs (Budiyono 2000), while a later study of seven BPDs concludes that their formation was undemocratic, and the ensuing politicization of the BPD political elites reduced the effectiveness of their control of village headman (Cahyono et al. 2004).[31] Political parties had too much influence on some BPDs, although more so in village head elections (Pilkades, Pemilihan Kepala Desa).[32] With political parties now able to campaign below subdistrict level, village councils could end up controlled by political parties, leading to increased conflict between members of village elites (Latief 2000; Suwondo 2000, 2001). There was concern BPDs would take over village lands used to pay the headman and other officials (*tanah bengkok*) or would act like courts and put a village head elected during the New Order on trial for past mistakes. As mentioned above, the name Village Representative Councils (BPD; Badan Perwakilan Desa), was changed jokingly (*diplesetkan*) to Badan Pemborosan Desa (Wasteful Village Councils) implying they had no financial management skills (Eko 2001).

The fifteen-member Cimacan BPD fit into a more progressive category of councils, which brought democracy to their village (at least before the council took the land compensation paid by the new developer, and lent this to a company owned by one of its members). The council was elected by popular vote. Those elected were one former village official, three former AMUK leaders (one of whom was a farmer), three youth leaders, a political party (P3) activist, an NGO activist, a mosque official, and five traders (Lucas 2003). It avoided fights with the headman, who first tried to ignore the BPD, but then decided to cooperate with it. The council's fifteen members were elected in a transparent process free of money politics.

During its five-year term (2001–6), apart from negotiating land compensation, the Cimacan BPD organized an election for the village headman, passed village regulations covering local parking levies, reformed village neighborhood associations (RT), and resolved smaller land manipulation cases by village officials, along with other governance concerns.[33] Despite the fact that the Cianjur district government tried to put obstacles in the path of the Cimacan BPD, its legitimacy as an elected body enabled it to resolve these various issues.

The Cimacan BPD was elected on 22 February 2001, but not formally installed by the Cianjur District government until 22 May 2001. Its fifteen members were chosen from thirty-eight candidates by direct election, in a "first past the post" (simple majority) system (the first fifteen candidates with the highest vote were elected). About 8,000 residents over the age of seventeen were eligible to vote, 6,000 registered, and 3,967 (49.5 percent) actually voted, not a bad proportion compared to local elections in most countries. None of the three women candidates was elected. Twelve of the thirteen members had nongovernment backgrounds. All were Muslim. Eight had some secondary education, two had primary school, and one had a degree in public administration. None of the elected members had any connections with the previous Cimacan village administration,[34] although one member had been involved in another Cianjur district village administration, including a year as village headman in the 1980s. All were working part-time in a range of occupations: two were farmers, and the chair (elected by the BPD) ran an ornamental bonsai plant business that was part of the lucrative Cimacan market extending to the outer islands, EU countries, and Japan.

The BPD had to find its own budget through fund-raising by contributions from owners of luxury holiday villas and small hotels. The village head provided a meeting room in the village administration office, which became the BPD headquarters. Of the elected members, four were from families who were involved in the original golf course dispute. Three members subsequently resigned, and were not replaced.[35] Three other members, who were among the founders of AMUK, formally resigned from AMUK before standing for election to the BPD, believing it was no longer possible to get the land back, and that the BPD should put its energies into getting a better compensation deal. Of those members whose political affiliations can be identified, two were PAN members, one was P3, one Golkar, one PKB, and others "non party," or of unknown affiliation, called Golput (*golongan putih*).[36] Out of thirty-eight candidates who stood for election, three were women. One came sixteenth, thereby just missing a seat.[37]

Under the Regional Autonomy Law, the BPD's role included supervision of village head elections. Before the Cimacan land compensation issue could be negotiated, a new village head had to be elected. This was the first matter that the Cimacan BPD had to deal with. The term of office of the retiring village head (Haji Dachlan) had ended in January 2001 but was extended for six months. As a caretaker headman, he had no authority to make decisions. In this vacuum, the BPD established its authority in village affairs by successfully running a democratic election for its village head in September 2001, the first village to be allowed to do so in Cianjur Kabupaten.

The Cimacan BPD's Role in the Land Dispute

The most pressing issue facing the newly elected BPD was the issue of compensation for loss of livelihood because of the expropriation of market garden land for the golf course. By 2001 no fewer than nine subdistrict officers, two district heads, two provincial governors, various district land office heads, heads of the National Land Agency (BPN) at provincial and national levels, district and provincial assemblies (DPRD), and the national parliament had all failed to resolve this dispute. For whatever range of legal or other reasons (such as corruption), they came to support the golf course developers (Bachriadi and Lucas 2001, 32–41).[38] What hope did the newly elected, inexperienced village BPD have of solving this dispute? They were young (average age thirty-seven, with six members under thirty), free of corruption, and had firsthand experience of the dispute and its impact on the livelihoods of their families and Rarahan hamlet community.

The economic situation in Cimacan and the election of a strong BPD were connected to its location at the center of the local tourism industry, as a gateway to the Botanic Gardens and the National Park. Located close to Jakarta, more than 100,000 visitors per year visited these attractions. The Puncak Pass region to the north of Cimacan was a popular destination for the Jakarta middle class on weekends, and for the seminar circuit. The horticultural industry—flower growers selling ornamental plants—by and large had weathered the 1997–98 economic downturn and developed markets outside Java.[39] By 2000 Cimacan had survived the 1997 economic crisis, while poorer villages in West Java had to implement similar decentralization and democratic reforms under less favorable economic conditions (Antlöv 2000).

Protests over the disputed golf course development had politicized Cimacan village since 1987. As a result of this long dispute, public expressions of dissatisfaction and conflict were not new phenomena in Cimacan. As BPD vice chairman and a founder of AMUK Dede Dachroni put it, "We were trained with conflict." Through their struggle for justice, involving many demonstrations and visits to the district assembly in Cianjur, the provincial assembly in Bandung, and to the national parliament, farmers and their leaders had learned new political skills. They learned how to mobilize fellow farmers and lobby politicians, NGOs, and students to support their struggle.[40] Several Cimacan BPD members were children or relatives of the original group of dispossessed landholders. They had grown up in households accustomed to conflict, angry and frustrated at being dispossessed of their livelihoods and the loss of educational opportunities for their children. For these reasons it was inevitable that the newly elected Cimacan BPD wanted to resolve the land issue, with or without the support of the village head.

Compensation Claims

Attempts to obtain additional compensation for farmers had begun early in the *reformasi* period, before the election of the BPD. In 1987 the golf course developer (PT BAM) paid Rp 15 million in compensation and a further Rp 5 million a year later—a total of $US 11,855 (Bachriadi and Wiradi 2001, 16–17). Opinions differ about what happened to the second lot of compensation in 1999 when the developer claimed paying Rp 600 million (US$76,384), to whom is not clear. One version was that it was paid to three farmers' representatives, to distribute to those cultivators who lost their livelihoods eleven years earlier. One of these representatives (Amir) absconded with Rp 100 million and left the village to get married. According to other informants (associated with AMUK), the developer had actually given the money to the head of the Cianjur District Office of Village Government, who had passed on only half to farmers. According to this version only Rp 70–80 million was actually distributed to farmers, while their leaders took at least Rp 70 million (interview, 24 August 2001; Lucas and Warren 2003, 93).

Although the Cimacan village BPD was keen to resolve the issue of compensation, this was complicated by money politics at the district level. Some Cianjur district government officials stood to gain a second time if the district government rather than the new village council negotiated a compensation agreement. According to a BPD member:

> There is a close connection between the [village] head election [*Pilkades*] and resolving the golf course dispute. There is someone in Cianjur regional government who wants to delay compensation settlement between the village and the developer, so he can get money from the developer. This person is the head of the [Cianjur District] Office of Village Government [Kabag Pemdes]. If BPD resolves the conflict, Kabag Pemdes can't ask the developer for money. That's why we want a quick election [for a new village head]. There are about five other land cases still unresolved [in Cimacan village] as well. Some involve village officials who put what is left of village land into their own names. BPD wants to investigate this. (Interview in Cimacan, 30 June 2003)

After it was elected, however, action by the developer in the Cianjur district court led the BPD to conclude that getting the land back from the developer was not politically or legally feasible.[41] In 2002, the developer sued the Cianjur district government in a district court civil action for compensation of Rp 30 billion if revocation of its two thirty-year leases on Cimacan village land was upheld. The court did not grant compensation to the developer, but did uphold the validity of the leases. This effectively put an end to the farmers' struggle to reclaim their land. The Cimacan BPD realized that the district administration would never agree to the village headman signing off on a cancellation of rights deed (*akte pelepasan hak*), because it could not afford to pay compensation. If the farmers continued to demand the return of their land they would have to wait fifteen years until the thirty-year lease had expired. The Village Council said fifteen years was too long to wait for a resolution of the conflict and instead decided to seek a fairer compensation agreement as soon as the village head election was held.

> If people keep demanding that the golf course land be returned under these political conditions, they might end up with nothing.... How long do the people have to keep up their struggle? I feel sorry for them having to wait another sixteen years till the leases end to get their land back. We have to use political power

[*kekuatan politik*], not legal power [*kekuatan hukum*]. Even if the court sits in session one hundred times, it won't solve the problem. (Interview with BPD member in Cimacan, 2 July 2003)

The issue for the BPD was getting the golf course operator to agree to an acceptable level of compensation for the community's loss of cultivation rights to the village land in 1987. It had become clear to BPD leaders (who had followed AMUK's failed attempt to get the village to revoke the lease in 2001) that farmers would not get back cultivation rights, because "the developer can still buy political power," and, as noted earlier, it had bribed the Cianjur district court to get a decision in its favor (interview, 28 August 2001).

In a nasty split AMUK (the NGO formed early in the *reformasi* period to resolve the land dispute) fell out with the Cimacan BPD over this issue. AMUK argued it represented the majority of farmers who wanted their land back. AMUK also wanted the village to keep its communal land. In the face of legal setbacks, the BPD wanted instead to negotiate a new compensation deal with the developer,[42] for both cultivators and the village based on the current market value of the land.

In March 2003 the BPD and the village administration successfully negotiated a compensation payment with PT Bukit Asri Padang Golf, the new leaseholder, of Rp 2.5 billion (or Rp 8,000 per square meter—US$0.95) for 231 "verified" families who had lost their cultivation rights seventeen years previously. But the long-term issue of lost village land and income from the alienation of village land was still unresolved. So the BPD negotiated a land swap (*ruislag*) to compensate for the loss of thirty-one hectares of village land to the original developer PT BAM, plus a Rp 2.5 billion cash payment to the village.

Students and NGOs in the Cimacan Dispute

In Indonesia NGOs and students have had a history of involvement in land disputes, starting back in the Suharto era (Lucas and Warren 2003, 115). In Cimacan, student nature lovers from a number of tertiary institutions, organized by SKEPHI (the NGO network for forest conservation in Indonesia), attended weekly climbing walks in the Gede-Pangrango National Park, where they learned about the land disputes from their local guides. Indro Cahyono, a cofounder of SKEPHI, recalls:

> We were training students from several universities as environmental activists. Then we would send them back to their old high schools as "environmental education facilitators" to give courses to nature lovers. Each week as part of their training the student nature lovers [*pecinta alam*] would climb up Gede Pangrango on Saturday nights. They often stayed in the houses of local villagers and talked about their concern for the environment. They took villagers as guides up the mountain. It was this group of nature lovers that found out about the plans to turn the national park buffer zone into a golf course. We told the people, "If you just hold meetings with the developer, [the struggle] won't get anywhere without any *solid* resistance. You won't be taken seriously." The case was presented at one of our training sessions for facilitators. So there was an environmental issue in the land dispute, the disappearance of the buffer zone for a golf course. And farmers were being evicted. (Interview, 25 March 1999)

SKEPHI began to issue press releases, accompanied farmers to make their case to the national parliament and to government departments, and organized seminars on the negative environmental impacts of golf courses. They alerted international NGOs about the case via *Setiakawan,* SKEPHI's English-language environmental human rights magazine[43] (Bachriadi and Lucas 2001, 176n58).

However, SKEPHI's involvement in the Cimacan dispute did not last. When the developer sued twenty-eight farmers in the district court for illegally cultivating its leased land, and the Jakarta Legal Aid Institute became involved, SKEPHI withdrew. According to the SKEPHI leader, Indro Cahyono, the SKEPHI "people's action" model, based on "how to give farmers courage to demand their land back" meant holding participatory training sessions, routine meetings, and fund-raising by the farmers themselves. Furthermore, Indro stated:

I was against the Legal Aid Institute involvement in the dispute. We needed a nonlitigation approach without LBH involvement. The legal struggle prevented people from demanding their "real" land rights via political struggle. It prevented them getting access to national and international NGOs, and access to important groups like journalists (so Cianjur would not be able to act in a too authoritarian way in future). The LBH approach had the effect that all the villagers were led to believe that resorting to the courts was an alternative to nonlitigation. Why didn't LBH explain the nonlitigation alternative? LBH wanted to show that Cimacan was part of their success story. But in doing so the crucial environmental and agrarian aspects of the dispute were lost under the banner, "This is a legal case." So this became a problem because it split the political movement in Cimacan. SKEPHI wanted advocacy not litigation. LBH came to Cimacan and said, "You can win this case legally." [But] we knew that behind the law there is power [in Indonesia]. (Interview, 23 February 1999)

However, from the farmers' viewpoint there was a downside to NGO and student involvement that was not village-based. Amir,[44] whose family were dispossessed farmers, was an original leader of the farmers' protest movement there, and had studied law at Pakuan University in Bogor. He expressed farmers' general frustration with these outside advocacy groups,

> Our struggle got support from many quarters. The first group to be involved came from the Student Nature Lovers group [SKEPHI]. Besides them there were activists from UNTAG [Universitas 17 Augustus 1945], UKI [Universitas Kristen Indonesia] (Jakarta) UNPAK (Pakuan University Bogor) and many others. It was a pity that the involvement of these groups was on and off [*terputus-putus*]. It was limited to organizing demonstrations to the national parliament, the Minister for Home Affairs, or to other government departments. They didn't check what happened after the demonstrations in a routine way. It was the same with the NGOs such as WALHI, SKEPHI, and YLBHI, which were active in the

beginning, but never contacted the community again for two years. (Amir 1995, 158)

Although SKEPHI's skepticism about litigation proved correct, and its analysis that farmers could never win in court because the "power" behind the courts was supported by the developer who "played with the law" (*main hukum*), the farmers' skepticism about NGOs' inability to sustain long periods of advocacy of the kind that, ironically, SKEPHI considered important, turned out to be well-founded, and continued into the *reformasi* period.

One reason why the BPD did not want to continue the struggle for land rights (as opposed to seeking compensation for loss of income and livelihood) was that they felt the community was reluctant to accept outside NGO involvement any longer. "We are sick of being exploited by NGOs from Jakarta," said Dede Dahroni, the BPD deputy chairperson. The same mistrust meant Jakarta-based NGOs such as SKEPHI faced an uphill battle in Cimacan. It was the same for WALHI (Indonesian Environmental Forum), which also publicized the dispute in a similar way to SKEPHI. Farmers were disappointed, feeling that outside NGO involvement was driven by other political motives, such as getting press coverage and funding for themselves.

Compensation for Farmers

Cimacan farmers put pressure on the BPD throughout 2002 to find a solution to the compensation issue. As mentioned earlier, the original developer had sold the leases and the ownership of the golf course to PT Bukit Asri Padang Golf, a bigger developer that was prepared to negotiate a compensation settlement. The BPD involved the farmers in the negotiations and, as already noted, the company agreed to a compensation rate of Rp 8,000 per square meter (US$0.95), without needing any pressure from the village government or the BPD. The BPD decided who qualified for compensation and reviewed each individual claim. Some farmers were claiming more land than they had originally cultivated, and new claimants, relatives of community leaders (*tokoh masyarakat*), had appeared on the register for compensation. To avoid further accusations of corruption and nepotism, the BPD asked the developer to pay the compensation directly into bank accounts of the original cultivators. At a ceremony, held ironically in the golf clubhouse, each landholder, after signing a release of cultivation rights (*pelepasan hak garap*) and a commitment to give up claims to land at the end of the original lease period, was given a Bank Mandiri pass book, with the compensation already deposited in it. The BPD encouraged the farmers to accept the offer "so we could be a harmonious community again (*kita bisa rukun kembali*)" (interview, Dede Dachroni, 10 August 2004). Eight original cultivators refused the compensation payment on the grounds it was too small.[45]

Compensation for the Village

The compensation for cultivators was only half the monetary compensation paid by the developer. It also agreed to pay a further Rp 2.5 billion to the village for loss of income from the rent that farmers would have paid to the village for cultivation rights. Rp 1.5 billion of this money was invested at 11 percent interest, in order to pay the wages of the village head and officials, and a stipend for the BPD itself.[46] An additional Rp 24 million was supposedly spent on grants of Rp 3 million to each of Cimacan's eight primary schools for financially disadvantaged students (*murid tidak mampu*), although the amounts are disputed. The remaining Rp 750 million were spent on village infrastructure, buying land for cemeteries in each of Ciamcan's five hamlets (Rp 50 million for each cemetery); construction of a new soccer field and access road; repairs to irrigation channels (Rp 17 million) and grants of Rp 1 million to each of Cimacan's twenty-eight mosques used for Friday prayers (interview with Cimacan BPD chair, 13 August 2004).

The BPD also negotiated compensation in kind for the loss of thirty-one hectares of village land in the form of a land swap (*ruilslag*) in a neighboring village. However, by mid-2003, community opinion was divided on this issue. A group of "idealists" not directly involved in the dispute wanted land values to be considered in deciding the land swap (i.e., that the land being offered as a swap should have a higher or at least equivalent value than the current golf course land).[47] A second group, the "realists" on the BPD, said that keeping village communal land (*tanah kas desa*) was more important than its market value. But even the realists said that the land swap was important because it was part of the moral solution to the land issue, which was not just an economic problem.

Other Missing Village Land

Other land was illegally taken by village elites and by the Cianjur district during the New Order. By 2003 the BPD had obtained back 2,400 square meters of village land that had been secretly put into the names of three former village officials (the former subdistrict head of Pacet, a former village headman, and a former head of Rarahan hamlet, where the golf course is located). The BPD has succeeded in getting this stolen land (which had no formal titles) returned to the village.[48] Other cases of land compulsorily acquired from the village without compensation during the New Order period, which were on the BPD's list of unresolved issues to be looked into once the golf course dispute was resolved, concerned a camping ground for the Indonesian scouts, and land expropriated without compensation by the Minister of Youth Affairs for a youth hostel.

The Future of the Golf Course

Since 2006 the number of tourists visiting the Cimacan golf course in particular, and the Puncak-Cibodas region in general, has declined. There are now longer, more professionally challenging golf courses closer to Jakarta.[49] The Cipularang toll road linking Jakarta to Bandung opened in 2005, and tourists now prefer to go to Bandung for the weekend instead of Puncak. The tollway is relatively free of the five- to ten-hour traffic jams experienced getting to and from the Puncak-Cibodas resorts. Investors buy weekend villas in Bandung rather than Cipanas. Hotel occupancy rates in the Puncak Pass and Cipanas region have declined from 90 percent to 20 percent (interviews in Cianjur, 16–18 August 2007).

This decline in tourism in the region has affected the Cimacan golf course. Although it is still the only course in Puncak, Jakarta weekend golfers now prefer to play on swankier courses nearer Jakarta, in Bogor (where there are now three golf courses), or Bandung. This has much reduced the demand for the Cimacan golf course and affected the livelihoods of its casual employees, most of whom have worked there for the last fifteen years at below standard minimum wages. In mid-2008 forty employees were laid off, leaving only forty-two employed by the development.[50]

"Half-Hearted Autonomy" (Otonomi Setengah Hati)

There was a widely held view in the Department of Home Affairs that the 1999 Regional Autonomy Act gave too much autonomy to district-level government. As we saw earlier, the first indication of this was the effort to "water down" local government authority in subsequent implementing regulations from the Ministry of Home Affairs. Five years later, in an effort to increase executive authority, a revised Local Government Act (No 32/2004) made the village-level elected BPD into a consultative rather than a representative council (Badan Permusyawaratan Desa), now appointed by "deliberation and consultation" (*musyawarah dan mufakat*). (UU32/2004, §209–10). In subsequent enabling legislation the emasculation of the BPD went further. While the BPD is defined as the body responsible for implementing village government, the restructured BPD would consist of the hamlet heads, "*adat* leaders, professional groups, religious leaders and other prominent persons" (PP 72/2005, §29 and 30). In Cimacan the first elected BPD's five-year term of office ended at the end of 2006. The succeeding council was not elected, but chosen by "mutual deliberation" as set out by the Cianjur District Regulation of Village Government. This meant

Cimacan's five hamlet heads each appointed four candidates, who then met and chose the eleven members of the new BPD. "The mechanism for choosing BPD members is not effective," said a former member; "the BPD is only a rubber-stamp forum (*ketok palu*) now" (interview, 17 July 2008), because members are appointed by hamlet heads who are themselves appointed by the village headman.[51] The headman now has the same powers that the headman had during the New Order. In short, the restructured BPDs are a return to the old village oligarchy structure and can no longer hold the headman to account.

With the loss of accountability in 2007, the newly appointed Cimacan BPD has since become embroiled in a potential financial disaster by lending the golf course compensation money paid by PT Asri Mulia Padang Golf to a BPD member whose company went broke.[52]

Elections for Village Headman

Since Suharto's downfall, Cimacan has held two elections for village head. Representatives of dispossessed farmers who stood for election have been unsuccessful both times. In 2001 a former "client of the State," a former member of the LKMD, won the election by 200 votes. He retired after one term, and in 2007 there were two candidates from Rarahan hamlet representing dispossessed villagers (Dede Dachroni and Ujar), which split the vote, so both were defeated by another client of the state and Muslim notable Haji Sofandi (a hamlet head for nineteen years). H. Sofandi won by 600 votes from Ujar (interview, 18 July 2008),[53] with Dede Dachroni (a younger-generation farmer) in third place.[54]

***

The elected Cimacan BPD was a more successful experiment in democratization compared with other villages in Cianjur and elsewhere Indonesia. The council was democratically elected in 2001, with a mandate to resolve the fourteen-year-long land dispute, and its effectiveness was further enhanced by the implementation of elections for the village headman (pilkades). Without the advocacy of the local NGO AMUK and the BPD, farmers would not have obtained compensation from the developer for loss of cultivation rights. However, the BPD was unable to find a way of breaking up Cimacan village into two new villages (*pemekaran*) that had the support of all the village. While direct elections were held for one hamlet head, the hundreds of kiosks and street vendors around the entrance to the botanical gardens, the national park, and the golf course have not been regulated. Attempts to gain compensation from former officials who stole village land were also unsuccessful, while attempts to raise money by imposing village levies (*retribusi*) were resented. Dede Dachroni, ex–BPD chairman, also failed to win the pilkades election, because of strong financial influence from PKS (Partai Keadilan Sosial) to ensure that former hamlet head H. Sofandi (a client of the state) easily won.

This failure by farmers' candidates to win village elections also reflects the limited numbers and power of farmer-based political organizations, not just in Cimacan village but throughout Cianjur district. This is apparently a general trend in districts with land disputes. Candidates representing farmers involved in land disputes have generally been unsuccessful in pilkades (village head elections) during the era of *reformasi*. There are several reasons for this. First, they did not have the financial backing needed to run a campaign.[55] Second, farmers and their supporters "were not used to fighting village elections" (interview in Cianjur, 16 June 2008). They had no political base with which to consolidate their election campaigns. The SPJB, formed in the mid-1990s, never had a branch in Cimacan. Although land disputes made local heroes, agrarian reform is not an issue that seems to get votes. As one district activist said, "Talking about land certificates doesn't get votes. What is the point of a candidate in a village election talking about agrarian reform if no one at the district or provincial levels ever talks about [i.e., is prepared to deal with] it?" Third, candidates are elected usually either because of their prominence in religious affairs or in village administration, because they are close family members with a previous village headman (*keturunan*), or because they have social standing in a strongly Islamic community, i.e., have been on the pilgrimage to Mecca.

Two development projects have emerged, involving former BPN members. The first is geothermal electricity (piping steam or hot water from within the national park to drive a power station outside the park), but it is not clear if permission will be forthcoming from the parks authority. The second project, promoted by the Deputy Bupati of Cianjur, and involving building a three-star hotel on the location of the parking lot and kiosks below the national park, did not get off the ground, partly because of the fear that protests would again erupt in Rarahan hamlet from the food-stall vendors and their supporters who faced eviction.

The Raptor Conservation Society thinks the golf course and villas are in danger of becoming obsolete. Reportedly, only a couple of players use the course daily during the week. There are better and bigger courses around Bogor, while in the Cibodas precinct the entrance to the golf course and the entrance to the national park are crowded and chaotic (*semrawut*) with street vendors and ticket sellers.[56] The land has only one alternative use now, and that is for luxury villas. But such a development would need approval from neighboring landholders, who in this instance are the national park and the forestry department. In theory approval may be difficult to obtain, as the golf course is built on land that is supposed to be a buffer zone for the national park. Whether or not money politics will prevail over zoning regulations remains to be seen.

Notes

1. For this often-quoted Javanese aphorism see Bachriadi and Lucas (2001, xiii) and *Setiakawan* (1991, 3).

2. The Sarekat Petani Jawa Barat was superseded by the Pasunden Peasants' Union—SPP, Sarekat Petani Pasunden.

3. Fidro and Fauzi (1995) identified twenty-eight long-running land disputes still unresolved by the mid-1990s.

4. *Setiakawan* no. 6 (July 1991) is a special issue on land cases in Indonesia.

5. The production was obtained from only 8 percent of the total area under vegetable cultivation in the province of West Java, reflecting the richness of Cianjur district soils and the high productivity of its vegetable growing industry (Hardjono 1990, 3–4).

6. With the exception of the Land and Buildings Tax (PBB—*Pajak Bumi dan Bangunan*) levied by the district government.

7. IPEDA—*Iuran Pembangunan Daerah,* regional development levies. For the system of land taxation under the New Order, see MacAndrews (1986, 62–68).

8. Villagers paid no other fees to cultivate this land apart from the IPEDA tax. Any income from *tanah kas desa* rents was in addition to and not in lieu of tax payments.

9. The village head accused farmers of failing to pay rent for the use of the land.

10. LKMD—village community security councils were set up by the New Order to implement government policy under the guise of consultation.

11. According to Amir, then leader of the protest movement, "No one has ever heard of the Rp 90 million (US$52,900) PT BAM paid to Cimacan village" (interview in Cimacan, 6 February 1999).

12. Annual Indonesian GDP per capita in 1989 was Rp 1,101,440 (or US$622). See http://www.economywatch.com/economic-statistics/country/Indonesia/year-1989/. Accessed 2 February 2012.

13. A "Ballad of the Evicted" recounts how day after day the developer bulldozed the terraced gardens and brought in soil to level the terrain, which later washed away, silting up the river and the lily pond in the botanical gardens (Bachriadi and Lucas 2001, 290–91). Thirty percent of the water flows of the Cikundul river (on the eastern side of the golf course) are taken by the golf club to water the fairways and greens; a small stream from the national park was moved; the highly endangered Javanese eagle (*elang Jawa*) nests less frequently nowadays (interview with RCS [Raptor Conservation Society] leader in Cimacan, 17 July 2008).

14. One *patok* is roughly 400 square meters. A *patok* literally means a boundary marker. Farmers estimated that the annual value of production from one *patok* in 1989 was roughly Rp 900,000.

15. Vegetable farmers are usually off to their fields after the 5 AM morning prayers.

16. Cibodas here refers to the botanical gardens, access to which is via Cimacan village.

17. That is, rebuild the stone terraces of his blocks again.

18. Cimacan farmers describe their plight in the poem "The Court of Conscience " (*Pengadilan Hati Nurani*) read out by protesters at the Indonesian Parliament on 15 December 1989 (Bachriadi and Lucas 2001, 300–303).

19. The market value of similar farmland in Rarahan hamlet was Rp 15–20,000 per square meter in the late 1980s. Farmers wanted Rp 5,000

per square meter as compensation for loss of livelihood. Today farmers say the land is worth Rp 60,000–300,000 per square meter, depending how close to the main road the land is (interview with BN, from one of the families who rejected compensation, Rarahan, 16 July 2008).

20. The village stated that they were supposed to receive Rp 2 million per annum from 209 farmers as rent payments, but actual rent received was half that amount. PT BAM paid a total of Rp 20 million in consolation money to farmers and a one-off payment of Rp 90 million to the village (referred to above) for leasing the land for thirty years.

21. In a letter to the governor of West Java in June 1988, Rudini said that before renting its land out to a third party: (1) the village had to pay the Cimacan farmers adequate compensation (*santunan*); (2) the village had to keep the land as a "village asset"; and (3) the rental agreement had to be reviewed every five years (Surat Mendagri No X.732.536/373/B. IV). These stipulations were never carried out. In July 1989 the developer erected a notice on the disputed land that said, "Farmers who have not taken their consolation money, and harvested their crops are obstructing development and opposing the government" (*Suara Pembaruan,* 20 July 1989). Three days later Rudini said, "What's going on here? Making an announcement which threatens poor people is not right. I've ordered the notice to be removed.... We have to use more humanitarian methods [we should treat farmers] the way we treat our own children" (*Media Indonesia* 25/July/ 1989). *Kompas* reported that Rudini had ordered the development of the golf course to stop (25 July 1989) (see Bachriadi and Lucas 2001, 262, 276), but four days later, after meeting with the governor of West Java (Yogie SM), the Bupati of Cianjur, and the village head of Cimacan, in Puncak, Rudini changed his mind. This was after the headman gave him false information about the amount of compensation paid to farmers by PT BAM, understating the number of families affected, and claiming that the golf course would employ four hundred locals (Bachriadi and Lucas 2001, 177n62). The Cimacan headman also often changed his evidence in court hearings, or said he "couldn't remember" inconvenient facts, behavior that drew the response, "Don't be inconsistent [*mencla-mencle*] when giving evidence" from the head of the judges' panel Benjamin Mangkoedilaga (Bachriadi and Lucas 2001, 37).

22. Oral histories record that a Chinese plantation owner, Babah Tjoan, kept livestock on the land and allowed farmers to plant vegetables; and that by 1937 a European planter, Georges Jean Marie Wahry, allowed farmers to plant vegetables between coffee plants (interviews in Rarahan hamlet, January–March 1999; Bachriadi and Lucas 2001, 256). Colonial records show that by 1940 the seventy-three-hectare Rarahan tea

plantation "fourteen kilometers northwest of Tjiandjoer" was leased by Tan Liok Tiauw (van Diessen et al. 2004, 251, quoting from the 1940 edition of *Handboek voor Cultuur- en Handelsondernemingen in Nederlansche Indie,* which lists the names of 2,400 plantations in the Dutch East Indies in that year).

23. Under KepPres 32/1979, §4 and PerMendagri No. 3/1979 (see Harsono 1996, 208–16; Bachriadi and Lucas 2001, notes 41 and 42, 136).

24. Cimacan village could not lease the land to the developer without first formally obtaining use rights (*hak pakai*) titles. The farmers were not allowed the mandatory time to lodge objections in this process. The leases nonetheless stated that if the land was not used for the stated purpose (agriculture), it had to be "returned to the government." A cynical response to this apparent contradiction in government policy would be that the developer had not been able to bribe the provincial agrarian affairs (later BPN) office to remove these conditions from the leases (SK Gubernor Kepala Daerah Tingkat I/ Kepala Direktorat Agraria No. 593.321/ SK.809 Ditag/1988, cited in Bachriadi and Lucas 2001, 261).

25. Article 28 of this decree said that farmers who had occupied former plantation land (which had been converted to Indonesian title after the 1960 Basic Agrarian Law was passed) could be given new rights to settle and work that land if land use and environmental conditions were met (Harsono 1996, 207–9).

26. For critical legal opinions on the Cianjur district court decision, see Bachriadi and Lucas (2001, 39–41) and Parlindungan (1994).

27. Cimacan Village Government Declaration no. 593/06/pm on 28 July 2000 canceled all agreements with BT PAM and both use rights certificates, asking BPN to do the same and to issue ownership certificates to the 287 original cultivators.

28. On the basis of the village declaration, Bupati Cianjur Decision No. 180/295-Huk 3 August 2000 revoked the leases and returned the land to the cultivators; the Cianjur district land office then requested revocation of the leases to the provincial BPN (SK BPN Cianjur Np100-1031-KP-2000, 31 July 2000) which recommended revocation of the leases (SK BPN Jawa Barat 540-1832/2000, 1 August 2000) to the national BPN whose deputy director (Luthfi Nasution) revoked Cimacan village use rights leases no. 8 and no. 9 (SK BPN No. 14-VIII-2000, 14 August 2000). However, the euphoric feeling that this was a tremendous development (*kemajuan yang luar biasa*) soon faded because the headman never signed the deed of revocation of rights (*akte pelepasan hak*). Undoubtedly, this was because of pressure from the district government, which did not want to pay compensation to the developer.

29. PT Argo Pantas, which also owns the nearby Koliba luxury real estate, has bought up all the vacant land in two villages, more than 150 hectares. The Argo Pantas land borders on the smaller of the two blocks "so they will build a resort near the golf course maybe." Fifty percent of the land in Cimacan is now owned by outsiders, and the remaining 50 percent by villagers, of which 60 percent is used for housing and 45 percent is farmland used for growing vegetables. "In the end money is more valuable than land." PT Argo Pantas is a company belonging to the Salim conglomerate owned by Sadono Salim, which was in the process of obtaining full ownership certificates in mid-2008 (interview with golf club employee in Cimacan on 17 July 2008).

30. Home Affairs Decree 64/2000 says village decrees should be drafted jointly with the headman and that the BPD is partner to the village government; the village budget is determined by the village headman (not jointly with the BPD); and each district has to make no fewer than twelve implementing decrees for village BPDs (Antlöv 2000, 2001).

31. A revised decentralization law (Law 32/ 2004) and government regulation (PP 72/2006) formally reduced the village democratization aim of the original Act 22/1999. This was reflected in BPD's new name, now the Badan Musyawarah Desa (Village Consultation Council), whose members were no longer elected but nominated by each hamlet head and approved by the village headman; and the headman's annual accountability report was no longer made to the BPD, but to the district head or mayor (Tjandra 2006).

32. According to one of the candidates who lost the 2007 Cimacan Pilkades, H. Sofandi won because of financial support from PKS (Partai Kesejahteran Sosial, the Islamic Social Welfare Party).

33. As well as regulations on sharing local taxes and levies (already mentioned), other duties included issuing identification cards by the village (not the district) and managing trader kiosks outside the entrance to the Cibodas Botanical Gardens and Gunung Gede Pangrango National Park (Lucas and Warren 2003).

34. At this time, this administration consisted of the village head, secretary, and eight village officials, five hamlet heads (*kepala dusun*), ten subhamlet (RW) heads, and fifty-seven neighborhood ward (RT) heads, who each received an "incentive payment" and were considered part of the village administrative structure. It also included two security officers left over from the New Order period. Outside the administration are the BPD and LPM (Community Development Board), a revised version of the old LKMD, and the PKK (Family Welfare Improvement Organization, a women's group).

35. One resigned because Cimacan BPD members were not paid; the second because he felt pressured by AMUK; and the third because he moved to another village.

36. Because the village head election (Pilkades) was held in September 2001, eight months after the BPD election, there were no unsuccessful *Kades* candidates standing in the Cimacan BPD elections.

37. In the subsequent village head elections, one of the five candidates was a woman. She received 66 votes, the winning candidate 2,732. In the 2006 Pilkades, there were no female candidates.

38. Momo Kosworo, a BPD member and one of the leaders of the struggle for farmers' compensation that set up AMUK, in a written statement to a Public Dialogue on "The Law, Human Rights and Justice" in Cimacan on 22 July 2000, recalls being told by an expelled director of PT BAM that the developer " bribed all the government agencies involved [with the dispute], and during the Cianjur court proceedings PT BAM gave money to both court [officials] and to the judges. On several occasions even the chairman of the panel of judges, Benjamin Mangkoedilaga asked for money for private expenses (a vehicle, soccer tickets, and *Hari Lebaran*)" (Kosworo 2000).

39. Lukmanul Hakim, chair of the BPD, said at the beginning of an interview that he had just struck a deal to send a truckload of ornamental plants worth Rp 35 million to Palembang in South Sumatra. His position on the new BPD was not unrelated to his prominence in the ornamental plants business.

40. For more details about how NGO-student alliances formed over land disputes during this period, see Lucas and Warren (2003).

41. As noted earlier, AMUK had almost succeeded in 2001, but the Cimacan headman in the end refused to sign the *Akte Pelepasan Hak* document revoking the leases, probably because of pressure from Cianjur district, as the developer had gone back to the Cianjur district court to reaffirm the validity of the leases and to claim compensation if they were canceled.

42. An additional issue for the community was compensation for crops planted during reclaiming actions at the start of the *reformasi* era, which had been destroyed during 2000 by the developer's *preman* gangs.

43. "Fourteen pictorial facts on the Cibodas golf course controversy" and "Cibodas farmers arrested for protest," in *Setiakawan*, no. 2, September–October 1989, 19–23; "Cibodas farmers on the move," *Setiakawan*, November–December 1989, 5–6.

44. As already noted, Amir later disappeared from Cimacan with part of the original compensation.

45. As of July 2008 these farmers still refused the compensation.

46. Monthly wages for officials include the village headman, who is paid Rp 750,000; village officials, Rp 250,000; RW/RT, Rp 30,000; BPD chair, Rp 500,000; BPD members, Rp 350,000. Village security personnel Linmas (formally Hansip), the village military presence (Babinsa and Babinmas), are also paid between Rp 80,000 and Rp 100,000 out of the interest on the golf course money.

47. The *ruislag* land, located in Sukoresmi village, is rain fed, not irrigated, and less fertile. The *ruislag* land being offered by the developer to the village was valued at Rp 10,000 per square meter, much less than the market value of the Cimacan golf course land of Rp 300,000.

48. Because the land stolen did not earn income, it was swapped for 1.5 hectares of irrigated rice land (with a gross return from three harvests per year of Rp 7.5–10 million) to augment the village budget.

49. A plaque in the nine-hole Cibodas golf course clubhouse says that the golf course designer was "Michael Coate and Assoc. Pty Ltd." An employee said this was an Australian company.

50. In 2008, thirty caddies were on call, but only a handful were finding work, basically for tips. There were twenty-one golf course and garden workers, nine security officers, and ten others working in the clubhouse and restaurant. Considering the promises of employment made by the first developer, very few local villagers have benefited from this so-called tourist resort. The daily casual wage when the golf course opened in 1989 was Rp 2,500 per day (US$1.41); in 2008 it was Rp 24,650 per day (US$2.55), or Rp 493,000 per month, well below the current Cianjur regional minimum wage of Rp 616,000 per month.

51. In contrast to Bali, in Java hamlet heads are appointed by the headman, not elected. Discussions about introducing elections for hamlet heads early in the BPD's five-year term of office came to nothing. One RT (*Rukun Tetangga,* neighborhood association) did hold elections for RT head, with a turn out of 76 percent of residents eligible to vote ("Berita acara pemilihan Ketua RT.06/02 Kampung Babakan Cikalong, Desa Cimacan Tahun 2001").

52. The bankrupt company shares were then bought by another local businessman who agreed to repay the Rp 500 million debt on the condition that he be given a second Rp 1 billion loan by the BPD to finish a market development. He now owes the village Rp 1.5 billion, and of July 2008 reputedly paid the village Rp 20 million per month interest (1.3 percent).

53. In the 2002 village elections, Ujar had also lost, but by a narrower margin of 400 votes. In at times an emotional interview, Ujar lamented the breakdown in communication between himself and Dede Dachroni over

who should run as the farmers' candidate, saying he did not understand why Dede, as the younger man, did not inform him that he was going to stand in the village election (interview, 18 July 2008).

54. Dede Dachroni was deputy chair of the elected BPD 2001–6. Haji Sofandi got 2,400 votes, Ujar 2,000, and Dede 1,000 votes. In Cimacan there were 12,000 registered voters and 60 percent turned out to vote in 2007 (interview with Dede Dachroni in Cimacan, 17 July 2008).

55. In the 2007 Cimacan elections, Dede's parents funded his Rp 50 million election campaign. The other farmers' candidate (Ujar) is said to have spent roughly the same. It was estimated by his opponents that Haji Sofandi spent more than Rp 100 million, "maybe Rp 150 million" (interview with Dede Dachroni, 17 July 2008).

56. Numbers of visitors to the national park have also been declining. Visitors have to pay twice to get in, with illegal ticket sellers and parking tickets (*pungutan liar*).

References

Amir. 1995a. "Rakyat Cimacan: hidup mati kami dari tanah ini, biarkan kami tetap bertani." In *Pembangunan Berbuah Sengketa: 29 Tulisan Pengalaman Advokasi Tanah*, ed. Boy Fidro and Noer Fauzi, 153–65. Kisaran: Yayasan Sintesa et al.

———. 1995b. "Kasus tanah Cimacan." In *Pluralisme Hukum Pertanahan dan Kumpulan Kasus Tanah*, ed. B. Harkam et al., 225–32. Jakarta: Yayasan Lembaga Bantuan Hukum Indonesia.

Antlöv, H. 2000. "Village Governance in Indonesia: Past Present and Future Challenges." Paper to the First International Seminar "Dinamika Politik Lokal di Indonesia: Perubahaan, Tantangan dan Harapan." Yayasan Percik and the Ford Foundation. Yogyakarta, 3–7 July.

———. 2001. "Village Governance and Local Politics in Indonesia." Paper to the Second International Seminar "Dinamika Politik Lokal di Indonesia Politik Pemberdayaan." Yayasan Percik and the Ford Foundation, Pekanbaru, 13–16 August.

AusAID. 2001. "Decentralisation in Indonesia: Options for Australian Aid." Appendix D. Translation of Law 25 of 1999.

Bachriadi, D., and A. Lucas. 2001. *Merampas Tanah Rakyat: Kasus Tapos dan Cimacan*. Jakarta: Kepustakaan Populer Gramedia.

"Berita Acara Pemilihan Ketua RT.06/02 Kampung Babakan, Cikalong, Desa Cimacan Tahun 2001."

Budiyono. 2000. "Reformasi di Pedesaan: Legitimasi Kekuasaan Elit Lokal di dalam Perubahan Sosial." Paper to the First International Seminar "Dinamika Politik Lokal di Indonesia: Perubahaan, Tantangan dan Harapan." Yayasan Percik and the Ford Foundation. Yogyakarta, 3–7 July.

Cahyono, H., et al. 2004. *Konflik Elite Politik di Pedesaan: Relasi antara Badan Perwakilan Desa dan Pemerintah Desa.* Jakarta: LIPI.

[Cianjur District Government] Bagian Pemerintahan Desa. 2000. "Himpunan Peraturan Daerah Kabupaten Tentang Pemerintahan Desa/Kelurahan." Cianjur.

Christina, M. 2001. "Kepentingan Masyarakat vs. Eksekutif, vs Legislatif." Paper to the Second International Seminar "Dinamika Politik Lokal di Indonesia Politik Pemberdayaan." Yayasan Percik and the Ford Foundation. Pekanbaru, 13–16 August.

DeTik. 1993. "Dja'i, 70-an tahun, petani Cimacan." 26 May.

Eko, S. 2001. "Badan Perwakilan Desa: Arena Baru Kekuasaan Baru." Paper to the Second International Seminar "Dinamika Politik Lokal di Indonesia Politik Pemberdayaan." Yayasan Percik and the Ford Foundation. Pekanbaru, 13–16 August.

Fidro, B., and N. Fauzi, eds. 1995. *Pembangunan Berbuah Sengketa: 29 Tulisan Pengalaman Advokasi Tanah.* Kisaran: Yayasan Sintesa.

Hardjono, J. 1990. *The Dilemma of Commercial Vegetable Production in West Java.* Bandung: Proyek Penelitian Sektor Non Pertanian Pedesaan Jawa Barat, Project Working Paper Series No B-2, Pusat Studi Pembangunan IPB dan Pusat Penelitian Lingkungan Hidup ITB.

Harsono, B. 1996. *Hukum Agrarian Indonesia: Peraturan-Peraturan Hukum Tanah.* Rev. ed. Jakarta: Penerbit Djambatan.

Kana, N., D. Pradjarta, and K. Suwondo. 2001. *Dinamika Politik Lokal di Indonesia: Perubahan, Tantangan dan Harapan Rekaman Proses Seminar.* Salatiga: Percik Press and the Ford Foundation.

Kosworo, M. 2000. "Pengantar sejarah kepemilikan tanah dan perjuangan warga Rarahan dalam mempertahankan haknya." Paper to the "Dialog Terbuka 'Hukum HAM dan Keadilan': Sebuah Tinjauan Kasus dari Perampasan Tanah di Cimacan." Ciamcan, 22 July.

Laporan Kasus/Case Reports Kedung Ombo, Kasus Arso, Cimacan. 1991. Vol. 2. YLBHI and JARIM.

Latief, M. S. 2000. "BPD, DPRK and DPRKGK: Legitimasi Kekuatan Elite Lokal dan Perobahan Sosial." Paper to the First International Seminar "Dinamika Politik Lokal di Indonesia: Perobahan Harapan dan Tantangan." Yayasan Percik dan Ford Foundation. Yogyakarta, 3–7 July.

Lucas, A. 2003. "Regional Autonomy and Village Governance Issues in West Java: Cimacan Village Council (BPD) in Cianjur Kabupaten in the Era of *Reformasi*." Paper to Seminar Internasional Ke Empat Yayasan Percik and Ford Foundation "Dinamika Politik Lokal: Partisipasi dan Demokratisasi." Salatiga 14–18 July.

Lucas, A., and C. Warren. 2003. "The State, the People and Their Mediators: The Struggle Over Agrarian Reform in Post-New Order Indonesia." *Indonesia* 76: 87–126.

MacAndrews, C. 1986. *Land Policy in Indonesia: A Study of Land Issues in the New Order Period*. Boston: Lincoln Institute of Land Policy.

Materi Rapat Rukun Tetangga 06 Kampung Babakan Cikalong RT 06/02, Desa Cimacan Kecamatan Pacet, Kabupaten Cianjur 43253, 2000. Minutes of meeting.

Parlindungan, A. P. 1994. "Kasus Lapangan Golf Cimacan." In *Bunga Rampai Hukum Agrarian Serta Landreform Bagian III*, 360–65. Bandung: Penerbit Mandar Maju.

Rencana Pelaksanaan Program Ke-RT-an 06/02, 2001. Program implementation plan.

Saragi, T. 2000. "Mencari Bentuk Otonomi Masyarakat Desa." Paper to the First International Seminar "Dinamika Politik Lokal di Indonesia: Perubahaan, Tantangan dan Harapan." Percik and the Ford Foundation. Yogyakarta, 3–7 July.

———. 2002. "Pemberdayaan Civil Society di Desa: Studi Kasus Kebijakan Desentralisasi di Kabupaten Bogor." Paper to the Third International Seminar "Dinamika Politik Lokal di Indonesia: Pluralitas Dalam Perspektif Lokal." Percik and the Ford Foundation. Salatiga, 9–12 July.

Setiakawan. 1991. "Land Is the Life of the People." No. 6 July.

Supini. 2001. "Faktor-faktor Penujang dan Penghambat Budaya Masyarakat terhadap Pengembangan Demokrasi Masyarakat Desa." Paper to the Second International Seminar "Dinamika Politik Lokal di Indonesia: Politik Pemberdayaan." Percik and the Ford Foundation. Pekanbaru, 13–16 August.

Suwondo, K. 2000. "Changing Patterns of Village Government and Local Leadership: The Case of Grundhul village." Paper to the First International Seminar "Dinamika Politik Lokal di Indonesia: Perubahaan, Tantangan dan Harapan." Yayasan Percik and the Ford Foundation. Yogyakarta, 3–7 July.

———. 2001. "Perkembangan Peran BPD: Studi Kasus di Beberapa Desa Klaten." Paper to the Second International Seminar "Dinamika Politik Lokal di Indonesia: Politik Pemberdayaan." Yayasan Percik and the Ford Foundation. Pekanbaru, 13–16 August.

Tjandra, W. R. 2006. "Desa, Entitas Demokrasi Riil." Kolom Demokrasi Desa. *Mudik*, no. 6 at http://forumdesa.org/mudik/mudik6/kolom.php accessed 3 February 2012.

Van Diessen, J. R., et al. 2004. *Grote Atlas van Nederlands Oost-Indie*. 2nd rev. ed. Zierekzee: Asia Maior; Utrecht: Koninklijk Nederlands Aardrijkskundig Genootschap (Royal Dutch Geographical Society).

Yayasan Pariba. 1999. *Undang-undang Pemerintah Daerah dan Perimbangan Keuangan Antara Pemerintah Pusat dan Daerah*. Jakarta.

Newspapers

DeTik
Kompas
Media Indonesia
Pikiran Rakyat
Suara Pembaruan

Chapter 5

OIL PALM PLANTATIONS, CUSTOMARY RIGHTS, AND LOCAL PROTESTS

A West Sumatran Case Study

AFRIZAL

Before its development in the 1980s as an oil palm plantation area, Nagari Kinali was in a relatively isolated region in the northwest of the Province of West Sumatra on the coastal lowlands, at the end of a minor road winding around Mount Ophir 75 km from its then district capital, Lubuk Sikapang, located in the highlands. Today Nagari Kinali has been transformed into the West Sumatran center of plantations development, mainly of oil palm. The first such corporation in the region was established in 1934 and, by the end of 2012, there were seven oil palm plantation corporations operating supposedly under the NES, or Nucleus Estate and Smallholder, plantations model of agricultural production. As a side effect of this large-scale plantation development, smallholder oil palm plantations have also flourished since the early 1990s.

This chapter will analyze how this oil palm "takeover" has occurred and the kinds of conflict that have arisen between the traditional customary (*adat*) landholders and the plantation corporations since the 1990s. Until mid-2012, many conflicts were still unresolved, particularly involving the provision of smallholder plantations (*kebun plasma*) under the NES scheme, which had originally been promised by investors and the district government to local customary landholders who provided their customary land to the large-scale oil palm plantation developers.

The Nagari Kinali Community

The *nagari* was the traditional administrative unit of the relatively decentralized Minangkabau society, made up of the people living in several adjacent hamlets under the authority of their hierarchical network of matrilineal kinship groups. After Indonesian independence the government of West Sumatra issued several regulations formalizing and modifying the nagari system. But during the New Order period there was an attempted standardization of the lowest levels of local government across Indonesia to subdistrict (*kecamatan*) and administrative village (*desa*) levels. This took away most of the nagari powers apart from matters of *adat* (customary practice), which, importantly, included rights over communal land. In 1983 the Provincial Government preserved and institutionalized the nagari as an *adat* body by establishing Nagari Adat Councils (*Kerapatan Adat Nagari,* KAN) as the officially recognized customary governing body of each nagari. Each KAN was made up of the *ninik mamak,* the leaders of nagari kinship groups. As with most organized activities under the New Order, the KAN were supervised and controlled by the state and the KAN heads' elections had to be approved by the central government–appointed district head (bupati) and could be, and were, sacked by him. KAN's main roles included representing the nagari community to the state and managing its property, particularly its customary land (*tanah ulayat*), if this existed at a nagari rather than a lower kinship level.

In 2001, as part of *reformasi,* new laws (UU 22/1999 and 25/1999) on decentralizing government were implemented, giving far more authority than before to district-level governments and providing (§93) for provincial and district governments to reform village-level government. Responding to this, the West Sumatra Provincial Government Regulation 9/2000 and its revision 16/2007, replaced the individual *desa* governments with nagari government. However, this regulation took authority, including over communal land, away from the lineage leaders in the KAN and gave it to these new nagari governments.

By 2001 most of Nagari Kinali's 49,000 hectares of customary land was being used for agriculture; 7.5 percent for rice (mainly irrigated), 15 percent for oil palm on smallholder plantations (with an estimated one thousand growers, each on less than 2 hectares) and 55 percent used by seven large oil palm plantations (six private, one state).[1]

According to customary law, all land in Nagari Kinali (apart from the Javanese transmigration areas)[2] is communal land of one or several matrilineages in a given hamlet.[3] Traditionally, no individual ownership of land is recognized in the nagari. An individual is understood to have only use rights over land, and these are obtained by permission from kinship group leaders. Recently local people have sold the land for which they had use rights either to other local people within Nagari Kinali or to outsiders. The sale of the land is done under the mechanism of customary law rather than state land law and approved by *ninik mamak*. In Nagari Kinali customary land consists of two types: clan customary land and subclan customary land. Both types of land are inalienable. However, both categories of land can be allocated to individual members of the clan or the subclan in the form of use rights. Under a permit from kinship group leaders and with consent of kinship group members, this land may become alienable.

In the West Pasaman District there are two types of communal land in terms of the authority of its management: *babingkah adat*, tenure authority which is held by the *Yang Dipertuan*, with other kinship group leaders' authority limited to decisions about the utilization of the land; and *babingkah tanah*, where it is the individual kinship groups that have tenure authority over their own group's land and where the *Yang Dipertuan* is limited to an advisory role. In case of *babingkah adat* the Yang Dipertuan is the decision maker about the transfer of communal land but the consent of other kinship group leaders should be sought. Conversely, in the case of *babingkah tanah* it is the individual kinship group leader who has authority over the disposition of communal land, but the consent of the Yang Dipertuan should be sought. Nagari Kinali Community applies the *babingkah tanah* principle.

Kinship group leaders, *ninik mamak,* are the customary authority holders over the land.[4] Alienation or pawning of communal land can be done only with their permission, on behalf of the kinship group. Outsiders who wish to use plots of communal land must ask for use rights from the appropriate *ninik mamak*.

Oil Palm in the New Order

The development of oil palm plantations was a major strand in the economic developmentalism of Suharto's New Order state. From the early 1970s its successive five-year plans involved the state itself investing in resource-based industries in rural areas (Bowie and Unger 1997, 49–52) and encouragement of foreign capital in what "really became a foreign investor's paradise" (Taylor 1974, 18). The decline in oil export revenue encouraged promotion of agro-industries as "a major catalyst for economic development" (Kuntjoro-Jakti 1981, 42). As a consequence, there was a dramatic growth in the number of large-scale palm oil plantation companies and the area under plantation.

First established in Indonesia in 1911, with only 1,200 hectares recorded in 1916, the area under oil palm plantation expanded to 110,000 hectares by 1940. It then doubled to 250,000 by 1978 and grew eightfold to over 2 million by 1998/9. By 2004 4.1 million hectares were under cultivation. By 2008 land used for oil palm plantation had again increased—to 7.33 million hectares.[5] The plantings were concentrated on the islands of Sumatra and Kalimantan, with about half controlled by large-scale private plantation companies (Badan Pusat Statistik 2009, xviii).[6] "Indonesia now leads the world . . . and is set to become the number one palm oil producer, overtaking Malaysia by 2010, or even earlier" (Colchester et al. 2006, 25).

Both the central and local governments had a major role in this development, encouraging and facilitating it by providing for the needs of investors: issuing permits, allocating land, and guaranteeing investors long-term control through commercial use leases (HGU).

The central government expected oil palm plantations to improve the national macroeconomic export performance (Basyar 1999, 49) and provincial and district officials expected them to improve the economies of their regions (Gunawan et al. 1995, 17–19; Afrizal 2005, 112–13; 2007, 95–96). To increase the benefit to local people a new mode of plantation production, called the Nucleus Estate and Smallholder (NES) plantation model was introduced in 1974–75 (Soetrisno et al. 1991, 94–95), supported by a presidential decree in 1986 (Asian Agri 2007). Under the NES program, a plantation has two parts: a nuclear estate that is the asset of the large capital investors and many smallholder plantations that belong to small farmers.

Both plantation investors and the state are supposed to play significant roles in the development of the NES system. The former is responsible for developing its nucleus estate and supporting the smallholders' plantations (*kebun plasma*) by improving their management quality and buying their production. The latter is responsible for recruiting the smallholders, organizing the land for their plantations and providing development loans for them. The recipients of smallholder plots are supposed to obtain a combined 3 hectares each from the state; 2 for oil palm plantation land; 0.75 for food crop farming, and 0.25 for settlement. The government loans are to be repaid through a charge of 30 percent subtracted by the plantation company from the amounts it pays the smallholders for the harvests it buys from them. (Soetrisno 1991, 95–101; Gunawan et al. 1995, 15–17, 20–23, 41–74; Basyar 1999, 66).

The NES program reached Nagari Kinali in the mid-1980s. The first palm oil plantation in West Sumatra, Ophier, was established on about 1,100 hectares in 1934, by a Dutch company; it had begun to produce during the Japanese Occupation but had been destroyed during the struggle for independence against the Dutch in 1948 (Kementrian Penerangan 1953, 730). In 1981 the provincial government of West Sumatra, supported by the West German Development Bank (KFW), had reestablished the now-nationalized oil palm plantation, introducing the NES model (Soetrisno et al. 1991, 104). Subsequently, the local district government (Kabupaten Pasaman at that time) invited private investors to set up plantations and provided Nagari Kinali's communal land for them (*Singgalang*, 29 October 1989; interview with *kabupaten* official 4 September 2002). A retired journalist, living in the area described what had happened.

> In the middle of the 1980s, after visiting the Ophier oil palm plantation that was run by PT. Perkebunan Nusantara VI [one of the state companies established to take over the nationalized Dutch plantations], private investors came to the Kinali subdistrict's lineage leaders, including those of Nagari Kinali, to ask for land. The lineage leaders told them to approach the Pasaman district officials for this purpose. At that time, local lineage leaders were supportive of the investors. . . . The district head (bupati) of Pasaman . . . said that the development of plantations would benefit lineage members . . . and that they would be provided with plantation partnership with corporations as had occurred at Ophier plantation. Accordingly, the kinship group leaders agreed to provide their communal land for private investors. (Interview, 7 May 2002)

In 1989 the district head, Rajuddin Nuh, said that the development of large-scale oil palm plantations in Nagari Kinali would apply the NES scheme. "Investors must involve the local community by providing a smallholder plantation, particularly to those whose land is utilised by the investors" (*Singgalang*, 29 October 1989). A month later, when he attended the ceremony to mark the beginning of oil palm planting by PT TSG, he reiterated that the company must organize smallholder plantations for landholders (*Singgalang*, 29 November 1989).

In general, the communal land allocated was previously nonfarmed swamp for which the plantation companies constructed new drainage systems. However, a small part was being used for rice or other farming.[7]

Two patterns of land transfer procedures occurred in Nagari Kinali, one direct and the other indirect. The first consisted of land transferred directly from local kinship group leaders to investors, formalized in signed land transfer letters and officially endorsed by the head of the Kinali Subdistrict and the leader of the Kinali Nagari Adat Council (KAN).[8] The second procedure took place when local kinship group leaders provided land for investors indirectly, via the Pasaman District government through its Land Appropriation Committee (*Panitia Pengadaan Tanah*) which under KepPres 55/1993 was made up entirely of district officials, chaired by the bupati.[9] In these cases, the kinship group leaders provided their group's communal land to the district head. Then the district head transferred the land to investors. In Nagari Kinali most of the communal land alienation from local landholders to private investors was carried out this way.

When the kinship group leaders provided communal land for the development of palm oil plantations they signed land transfer letters (*Surat Penyerahan Tanah*). In the letters kinship group leaders agree to allow the head of Pasaman District to allocate the land to palm oil plantation investors: "The first party (kinship group leaders) gives authority over the utilization of our communal land to the second party (the Head of Pasaman District . . .)."[10] However, on request by palm oil plantation companies, the land rights release agreements (*Surat Pernyataan Pelepasan Hak*) were issued by kinship group leaders, clearly declaring that they transferred their rights of ownership over the land to the district government. In one example of the letters, the kinship group leaders say, "We whose signatures below [as] kinship group leaders . . . transfer our right over communal land to. . . . Henceforth we and our kinship group members no longer hold rights over the land."[11]

The oil palm companies then used the land release agreements and the land rights transfer agreements to apply to the national Ministry of Agrarian Affairs/Head of BPN (National Land Agency) for commercial use leases, with these letters being one of the considerations for issuing such leases. At the same time, the ministry used these letters as the legal basis for claiming that the land had become state land.[12] Since HGU can only be issued on state land, communal land had to be legally converted to state land before a HGU lease could be issued. This was one example of how the government was pursuing a more general policy of conversion of communal land into state land at the time. This mechanism of providing an HGU (commercial use) lease on what had been nonstate land was legitimized by the central government in 1996 with its Law No. 40/1996 on Commercial Land Use. According to this law a commercial use lease can be provided on nonstate land directly controlled by the state through the technique of rights renunciation (*pelepasan hak*).

However, Nagari Kinali's kinship group leaders' interpretation of the land release involved has been that neither of the two procedures through which they had provided communal land to the local government and to oil palm plantation companies involved permanent sale. Therefore, most kinship group leaders believed that they retained ultimate ownership of the land.[13] This is contradictory to the *Surat Pernyataan Pelepasan Hak* as mentioned earlier. However, the belief that kinship group leaders retain ultimate ownership of the land in question is understandable as the letter is signed by only a few kinship group leaders with doubtful awareness of legal consequences of the letter they signed.

The Agrarian Protest: Two Contrasting Customary Leaders

It is useful to present the contribution of two influential *adat* leaders of Nagari Kinali in the nagari community's agrarian struggles to show how local *adat* leaders contributed to the conflict between palm oil plantation companies and local people. As will be demonstrated below one *adat* leader was part of the problem, while another was part of the solution.

In Nagari Kinali, the head of the Nagari Adat Council[14] is the highest *adat* authority. The position has been a powerful one with its occupant being treated by state authorities as the overall representative of the Kinali customary community. From the beginning of the oil plantation expansion in the mid-1980s until 2001, the position was held by Tk. ZB,[15] who held the position of Yang Dipertuan Kinali that is traditionally the highest *adat* authority in the nagari.

When local officials and representatives of private investors approached kinship group leaders of the Nagari Kinali about obtaining *ulayat* land, Tk. ZB acted as a mediator and effective holder of customary authority. It was he who organized meetings of kinship group leaders to decide on what *adat* payments should be asked for transferring their customary communal land rights, took these decisions to the district government, received the payments, and transferred them to the respective land right holders. But he was subsequently accused by customary landholders of having colluded with the companies and having withheld payments; it was also claimed that he had received a 2 billion rupiah payment from one company.[16]

It was Tk. ZB who was mandated by the customary leaders to draw up the lists of those who were eligible to be allocated plantation land (*kebun plasma*). He was accused by local *adat* leaders of changing these lists to suit his personal interests, including changing some names of customary communal land rights holders to his own. In his position as head of the Nagari Adat Council, he signed the various land alienation agreements with representatives of the government; including some falsely claiming he had been among the providers of land. He also secretly agreed to the transfer by sale of some land between two plantation companies. By the late 1990s many lesser customary leaders, other individuals, and the Nagari Kinali Community Rights Advocating Team had sent formal protests to subdistrict and district heads, and even to the prosecutor's offices of both the district and provincial governments, requesting he be replaced or prosecuted. The various state authorities did not respond to these requests and continued to recognize him as the formal *adat* leader until he died in 2001,[17] because he helped them obtain customary land for the nuclear palm oil estates.

In contrast, Tk. ZB's successor as KAN leader, Datuak BBS, had been a long-time activist on behalf of the interests of Nagari members. He was not a Yang Dipertuan Kinali, but a lineage leader, one of the four Nagari *adat* formal dispute resolution judges (*Hakim Nan Barampek*), and had been the vice-head of the KAN. In 1991 he had been appointed by the KAN to organize land alienation for outsiders, and was the leader of the Nagari Kinali Community Rights Advocacy Team. A primary school graduate and low-income farmer living in a very basic house, he had written several letters to the plantation companies and the different levels of government voicing concerns of local land rights holders and demanding compensation; he had been a public representative in land rights struggles against the companies and the protests against Tk. ZB, and publicly supported two local farmers' associations in their dispute with one of the plantation companies. Because of these activities he had been interviewed by the police several times, and had also supported others who had been detained. He had written to the West Sumatra governor in a successful attempt to gain the release, under the guarantee of himself and two other Nagari figures, of five local protesters who had been arrested by the district police for cutting down the oil palms of the nucleus estate company that had taken over their customary land because their demand for compensation was not met.

It is obvious from the above discussion that the two influential *adat* leaders had antithetical approaches to their responsibility for their community's affairs. Tk. ZB facilitated the presence of palm oil companies and made use of them for his own economic interest. In contrast, Datuak BBS led local people in their struggle against local government and palm oil companies. It seems that the factors that are responsible for the differences between the two *adat* leaders are their social positions at the time of the coming of palm oil investors to Nagari Kinali, their power in the community, and their personal background. Tk. ZB was a Yang Dipertuan Kinali and a leader of Kerapatan Adat Kinali. This made his power as the highest community leader uncontrollable. The local government officials co-opted him to make their task of organizing land alienation easier. This situation opened an opportunity for Tk. ZB to corrupt his authority. This was compounded by his personal lifestyle. Tk. ZB had five wives and provided each wife with a luxurious house, excessive by Nagari Kinali community standards.

Different from Tk. ZB, Datuak BBS was a local intellectual with a modest lifestyle (he has one wife). He was not a Yang Dipertuan Kinali and held the position of KAN leader in 2001 at the time where many people in Nagari Kinali were influenced by *reformasi* and were critical of their leaders. As the vice-KAN leader, he was sidelined by Tk. ZB who, as KAN leader, controlled land alienation to palm oil investors in the early 1990s. Besides that, both he and his kinship group were among the victims of Tk. ZB, since his own kinship group's customary land (amounting to several hundred hectares) was part of the area transferred to the company (interviews in July 2002 and November 2008).

As of November 2008, Datuak BBS still holds the position of kinship group leader, but is no longer the head of KAN, since his term as a KAN leader ended in 2006. By then his economic position was considerably improved, as he has an independent (not *plasma*) smallholder palm oil plantation. He also received payment from one nucleus estate (PT AMP) as compensation for smallholder blocks not yet transferred (see below under company's responses). With a total income of 4–6 million per month[18] he was able to renovate his house. However, he also stopped campaigning for smallholders' claims to obtain *plasma* blocks from the nucleus estate.[19]

Thus it seems that when a company pays compensation to community leaders, community land struggles in the wider long-term interest are weakened. As we have seen, this happened twice in Nagari Kinali, under the two different Nagari leaders (Tk. ZB and Datuak BBS). Clearly palm oil companies have the power to control local leaders and the outcome of the land struggles, whether through outright corruption, or manipulation of compensation payments, a widespread phenomenon not restricted to Nagari Kinali.

Community Protests

Nagari Kinali is under the administration of the Kinali Subdistrict (*Kecamatan*), which, in turn, is now under the West Pasaman District (*Kabupaten*). The new district capital, Simpang Empat, is about 15 kilometers away. However, this district was created only in 2003 when the single Pasaman District was divided into two, so during most of the protests the district's central administration (in Lubuk Sikaping) was 75 kilometers away, in the highlands.

Nagari Kinali members had three main goals in their various struggles with oil palm plantation companies—(a) obtaining compensation for released communal land, (b) gaining smallholder plantations, and (c) the ultimate return of their land.

Compensation for Cultivated Communal Land

Under local customary laws, payments, usually called *adat diisi limbago dituang*,[20] are made when rights to use a plot of customary land are provided to a member of the community by kinship group leaders. If such a right is provided to an outsider, the payment may be called a *bungo siriah*, symbolizing the traditional welcoming into the community,[21] or it may be more prosaically called *uang adat* (customary payment). All these customary terms appear in the documentation and discussion of the payments made by the plantation companies to the kinship groups through their leaders. This is critical in relation to claims that it was use rights not ownership that was being transferred, as has been discussed above.

The various successive provisions of land rights to the companies involved agreed-upon payments to local communities for use (not sale) of their communal lands. Subsequently, *adat* communities demanded additional payments in compensation for use of land that had previously been cultivated and so would have had improvements made, such as irrigation or tree-planting. In one case, after twenty lineage groups had agreed in 1989 to provide a total of 7,000 hectares to the TSG Company for its nuclear estate in return for a *bungo siriah* payment, one of the lineage leaders, on behalf of his group, requested an additional payment in 1994 as the 900 hectares it had provided had not been "wasteland" but their cultivated land. They were successful in this claim. In 1998 the same group demanded they be given smallholder plantations as had been originally promised in a verbal agreement by the company and the district head, but they were not successful in this claim.

There were a number of cases of claims, regarded with varying degrees of legitimacy for additional compensation. In the 1970s, one kinship group had agreed with another, through their respective customary leaders, to be provided with the use of half the latter's communal land in return for building an irrigation scheme for the entire area. However, in 1989, with the irrigation works only half completed, the land was transferred by its kinship group, through the district head, to be a part of the 7,000 hectares for the use of the TSG Company. In mid-1991 the leader of the irrigation-building group protested successfully to the company for an additional improvement payment for the incomplete work done by the time the land had been transferred. It was known that he then kept the communal land improvement payment and did not pass it on to his kinship group members. This leader died, and in 2002 another local man, claiming to the company to be his successor, demanded another payment for the same reason. He had been previously making the same claim of status locally, but this had not been accepted by other customary leaders who recognized him as only an assistant to the true leader who lived elsewhere. The company refused his demand. He was later imprisoned by the Kinali subdistrict police without trial for harvesting the plantation's oil palm.

Provision of Smallholder Plantations (Kebun Plasma)

As part of the original negotiations between district officials, plantation companies and communal land rights holders, promises were made to the latter that they would receive *kebun plasma* under the NES system. In some cases these promises were written into the transfer agreement; in other cases they were verbal agreements.

In one case a kinship group leader provided 350 hectares of his customary land in 1989 to the TR Company, receiving both the basic payment and improvement supplement for this. The company also verbally promised the kinship group leader that it would provide his group with 100 hectares of smallholder plantations. The district head also publicly acknowledged the agreement. In 1993 the TR Company sold the transferred land to the TSG Company without the consent of the kinship group leader and perhaps the district head as well. In doing so this added another 165 hectares of the group's adjacent rice fields to the sale without the kinship group leader's knowledge. In 1994 the kinship leader and his group demanded that TSG provide *kebun plasma* to landholders as had been promised in the original agreement. TSG's local management suggested that the kinship group leader discuss the matter with its Jakarta head office, which he did, accompanied by Datuak BBS as KAN vice-head. It was agreed in Jakarta that the company would provide half the original land to the kinship group for smallholder plantations and that it would make additional payment for the newly included rice fields.

Because the company did not follow through on the agreement mentioned above, in 1998 Datuak BBS and his group protested again, with four members harvesting some of the company's oil palms, chopping down others, and consequently were arrested by district police.

The next year the kinship group leader threatened to occupy the land and take over the plantation now established there. A few months later, at the beginning of 2000, the company offered to transfer 100 hectares of *kebun plasma* as soon as their oil palms started producing and make monthly compensation payments for income lost until the end of the year. However, this offer was only verbal, and, despite further protests by the leader and his kinship group in early 2002, it was not carried out. This remains the situation until mid-2011. In the same period of political ferment (June 1998), another kinship group protested the failure of TSG to fulfill the oral agreement to provide 900 hectares of smallholder plantation. The company responded and signed an agreement to develop the 900 hectares of *kebun plasma,* but again the agreement has not been realized to date. During 1998 some twenty lineage leaders asked the company's management to develop 7,000 hectares of smallholder plantations as compensation for another 7,000 hectares of their customary land that had been provided to the company for its nucleus estate. It was found in mid-2008 that instead of establishing the smallholder plantations the company was paying Rp 30,000,000 a month to the twenty kinship group leaders (see the section on company's responses).

In several other cases the provision of *kebun plasma* was written into the original agreements. For example, the 1993–94 letters of communal land release involving eleven Nagari Kinali kinship groups mention that 60 to 70 percent of total land provided for the plantation company was for the nucleus estate, while 30 to 40 percent was for smallholder plantations. In May 1997 and in December 1999, Datuak BBS, acting as the vice-head of the Kinali KAN, together with the leaders of a local cooperative, sent the director of the plantation company a letter stating that the company must transfer to local people the smallholdings that had been developed and begun to produce. But the company argued that it was the duty of the local government to organize the transfer of the smallholder plantations. This was based on stipulations in these letters of agreement that the second party (the head of Pasaman District) has an "obligation to organize the development of [smallholder] plantations."

In a more general protest, on 1 and 4 November 2002 the people of Nagari Kinali demonstrated to the Pasaman district head and to the Pasaman District People's Representative Assembly (DPRD), expressing their concern that oil palm companies operating in their nagari had not transferred the smallholder plantations that had already begun producing palm oil fruits. They also requested that the head of the district and the DPRD press the oil palm plantation companies to keep their promise (*Padang Ekspres,* 1 and 4 November 2002).[22]

The Return of Land

As well as demands for more appropriate compensation and for the allocation of promised smallholder plantations in return for transfer of their communal land, there were also protests complaining that companies had taken their land by force and demands for its return. Cases recorded by 2002 are shown in table 5.1.

Protest Methods

The various tactics employed by the people of Nagari Kinali to defend their land and rights during the late New Order and in the early *reformasi* period include lobbying companies and state officials;[23]

TABLE 5.1
Local people's protests over illegally taken land in Negari Kinali

Protesters	Date	Complaint	Hectares
Seven farmers	19 June 1996	Rice fields taken without their consent (PT PMJ)[1]	Unknown
Eight kinship group leaders	25 October 1996	Company planting beyond land provided and hiding documents showing the real size of its plantation (PT AMP)[2]	Unknown
A hamlet farmers' association	3 October 1997	Backed up by two army personnel, fish ponds taken by force (PT TR[3])	70
130 Javanese transmigrant farm-households	17 July 1998	Land taken without their agreement (PT TSG)[4]	87
A Nagari kinship group leader and two members	24 October 1999	Farming land taken without their consent (PN VI)[5]	Unknown
Farmers' associations of two hamlets	10 April 2000	Farming land taken by force (PN VI Company)	197

Sources: Letters to local police 16 October 1997 and to a company director 10 April 2000; *Daftar Investor Perkebunan Sawit Di Kecamatan Kinali 2001*; interviews April–May 2002.

Notes: PN (Perusahaan Negara) are state-owned companies.

[1] A company owned by a foreign Investor
[2] A member of Wilmar Group and owned by a foreign investor
[3] Owned by a national investor
[4] Owned by a foreign investor
[5] Owned by the Indonesian government

establishing an activist organization;[24] receiving help from NGOs;[25] trying to stop companies from working on disputed lands;[26] cultivating and harvesting palm fruits on disputed lands;[27] destroying company plantations;[28] public demonstrations;[29] and bringing cases to court. The court case demonstrates the difficulty of using the legal system to obtain justice for local people in land cases.

In April 2002, the local kinship group leader, ABMA, and members prevented PT TSG from harvesting oil palm plantation on the 516 hectares of disputed land, and erected a barricade, blocking the way to the plantation for five days. On the sixth day five trucks with police from Padang came to the site, destroyed the barricade and interrogated the lineage group leader. Being advised beforehand, the protesters had stayed away; so there was no resistance and no violence.[30] The kinship group leader then demanded that the company pay his group for all the harvests on the disputed land and for all the costs of planting and maintenance of the palms. Moreover, because the police had supported the company and destroyed the barricade, ABMA demanded that the police pay compensation as well. He then took the matter to court. In April 2002, supported by the Padang Legal Aid Institute Office (LBH-Padang) (his lawyer being the previous leader of the LRA NGO), he lodged his case, suing the company management and police and demanding Rp 2.5 billion from the company for harvesting, planting, and maintenance of oil palms; Rp 5.1 billion from the national, provincial, district, and subdistrict police for harvesting oil palms; and Rp 5 billion for damaging the prestige of his lineage (*Singgalang,* 23 May 2002, and *Padang Ekspres,* 25 June 2002).

In November 2002 the Padang district court decided that ABMA's claims could not be accepted by the court because they were incomplete and vague in that he could not provide written evidence of his agreements with the company management, and it was unclear who the accused agents were. However, the court allowed him to appeal, but ABMA did not follow up on this[31] because he thought that he would not be succesful.[32]

The Impact of Reformasi and the Role of the Media

The national political reform movement after mid-1998 affected Nagari Kinali's agrarian struggles. Based on data gathered by the staff of Kinali Subdistrict, fifty protest actions had been carried out by local people against oil palm plantation companies between 1990 and 2002, thirty eight (76 percent) of these after June 1998.

As can be seen from table 5.2, tactics changed after mid-1998. Before then local protests were in the form of lobbying by sending letters and

TABLE 5.2
Protest tactics of the people of Nagari Kinali

Actions	Number of actions		
	Before mid-1998	After mid-1998	Total
Writing letters and holding meetings	10	17	27
Prohibiting companies' activities	1	1	2
Harvesting companies' plantations	0	4	4
Destroying companies' plantations	1	2	3
Cultivating reclaimed land	0	3	3
Obtaining support from local and provincial state officials	0	6	6
Asking for assistance from outside NGOs	0	1	1
Demonstrations	0	4	4
Bringing cases to court	0	1	1
Total	12	38	50

Sources: Compiled from *Daftar Investor Perkebunan Sawit Di Kecamatan Kinali 2001; Padang Ekspres*, 25 June, 4 July, 2 November, and 5 November 2002; *Singgalang*, 25 June 1998 and 23 May 2002; Letters of Nagari Kinali Community Rights Advocacy Team to West Sumatran Public Prosecutor, 17 June 1998, and to Pasaman District Public Prosecutor on 3 August,] 1998; Interviews with *datuak* BBS, 24 April 2002, and ABMA, 27 April 2002, in Kinali.

expressing demands privately in meetings. After *reformasi* local people carried out more public and more violent actions such as cultivation of disputed land, blocking company access to their plantations, harvesting company oil palm fruits, and destroying company plantations. Of the fourteen cases where these tactics were employed only one case occurred before mid-1998. Asking for help from the local state officials, demonstrations, asking for NGO support, and bringing a case into court were also carried out after *reformasi* had commenced. Moreover, protest letters and speeches started to include references to "reform."[33]

The media contributed to the Nagari Kinali agrarian protests. First, local people knew about *reformasi* from watching television. Datuak BBS, one of the Nagari Kinali people's protest leaders, said, "Television informed us about student protests and local community protests in many places in Indonesia," and many people in Nagari

Kinali recognized *reformasi* from watching television. Second, the media reported the protests of the people of Nagari Kinali as public issues in West Sumatra. With NGO assistance (before LRA was disbanded), the leaders of the Nagari Kinali Community Rights Advocacy Team used newspapers to publicize their cause. Newspapers, mostly Padang-based, reported protests and the court case by the lineage leader against the PT TSG plantation company and the subdistrict, district, provincial, and national police.

The Achievements of Protesters

Local people were successful in gaining some but not all of their demands. They received land improvement compensation, and although the land they claimed had been illegally taken was not returned, some monetary compensation was made. Nevertheless, the demands for smallholder plantations, although part of all original agreements between the nagari and plantation owners, were not successful. Additionally, when HGU leases expire in the future, new problems will occur in Nagari Kinali as the people believe that they retain ownership to their ancestral land while acceding to the goverment that the land is state land.

Responses of Companies

Several of the plantation companies did plant the areas they had promised to smallholders but failed to transfer them to local people. In mid-1999 the head of Pasaman District expressed his support for the transfer of such areas when they began to produce. To this end he wrote to the leader of the Nagari Kinali Community Rights Advocacy Team stating that there had been an agreement about this between his government and the companies on 30 July 1999. By mid-2011, twelve years later, none of the planted and producing smallholder plantations had been transferred to local people.

Companies gave several justifications for not releasing smallholder plantations. The first, from PT AMP, was that it was the district government's responsibility to organize the smallholder plantations, not theirs. PT AMP also claimed that the requisite smallholder farmer cooperatives for recipient allocation and marketing had not been formed. However, farmers counterclaimed that lists had been drawn up and given to the district head, and that cooperatives had been formed. Certainly at least two had been, one for prospective recipients from PT PMJ and one from PT AMP. In 2008 PMJ, AMP, and TSG managements were arguing that there was not enough land available for the list of proposed recipients, and they were asking the relevant kinship group leaders to find more. This was proving extremely difficult as there was now no unused communal land as so much had already been transferred for use as nucleus estates and cultivated by local people for their own palm oil plantations.

A supposedly temporary resolution had been introduced by companies that had already planted smallholder plantations, such as PT AMP. Instead of being given control of smallholder plantations, the proposed recipients were receiving a monthly payment of Rp 150,000 in 2002, increased to Rp 300, 000 by 2008. PT AMP spent about Rp 90 million a month for the three hundred households that were proposed recipients of *kebun plasma*. Compared to company profits from palm oil these payments are minuscule.

PT TSG had barely developed any *kebun plasma* in spite of its 1998 written agreement to develop 124 hectares for sixty-two members of one kinship group, paying all costs, which would be repaid by the recipients after the palms started producing. Ten years later none of this had been done. This happened because both the local government and local people did not push the company to realize the agreement. It had also promised to develop and transfer another 3,000 hectares but had done so for only 200 hectares by the end of 2002 and no more by mid-2008. PT TSG was sold to PT Lintas Inter Nusa (LIN) in early 2005 without the prior knowledge of the relevant kinship group leaders and with no approval of local government. At the time, these leaders did not react because their regular monthly payments of Rp 40 million continued, but protested and organized roadblocks after the payments were stopped two months later (Hildayana 2007, 44–81).[34]

In 2002 the company had justified its not having developed the 3,000 hectares of smallholder plantations by pointing out that the central government had stopped providing credit, namely, *Kredit Koperasi Primer untuk Anggota* (Credit for Primary Cooperative Members, KKPA) for this from 1998. It was true that the central government stopped KKPA in that year throughout Indonesia.[35] But the then Pasaman district secretary (*Sekwilda*) said that the plantations should have been developed before 1998. The TSG nucleus estate had been completed in 1995, so there had been several years for *kebun plasma* development during which government credit would have been available.

The company also blamed the 2001 occupation of the land by local people as a reason for being unable to develop it as *kebun plasma*. However, this occupation and subsequent partial cultivation by members of a protesting lineage had been in response to the lack of company planting. Another argument by the company was that the original written transfer agreement did not contain a reference to *kebun plasma*. Although true, there had been verbal public promises about them at the 1989 ceremony for the first plantings at the TSG nucleus estate; a 1998 written agreement between the company and one kinship group leader; a 1999 agreement between management and nagari leaders over the development of 3,000 hectares for *kebun plasma,* and a 2000 agreement with the kinship group leaders of one hamlet for the development of another 200 hectares. Subsequently, a company public relations officer attempted to explain these away because "the management of PT TSG was under pressure at the time agreements were made" (interview, Kinali, 20 April 2001).[36]

At the end of 2004, facilitated by the government of the newly established West Pasaman District, a solution was agreed between PT TSG and the leaders of the kinship groups who had originally (in the early 1990s) provided 7,000 hectares for the PT TSG nucleus estate. The company agreed again to develop 3,000 hectares for *kebun plasma* (for these kinship groups). However, the land for this 3,000 hectares could not now be found, meaning there was no more ulayat lineage land in

Nagari Kinali. So the kinship group leaders asked the company to resurvey its nucleus estate areas. They suspected that TSG was already cultivating the promised 3,000 hectares of land, which was outside of the original 7,000 hectares as part of its nucleus estate. The company refused to do this. Four years later (mid-2008), PT LIN, the new owners, had still not agreed, as it did not want to disturb its own nucleus estate. They wanted any smallholder development to be outside of what it was already using, which they claimed was 7,000 hectares but which kinship group leaders suspected was closer to 10,000 hectares. PT LIN, probably realizing what PT TSG had done, agreed to pay local people Rp 40 million a month in compensation through their respective kinship group leaders, until another solution can be found. As mentioned previously, PT LIN had stopped these monthly compensation payments after buying the company in 2005. However, after kinship group members blocked access roads and threatened to take over the nucleus estate, PT LIN resumed a reduced monthly payment of Rp 30 million (Hildayana 2007, 53–54, 56, 62), continuing to the present.

Responses of the State

As mentioned earlier, in their efforts to resolve their conflicts with oil palm companies, from 1998 to mid-2008 the people of Nagari Kinali attempted to get help from provincial and local state officials, including the elected local assembly (DPRD) members. However, their demand for smallholder plantations was given little genuine support at either the district or the provincial level.[37] The DPRD representatives made no attempt to mediate between the people of Nagari Kinali, the companies, and local state officials; instead they merely urged the officials to resolve the conflicts or, as in a 2002 interview with the DPRD chairman, blamed the previous New Order Pasaman government for its apparent lack of knowledge and interest in local rights. This tells us that *reformasi* and the 1999 decentralization laws did not cause the Pasaman District Parliament (DPRD) to become responsive and to get involved in the Nagari Kinali community's struggle.

Although the local district government has a duty both to recruit the recipients of smallholder plantations and to organize the transfer of *kebun plasma* to them, up to mid-2008 the local state apparatus had not carried out this responsibility. In the second half of 1999 the district head expressed his agreement to transfer to local recipients smallholder plots that were already producing and by 2001 the Kinali Subdistrict office reported that about 1,120 hectares of smallholder plantations were ready for transfer, which the district government never implemented. This confirms others' findings that the process of transferring smallholder plantations from the control of a nucleus estate corporation to their expectant recipients is problematic, because it is not in the interests of the companies that stand to reap better profits from greater control over the production process.[38] Additionally, the more recent government regulations that shift the minimum proportion of *plasma* estate down to 20 percent[39] is an indicator of the inclination of the national government to pander to the interests of big companies rather than smallholders.

Additionally, the district government of Pasaman objected to pushing PT TSG to develop smallholder plantations, claiming that there had been no written reference to it in the communal land transfer agreement between the kinship group leaders in question and the companies at the time of the land alienation process. Although true, this had been a "mistake" made by the local government officials responsible for drawing up the agreement.[40] The district head himself had asserted there would be such plantations in his 1989 public speech at the PT TSG nucleus estate's planting commencement ceremony (*Singgalang*, 29 November 1989).

As a result of *reformasi* and the ensuing fission of regional areas (*pemekaran*), in 2003 Pasaman District (capital Lubuk Sikaping) was divided into Pasaman District (population about 243,000) and West Pasaman District (capital Simpang Empat, population about 290,000). The area of Nagari Kinali is in West Pasaman, less than 15 kilometers, rather than the previous 75 kilometers, from its district capital. However, it appears that the change did not help the people of Nagari Kinali in their struggle against the oil palm plantation companies.

The new district government first tried to resolve these plantation conflicts in 2004 by setting up a committee of representatives of the district and subdistrict administrations, PT TSG,[41] Nagari leaders, local police and local military. This committee recommended that the company should develop 3,000 hectares of *kebun plasma* but, as described above, such an area of available land could not be found. In 2005 the government set up a new committee, this time representing the district and subdistrict administrations, the elected district assembly, the local government plantation and land agencies (*Kantor Pertanahan*), police and military, the Nagari's governing council and *adat* leaders. However, its only result was a clarification of the location of the company's nucleus estate.

It is likely that the main factor behind the failure of the above committee to resolve the conflicts was that the local government was not supportive of the Nagari Kinali people's demands for *kebun plasma*. For the local government the expropriation of revenues from the oil palm plantation companies appears to be more important than supporting their demands because of its reliance on those revenues. Both before and after Pasaman was split into two new districts, the local government needed palm oil companies for generating its own revenues.

This was partly due to the structure of local government financing after *reformasi*. For example, in 2000 before the *pemekaran*, the government of Pasaman District received Rp 618.5 million (from all oil palm plantation companies operating in the district). This was 58 percent of its total locally raised income (*Pendapatan Asli Daerah*, PAD) that year and was proudly reported in 2001. Similarly, palm oil companies continued to make an important financial contribution to the newly formed West Pasaman District government's income after 2003. Although in 2007 the West Pasaman District government obtained only Rp 876 million from palm oil plantation companies, and this was 7.3 percent of its PAD in that year, in 2008 the amount received by the local government from the companies jumped to Rp. 4.5 billion, 23.5 percent of its PAD. Local government planned to increase its income from the sector to 30 percent of its PAD in 2009.[42] This shows how difficult it is to resolve these disputes given the level of revenue that palm oil generates for district budgets.

Before and after the division of Pasaman District, the regional government issued a regulation to legitimize its expropriating revenues from agriculture, including plantations, which did not mention local community's land rights.[43] Although, according to interviews with district officials in 2002,[44] the central government prohibited local governments from collecting payment from the exploitation of natural resources, including from plantation companies, the district government avoided this prohibition by collecting payments from the companies indirectly in the form of a third party's "voluntary" financial contribution, that is paid to the Regional Government Finance Agency (*Badan Keuangan Daerah*).

The Nagari Kinali case demonstrates the problems of the development of large-scale oil palm plantations on land over which the local community has customary rights, despite recognition by local government. The development of the large-scale oil palm plantations that were supposed to be run in the form of Nucleus Estate and Smallholder Plantations (NES) created conflicts between local customary landholders, who were supposed to be smallholder plantation recipients, and the plantation companies. The conflict is complex, related to local land tenure, local social structure, political change, and the behavior of both the companies and the state during the New Order and *reformasi*.

The people of Nagari Kinali protested about all seven oil palm plantation companies operating in their nagari and asked for help from the state government. Protesters were members of kinship groups, and the leaders of these groups played very important roles as leaders of these protests. Lineage group protests have been linked to the customary *adat* rights they traditionally held on the land utilized for the plantations. They protested to demand both communal land improvement compensation (and in some cases the return of land) and to obtain smallholder plantations, but the latter demand dominated. Some of the other demands have been settled through monetary compensation but the promised transfer of smallholdings after development into productive oil palm has not occurred, in some cases up to two decades after the public commitments.

The state played a significant role in these developments. It was the Pasaman District government that brought oil palm plantation investors to Nagari Kinali, with local state officials organizing local kinship group leaders to provide their communal land for large-scale oil plantation development and also making possible the claim by the Ministry of Agrarian Affairs/Head of National Land Administration (BPN) that people's customary land (*tanah adat*) had thereby become state land (*tanah negara*) through local agreements and the issue of HGU certificates. The district government promised local people that they would get smallholder plantations in return for agreeing to transfer use of their communal land but then showed little willingness to force company management to deliver these *kebun plasma,* and so far has failed to perform its duty. Decentralization and the establishment of a smaller district government covering the Nagari Kinali lands should theoretically have made the district government more responsive to the Nagari Kinali people; but at the same time, it made the new district more dependent on the plantations. It has to support the oil palm plantation companies, which provide the largest contribution to locally raised income, to meet its own financial needs.

The Nagari Kinali case shows that *reformasi* brought national political change and was a positive influence in local people's land struggles as it opened political opportunities for locals to express their interests. This is indicated by the fact that although local protests against oil palm plantation corporations had begun in 1993 and several important events had occurred at the beginning of 1998, it was after mid-1998 that the struggles found extra momentum and protest became more overt. By 2001 there had been two significant outcomes of agrarian protests in Nagari Kenali. In the first case, 197 hectares of land taken by force from fourteen kinship groups for a HGU leased to PN VI company was returned. In the second, compensation was paid by PT TSG to three kinship group leaders (of Rp 9, 25, and 55 million respectively) and Rp 58 million to two farmers' associations for 70 hectares of illegally expropriated fish ponds (Daftar Investor Perkebunan Sawit di Kecamatan Kinali 2001).

The case also reveals the weakness of customary society struggles. The media, mainly newspapers, helped the people of Nagari Kinali, first by bringing the issues to public attention and then by covering and reporting local actions, so that Nagari Kinali claims became and continued to be connected with wider public issues. There was involvement of civil society elements in the Nagari Kinali people's struggles with city-based NGOs providing some assistance through publicity and legal support, to elements of the people's struggles, but they did not contribute toward wider organization of the nagari community as a whole; nor did they maintain a continuing role in negotiations of their demands to oil palm companies and the local government. In most of their continuing struggles, the people of Nagari Kinali, have had to rely on their own resources—in particular their own customary leaders, who were often co-opted by business and state interests for private reward.

Notes

This chapter is based on the author's PhD research and is a revised version of Afrizal 2007.

1. Official statistics are from *Dinas Pertanian Kecamatan Kinali 2001*, *Monografi Kecamatan Kinali 2001* or *BPS Pasaman Barat 2007*. Other information was drawn from interviews.

2. Nagari Kinali's 2007 population of about 48,000 was about two-thirds ethnic Minangkabau and a third ethnic Javanese. The latter were settled in a state transmigration program from 1961 on about 4,000 hectares given, without payment, by the appropriate kinship group leaders.

3. Unlike other West Sumatran nagari there is no recognized communal land belonging to the whole nagari community (*ulayat nagari*) or to the whole clan (*ulayat suku*).

4. For marriage or other reasons these customary leaders may not live in their natal hamlets.

5. For more details see Colchester et al. 2006 and Badan Pusat Statistik 2009.

6. There were 170 estates recorded in 1985, 683 by 1999, and 1,197 by 2009 (Biro Pusat Statistik 1985, 248; 1999, 208–9; Soetrisno et al. 1991, 72–75; Basyar 1999, 35; Colchester et al. 2006, 21–22; Badan Pusat Statistik 2010).

7. Informants estimated that previously about a hundred local people had used the swampy areas for fishing and rattan collecting. Information

about previous uses and initial developments came from interviews with several company and official representatives as well as lineage leaders.

8. These letters and transfer statements are still available. Other information on procedures was derived from interviews with relevant officials.

9. On Indonesian land acquisition laws see Fitzpatrick (2008, 227–233); on Presidential Decision No. 55 of 1993 and the functions of the land appropriation committees see Sumardjono (1995, 19–32; 2001, 72–92).

10. *Surat Pernyataan Pelepasan Hak* by twenty kinship group leaders of Nagari Kinali for PT. TSG.

11. "Kami yang bertanda tangan di bawah ini ninik mamak . . . menyerahkan hak kami atas tanah ulayat kepada. . . . Setelah diserahkan kami dan anak cucu kemanakan tidak berhak lagi atas tanah tersebut." *Surat Pernyataan Pelepasan Hak* by three kinship group leaders of Nagari Kinali for PT. TSG.

12. They included the statement that it "fulfilled requirements to obtain an HGU lease on state land that was former *ulayat* land" (see, for example, *Keputusan Mentri Negara Agraria/Kepala Badan Pertanahan Nasional* No. 37/HGU/BPN/94 about the HGU for PT TSG). At the end of 1989 the head of Pasaman District, Rajuddin Nuh, had made it clear to journalists that the land on which an HGU was issued by the government becomes state land. He said, "When investors no longer need the land, the land must be returned to the head of district" (meaning to the state) (*Singgalang,* 29 October 1989).

13. Analyses of six agreements for about 30,540 hectares of communal land signed by kinship group leaders of Nagari Kinali for plantation companies showed they included no references to purchase and sale of land. The same was found in a succession of letters from kinship group leaders of another nagari providing land to one of the companies involved with Nagari Kinali. Several recent interviews with kinship group leaders confirmed this belief in the absence of any mention of selling in these other land alienation agreements.

14. KAN is the adat leader's organization that is recognized by the West Sumatran government.

15. Tk. ZB, who was also a leader of his kinship group, was a farmer and primary school graduate.

16. Letter from the Nagari Kinali Community Rights Advocacy Team to the head of Provincial Prosecutor's Office 17 June 1998; interviews with lineage leaders and KAN head April–May 2002.

17. The claims about Tk. ZB were made in several interviews with local leaders in 2002 and in documents sent to the various state authorities. His signature as KAN leader appears on the various transfer statements and agreements of the time.

18. I have no information about whether he shared this income with his kinship group. I suspect the income was regarded as personal, since similar payments are made by palm oil plantation companies in Nagari Kinali to many *ninik mamak* (information obtained from informal focus group discussion in the house of the head of Nagari Kinali in May 2011 with the head of Nagari Kinali and five informal leaders of the nagari).

19. Interviews with Dt. BBS and the head of Kinali subdistrict, November 2008.

20. Literally "tradition is followed and agreements made."

21. *Siriah* or *sirih* is a kind of leaf chewed locally, which is presented in ceremonial events to welcome guests or to invite people to attend a ceremony. *Bungo* means flower.

22. The local government's responses will be discussed under the section "Response of the State."

23. Lobbying was mostly by letters. In 2000 two hamlet leaders wrote to the director of PN VI Company demanding the return of land taken by force in 1984. In 1998 the Nagari Kinali Community Rights Advocacy Team (Tim Pembela Hak Masyarakat Kenagarian Kinali) sent the West Sumatran public prosecutor a letter requesting that he seek resolution to their disputes with all oil palm plantation companies in their nagari. A few weeks later the team also sent the Pasaman District public prosecutor a similar letter stating that palm oil companies had expropriated land from local people and had not kept their promises to develop and transfer smallholder plantations. In 2000, sixteen kinship group leaders wrote to the head of Pasaman District to help solve their disputes with the PN VI Company, which they claimed had taken over long-cultivated land. In mid-2007 it was reported that this letter writing to officials was still continuing (Hildayana 2007, 44–71).

24. In mid-1998 the Nagari Kinali Community Rights Advocacy Team was set up by ten people. This organization was led by the influential kinship group leader and KAN vice-head, Datuak BBS. However, despite its name, this organization was never effective in organizing broader Nagari Kinali community struggles. This was because it was established by a group of local kinship group leaders to facilitate their own struggles to get individual smallholder plantations from the palm oil company.

25. Nagari Kinali got assistance from two Padang-based NGOs, the West Sumatran University Students Communication Forum (FKMSB, Forum Komunikasi Mahasiswa Sumatera Barat) and the Advocacy and Research Institute (LRA, Lembaga Riset Advokasi) who protected kinship group leaders from threats of police arrest over harvesting and cutting down of oil palm trees on disputed PT TSG plantation land. NGO

members told the police in Kinali that many more protesters would become involved if arrests occurred. The LRA focused its attention on local rights to natural resources, limiting its support to the particular conflict that had first attracted the support of the FKSMB and to assisting the Nagari Kinali Community Rights Advocacy Team. This included assistance in the writing of the 1998 letters to the provincial and the district public prosecutors (see note 23 above); holding a media presentation at its office when the complaints were publicized (*Singgalang,* 25 July 1998) and, through the contacts which had been made with its legally trained personnel, enabling the kinship group's dispute to be taken to court. However, support from this source disappeared in 2001 when the LRA (like its predecessor the FKMSB) disintegrated because of disagreements among its leaders. The subsequent organization formed by several of its members was more interested in developing organic farming. This issue is very typical of Indonesian NGOs, which are often disintegrating and reforming. Many NGO organizations are weak, relying too much on their founders and used by activists as a temporary workplace.

26. Locals used both letter writing and direct action (roadblocks) to try to stop land clearing, planting, and harvesting on Nagari Kinali land, but these actions had limited success, In 1996, after PT AMP did not respond to their claims, two kinship group leaders sent a letter to its director asking the company to stop working on their 700 hectares. The company did not take any notice. In 2002 another kinship group blocked the road to PT TSG plantation on disputed land to support their order prohibiting the company from harvesting. As the matter remained unresolved there was another roadblock protest four years later (Hildayana 2007, 67). The kinship group leaders did not ask the police to intervene, probably because they expected the police would support the palm oil companies.

27. Nine years after the transfer of about 1,500 hectares of former swamp from local landholders to PT TSG, the promised 1,500 hectares *kebun plasma* area had been cleared and drained but not further developed. So about 100 members of traditional lineage landowners took over and cultivated about 300 hectares (*Daftar Investor Perkebunan Sawit Di Kecamatan Kinali* 2001). Where promised *plasma* land was already developed but not transferred to smallholders, local people began harvesting palm oil crops to pressure the companies. In 1998 the leaders of the Nagari Kinali Community Rights Advocacy Team instructed the proposed recipients of PT AMP's smallholding program to harvest the oil palm fruits located within their proposed area. And in 2000 a group harvested fruits from the PN VI company's nuclear estate. According to officials these

activities constituted theft, whereas according to the harvesters what was taken was their rightful property.

28. In a few protests against a nonresponding company oil palms were burned or chopped down. For example, one individual burned 35 oil palms on PT PANP's plantation because his demand to be given land alienation compensation for about 70 hectares was not approved; in 2000 an unknown number of people from a local hamlet chopped down 535 oil palms on the same company's plantation; then about three weeks later, 3 hectares were burned by the hamlet's farmers' association (*Daftar Investor Perkebunan Sawit Di Kecamatan Kinali* 2001).

29. The people of Nagari Kinali also used public demonstrations to press provincial or local state officials and the local elected District People's Representative Assembly (DPRD) into finding solutions to their disputes. For example, in mid-1998, led by the Nagari Kinali Community Rights Advocacy Team, the people of Nagari Kinali demonstrated to the governor of West Sumatra to express their concerns (*Singgalang,* 25 June 1998). In 2002, led by a kinship group leader, 200 people demonstrated to the head of Pasaman District to ask him to free three Kinalians arrested by police and to transfer *kebun plasma* land that was already producing (*Padang Ekspres,* 2 November 2002). Three days later another group of 250 demonstrated to the Pasaman DPRD to find a solution for the transfer of *kebun plasma* (*Padang Ekspres,* 5 November 2002).

30. Interview with ABMA and a number of his relatives gathered at his house at the time of interview, 27 April 2002, in Kinali.

31. *Singgalang,* 23 May 2002, and *Padang Ekspres,* 25 June 2002.

32. Personal communication with Jomi, an LRA activist, in January 2012.

33. Such as "In line with the aim of total reform (*reformasi total*) expressed by Indonesian society, allow us on this occasion to report our complaints and suffering . . . ," and "We, the farmers, hope that in this reform era the government will not allow . . . (company) to continue to ignore the law by expropriating land from us" (letters of Nagari Kinali Community Rights Advocacy Team to West Sumatran Public Prosecutor, 17 June 1998, and to Pasaman District Public Prosecutor on 3 August 1998).

34. Interviews with the head of Kinali subdistrict and TMM Nagari Kinali, August 2008.

35. Personal communication with Dr. Ira Wahyuni, an agricultural economist, November 2008.

36. What he meant was that during 1998 local protests occurred frequently in Nagari Kinali directed toward the management of PT TSG.

37. According to the head of the Development and Planning Division of the West Sumatran Provincial Agriculture and Plantation Office, the

local district (kabupaten) bureaucracy carries the responsibility of solving plantation land disputes, not the Province of West Sumatra (interview, 12 February 2002, Padang).

38. There have been earlier reports that state bureaucracy plays a role in the problem, partly as it is very slow in completing the paperwork needed because of a lack of coordination (see Soetrisno et al. 1991, 115; Gunawan et al. 1995, 68; Ahmad 1998, 137).

39. See article 10 of Peraturan Menteri Pertanian Nomor 26/Permentan/OT.140/2/2007 tentang Pedoman Perizinan Usaha Perkebunan.

40. It was also possible that this was a deliberate "mistake," since PT TSG may have paid these officials to exclude reference to small holder plantations.

41. The company with which the Nagari Kinali kinship groups were most in dispute over the lack of provision of shareholder plantations.

42. The data were obtained from the public relations head of the West Pasaman district head's office.

43. There was a similar regulation about raising revenue from the collection of birds' nests from caves, with no reference to the communal rights of the *adat* land rights holders, only of government, in the specifying of required payments.

44. Interviews with senior officials in the District's Regional Income Agency and the Agricultural and Plantation Office, April and May 2002.

References

Afrizal. 2005. "The Nagari Community, Business and the State: The Origin and the Process of Contemporary Agrarian Protests In West Sumatera, Indonesia." PhD diss., Flinders University, South Australia.

———. 2006. *Sosiologi Konflik Agraria: Protes-Protes Agraria dalam Masyarakat Indonesia Kontemporer.* Padang: Universitas Andalas Press.

———. 2007. *The Nagari Community, Business and the State: The Origin and the Process of Contemporary Agrarian Protests In West Sumatra.* Bogor: Forest People Programme and Sawit Watch.

Agri Asian. 2007. "Smallholders's Mission: Harmonious Partnership Sustainable Plasma." *Agri Asian Fact Sheet,* November.

Ahmad, R. 1998. *Perkebunan: Dari NES Ke PIR.* Jakarta: Puspa Swara.

Badan Pusat Statistik. 2009. *Statistik Kelapa Sawit Indonesia.* Jakarta. Badan Pusat Statistik.

———. 2010. *Direktori Perusahaan Perkebunan Kelapa Sawit 2009.* Jakarta. Badan Pusat Statistik.

BAPPEDA Propinsi Sumatera Barat and BPS Propinsi Sumatera Barat. 1994. *Produk Domestik Regional Bruto (PRDB) Menurut Lapangan Usaha Propinsi Sumatera Barat, 1989–1993*. Padang: BAPPEDA Propinsi Sumatera Barat dan BPS Propinsi Sumatera Barat.

Basyar, H. A. 1999. *Perkebunan Besar Kelapa Sawit: Blunder Ketiga Kebijakan Sektor Kehutanan*. N.p.: E-Law and CePAS.

Benda-Beckmann, F. Von, and K. Von Benda-Beckmann. 2001. "Recreating the Nagari: Decentralization in West Sumatra." *Max Planck Institute for Social Anthropology Working Paper*, no. 31. Halle.

Biro Pusat Statistik. 1985. *Statistik Indonesia*. Jakarta: Biro Pusat Statistik.

———. 1999. *Statistik Indonesia*. Jakarta: Biro Pusat Statistik.

Bowie, A., and D. Unger. 1997. *The Politics of Open Economies: Indonesia, Malaysia, the Philippines, and Thailand*. Cambridge: Cambridge University Press.

BPS Pasaman Barat. 2007. *Pasaman Barat Dalam Angka*. Simpang IV: BPS Pasaman Barat.

Colchester, M., et al. 2006. *Palm Oil and Land Acquisition in Indonesia: Implications for Local Communities and Indigenous Peoples*. Bogor: Forest People Program and Sawit Watch.

Fitzpatrick, Daniel. 2008."Beyond Dualism: Land Acquisition and Law in Indonesia." In *Indonesia Law and Society*, 2nd ed., edited by Tim Lindsey, 224–46. Sydney: Federation Press.

Gunawan, R., et al. 1995. *Dilema Petani Plasma: Pengalaman PIR-BUN Jawa Barat*. Bandung: Akatiga.

Hildayana, F. 2007. "Daya Tanggap Pemerintah Kabupaten Pasaman Barat Dalam Menyelesaikan Konflik (Studi Kasus: Penyelesaian Konflik Antara PT. Trisangga Guna/PT. Laras Internusa dengan Masyarakat Kinali." Skripsi, Program Studi Politik Fakultas Ilmu Sosial dan Ilmu Poitik Universitas Andalas.

Kasri, A. 2000. "Tanah Ulayat dalam Problematik Pembangunan." Paper presented to seminar Reaktualisasi Adat Basandi Syarak, Syarak Basandi Kitabullah, Bukitinggi, 22–23 January.

Kementrian Penerangan. 1953. *Republik Indonesia: Propinsi Sumatera Tengah*. Bandung: Djawatan Penerangan Propinsi Sumatera Tengah.

Kuntjoro-Jakti, D. 1981. "The Political Economy of Development: The Case of Indonesia under the New Order Government, 1966–1978. PhD diss., University of California.

Langill, L. R. 1978. "Military Rule and Development Policy in Indonesia under the New Order: 1966–1974." PhD diss., American University.

Mirwati, Y. 2000. "Analisis Yuridis Reformasi Hak Ulayat dan Masa Depannya di Sumatera Barat." Paper presented at the seminar Reaktualisasi

Adat Basandi Syarak, Syarak Basandi Kitabullah, Bukitinggi, 22–23 January.

Nuh, J. M., and E. Collins. 2001. "Land Conflict and Grassroots Democracy in South Sumatra: The Dynamics of Violence in South Sumatra." *Antropologi Indonesia.* Tahun 35 (64):41–55.

Singgalang. 29 October 1989. "Tanah Ulayat di Sumbar, Untuk Kesejahteraan atau Perpecahan."

———. 29 November 1989. "Tanah Ulayat di Pasaman Mulai Diselimuti Pohon Sawit."

———. 25 June 1998. "Hentikan Intimidasi: Rakyat Kinali Tuntut Pengembalian Hak."

Soetrisno, L., et al. 1991. *Kelapa Sawit: Kajian Sosial Ekonomi.* Yogyakarta: Aditya Media.

Sumardjono, Maria SW. 1995 "Pengadaan Tanah bagi Pelaksanaan Pembangunan untuk Kepentingan Umum" (Bagian 1 dan 2). In *Pluralisme Hukum Pertanahan dan Kumpulan Kasus Tanah,* ed. Benny K. Harman et al., 19–32. Jakarta: Yayasan Bantuan Hukum Indonesia.

———. 2001. *Kebijakan Pertanahan Antara Regulasi dan Implementasi.* Jakarta: Pernerbit Buku Kompas.

Taylor, J. 1974. "The Economic Strategy of the 'New Order.'" In *Repression and Exploitation in Indonesia,* ed. The British Indonesian Committee, 13–28. London: Spokesman Books.

Newspapers

Padang Ekspres
Singgalang

Chapter 6

TENURE AND TRANSFORMATION IN CENTRAL KALIMANTAN

After the "Million Hectare" Project

JOHN MCCARTHY

At the time of the widespread interethnic conflict in Central Kalimantan during March 2001, more than one report evoked the classical image of the frontier, comparing the province to the Wild West. The frontier is characteristically a physical place in rapid transition. Frontier areas tend to have low population densities and high rates of in-migration; the organs of the central state tend to be weak and consequently the law an abstract concept. Different actors compete to establish claims over the abundant natural resources that are up for grabs in a frontier context. Accordingly, violent conflicts can erupt between actors—indigenous people, pioneer farmers, bureaucrats, loggers, miners, and developers—attempting to secure their claims over natural resources.[1]

Transformative Processes in Central Kalimantan

Consequently, as Schmink and Wood (1992) have noted, the frontier has rich metaphorical meanings. The frontier can be viewed as reflecting both a division between competing claims over resources and a conflict over alternative definitions of what actually constitutes a "resource." For "what are considered 'natural' resources are in fact social as well as natural; they are products of historically contingent sociocultural definitions just as much as they are products of biogeochemical processes."[2] As states, corporations, migrants, and customary landowners assert their claims over a resource, they advance alternative definitions of the value of native forest, the worth of indigenous cultural practices compared to modern technology, and the legitimacy of alternative forms of land tenure. In other words, occurring in contexts of institutional pluralism, the conflict over resources at the frontier is as much as anything a struggle over the discourse and the legal regime that defines and gives value to particular patterns of resource use.

Although a frontier "can be figurative, temporal or spatial," the "frontier" has historically also served to delineate a binary opposition between "secure tenure, freehold ownership, and State-guaranteed rights to property" and "uncertain and undeveloped entitlements, communal claims, and the absence of State guarantees to property" (Blomley 2003, 124). By separating statutory forms of property considered "legal" and modern from their antithesis (forms of property relations associated with ambiguity and uncertainty and hence too often conflict), legal property discourse plays a foundational role in "the construction of a constitutive outside to property and its violence" (Blomley 2003, 124). This frontier metaphor obscured the specific circumstances in which the dualism of statutory and customary property emerged. Processes of alienation and enclosure have historically (and more recently in this case) depended on various forms of explicit, implied, or structural violence that underwrite processes of expropriation and transfer of resource rights (Blomley 2003). Is it surprising that "frontiers" tend to be associated with conflict?

This chapter considers the specific case of Central Kalimantan's southern peat forests, a frontier area renowned during the 1990s for Suharto's "Million Hectare" Peat Land Development Project (Project Pengembangan Lahan Gambut, or PLG). Encompassing an area of 1.7 million hectares lying between the Java Sea to the south, the Sebangau

River and Palangkaraya to the west, the Barito River to the east and the proposed Palangkaraya-Buntok road to the north (Herman 1998), this megaproject aimed to convert one million hectares of peat swamp forest to rice and other crops. After these peatlands went up in flames ecologists have estimated that the fires released at least one billion tons of carbon, adding "about 0.5 parts per million carbon dioxide to the atmosphere." This is the equivalent of "an estimated ten years of carbon fixation by all of the world's pristine peat bogs" or "more than that released by the fossil fuels the European Union burns in a year" (Rieley 2001, 16). Considering the environmental costs together with the social and economic costs, PLG has been considered one of the great environmental disasters of the twentieth century (Ginting 2000).

PLG represents a particular local transformation of the peat forest frontier of Central Kalimantan, but it also fits into a set of wider tenurial transformations occurring in outer island Indonesia. Before proceeding further, it is important to consider schematically the general dynamics shaping this transformation. First, as technology and infrastructure develops, there is a change in the resources that actors can extract from or utilize in an area. Second, as this gives rise to new market opportunities, there is a shift in what is valuable and hence worth extracting or otherwise using. Third, state policies and laws that have long provided for the assertion of eminent domain, enabling the allocation of lands to plantations, tend to be used in new ways to support national development strategies that reflect and reinforce these changes. Of course, what passes for national development, particularly during the Suharto period, tended to be colored by the interests of the politico-bureaucrats at the apex of the state and the corporate actors on whose "generosity" the wheels of a clientelist system turn. In this context, like the parallel lines of a railway, national development strategies that depend on revenue generation run alongside capital accumulation strategies. Fourth, these changes entail a series of redefinitions. Areas to be exploited need to be mapped in accordance with state planning categories, a process that reifies property, replacing a native place "dense with meanings, stories and tenurial relations" with an abstract space, the process thereby making it available for enclosure and privatization

(Blomley 2003, 129). As this is worked through legal categories, local sociocultural definitions of appropriate uses of resources and indigenous tenurial regimes tend to become invisible, with state law serving as "a form of organized forgetting" (Blomley 2003, 128). Consequently, as these cumulative changes are worked out on the ground, both the landscape and local patterns of resource uses are transformed.

The workings of these dynamics are apparent in the transformative processes typically found in Kalimantan.[3] First, with the rise of markets for timber and the emergence of technologies to exploit forests on a large scale, beginning in the late 1960s the interests of the alliance between politico-bureaucrats and corporate groups focused on industrial logging. State planners facilitated this by redefining large regions—including areas subject to extensive local land uses—as state "forest zone" and granting timber concessions.

Second, as part of the government development strategy, the state also embarked on a large-scale government-administered colonization project, the well-known transmigration program. Transmigration involved both a demographic shift and the emergence of a new form of resource exploitation (Pannell and Benda-Beckmann 1998). It combined the opening of agricultural rice lands in sparsely populated regions with the settlement of farmers from densely populated areas of Java, Madura, and Bali who would form a readily disciplined labor force for the plantations to which many transmigration schemes were twinned. The idea was that these transmigrants would carry agricultural techniques, cultural refinements, and economic entrepreneurship to the "outer islands," thereby indirectly raising the level of development in the periphery. As transmigration entailed replacing extensive swidden and agroforestry systems with intensive wet rice cultivation, it also entailed a redefinition of the optimal form of agriculture.

Third, in the 1980s we see the beginning of a process that had much more significant consequences for local tenurial regimes when the development of private oil palm and timber estates became a particular focus of New Order policy (Casson 2000). At this time the government came to understand the possibilities for revenue generation from tree-crops involving large-scale capital intensive ventures.

Directing investment to oil palm, which was believed to have the highest economic potential of any of the estate crops, the government stimulated the development of large-scale private oil palm plantations and nucleus estate schemes, typically integrated with the transmigration program. This involved attracting domestic and foreign investors by offering access to credit and interest subsidies for the establishment of plantations and associated facilities as well as reclassifying areas of state "forest zone" for agriculture.

With the ongoing depletion of forest resources, during the late 1980s, the state also began to promote the development of timber estates (HTI) with the aim that Indonesia would become the world's largest pulp and paper producer (Gellert 1998). This involved replanting forest areas with a monoculture of quick-growing exotic species. This period also laid the foundation for a boom in palm oil, with large areas allocated for plantation development. However, with these processes occurring simultaneously in the same landscapes, these were not necessarily discrete or uniform processes.

Many of these areas of Central Kalimantan peatlands were subject to local customary (*adat*) tenurial uses. Indeed, the Basic Agrarian Law (UUPA 5/1960) allowed for limited recognition of these customary rights. Beyond the expense and difficulty of obtaining a certificate granting permanent registered property land use rights (*hak milik*), the difficulty that Dayak landholders experienced was that their extensive land uses combined rubber cultivation and other tree crops in more permanent mixed forest gardens with swidden agriculture that involves leaving swiddens fallow for at least five years. Agrarian law stipulates maximum permitted landholdings of twenty hectares for dry land (*ladang*), inadequate for extensive forms of swidden agriculture (JICA and Bappenas 1999). The tenuous customary rights that the agrarian law might afford Dayak landowners were further weakened as the Basic Forestry Act (UU 5/1967) established a state territorialization regime (Tata Guna Hutan Kesepakatan, or TGHK) that allowed for only very limited rights in areas classified as "forest estate." This framework allowed state planners to allocate "forest areas" to agricultural development schemes and timber or oil palm plantations.

Nonetheless, there is a significant difference between the timber concession system, on the one hand, and land clearing for transmigration settlements and plantations, on the other. The timber concession system allowed for the de facto coexistence of overlapping property regimes with local communities and state and commercial interests, in many cases enabling swidden agriculture and the cultivation of tree crops by Dayak farmers to coexist with logging from natural forests for over thirty years. In contrast, the development of plantations or food estates requires much more of a revolution in tenurial relations—not to mention in ecological impacts—replacing the overlapping situation with a more exclusive form of property rights that typically extinguishes long-standing tenurial regimes (JICA and Bappenas 1999). As we shall see, these transformative processes were played out in the peatlands of Central Kalimantan prior to PLG.

Before PLG:
Transforming the Peat Swamp Forests of Central Kalimantan

According to a study conducted during the 1980s, 45,536 square kilometers—or 30 percent of the province—consists of extensive swamp forests, an area lying between sea level and five meters elevation subject to tidal and seasonal flooding.[4] These peat forests are inaccessible and fragile ecosystems that are not well suited to conventional agriculture. In areas behind the coast, layers of peat have developed to a depth of more than fifteen meters. At maximum development, these thick areas of peat form convex or domed surfaces with flattened tops that are the substrate of mature, tall rain forest.

Despite the apparent obstacles to productivity, the Ngaju Dayak resident along rivers in the peat swamps of Central Kalimantan adjusted to these conditions, developing a system of resource management known as *petak danum*. These extensive systems of agriculture, agroforestry, and aquaculture enabled the Ngaju Dayak to sustain low population densities in the apparently marginal peatlands.

A 1997 report into land-use practices in the Mengkatip area (Kecamatan Dusun Hilir, Kabupaten Barito Selatan) described how soils up to one meter deep were found for a distance of about two to three kilometers from the banks of the rivers. Farmers had long found that they could cultivate rice in these shallow soils, planting local varieties of rice adapted to the area and avoiding tilling practices that would disturb underlying peat layers. As rice fields in these conditions tended to be productive for only a few years, farmers followed a natural succession, planting tree crops in former rice fields, including rattan, *purun* (a palm used for weaving mats), and rubber. Ngaju Dayak combined rice agriculture and the cultivation of gardens with fisheries production from managed peat swamp ponds known as *beje*. Further away from the banks, in the area up to approximately three kilometers from the river, lay the lands considered to be the common property resources of the village (*hutan kesepakatan adat*), to which villagers could obtain use rights under *adat* arrangements. Beyond this area lay peatlands ranging from three to twelve meters in depth. Although this land could not be used for gardens or wet rice cultivation, villagers used the area for the production of valuable forest products (Tim Pemantuan Kawasan Konservasi Air Hitam 1997). Similar forms of land use were found across the network of major rivers—the Kapuas, Kahayan, and Barito Rivers—and their tributaries that cut through the peatlands of Central and South Kalimantan (Schlapfer and Marinova 1999). These systems ultimately depended on the extensive peat forest ecosystem for both subsistence and the production of commodities for local and regional markets.

As with other societies in Kalimantan (see, e.g., Colfer and Dudley 1993; Padoch and Peluso 1996), over time the Ngaju had developed customary practices regarding tenure. These recognized individual rights to particular things as well as providing notions of territoriality involving the assertion of common property rights of particular Ngaju groups over specific geographical areas adjacent to their villages.

Local *adat* heads recount that the Dutch colonial regime had taken steps toward recognizing the tenurial rights of the Ngaju over the riverbank areas. For example, in the Mengkatip area, Dutch authorities entered into agreements with the local inhabitants, establishing the extent of the corporate rights of the Ngaju Dayak villages. The Ngaju

Dayak retained rights over three to five kilometers to the left and right of the river, or as far as the sound of a gong could be heard. Beyond this point the land was considered to be the territory of the Dutch colonial state (Wirasapoetra and Nathalia 1998). Contemporary spatial plans continue to distinguish between areas under local tenure along the banks of the major rivers and state "forestry estate" beyond.

However, the situation in the peat forests changed after the late 1960s. At this time the forestry department began granting logging concessions (Hak Pengusahaan Hutan, HPH) to private firms, as one informant observed, transforming Central Kalimantan into the "kitchen of the logging companies."[5] Of the 561 concessions operating in Indonesia in 1990, some 115 logging concessions operated in Central Kalimantan, including 12 concessions in what later became the PLG area (McCarthy 2001a; McCarthy 2001b). These concessions involved the indiscriminate expropriation of lands, including villages, traditional lands, forest gardens, and sacred sites (*keramat*): a forestry map from the 1970s showed that a concession had even been granted over the provincial capital, Palangkaraya. Over ensuing decades, as industrial logging extracted timber from the forests, the ecology of large areas of the province was transformed.

In the Mengkatip area, for instance, as early as 1969 PT Jayanti Group obtained a concession that encompassed the subdistrict (*kecamatan*) of Dusun Hilir, operating in the area for some twenty years. Djajanti, owned by Burhan Uray, was one of Indonesia's biggest timber groups, holding twenty-five concessions covering 2.8 million hectares of forest.[6] PT Jayanti harvested ramin (*Gonystylus*), kapur (*Calophyllum saulatri*), meranti rawa (*Shorea* spp), and jelutung (*Dyera costullata*) from an area where the peat reached up to seven meters in depth. After the initial years, between 1975 and 1982, PT Jayanti subcontracted its timber concession to PT Mengkatip (Tim Pemantuan Kawasan Konservasi Air Hitam 1997). However, by the mid-1990s the logging concessions had exhausted the major timber stocks in the area. At the inception of PLG only five concessions were still active.

Central Kalimantan, including the southern peat forest area, had first received transmigrants during the colonial period. This program was reintroduced during the Suharto period, and the area absorbed 189,977 transmigrants by 1995. During the New Order, transmigrant schemes in the PLG area—some of them already fifteen years old at the time—formed part of an 80,000-hectare swamp reclamation program (Herman 1998; Tim Ahli Pemgembangan Lahan Basah Terpadu 1998).

These transmigration schemes in peat swamp areas had a checkered history. Technocratic planners were slow to learn the lessons offered by traditional farming techniques regarding choice of plants and cultivation methods on marginal soils.[7] Consequently, many sites—especially those in the peatlands—still remained "at the stage of trial and error, and in some cases had failed completely" (Schlapfer and Marinova 1999, 59). Transmigrants unable to eke out an existence cultivating rice on this marginal land using methods imported from Java took up "fugitive strategies," moving up logging roads into areas of forest to open new plots and plant cash crops. When the fertility of a plot began to decline, these farmers shifted from one site to another "without apparent concern for its future productivity" (Abdoellah 1996). Transmigrants also became involved in exploiting surrounding forests, supplying the illegal timber and wildlife trades to survive (SKEPHI 1998). Transmigration created an exploitative "frontier agriculture which leads to partial resource depletion or long-term ecological degradation" (Abdoellah 1996, 277).

State Developmentalism, Accumulative Strategies, and PLG

Rationale

In establishing its legitimacy during the late 1960s, the Suharto administration set about becoming an agent of development. A central part of its efforts to kick-start the process of economic growth in Indonesia through successive five-year plans involved national programs to raise rice production and reduce dependence on imports. In the short term these efforts (mainly achieved through "Green Revolution" technologies) succeeded in moving Indonesia from its status as the world's largest importer of rice during the late 1960s to self-sufficiency in 1984. In 1985 President Suharto proudly accepted an award from the United Nations Food and Agriculture Organization for these efforts (*Tempo* 12 April 1999).

But housing, factories, tollways, industrial complexes, and other development projects during the capital-intensive transformation of the late 1980s and early 1990s diverted large areas of Java's rich agricultural lands to other uses and led to the loss of an estimated 20 percent of its agricultural land, including fertile rice lands for which irrigation had been provided between 1969 and 1985 (*Kompas*, 16 April 1999). These changes—along with increased rice consumption associated with population growth and lost production due to droughts and pest infestations—meant that Indonesia began importing rice once again. In 1995, in commemorating World Food Day, the FAO listed Indonesia among eighty-eight nations threatened by food shortages (Tim Teknis KepPres RI. No. 82/1995 1995).

The loss of rice self-sufficiency undermined New Order legitimacy and Suharto's credentials as "the father of development." On 5 June 1995, Suharto responded with a new strategy to expand rice production by 5.1 million tons annually, by designating an area of 5.8 million hectares in Central Kalimantan for conversion to rice production.[8] As Suharto demanded that the first harvest occur in time for the 1997 presidential elections, work needed to begin immediately.

Well-connected corporate groups became partners in the design and implementation of PLG. With headquarters in Singapore and former generals and New Order figures with links to Suharto sitting on its board of directors, the Sambu Group had significant plantation interests. The proposal for peatland development originally came from the director of Sambu Group's PT Sumatera Timur, Tay Juhana. PT Sumatera Timur had earlier developed a successful oil palm plantation on 60,000 hectares of peat soils. After visiting Riau to see the project firsthand, Suharto asked PT Sumatera Timur Indonesia to produce a concept for a megaproject involving wet rice agriculture on peat soils. The governor of Central Kalimantan at this time, Warsito Rasman, lobbied persistently to obtain the project for Central Kalimantan, guaranteeing that his province would be able to provide the land (*Kompas,* 8 April 2000).

Alongside the developmental discourse that underpinned the project by providing the proclaimed rationale—rice production—lay a second unstated objective. Timber interests close to Suharto had invested heavily in the capital-intensive pulp and paper sector, developing production capacities in sawn wood, plywood, and pulp industries, and creating a demand for logs and fiber that substantially exceeded the timber supply produced from timber concessions that were by now often heavily logged over. To support these highly leveraged business ventures, the politico-bureaucrat patrons of these corporate groups needed to take steps to source timber. The PLG project would involve clear-cutting a million hectares of peat swamp forest that would generate large amounts of timber (Barr 2000, 9).

Redefinitions

In manipulating the ecological and social "facts" in the area, PLG planning once again engaged in a process of "organized forgetting." A planning document prepared by the cabinet team implementing the project revealed that the area was suited for the project because:

1. "it represents one area" (*hamparan*);
2. the land is suitable for food crop agricultural cultivation, horticulture, and plantations;
3. it does not represent a protected area or limited production area;
4. it does not represent an area that is already owned or already cultivated by local people and it is not an area that is already used for settlement or other uses. (Tim Teknis KepPres RI. No. 82/1995)

This way of seeing the peatlands of Central Kalimantan ignored the obvious ecological features of the area revealed by decades of attempts to transform peatlands into permanent rice land. Peat soils lack essential nutrients such as silicon, copper, magnesium, potassium, and phosphorous, are highly acidic, and will become toxic under certain conditions. Reclaiming this type of land for agricultural development can generate toxic, unproductive acid sulphate soils. Consequently, implementation of peat conversion projects present considerable technical, engineering, and other problems that require very careful consideration and preparation. In particular, sustainable water management and amelioration of soil fertility in order to allow crop-production of any significance present far more important and difficult problems than the technical work of preparing the drainage ditches and dykes.

This "re-seeing" of the peatlands as potential rice lands also involved redefining the area in terms of the state's planning categories. In order to facilitate land conversion, the Ministry of Forestry needed to cancel its stated intention to "rehabilitate" the area of the forestry estate, release the area from the "forest zone" and set in motion the process of granting forest usage permits (IPK) (Bappeda Propinsi Daerah Tingkat I Kalimantan Tengah 1996). These plans also contradicted existing forestry and spatial planning laws, which protected peat areas deeper than three meters.[9]

Indeed, in accordance with the spatial planning act, the district governments in Barito Selatan and Kapuas had already completed elementary regional spatial plans (Rencana Tata Ruang Wilayah Kabupaten, RTRWK) before the inception of PLG. However, in classic top-down fashion, Bappeda Planning Department offices in both districts had to revise their district RTRWK plans recategorizing areas irrespective of their physical conditions, including approximately 473,700 hectares of the PLG area containing peat greater than three meters in thickness (*Kompas,* 8 May 2000).

Furthermore, this process disregarded local tenurial regimes. If the principles laid down in the spatial planning were rigorously applied, local people would participate in the preparation of spatial plans and would receive "fair compensation for any loss suffered arising from the implementation of development activities complying with the spatial plan" (UU 24/1992, §4). To be sure, the project plan did set aside some one to three kilometers of "green belt" river corridors along major rivers in accordance with the law. However, this did not adequately accommodate extensive areas of deep peat or protect existing rattan and rubber gardens, local rice fields, and fishponds (Herman 1998, 5) that were destroyed to make way for the Mega Rice project. Nor did local communities receive compensation for areas already cultivated or otherwise used and now to be transformed into rice fields, irrigation canals, and transmigrant settlements.

PLG involved imposing what the state considered an optimal form of agriculture—wet rice cultivation—on the area. For, as indicated in a PLG report, planners considered the existing pattern of land use deficient, because of what they considered to be the lack of farming capacity among local communities (Bappeda Propinsi Daerah Tingkat 1 Kalimantan Tengah 1996, 1).

In other words, the peat swamp lands of Central Kalimantan represented a frontier area—or what Scott has called a "nonstate space"—where the population was sparsely settled and maintained a traditional extensive form of agriculture that limited "the possibilities for State appropriation." PLG would transform this area into a "state space" of regularly settled communities producing a surplus of rice that could be appropriated by the state (Scott 1998).[10]

PLG also involved an expansion of this state-funded and -administered colonization project, with planners originally aiming to settle 1.7 million transmigrants. In the past, transmigration entailed bringing in farmers practicing the state planners' preferred model of agriculture—*sawah* cultivation—and hoping that these methods would diffuse into surrounding communities (Dove 1985). However, during the 1990s, transmigration schemes had shifted toward recruiting the local population. It was originally envisaged that 60 percent of the transmigrants involved in PLG would be local people. However, PLG ignored indigenous sociocultural definitions of what could or should be exploited. Local people familiar with the agroecology of the area and the fate of previous transmigrant schemes in the peatlands were reluctant to join the project. As sustenance allowances and new housing were offered to smallholders agreeing to join the project, 20 percent of the 54,000 transmigrants that became involved were "local transmigrants" (*Kompas,* 8 May 2000).[11]

Implementation

Writing of other tragic episodes of state-initiated social engineering, Scott has observed (1998) that such "developmentalist" projects are characteristically driven by a modernist ideology that placed unbounded faith in "scientific and technical progress, the expansion of production, the growing satisfaction of human needs, the mastery of nature . . . and, above all, the rational design of social order commensurate with the scientific understanding of natural laws." This ideological perspective leads to disaster because it is "uncritical, unskeptical, and thus unscientifically optimistic about the possibilities for the comprehensive planning of human settlement and production" (Scott 1998, 4). The possibility of catastrophe is exacerbated when it is an authoritarian state that has resolved to embark on such an ideologically driven program. This is because authoritarian states suppress the criticism that might otherwise check an ill-advised development project.

In many respects, PLG presents a caricature of high modernist planning. Behind the rhetoric of technocratic planning and its articulation in planning documents justified in legalistic terms, Suharto had made a political decision: political considerations totally eclipsed technical planning. As a report in *Tempo* (12 April 1999) noted, the project exemplified the excesses of top-down, centralist planning. The principle of pleasing the superior—"as long as the boss is happy" (*asal bapak senang*)—governed implementation, ensuring that lower-level officials with considerable knowledge of the problems facing PLG were too afraid to raise any questions. A scientific expert from the World Bank who visited PLG in 1998 stated that "political forces" beyond the control of those government officials charged with carrying out the project had accelerated implementation, forcing a project timetable on these officials against their professional judgment (Herman 1998, 9). Planning and decision making against the evidence on this scale involved the exertion of power expressed in control of land and ideas by an authoritarian and highly centralized state. As an official in Bappeda's Kuala Kapuas office later reported:

> We couldn't say anything at the time. . . . When they took photos from the air during the planning stage, they didn't see the villages on the river or people's gardens. It was taken as empty land.[12]

As it was not possible to contradict or even delay Suharto's plans, technical considerations were pushed aside. In January 1996 work began on the infrastructure before the planning process was completed. PLG proceeded without cost-benefit analysis, engineering studies, or effective environmental impact assessments.

In large state-initiated social engineering projects of this type, planners can more readily believe a plan is efficient and rationally organized if it looks "regimented and orderly in a geometrical sense" (Scott 1998, 4). Ironically, while planners can develop attractive design documents, a project itself can be badly designed. A major component of PLG involved building a system of canals through the whole area, including dual primary canals linking the Kahayan, Barito, and Kapuas Rivers and a series of north-south main canals. The project designers envisaged that the main canals would feed fresh water, through gravity supply, to rice fields "outside the range of tidal fluctuation" (Herman 1998, 2). However, construction of the primary channels cut through deep peat areas, including peat domes eleven meters above the surrounding areas. This caused oxidization of organic matter, acid formation, and drying out of the peat, leading the peat to rapidly subside and decompose, making the area subject to drought and flood, as well as increasingly prone to fires. As the drainage system had not been built in accordance with the soil and topography, it would not be possible to irrigate most of the area designated for agriculture. At the same time, large quantities of acidic water displaced from the peat areas reduced the suitability of the area for agriculture and killed off fish life in surrounding rivers (Herman 1998, 1–2).

Corruption and the misuse of state funds marked implementation to the extent that the national weekly *Tempo* later described the project as a "money party" (*pesta uang*) (*Tempo,* 12 April 1999). Huge state investments reduced the incentive for efficient planning and implementation because, with large benefits derived from involvement in the project, those involved would not bear the cost of failure. The project cost US$2 to 3 billion (at 1995 exchange rates). In another twist of irony, PLG derived Rp 527 billion of its costs from the "reforestation fund," with the remainder paid from the state budget. When government departments let contracts for the opening of the forest, the development of secondary channels, housing for transmigrants and agricultural equipment, the development of rice fields, and the development of irrigation, the process occurred without tendering, through a subcontracting process "colored with practices of unrestrained corruption" (*Tempo,* 12 April 999). For instance, subsidiaries of Bob Hasan's (Suharto's golfing partner) Nusamba Group obtained the contracts for developing topographical maps and preparing equipment for the transmigrants. When the state funded the digging of channels into the peat swamps, it subsidized access to otherwise inaccessible strands of valuable peat swamp timber, including ironwood (*ulin*), *ramin,* and *meranti* trees (*Kompas,* 8 May 2000). More than ten powerful timber companies pocketed the IPK permits given out by the forestry department to clear-cut the forest or subcontracted IPK operations from the state forestry company Inhutani III (*Tempo,* 12 April 1999). Major corporate beneficiaries included the Barito Pacific Timber Group, the Jayanti Group, subsidiaries of the Salim Group, and PT Tante Mario, a branch company of Humpus Group owned by Tommy Suharto (Rijksen 1998).

Land clearance utilized fire, the cheapest method. In the dry conditions generated by the El Nino event of 1997–98, these fires readily spread through the drained peatlands, destroying remaining community rubber and rattan gardens. By August 1997, satellite images showed that the whole PLG area was covered by dense smoke and haze. Through the thick haze, satellite photos revealed that nearly all of the vegetation and peatland in the project area and near the river was burning (Boehm 1998).

Impact on Communities

During late 1997 a team of NGO fieldworkers visited an area of small tributaries, deep peat, and small lakes between the Kahayan and Barito Rivers sandwiched between the Mengkatip and Mantangai Rivers. In 1996 this area found itself located in Zone A of the project, 305,195 hectares slated for immediate conversion. The environmental impact assessment (AMDAL) carried out early in the project implementation stage had identified the ecological value of the black-water area of very deep peat found along this river, creating a conservation corridor along the Mengkatip River and a section of the Mantangai River (Herman 1998). Nevertheless, in 1996 the state timber company PT Inhutani III obtained forest use permits (IPK) over the area and subcontracted these to PT Rente Mario and a number of other timber operators. In 1996 migrants from Banjarmasin and from the downstream towns had moved into Mengkatip area, working directly for timber companies with the IPK licenses or supplying timber to contractors developing transmigration sites.

This encompassed the resource base of the Dayaks in the Mengkatip area. Using fire to clear the land, contractors burned down community rattan gardens. The opening of the canals to drain the peat area depleted the river system, undermining the village fishery. In the absence of compensation for lost livelihoods, the Dayak were left with no choice but to take up logging, adopting opportunistic strategies and becoming heavily involved in the unfettered logging of surrounding forests (Tim Pemantuan Kawasan Konservasi Air Hitam 1997).

In 1997 timber companies, together with the in-migrants and local villagers, busily extracted the timber from peat forests. The company laid train rails along the floor of the peat forest, using large amounts of timber extracted from the forest for sleepers. Loggers would take the logs out in rail carts to temporary collection points at the intersection between rail branches. Some of these rail networks were very extensive. Villagers in the Mengkatip area reported that in 1997, without counting the length of branch railways, PT Tante Mario had developed a thirty-kilometer railway in its IPK concession. Logging crews then took the logs down these railways to log ponds on the banks of the tributaries, tied them together in lines, and towed them by motor boat down to the Mengkatip, Barito, and Mentangai Rivers. From here workers deposited the logs in large log ponds before loading them onto ships for transportation to port. Alternatively, logging teams unloaded the logs at local sawmills for direct processing (Tim Pemantuan Kawasan Konservasi Air Hitam 1997). During this time scores of sawmills began operations along the rivers and tributaries of southern Central Kalimantan.

In addition to the formally legal operations of companies with valid IPKs, a parallel extralegal network of timber extraction developed, similar to that found elsewhere (McCarthy 2006). From the beginning of 1996, community loggers worked along the black-water conservation corridor, selling the timber to brokers. The team of fieldworkers calculated that, at the end of 1997, 1,000 people were carrying out this logging in the Mengkatip area alone, producing an estimated 100,000 logs per month. Timber brokers would provide advances to loggers in the form of food or cash, or buy the timber directly from villagers. Timber brokers connected to companies would buy *ramin,* one of the most valuable varieties of timber, from loggers for Rp 72,000/cubic meter, while *ramin* could be sold in Banjarmasin for at least Rp 700,000/cubic meter (Tim Pemantuan Kawasan Konservasi Air Hitam, 1997, 12).

A complex timber trade operated in the area. Stretching from this chain of buyers and sellers that had previously operated in the area, villagers and in-migrants logging outside legal concessions were connected with timber companies protected by HPH or IPK permits. This network had become increasingly active after the inception of the PLG project in 1996. Along the river, transactions occurred openly on rafts, traditional schooners (*pinisi*), and pontoons, as though the timber had been produced legally. Entrepreneurs in the ports, funded by financiers from the timber companies, placed orders with local loggers for timber to be sent to Banjarmasin, Sampit, or Palangkabun or further afield to Surabaya and Jakarta. These transactions occurred in collusion with district and provincial forestry staff, local military officers, the police, and other local government staff. As these officials received extralegal payments on a regular basis, loggers had early warning in advance of any law enforcement actions, and cases of illegal logging were "solved" in local coffee shops (Tim Pemantuan Kawasan Konservasi Air Hitam, 1997, 12).

Aftermath

Plagued by these problems at the time Suharto was forced from office, the project had not met its stated agricultural objectives. President Habibie put the project on hold in 1998, and finally canceled it in July

1999. In August 1999, the forestry department revoked all the timber use permits (IPK). At its conclusion, the project had prepared 70,000 of the projected million hectares for agriculture. However, the engineering failures left upstream areas drought-stricken in the dry season and flooded in the wet. This, together with the fires that destroyed rattan and *purun* gardens, ensured that the livelihoods of Dayak people over a wide area virtually collapsed (*Kompas*, 7 July 2000).

As a plague of rats infested the area, the agricultural efforts of many transmigrants were unsuccessful, and the period of government support ended in December 1999. Subsequently, the transmigrants who had settled in the southern swamplands faced considerable hardship (*Banjarmasin Post*, 18 August 2000). Even the transmigrants who had succeeded in harvesting their crops faced problems. The high price of taking agricultural products to market and the poor demand in local cities meant that many crops were left rotting in the fields (*Kompas*, 7 August 2000). After the end of the project, transmigrants—alongside the local population whose productive lands had been destroyed—were largely left to their own resources. Although many returned to their places of origin, others left destitute by the project took up fugitive strategies, continuing to engage in logging of surrounding forests (Yayasan Betang Borneo and Netherland Committee for IUCN 2000). The channels constructed during the project have become conduits along which people gain access to the interior. As a result, during 1999 all remaining timber was being removed (Rieley 1999).

In response, during 1999 the Dayak communities began taking action, demanding compensation from the central government and threatening to force the transmigrants to leave if these demands were not met (*Banjarmasin Post*, 17 February 1999). Over that year the numbers of people claiming compensation continued to climb. With the government facing 34,000 legal claims amounting to Rp 300 billion for lost property and lost opportunity of income, a long bureaucratic process began to check the authenticity of these claims and work out a compensation process (Muhamad 2001).

In March 2001, the conflict between ethnic Madurese and indigenous Dayak groups spread from neighboring Sampit and Palangkaraya into the PLG area, leading to house burning, an unknown number of deaths, and the ethnic cleansing of Madurese by Dayak groups. Various accounts found the root of this Dayak-Madurese conflict in a cocktail of problems. These include the systematic "denial of Dayak land and resource rights," the marginalization of Dayak groups, the erosion of informal and traditional authority systems, including institutions for managing conflict, and the perception of powerlessness among Dayak unable to compete with "aggressive" Madurese in-migrants (*Down to Earth* 2001).[13] As in the neighboring province, such grievances may have set the context for ethnic mobilization (Davidson and Henley 2007), but local actors jockeying for power during a phase of intense local political competition under regional autonomy seem to have initiated the mobilizations that provided the point of combustion (Klinken 2002).

At the same time, PLG had transformed rural producers into a labor force that depended on forest clearing, instead of forming an agricultural population of transmigrants and indigenous landowners tied to rice production. It had created a large-scale illegal logging system, leading to a phase of resource opportunism where local villagers and in-migrants join in logging on an increasingly uncontrolled and large scale.

By 2000 most of the PLG area had been logged and cleared, leaving a devastated landscape approximately the size of Northern Ireland (Rieley 1999). After the timber was exhausted from the PLG area, loggers moved west into a large neighboring area of peat swamp forest between the Sebangau and Katingan Rivers. An aerial survey of this vast landscape in 1999 found sixty-six locations where loggers—using logging skids, small canals, and huts visible from the air—were extracting timber inside this area of production forest (Rieley 1999). This was occurring in an area where most official timber concessions had expired. Rafts of logs were towed down the Sebangau River to a pocket of sawmills that lined the banks along a stretch of river. A local government official interviewed in Kuala Kapuas during August 2000 reported that, although there were too many sawmills here to estimate accurately, the number ran to over a hundred.[14] Another report noted that at least 125 sawmills were operating in the Sebangau estuary. As each sawmill was able to produce between 20 and 30 cubic meters of sawn timber each day, the report estimated that no less than 2,000–3,000 cubic meters of timber were being produced daily (Yayasan Betang Borneo and Netherland Committee for IUCN 2000).

Some five years later the logging epidemic rapidly abated when the new president, Susilo Bambang Yudhoyono, embarked on a high-profile crackdown. In 2005 police operations reportedly had an immediate impact on illegal logging (Soetjipto 2005). Although these operations characteristically did not succeed in netting the leaders of the major timber networks, higher transaction costs for illegal logging networks due to police enforcement, combined with the increasing scarcity of timber and government persuasion, convinced those with capital in timber operations to move into other booming sectors of the economy, principally oil palm.

Earlier, under the Habibie government, a proposal had emerged to expand PLG by developing a total of 2.8 million hectares of surrounding peatland. Known as the "Integrated Economic Area within the Kapuas, Kahayan and Barito Catchments" (Kapet Das Kakab),[15] the project favored oil palm and rubber development, justifying the "removal of a further half million hectares of pristine peat swamp forest, as well as to launder money to certain business enterprises and government officials under the guise of land clearance, infrastructure provision and planting incentives" (Rieley 2001). The cancellation of Kapet under President Wahid then "created a vacuum of indecision" where other land development schemes were able to emerge (Rieley 2001). Into this vacuum stepped district governments that had gained discretionary authority over key permits under regional autonomy, including over *izin lokasi*. As these "location permits" were the first step in obtaining thirty-five-year plantation concessions, pocketing one effectively provided a plantation company with a development option over an area. The price for palm oil boomed at a time when Indonesia was projected to emerge as a major global player in the biofuel markets (FAO 2008). With large areas reserved by state planners for oil palm, Central Kalimantan became a strategic frontier for oil palm development. Investor interest led to a race to obtain these *izin lokasi*. By July 2008, governments had issued 334 plantation permits over an area reaching 4.2 million hectares. With some 130 plantations already in production, there were now said to be 204 permits issued over areas yet to come into operation.[16] While the provincial government sought to have dormant ("sleeping") permits canceled, the districts with the most suitable land were now unable to allocate new land to investors.[17]

While state plans to "revitalize" the PLG area hardly proceeded due to lack of funding,[18] in 2007 Susilo Bambang Yudhoyono issued a presidential instruction (Inpres),[19] directing that 1.1 million hectares of the PLG peat area should be conserved and returned to its original status. The remaining 300,000 hectares would be allocated to agricultural production, with only 10,000 hectares to be allocated for oil palm. By now, district governments (Pulang Pisau, Kapuas, and Barito Selatan) in the ex-PLG area had issued location permits for oil palm and rubber over 369,400 hectares and mining licenses over a further 41,536 hectares.[20] And as the minister of national planning remarked, development permits already issued could not be canceled.[21] Although district governments and plantations sought to defend existing permits, it was alleged that location permits continued to be issued for some time.

With claims to property a stimulus to popular mobilization, during the "vacuum of indecision" described earlier new community-based initiatives also emerged. These included Yayasan Petak Danum (YPD), a local organization working with the Dayak farmer groups whose livelihoods had been displaced by PLG. Despite limited resources, by 2008 YPD had reconstructed 125 hectares of sawah, planted 2,000 rubber trees, 100,000 rotan seedlings, and 50,000 forest trees. These efforts aimed to meet the aspirations of local Dayak to reconstruct their livelihoods. In parallel with these efforts, Wetlands International helped local farmer groups create small-scale dams (*tabat*) over 20,000 hectares. The *tabat* causes water to well up in PLG channels, in the process reconstituting the ecological function of surrounding peat and facilitating the re-creation of village gardens and fisheries.[22]

In parallel with these efforts, The Borneo Orangutan Survival Foundation (BOS) began working what had been PLG's E Block, which originally encompassed 377,000 hectares. This area of deep peat retained a relatively high level of biodiversity and approximately 3,000 wild orangutans. BOS has proposed that this area of the PLG area be transformed into Mawas National Park, a scheme that competes with various oil palm and timber plantation plans. However, the six leaders of the *adat* areas (*kedamangan*) encompassed by the Mawas proposal have publicly repudiated it on the grounds that it was developed without the consent of the customary landowners, that it would eliminate *adat* property rights and negatively affect the continuation of existing livelihoods. In the meantime, while the legal status of BOS's 280,000-hectare conservation area had not been settled, BOS activities had already led to conflict. According to an open letter from the six *damang* (customary leaders) to BOS, the project has caused "unrest" among the communities who have been intimidated by BOS's use of police and the army to prohibit them from entering the area enclosed by Mawas to fish and collect forest products.[23]

During 2008 a working group involving the Departments of Agriculture, Forestry, and Public Works, the National Planning Agency (BAPPENAS), and the provincial government developed a master plan for the rehabilitation of the degraded peatlands and for a pilot Reducing Emissions from Deforestation and Degradation (REDD+) project.[24] Given that the PLG site still comprised such an enormous carbon sink, and that the areas had emitted enormous amounts of greenhouse gases, the PLG site was an obvious target for an REDD+ scheme. A large AusAID program, working with international NGOs and provincial agencies, has been developing carbon sequestration and forest conservation projects. In the meantime, BOS has already explored a Carbon Offset Agreement with Shell Canada and attained a provisional agreement from the Ministry of Forestry in Jakarta (Smitt n.d.).

The government regulation (PP No. 6/2007) that provides a legal basis for REDD+ pilot projects authorizes provincial and district governments to issue licenses, including permits for storing and absorbing carbon in production and protection forests. It is envisaged that this will allow large landholders and leaseholders, including actors with oil palm and timber concessions, to obtain licenses for the sale of carbon stocks in their areas. At the same time a draft forestry ministry regulation for implementing REDD+ places authority for REDD+ firmly in the hands of the Ministry of Forestry. Critics have argued that the emerging REDD+ policy framework continues to work on the assumption of the state right of control over areas mapped in the national forestry estate, maintaining that this may well allow "those wishing to implement REDD initiatives" to "ignore Indigenous Peoples and local community rights," in the process further marginalizing customary landowners (Anderson and Kuswardono 2008, 5). Noting that Payment for Environmental Services schemes have impacted negatively on land reform programs and campaigns for recognition of indigenous title in other countries, land rights advocates worry that Indonesia's REDD+ program will complicate efforts to redress the critical tenurial challenges facing customary landowners (Anderson and Kuswardono 2008). With framework laws still in contention, it remains unclear how REDD+ initiatives will recognize the entitlements of customary landowners, settle outstanding claims to resources locked up in areas mapped as "forestry estate," or resolve new disputes that may emerge if REDD+ programs are unable to deal with the problem of overlapping property rights.[25]

Pricing the carbon sequestered in these peat swamps and assigning property rights to them appears to be a novel turn. It might be argued that, in key senses, this "commoditisation of nature" continues earlier processes involving the enclosure and privatization of lands (Nevins and Peluso 2008, 19). Nonetheless, it does prefigure a further transformation of the PLG area as an enclosed "natural site" where carbon is conceptually abstracted from its specific local context and traded internationally for the sake of preserving the "global commons."

This turn may yet provide effective incentives for conservation to land managers, creating a carbon store and active carbon sink, and halting the fires from dried-out peatlands that can release fifty tons of carbon per hectare. Further, these schemes could channel the benefits of international carbon trading to local communities. Yet the challenges, as in other cases, include procedural complexity, lack of integrated institutional arrangements between the different actors and agencies involved, deficiencies in organizational capacity within the state and civil society, and the underlying conflicted property system (Kosoy, Corbera, and Brown 2008). The new initiatives will need to ensure that the legal framework works for, rather than against, local landowners lacking the formal land tenure rights to access payments. The challenge will remain that of breaking out of past sociopolitical and legal patterns to ensure that the Ngaju Dayak do not experience the trade in carbon credits as yet another process involving "outright theft of their land, resources and sovereignty" (Nevins and Peluso 2008, 18).

* * *

The transformation in the southern peatlands of Central Kalimantan illustrates a wider process where the emergence of new state development strategies occurs alongside changing political structures, clientelist networks, capital accumulation strategies, and international pressures. With struggles and contests turning on issues of land and resource rights, property and social relations exist in dynamic interaction, ensuring that tenure cannot be considered "a static, pre-given entity, but depends on a continual, 'active doing.'"[26] This means that state and corporate strategies alter with the changing utility of local resources (including for conservation and environmental services), necessitating a continued reworking and reapplication of state notions of territoriality and tenure developed to control access to productive resources pertaining to the same "nature." This "active doing" can also encompass renewed local responses to mobilize people, develop community organization, resist dispossession, and create more productive and potentially sustainable agro-ecological futures.

The Central Kalimantan experience parallels transformations elsewhere. Historically, the "expropriation of the self-supporting English peasants" during the enclosure of the English commons is the classical example, involving the usurpation of common property supported by "parliamentary forms of robbery" (Glassman 2006, 610). Here the "removal of agricultural producers from the countryside and consolidation of more privatized control over resources," affected changes in property relations, transformations in human-environment relations, and the consolidation of capital (Glassman 2006). In Southeast Asia, colonial regimes also enclosed land "to enable primitive accumulation of various sorts" (Nevins and Peluso 2008, 12). Using laws that created categories of "free," "unencumbered" land, colonial territorialization processes enclosed vast tracts of land and resources as forest and nature reserves and to make them available for commercial agricultural enterprises.

Developments in Central Kalimantan's peatlands both compressed and speeded up these transformative processes. With changing property relations inscribed on the landscape over just a few years, this entailed a physical transformation in perhaps the most dramatic fashion of the epoch. In this process customary landowners with long-standing and ecologically adapted practices were induced to follow in-migrants, changing their labor practices to become opportunistic workers in the short-term extraction of local resources. After the liquidation of extensive forest resources during the rather chaotic transitional period following the resignation of Suharto and the decentralization of authority, the boom in palm oil prices up to late 2008 extended the process of enclosure and plantation development. Now, with global warming and the advent of global markets for environmental services, the peatlands of Central Kalimantan have emerged as the newest frontier for investment, an outcome that will entail once again remapping local landscapes to resituate the ex-PLG area within global carbon markets and state planning categories.

In sum, as in other cases on the island of Borneo, PLG has seen the imagination of a landscape, a forested frontier or tabula rasa of "waste lands" on which, with the implementation of the right policies, improved developmental futures might be inscribed (cf. McCarthy and Cramb 2009; Dove 1983; Colfer and Dudley 1993). Here, the process took rather an extreme form both because of the scale involved and the degree of power and prestige Suharto personally had invested in the project. The latter factor more or less impelled state officials entrusted with planning the project, in the most blatant and dramatic fashion, to reverse the formal processes of evidence-based planning (such as there were) incorporated in state planning and environmental laws that were supposed to avoid planning disasters on this scale. Here, rather than building on existing assessments of the particular situation, or carrying out new ones to anticipate problems, and then ensuring that plans were developed to accord with the area's specific ecological and social characteristics, existing tenurial arrangements were overlooked and areas were remapped to make the landscape accord with the political and economic plans of the president. Subsequently, this work of imagination ran up against reality, culminating in environmental and social disaster. The PLG project set out to transform the tenurial rules and practices specifying who could access and use land and under what conditions on a grand scale. It remains to be seen how current plans to regenerate the peatlands and use them as sink and store of global carbon can deliver a happier outcome for local landowners and ecology alike.

Notes

1. Research for this paper was carried out in Central Kalimantan between 1999 and 2001 in the course of conducting research into decentralization processes in Central Kalimantan for the Centre for International Forestry Research and further research subsequent to this.

2. Freudenbury, Frickel, and Garmaling (1995), cited in Ciccantell (1999).

3. For a similar account, see Mayer (1996).

4. The RePPProT study (JICA and Bappenas 1999).

5. Interview, Palangkaraya, 28 June 2000.

6. "Kalimantan: Pulp and Paper Invasion," *Down to Earth* 32, February 1997.

7. In contrast, later transmigration programs involving oil palm achieved success in many cases (Levang 2003).

8. Although the concept initially projected conversion of 5.8 million hectares of Kalteng's peat swamp forests into rice paddy, this was later scaled down to 1.4 million hectares.

9. A 1990 presidential decision (KepPres No. 32/1990 tentang Pengelolaan Kawasan Lindung) and 1992 Spatial Planning Act (UU No. 24/1992).

10. This parallels similar attempts to develop the Meratus hill people described by A. L. Tsing (1993).

11. While PLG planners originally aimed to settle 1.7 million transmigrants, by 1997 only 54,000 transmigrants had been moved into the area (*Kompas,* 8 May 2000).
12. Interview, official, Bappeda, Kuala Kapuas 28 July 2000.
13. See Klinken (2002).
14. Interview, local government official, 1 August 2000.
15. Kawasan pertumbuhan ekonomi Daerah Aliran Sungai Kapuas, Kahayan dan Barito.
16. 23 July 2008. "Api dalam Sawit." http://budidayak.blogspot.com/2008/07/api-dalam-sawit.html.
17. "Potensi Pengembangan Investasi Perkebunan Provinsi Kalimantan Tengah." http://www.kalteng.go.id.
18. See *Suara Pembaruan,* 6 March 2008.
19. Instruksi Presiden Nomor 2 Tahun 2007 tentang Percepatan Rehabilitasi Dan Revitalisasi Kawasan Pengembangan Lahan Gambut di Kalimantan Tengah.
20. *Kalteng Pos,* 20 October 2008.
21. *Kompas,* 25 September 2007.
22. *Kompas,* 25 April 2008.
23. Peserta Temu Rakyat Pengelola Gambut 2009; Damang Dusun Hilir Jenamas n.d.).
24. See Anderson and Kuswardono (2008).
25. See http://www.downtoearth-indonesia.org/theme/redd?page=3. Accessed 1 May 2008.
26. Blomley (2003) after Rose (1994).

References

Abdoellah, O. S. 1996. "Social and Environmental Impacts of Transmigration: A Case-study in Barambai, South Kalimantan." In *Borneo in Transition People, Forests, Conservation and Development,* ed. C. Padoch and N. L. Peluso, 267–79. Kuala Lumpur: Oxford University Press.
Anderson, P., and T. Kuswardono. 2008. *Report to the Rain Forest Foundation Norway on Reducing Emissions from Deforestation and Degradation in Indonesia.* Jakarta.
Bappeda Propinsi Daerah Tingkat 1 Kalimantan Tengah. 1996. "Pengembangan Lahan Gambut Satu Juta Hektar untuk Pertanian Tanaman Pangan di Kalimantan Tengah." Palangkaraya.

Barr, C. 2000. "Will HPH Reform Lead to Sustainable Forest Management? Questioning the Assumptions of the 'Sustainable Logging' Paradigm in Indonesia." In *Banking on Sustainability: A Critical Assessment of Structural Adjustment in Indonesia's Forest and Estate Crop Industries*. Unpublished manuscript, CIFOR and WWF-International's Macroeconomics Program Office.

Blomley, N. 2003. "Law, Property, and the Geography of Violence: The Frontier, the Survey, and the Grid." *Annals of the Association of American Geographers* 93:121–41.

Boehm, D. V. 1998. "Explanation for the Following 5 Satellite Images." In *The Mega Rice Project Central Kalimantan Indonesia—An Appeal for Intervention to the International Community*. Jakarta: SKEPHI.

Casson, A. 2000. *The Hesitant Boom: Indonesia's Oil Palm Sub-Sector in an Era of Economic Crisis and Political Change*. Bogor: CIFOR.

Ciccantell, P. S. 1999. "It's All About Power: The Political Economy and Ecology of Redefining the Brazilian Amazon." *Sociological Quarterly* 40 (2): 293–315.

Colfer, C., and R. G. Dudley. 1993. *Shifting Cultivators of Indonesia: Marauders or Managers of the Forest?* Rome: Food and Agriculture Organization of the United Nations.

Damang Dusun Hilir Jenamas. (n.d.). "Surat Penolakan Damang Kepala Adat Terhadap Keberadaan BOS MAWAS." http://waseng.wordpress.com/2006/12/01/surat-penolakan-damang-kepala-adat-terhadap-keberadaan-bos-mawas/.

Davidson, J. S., and D. Henley, eds. 2007. *The Revival of Tradition in Indonesian Politics: The Deployment of Adat from Colonialism to Indigenism*. London: Routledge.

Dove, M. R. 1983. "Theories of Swidden Agriculture, and the Political Economy of Ignorance." *Agroforestry Systems* 1:85–99.

———. 1985. "The Agroecological Mythology of the Javanese and the Political Economy of Indonesia." *Indonesia* 39:1–36.

Down to Earth. 2001. "Behind the Central Kalimantan Violence." 49 (May). http://www.downtoearth-indonesia.org/story/behind-central-kalimantan-violence. Accessed 1 May 2008.

———. 2002. "Forestry in the Suharto Era." In *Forests, People and Rights. Down to Earth* Special Report: June 2002. http://dte.gn.apc.org/srf1.htm#cmp.

FAO. 2008. "Biofuels, Prospects, Risks and Opportunities." In *State of Food and Agriculture*. Rome.

Gellert, P. K. 1998. "A Brief History and Analysis of Indonesia's Forest Fire Crisis." *Indonesia* 65:63–85.

Ginting, L. 2000. "Indonesian Forestry: How to Move Forward." The Indonesian Forum for Environment/Friends of the Earth Indonesia, WALHI's Position on the CGI Forestry Meeting, 26 January.

Glassman, J. 2006. "Primitive Accumulation, Accumulation by Dispossession, Accumulation by 'Extra-economic' Means." *Progress in Human Geography* 30:608–25.

Herman, T. 1998. "Million Hectare Swampland Project: Field Visit Observations and Recommendations." World Bank Unpublished Report IBN-DLO (1998). Central Kalimantan Regional Ecological Planning in the Service of Development. Proposal for Expert Support.

JICA and Bappenas. 1999. "The Development Study on Comprehensive Regional Development Plan for the Western Part of Kalimantan SCRDP." Kaltengbar Japan International Cooperation Agency (JICA), National Development Planning Agency (BAPPENAS). Government of Indonesia.

Klinken, Gerry van. 2002. "Indonesia's New Ethnic Elites (Central and East Kalimantan)." In *Indonesia: In Search of Transition,* ed. H. S. Nordholt and I. Abdullah, 67–105. Yogyakarta: Pustaka Pelajar.

Kosoy, N., E. Corbera, and K. Brown. 2008. "Participation in Payments for Ecosystem Services: Case Studies from the Lacandon Rain forest, Mexico." *Geoforum* 39:2073–2083.

Levang, P. 2003. "Ayo ke Tanah Sebrang : Transmigrasi di Indonesia." Jakarta: Kepustakaan Populer.

McCarthy, J. F. 2001a. "Decentralization and Forest Management in Kapuas District." http://www.cifor.cgiar.org/publications.

———. 2001b. "Decentralization, Local Communities and Forest Management in Barito Selatan." http://www.cifor.cgiar.org/publications.

———. 2006. *The Fourth Circle: A Political Ecology of Sumatra's Rainforest Frontier.* Stanford: Stanford University Press.

McCarthy, J., and R. Cramb. 2009. "Policy Narratives, Landholder Engagement, and Oil Palm Expansion on the Malaysian and Indonesian Frontiers." *Geographical Journal* 175:112–23.

Mayer, J. 1996. "Impacts of the East Kalimantan Forest Fires of 1982–1983 on Village Life, Forest Use and Land Use." In *Borneo in Transition,* ed. C. Padoch and N. L. Peluso, 187–218. Kuala Lumpur: Oxford University Press.

Muhamad, N. Z. 2001. "Management of Tropical Peatlands in Indonesia: Mega Reclamation Project in Central Kalimantan." School of Geography, University of Nottingham.

Nevins, J., and N. L. Peluso. 2008. *Taking Southeast Asia to Market: Commodities, Nature, and People in the Neoliberal Age.* Ithaca, NY: Cornell University Press.

Padoch, C., and N. L. Peluso, eds. 1996. *Borneo in Transition: People, Forests, Conservation and Development.* Kuala Lumpur: Oxford University Press.

Pannell, S. N., and F. v. Benda-Beckmann, eds. 1998. *Old World Places, New World Problems: Exploring Issues of Resource Management in Eastern Indonesia.* Canberra Centre for Resource and Environmental Studies, ANU.

Peserta Temu Rakyat Pengelola Gambut. 2009. "PETISI GAMBUT." http:// groups.yahoo.com/group/rimbawan-interaktif/message/2347. Accessed 1 March 2004.

"Potensi Pengembangan Investasi Perkebunan Provinsi Kalimantan Tengah." http://www.kalteng.go.id. n.d.

Rieley, D. J. 1999. *Death of the Peat Swamp Project.* http://www.geog.nottingham.ac.uk/~rieley/Dartrop/dartrop.htm.

———. 2001. "Kalimantan's Peatland Disaster: Greed and Stupidity Destroy the Last Peatland Wilderness, Home to Thousands of Orangutan." *Inside Indonesia* 65, available at http://www.insideindonesia.org/feature-editions/kalimantans-peatland-disaster.

Rijksen, D. H. D. 1998. "Brief on the Mega-Rice Project in Central Kalimantan." In *The Mega Rice Project Central Kalimantan Indonesia—An Appeal for Intervention to the International Community.* Jakarta: SKEPHI.

Rose, C. M. 1994. *Property as Persuasion: Essays on the History, Theory, and Rhetoric of Ownership.* Boulder, CO: Westview Press.

Schlapfer, A., and D. Marinova. 1999. "Tidal Swamp Development in Kalimantan." *Journal of Policy Studies* 7:57–66.

Schmink, M., and C. H. Wood. 1992. *Contested Frontiers in Amazonia.* New York: Columbia University Press.

Scott, J. C. 1998. *Seeing like a State: How Certain Schemes to Improve the Human Condition Have Failed.* New Haven: Yale University Press.

SKEPHI. 1998. "The Mega Rice Project Central Kalimantan Indonesia—An Appeal for Intervention to the International Community."

Smitt, W. n.d. "The BOS 'Mawas' Debt for Nature Swap and Carbon Offset Agreement." http://www.peat-portal.net/view_fileid=273. Accessed 1 March 2004.

Soetjipto, T. 2005. "Indonesia Timber War Misses Top Smugglers—Activists." Jakarta: Reuters.

Tim Ahli Pemgembangan Lahan Basah Terpadu. 1998. "Analisis Kebijakan Pemerintah dan Strategi tentang Proyek Pengembangan Lahan Gambut." Jakarta.

Tim Pemantuan Kawasan Konservasi Air Hitam. 1997. "Lindungilah Ekosistem Air Hitam dari Ancaman Proyek Lahan Gambut (PLG) Satu Juta Hektar di Kalimantan Tengah." Unpublished report. Jakarta.

Tim Teknis KepPres RI.No.82/1995. 1995. "Perkembangan Proyek Pengembangan Lahan Gambut di Propinsi Kalimantan Tengah." Jakarta.

Tsing, A. L. 1993. *In the Realm of the Diamond Queen: Marginality in an Out-of-the-Way-Place*. Princeton: Princeton University Press.

Wirasapoetra, K., and I. Nathalia. 1998. "Pengetahuan Lokal Masyarakat Adat Ngaju dalam Pengelolaan Sumberdaya Alam di Kalimantan Tengah." Seminar Nasional Dampak Lingkungan dan Sosial Proyek Pengembangan Lahan Gambut 1 Juta Hektar Jakarta: Wahana Lingkungan Hidup.

Yayasan Betang Borneo and Netherland Committee for IUCN. 2000. "Tragedy of the Rain forest: Illegal Logging Investigation and Wildlife Monitoring in the River Sebangau Catchment area of Central Kalimantan." Yayasan Betang Borneo and Netherland Committee for International Union for Nature Conservation (IUCN).

Newspapers

Kalteng Pos
Kompas
Suara Pembaruan

Chapter 7

LAND DISPUTES AND THE CHURCH

Sobering Thoughts from Flores

JOHN MANSFORD PRIOR

Land disputes are dramatically on the increase in Flores, and the Catholic Church is closely involved. Land disputes are a vital issue, and not only because land with its natural resources is the foundation of the local economy. Just as important, land, village, and house map out the religious, cosmological, and cultural values of the indigenous people of Flores (Erb 1999; Lawang 1999; Prior 1988; Tule 2004). Land disputes also focus our attention on the globalizing market and the local economies of Flores as they are appropriated by wider commercial concerns. In addition, land disputes reflect a resurgence of local culture and the demand for both dignity and identity by the Florenese peoples. They also might indicate the breakup of the indigenous communities of Flores as we have known them.

In this chapter I examine two cases. In the first I look at a clash between the government and people in Western Flores regarding the use of land claimed by both sides. In the second I turn to the church as landowner and look at a move by indigenous people in central Flores to reclaim land that has been used by the church for over seventy years.

Flores is a long and narrow island, 360 kilometers long and twelve to seventy kilometers wide, mainly mountainous with large forest reserves. Its economy is largely small-scale agricultural with some plantations, especially of coffee. Part of the Province of Nusa Tenggara Timur (NTT), until recently Flores was divided into five districts (*Kabupaten* or regencies).[1] Manggarai in the west has Ruteng as its district capital, and Sikka in central Flores has Maumere. For centuries the coastal regions of Manggarai were claimed by the Sultan of Bima from the neighboring isle of Sumbawa; ties with Bima were formally broken only in the 1920s. There have been smaller settlements of Macassarese and Buginese Muslims in Geliting to the east of Maumere since at least the nineteenth century (Steenbrink 2007, 85–86). After two centuries of rivalry in the area, the Portuguese sold Flores to the Dutch in 1859. The state's role in the subsequent colonization was fairly minimal; it was the Catholic Church that brought the modern world to Flores through schools, health centers, and social outreach. Only in the mid-1970s did the government budget overtake that of the church in social and economic development. The population is predominantly Catholic, with various fusions of local traditional beliefs.

Case One: Outside Interests versus Indigenous Communities

In this clash over land use, ethical principles and ecological rights can be found on each side. The case highlights conflicts involving local people and NGOs versus government, ecology versus economy, local versus global interests, positive law versus *adat,* and the institutional church versus its own members.

Before its division in 2003, Manggarai was the largest regency in the Province of Nusa Tenggara Timur, which is a little over 7,000 square kilometers with a population of about 600,000, of whom nearly 90 percent live from the soil. Fifteen percent of this large upland area of western Flores has inclines above thirty degrees. There is wetland rice cultivation, shifting dryland cultivation, and land for grazing water buffaloes, goats, and cattle. The Forestry Department has classified 40 percent of Manggarai as covered by forest under seven categories: Protected Forest, Forest of Natural Importance, National Park, Tourist

Natural Park, Production Forest, Limited Production Forest, and Conservation Production Forest. Thirty percent is Protected Forest (Tim Advokasi 2003, 1).

In 1937, in consultation with the local population the Dutch authorities declared some 3,000 hectares of Manggarai forest "closed."[2] In 1972 a team was established by the provincial government to redraw forest boundaries. In October 1984 the boundaries of Kuwus forest were extended,[3] thereby encroaching on cultivated land. Documents state that the redrawing was made with the agreement of the local population, but the only fingerprints on the document are those of the administrative village head (*kepala desa*). According to the government, the *kepala desa* signed on behalf of the villagers, but according to the indigenous community a village headman has no right to sign on their behalf, only the traditional village head (*tu'a golo*)[4] and ritual land guardian (*tu'a teno*) can do so after consultation with community members. Nevertheless, on 21 January 1986 these extended boundaries were confirmed by the Minister of Forestry in Jakarta. The villagers claim that the new Protection Forest boundaries do not conform to those agreed to by the Dutch in 1937, and were made without due consultation (Erb 2008, 225–27). As a result of the redrawing, coffee trees planted in the extended Kuwus forest became illegal. Forestry Law No. 41 (1999) became the legal basis for the clearing of the villagers' coffee trees to make way for hardwood reforestation.

For many years indigenous communities in Manggarai have been planting coffee in protected forestry areas, claiming that the land belongs to them. Also, they allege that they received explicit permission in 1977 from the former Bupati of Manggarai, who gave them Forestry Use Rights (Hak Pakai Kawasan Hutan, HPKH) on the condition that 60 percent of produce was handed over to the district administration. The villagers agree that they have not handed over the government's portion for some years.[5]

The alleged deal led to an ambiguous situation whereby the villagers continued to claim the land as theirs by traditional right, while the HPKH could be evidence that their "ancestral lands" in fact belong to the state. Parts of the area now classified as protection forest have been populated and farmed for generations. Cash crops in the forest include cloves, coffee, vanilla, and coconut. Trees more than a hundred years old grow beside banana trees and close to crops such as maize and groundnuts. The villagers also gathered wood, rattan, and medicinal plants. However, the ancestors had declared other areas as sacred and therefore protected (Mirsel 2004, 43–45), and these areas have been maintained uncultivated to date.

The ecology of Flores is fragile, and severe rain erosion is averted only by undergrowth rather than larger trees. For this reason, soil on Florenese hillsides with gradients over forty degrees should never be cultivated (Braman 1991, 5, 8; *Pos Kupang* [hereafter *PK*], 6 November 2003). Crucially, given the geology, geography, and climate of Flores, any form of monoculture, whether the villagers' coffee or the Bupati's teak, is unsuitable for long-term conservation (*PK*, 11 November 2003).

On 14 October 2002, Manggarai Bupati Antony Dagur Bagul[6] signed an instruction (Dk 522.11/1134/10/2002) to implement a reforestation program by the District Forestry Department. He instructed that registered forest areas be cleared of all trees planted by the local villagers in designated areas, and that any villager who opposed the program should be arrested. The first phase of clearance was executed in October 2002, with subsequent phases completed in early December 2003. The department planned to replace the thousands of coffee trees with mahogany, two types of teak, and sandalwood. The coffee was in the hands of the local villagers, but the hardwoods would belong to outside businesses working with government contracts. Six such permits had been signed by the district government in "protected areas" (Walhi 2003, 39). Thus the politics of conservation were supporting capital investment and not the local economy of the farmers' or people's customary rights. Local villagers suspect that coffee trees were being cleared not only in protected areas but also in sites that have been designated as *"wisata alam"* (nature tourist areas), because they contained mineral deposits including magnesium and gold.

The felling of villagers' coffee trees began on the day of the signing of the bupati's instruction, 7 October 2002.[7] The bupati himself was present, as were other members of the Area Leaders Council

(Muspida), comprising senior local government and security officials. The bupati declared, "First, the confiscation of unauthorized chain saws; second, the regulation of wood products such as planks and posts and unauthorized non-wood produce such as candle-wood nuts, rattan, sandal-wood, ebony, cinnamon bark and honey; third, the protection of the forest from the inhabitants who steal wood, unlawfully destroy trees and move the border markers."[8]

A joint team, consisting of the district police chief, military chief, forestry police,[9] subdistrict head, village heads, and officials of Manggarai District, oversaw the implementation of the instruction. The first phase was carried out by a 356-person team (eighty soldiers, fifty police, three personnel from the district public prosecutor's office, eleven from the Agency for the Conservation of Natural Resources (BKSDA) and 212 from the district office (FP 22 October 2002). Also present were *preman* (hired youth gangs) sporting red headbands to show they were ready to fight, and hundreds of students from a state senior high school as a lesson in forestry conservation. Rumors abounded about certain villages whose fields would be exempted, thus raising tension with villages whose trees had already been cut down (*PK*, 6 November 2003).

The head of the District Forestry Department and coordinator of the joint team subsequently explained the three objectives of the total operation: (a) to protect the forest, land, and water by restoring the rights of the state over the forest, which had been irresponsibly encroached upon by the local population; (b) to "sterilize" (*men-steril-kan*) the Protection Forest from the villagers' plants; and (c) to restore the ecology of the forest (cited in Walhi 2003, 25). The Forestry Department head had no problems with the threatened court case brought by Colol village, as he was convinced that he was working within the law, and even that "God's law" was on his side (*PK*, 8 December 2003).

During the first phase in October 2002, some 4,000 hectares of coffee were cut down (*PK*, 21 October 2003) across several subdistricts. By the end of the program in December 2003, nearly 87,000 hectares had been targeted (Mirsel 2004, 47). Several phases of the clearing process have been reported by NGOs.[10] One well-reported case involved about 1,100 hectares of the RTK's 118 forest areas in several subdistricts, when the Colol villagers lost their main source of livelihood. It was claimed that Colol's annual coffee harvest had enabled its expansion from about seventy inhabitants in the 1960s to 2,000 at the time of the dispute, but the district lost an estimated 4,000 tons or 52 percent of Manggarai's recorded annual harvest.[11] One hundred sixty families had their coffee trees cut down, while bananas, avocados, taro, tobacco, beans, and maize were taken by members of the joint team clearing the forest; fifty-one huts were burned; chicken runs were destroyed, and the chickens taken, as were fish from the villagers' ponds. The government was acting "to restore a protected forest area," but the villagers claimed the land as theirs, "the ancestral lands of Colol," an "inheritance from many generations back" (Embu 2004, 114).

The presence of the military meant that, at first, local villagers "could do little but weep" (*PK,* 20 October 2003). A 300-member joint team moved into the Colol area on 6 October 2003. The clearing operation took place over a succession of two to three days, from 14 October to 23 October, in each of several villages, amid protests and the beating up of one of the team. On 22 October around 1,000 people from three villages massed in the forest to thwart further destruction of their coffee trees in the Colol area; their sheer numbers prevented the forestry police from felling more trees.

Public statements, protests, demonstrations, and threatened court action were legion. The Manggarai University Students Alliance Forum (Aliansi Forum Mahasiswa Manggarai, Siomama) and the Socially Concerned University Students Forum (Forum Mahasiswa Peduli Sosial, FMPS) in the district capital Ruteng held a "long march" demanding that Bupati Bagul be "tried in a full session of the District Assembly" (*PK,* 20 October, 30 October, 7 November, and 14 November 2003). Their demands ignored, they briefly "took over" the assembly building a week later. The NTT Islands Indigenous *Adat* Community Movement's Network (JAGAD-NTT)[12] and the Council of the Alliance of Indigenous Peoples of the Archipelago Region (AMAN NTT), released studies and statements. A lawyer and member of the Provincial Assembly in Kupang, Servas Lawang,[13] personally inspected the situation in Colol (*PK,* 4 November 2003) and helped prepare a court case on the people's behalf, which was lodged in Kupang District Court on 8 December 2003 (*PK,* 9 December 2003). The judge concluded that the farmers did not attack the police station, but found them guilty of causing damage.

On the ground in the forest, however, Colol villagers had to struggle largely on their own, with moral support from the parish priest, while up against not only the whole apparatus of the district government but also the hierarchy of their diocese (*PK,* 20 November 2003).[14] Despite protests, the clearing of all the projected areas was completed by the first week of December 2003. As the coffee trees were deemed "illegal" (because located in restricted areas), no compensation was given to the villagers who had lost their main means of livelihood. The district government made no effort to suggest, let alone provide, any alternative sources of income apart from proposing that the affected communities migrate. Some 1,600 families from one area (the Meler-Kuwus) alone have relocated nearby.[15]

The story did not end with the last of the coffee trees felled. On 4 March 2004 a group of officials, some armed, went to two locations to disperse villagers who were collecting wood and cassava on disputed land; the villagers drove them away as the case was still *sub judice*. A few days later the district assembly (DPRD) discussed the issue and recommended that the bupati himself inspect the site. The next day he did so, in a party of nine vehicles, supposedly unannounced. However, word had already reached the area and no one was to be found. The party then went on to Colol, found two women digging up tubers on what they claimed was their land, fired warning shots, and took them into custody. Subsequently a total of seven farmers, four of them women (two mothers, two teenagers), were taken to the police station in the district capital, Ruteng.

The next day villagers gathered in their clan house and decided to go to Ruteng to demand that the seven be freed. Early that morning 120 people in three trucks left, arriving in Ruteng at 9 AM. The police had been warned that 400 were coming. As the villagers were climbing off the trucks, the police fired warning shots, and someone threw some rocks from behind the police station onto its roof. Later the villagers were convinced it was the police themselves who had thrown the stones because the villagers were too afraid even to go into the police compound. The police started firing at the villagers, killing six and wounding twenty-eight others. The regional press reported only the police version, which was supported by both the district government and Ruteng diocese, namely that the police were defending themselves from a savage attack by angry demonstrators (Embu 2004, 248–300).

The police took some internal disciplinary measures against a few individual police, but there was no public court case. The Ruteng police chief was speedily transferred away to the provincial capital, but later promoted. The one police officer later brought to trial in Kupang was freed without condition. The bupati, despite a heavy dose of "money politics," lost the election later that year and has since disappeared from the political scene. A month after "Bloody Wednesday" a team from the National Commission on Human Rights (KomnasHAM) made a five-day visit to investigate the incident. Fifteen months later another team went to Kupang for a three-day visit to establish a Regional Commission of East Nusa Tenggara. The commission's subsequent 700-page report in 2005 concluded that human rights had been seriously violated but also that damage had been committed by the demonstrators, although the contention that they "attacked the police" had not been proven. However, the conclusion that there had been a serious violation of human rights was subsequently watered down in the final plenary meeting of the commission in Jakarta.[16] In 2005 the head of the District Forestry Department was replaced. The new bupati, Christian Rotok, has allowed the farmers to make use of the land again through the community-based forest management (PHBK) program. However, ownership of the land is still in dispute.[17]

Case Two: Church Land in Dispute

The people of Utan Wair village, in the Tana 'Ai region on the northern coast of Sikka District in central Flores, are trying to reclaim about

800 hectares of land that has been used by the church as a coconut plantation since 1926.[18] They also had a dispute with the Forestry Department over two unilateral extensions of a protected forestry area into their claimed *adat* land in 1967 and 1984, which was settled in 2001 when the NTT governor agreed that the forest boundary would revert to that established by the Dutch colonial authority in consultation with the local people in 1932. The conflict with the Ende diocese continues, although elders and indigenous communities seriously differ among themselves over their claims to the land and over the best strategies and tactics to use to get the land back.

The case involves the Soge cultural domain at the western edge of Tana 'Ai where the two villages of Utan Wair and Likong Gete are demanding the return of land that had been granted for long-term commercial enterprise leases (HGU) by the Dutch colonial government and which is leased by the Archdiocese of Ende, and since 2005 by the new Diocese of Maumere.

The Soge people still live partly by shifting cultivation, hunting (wild boar, monkey, deer, and porcupine pig [*babi landak*]), and by handicraft production, in particular *ikat* cloth. The forest is used for building material, rattan, and firewood. However, *adat* taboos protect both the forest and the water supply. Many villagers cultivate the land beneath the diocesan plantation's coconut trees, paying a small rent for each ten square meters (the distance between the trees) plus twelve days of labor a year in the plantation.

The Tana 'Ai clans have their oral historians, whose narratives rely on the inspiration of the ancestors rather than documentary proof. The claim of the Soge ceremonial domain over part of the protected forest, and in particular the claim of Utan Wair village over the diocesan plantation, is based on oral history as well as ancestral graves, ceremonial altars, ritual land markers,[19] and signs of the former village of Liri Watu, all found within the plantation area. Also the presence of groves of trees on the north coast, such as coconut, tamarind, lontar, and mangoes, are cited in support of their claim.

The Soge people claim to have been the first of the twenty-two clans of Tana 'Ai to have arrived in Flores, originating from the Moluccas

(Silamurti and Tasnim 2001). They have a variety of stone altars where they celebrated annual cleansing rituals, fertility rites, and good harvests, and once celebrated war victories. Since 1969 the government and the church have forbidden these *adat* rituals, but they have continued somewhat surreptitiously, with bribing of the government authorities.[20] With the post-1998 political reformation there has been a cultural renaissance and a receding of the fear of being stamped "*kafir*" (unbeliever).[21]

According to the local indigenous community, Raja Nai Roa forcefully pushed the Soge people into the interior,[22] stating that the land of Nangahale was unhealthy (malaria), frequently flooded, and little more than a battleground for the local villages. As they were unwilling to migrate to the hills, Nai Roa, with Dutch connivance, burned down their village. Having thereby cleared the land, in 1912 he leased some 1,450 hectares to a Dutch private company for a coconut and cotton plantation. The cotton failed, and by 1915/16 the plantation was given over entirely to coconuts and has remained so ever since.

In 1926 the company was sold to the Apostolic Vicariate of the Lesser Sunda Islands. Since then the church has gradually subdivided its administration, and what was the vicariate now consists of eight dioceses.[23] The local legal successor to the vicariate, the Archdiocese of Ende, formed the diocesan plantation authority (PT Diag) to manage the plantation. On 5 January 1989 PT Diag obtained the right to use 655 hectares under commercial use rights (HGU) for twenty-five years from the National Land Agency (BPN), that is, until 13 December 2013. In 2005 the area covered by the district became an independent diocese, and ownership of PT Diag passed to this new Diocese of Maumere, although in a continuation of a previous arrangement, some 270 hectares is being used as a farm by St. Paul's Seminary, Ledalero, which is owned not by the diocese but by the Divine Word Missionaries (SVD).

In 1971 the village of Wetak Lahon was burned down when the diocesan plantation cleared away some nearby scrub. The plantation authorities claimed it was an accident. The villagers, who have continued to believe it was deliberate, established a new village, Utan

Wair, in a low-lying area, which is flooded in most years during the monsoons and which experienced serious flooding in 1998.

In December 1991 a major earthquake off the north coast of Flores caused a tsunami that hit the coast and swept over the small island of Babi. The diocesan authorities donated five hectares of the plantation to relocate the survivors. Some of these Bajo (sea gypsy) people subsequently sold their houses and plots to outsiders. Another hectare was rented by the diocese to a private pearl farming company, while fifteen hectares were rented to the Sikka District's Plantation Authority (Dinas Perkebunan) for a hybrid coconut laboratory. Meanwhile, full-time workers on the plantation, all of whom come from outside the Kabupaten, have been granted plots to build permanent housing and cultivate gardens for their families.

In the 1990s Josef Lewor Goban of Likong Gete village took the initiative to establish a number of Lembaga Persekutuan Masyarakat Adat (LPMA) or customary law community organizations, in the central Flores cultural domain of Tana 'Ai.[24] They were intended to represent the *adat* communities to other bodies, including the government bureaucracy. There were four of these LPMA based in Utan Wair, Likong Wete (Josef Goban's village), Runut, and Blidit villages, which collaborated with similar *adat* community organizations across the district border in East Flores. The Utan Wair LPMA spearheaded the attempts to have the diocesan plantation land returned. Such indigenous community organizations were first seen by interested outsiders as part of a more general cultural renaissance. John Bala of the Nusra Legal Aid Society and other NGO activists thought that a new generation of indigenous peoples was rediscovering its cultural identity, as expressed in a certain set of values embedded within a traditional economic and political system. The establishment of the LPMA coincided with the revival of *adat* ritual sites and cycles that had been in abeyance by the people of Utan Wair.

In 1996 representatives of the villages of Utan Wair, Likong Gete, and Runut asked the district head of Sikka to return the Nangahale land and its resources to the Soge people. On 2 February 1997 they wrote to Vice-President Try Sutrisno. Hopes rose two years later when the director general of Public Administration and Provincial Autonomy, on 26 May 1999, asked the NTT governor to settle the dispute. No action was taken.

On 22 March 2000 Josef Lewor Goban, with two other representatives of LPMAs, met with the Sikka District Assembly (DPRD) in the capital, Maumere. A few weeks later three LPMA representatives met the speaker of the provincial assembly who was visiting the district from which he hails. In June the district government invited the minister for environment, Soni Keraf, a Florenese from Jakarta. They listened to the demands of a delegation from Tana 'Ai, but no decisions were made because the ministers insisted on more concrete data. Also in June, a large meeting was held in the district head's conference room between representatives of the provincial and district forestry departments, the district public prosecutor, the sociopolitical affairs office, the military chief, and the chief of police, as well as expert staff and representatives of the Tana 'Ai *adat* community. Much information was shared, but again no concrete resolution resulted.

Seeing no tangible results from delegations, written appeals, and discussions over the years, on 26 August 2000 some forty families from Utan Wair cleared land within the diocesan plantation in order to establish a new village to replace flood-prone Utan Wair, and to return to the land of their ancestors after nearly a century.

The diocesan plantation authorities reported the illegal occupation to the police. On 13 September three residents of Likong Gete, the wife, son, and sister of Josef Lewor Goban (who was in Jakarta at the time) were arrested for logging in a protected forest area and taking fruit belonging to the diocese. In solidarity, around 300 villagers from Utan Wair, Likong Gete and Blidit went to the police station in Maumere, shouting "To arrest one is to arrest all." Interrogations began of four to six people a day. Two days later the detainees were released with the help of the Nusa Tenggara Legal Aid Society.

On 28 September the Utan Wair LPMA was called to Maumere by the Sikka District Assembly for a discussion about the illegal establishment of a settlement on the Nangahale land. Also present were the head of the Sikka branch of the National Plantation Authority, the director of the Diocesan Plantation Authority (PT Diag),²⁵ and the district's chief of police. On 11 November a meeting was held between the Utan Wair LPMA and the forestry minister, with the Sikka district government represented by the NTT governor. A team was formed with members from the LPMA and the district government to solve the problem. It was agreed that the activities of the *adat* organization would not be interfered with.

However, the forty families were detained, interrogated by the police, and accused of taking over land used legally by the archdiocese. On 12 December the Tana 'Ai LPMAs demonstrated at the Maumere police station, demanding that the ten remaining detainees be released. Some of the demonstrators camped outside the police station for a week, demanding to be arrested as well, as they also worked the Protection Forest area. They were ignored and had to return home empty-handed.

In 2001, with the assistance of the Participatory Mapping Work Network (JKPP) and the Maumere-based Nusra Legal Aid Society, the people of Utan Wair formed a joint team and mapped out the whole of the land of the Soge people, including that within the boundaries of the disputed plantation. A community mapping strategy was used in which initial information came from "local intellectuals," and the area was mapped by the villagers themselves with many more observing.²⁶ However, the process came to a halt, and subsequently the map was neither legalized nor published, as clan elders from each of the villages protested that it was not right to publish "*adat* secrets" concerning land and its natural resources.²⁷

On 22 November 2003 a weeklong consultation between the Tana 'Ai communities was held with representatives from seven LPMAs, including a women's organization. The increase in the number of LPMAs participating indicated that the *adat* community network was becoming more extensive. A number of NGOs were also invited, as well as the director of the Candraditya Research Centre, and several "prominent persons" such as elders, village heads, and a local parish priest.²⁸ The government advised the community to be patient and wait for the HGU land to return to the community in 2013.

Bupati Paulus Moa established two teams: one team to investigate the altered forest borders from those of 1932 to those of 1984,[29] the second to investigate further the demand that Nangahale land be returned to the community. The second team met with Archbishop Abdon Longinus da Cunha. The bishop, who had studied law at the University of Indonesia in Jakarta, defended the diocese's legal right over the land and stated: "If you are not satisfied, then go to court!" As the bishop is thought "to hold the keys to heaven," the team felt powerless and disbanded. Another key factor that has prevented, so far, the Soge clan from increasing effective pressure on the diocese to return their land is that they have contradictory stories supporting their individual claims. There is no clear account that can convince all interested indigenous parties.

Whereas elders are reclaiming land taken away a hundred years previously and buttress their claim by reviving *adat* rituals long since prohibited or simply neglected, their action is viewed by the "little people" in this community as little more than a manipulation of *adat* for a land grab. This is Flores' local version of "ethnic elite politics" (van Klinken 2002, 67–105). Land was traditionally held by the whole clan, not as the private property of the elders. These days, when opportune, the LPMA claim *hak ulayat* (holdership rights), but when it is to their personal advantage, elders claim family ownership.

LPMA community organizations were welcomed by the 1999 Congress of AMAN (Alliance of Indigenous [Adat] Peoples of the Archipelago) as an emerging social and political force that would have to be reckoned with in solving conflicts and reclaiming *adat* rights for their people, as bodies that would "re-vitalize, re-activate and re-actualize" their communities, a necessary balance to outside commercial and political interests. This hope has now faded.[30] Indigenous activists advancing *adat* revival movements that emerged in the 1990s (who were themselves returnees from work in town or from Malaysia) have morphed into instruments that control the local community to their own benefit. Also many traditional leaders have turned out to be little more than opportunists exploiting *adat* to advance their own interests. Many LPMAs in Maumere are interested only in consolidating the claims of the landholders/owners themselves, and not in land redistribution. Perhaps the three remaining LPMAs that continue to work for their members are those of Utan Wair, Hikong, and Pigan Bekor; each of these is accompanied by a committed NGO. NGOs such as LBHNT no longer find LPMAs a vehicle for furthering human rights, democracy, and ecological concerns. NGO/LPMA collaboration would be closer if the *adat* communities were open to cultivating their lands more intensively yet in ecologically friendly ways, rather than simply claiming their traditional rights. While their struggle has succeeded in winning acknowledgment for their village relocated on HGU land, to date church diocesan authorities and the local government have not included the local people in their negotiations for a renewal of the diocesan lease on part of the land. Whether the remaining land is returned to the local people or is expropriated by the government will be determined in 2013 when the boundaries of any diocesan HGU lease renewals are made known. Return of HGU land is still an issue that, if not solved beforehand, will come to a climax in 2013 when the HGU contract ends.

Reflections on Land Disputes in Flores

Adat Law and Positive Law

There is hardly a traditional elder or government official who applies customary or positive law for the common good rather than for his own individual interests. History has bequeathed a web of confusion that makes land disputes today apparently unsolvable by traditional leaders, the government, NGOs, or the church.

National law, as interpreted by government, views the problem as one of individual rights, whereas traditionally the local *adat* community recognized communal rights. Land was redistributed regularly by the elders according to each family's need. Today neither the government nor the *adat* community is adept at interpreting national or traditional law critically and implementing the law according to the purpose of the lawmakers within changing contexts.

Under *adat* law, virtually all land in Flores, including mountainous forestry regions, belongs to indigenous communities. Although the potential claim of indigenous communities over particular forests based on customary law is acknowledged by the 1960 agrarian law, the law's conditions can readily be used to override such claims. Customary laws are acceptable only "in so far as they are still seen to be present," "not contrary to the national interests of the State," and "not contrary to Indonesian socialism" (Hooker 1978, 111–26).

A Monetized Local Economy

An increasingly monetized local economy has been driving villagers even further into forestry areas over the last few decades. As land has become a commodity, land disputes have intensified, with increasing intervention by outsiders who have commercial interests in acquiring the land. As monetary needs increase by the year, the unity of the village is strained by the competing needs of individual families who feel that they need to sell land; this intensifies struggles within and between villages over land claims. Insistence on the traditional inalienability of *adat* land is seen to benefit only the elders, who increasingly claim ownership rather than guardianship of what has now become a commodity.

Weakness of the Court System

Recourse to the courts inevitably complicates and prolongs disputes. The legal bureaucracy, including defense lawyers, prosecutors, and judges, all encourage use of the courts. And so each dispute, which is never concluded to the satisfaction of the losing party, sows the seeds of retaliation. Conflicts "concluded" in the district court often continue unabated in the village. Although the Colol case was brought to the Manggarai District Court in Ruteng, the people were powerless, as the decision to clear the coffee trees had been signed by the entire district leadership (*Muspida*), including the judiciary; and so there was no independent authority to whom they could turn. In the case of the disputed diocesan plantation, if the claimants should decide to go to the Sikka

District Court in Maumere, they will have to take on the diocese, their own religious authorities. The Utan Wair villagers hesitate to do this, and moreover this option is not open as long as they are internally divided. As the management of the HGU land under dispute will return to the National Land Agency's district land office (*kantor tanah*) in 2013, there is little pressure on the government to intervene until then.[31]

The Role of Nongovernment Organizations

In the two disputes discussed above, NGOs were vital in collecting and distributing detailed data to both the regional media and government, and also in giving voice to viewpoints other than those of the government and the institutional church. They brought each of the cases to district courts and, in the case of Colol, to the notice of the National Commission for Human Rights. They have also held leadership and organization workshops for the *adat* communities.

Whereas most *adat* leaders confine themselves to defending their traditional land rights, the government is project-oriented, and the church is concerned with balancing its budget through retaining use of HGU land. At their best, NGOs combine support for *adat* rights with training in ecologically friendly development alternatives. Nevertheless, in Flores most NGOs end up working for their administrators rather than for the people they were established to serve. There are three key issues here. First, few of the NGOs are motivated by a clear ideology or a firm commitment to the whole community (as many are in Java), as a result of the lack of any critical education during the Suharto regime and a faith-formed social conscience. Second, the NGOs are financially insecure and are not professionally managed. Third, NGOs tended to become involved in land disputes only in the short term, before moving on to the next project.[32] Although the project-oriented NGOs have made valuable contributions in collecting data and initial advocacy, after conflicts die down and project money is finished they fade from the scene. In general, NGOs rarely have adequate conflict-resolution skills and find the lack of local solidarity difficult to engage with.

The Church: A Party to the Land Disputes

Although a few individual local pastors have tried to articulate and support village grievances, the institutional church in Flores has invariably defended its own interests and in doing so, interprets positive law narrowly, readily calling on the police to enforce its claims. There is no indication yet of church leadership open to becoming a voice for agrarian reform.

If pastors on the ground have had little success as mediators, the dioceses have had even less, during their rare occasions when they have attempted it. In the Colol coffee tree–clearing dispute, a compromise offer was drawn up by the district government with the support of the Ruteng diocese[33] and taken to the villagers by the Diocesan Justice and Peace Commission with its recommendation of acceptance. The offer was rejected, as diocesan involvement was interpreted by the village not as mediation but as a move to "sell" the government program. The villagers feared that acceptance would have lost them any *adat* rights over the disputed land (*PK*, 8 November 2003, 9 November 2003). The government then went ahead and completed its clearance program.

The introduction of the 1999 Regional Autonomy Law (implemented from 2001, amended in 2004 [UU 32/2004]), in which the district government takes over many of the powers of the central government, is causing concern about what will happen to the Nangahale land when the commercial use rights run out in 2013, as its control will then revert to the district government. In what could be a precedent, in the late 1980s, more than 200 hectares of expired HGU land which had previously been used for a diocesan coconut plantation, but which now came within the Maumere town boundary, was split fifty-fifty between the church and the district government.[34] When the current HGU lease expires in 2013, it is not clear who will then obtain use of it and for what purpose.

While the 1999 autonomy law established the village as a legal body with an elected council (Badan Perwakilian Desa, BPD), the amended law of 2004 has, in practice, reduced the council to little more than an advisory body (Dewan Permusyawarahan Desa) and has required that the village secretary, who now has to be a government employee, be appointed by the district government.[35] These two changes have undermined an emerging alliance between villages to campaign for their land rights.

The institutional church in Flores rarely campaigns on social issues, except in partnership with a government program. None of the bishops of Ruteng, Ende, and since 2005, Maumere has responded to key economic, political, cultural, and ethical issues. Over the years, bishops in Flores have worked closely with government while spearheading modernization through schooling and socioeconomic development. The institutional church in Flores has yet to decouple itself from the 150-year "partnership" with the state, let alone reposition itself as a movement for cultural renewal and political reform.

A Future for *Adat* Land Law?

There has been an obvious lack of success in solving these disputes by appealing to customary law. *Adat* law is simply overridden by the application of the positive law of the state and undermined by the informal manipulation by private interests. An increasingly contentious issue concerns what the local *adat* actually is, with mounting skepticism about claims allegedly based on "custom" and "community" being put forward by actual or intended ethnic elites who would benefit personally. This is in spite of proposals lodged by legal academics (such as the teams from the Law Faculty of the University of Nusa Cendana in Kupang, West Timor, and the University of Indonesia in Jakarta), and by several NGOs and Catholic organizations and centers, calling for legal clarification.[36] Both church and state have long undermined the integrity of *adat* institutions. Customary land rights originally involved fairer distribution and resource access to local people, but it is difficult to see how the communal vision and fair principles of the *adat* can counter the individual interests and commercialized values of the various stakeholders today.

This study has focused on the ambiguous role of the church in land conflicts in Flores. The dramatic rise in disputes after 1998 is an expression of the rejection of the repressive political culture of the Suharto regime, and a reflection of the damaging structural relations it set in place. Recent land conflicts are a response by indigenous communities to landgrabbing through the legality of national law supported by government bureaucracy and the forces of "law and order." Aside from a few NGOs and members of some religious orders or congregations, the institutional church in Flores has yet to engage in this struggle to reclaim land by indigenous peoples, virtually all of whom are Catholic, or even to acknowledge the legitimacy of the struggle and to act in solidarity with local community organizations.

If the *adat* communities, NGOs, the government, and the church, as stake-holders in these disputes, held a clear consensual ideology such as a fundamental commitment to act for and with the powerless, with a common appreciation of cultural/human values and a shared ethical stance in the face of the accelerating clash of cultures and economies that is engulfing Flores, then there might be hope of an equitable way forward. This is where academics, in the church and the wider society, listening closely to the villagers, could make a much-needed contribution.

Notes

1. Since 2003, Manggarai has been split into the three regencies of Manggarai, Western Manggarai, and Eastern Manggarai.

2. It is not clear whether *adat* leaders were involved or whether there was an *adat* ceremony to seal the agreement (Suryaalam 2003, 2–3). Some areas, such as Colol, claim their ancestors were forced to accept the forestry borders. On the substantial changes made in 1979–81 and the major discrepancies between borders to ancestral land marked by certain trees, markers erected by the Dutch in the 1930s, and the more recent markers placed by the District Forestry Department, see Erb and Jelahut (2008, 226–27).

3. RTK, *Register Tanah Kehutanan* (1984, 111).

4. The *kepala desa* (village head/administrator), installed by the Indonesian district government, has no rights or obligations under *adat*. However, as the influence of *adat* and *adat* ritual land guardians (*tu'a teno*) declined, and the role of traditional village heads (in Indonesian *kepala*

kampung, in Manggarai language *tu'a golo)* was eclipsed by both the Dutch-instituted rajadom (1924) and the New Order local administration (*kepala desa),* these village heads were increasingly called on to manage ongoing disputes.

5. There was little effort to collect the coffee from the farmers, and the farmers themselves made no effort to hand it over to the government.

6. Interestingly, just prior to being elected bupati in 1999, he had published his academic thesis on the culture of Manggarai (Bagul 1998).

7. See also the account and analysis by Maribeth Erb and Josep Jelahat (2008).

8. Surat Perintah Tugas Bupati Manggarai No: DK.522.11/1143/IX/2002, 7 October 2002.

9. The forestry police have little interest in conservation; not infrequently they allow villagers to fell trees that they then confiscate and sell.

10. See Walhi (2003) for details on the Kuwus conflict, and Suryaalam (2003) for the Golo Mese case. The ongoing saga was reported almost daily in the regional press, *Pos Kupang* (PK) and *Flores Pos* (FP), particularly the Colol case (October–November 2003).

11. Colol was the only major coffee-producing area, harvesting over 50 percent of the total legal annual production of Manggarai District.

12. JAGAD-NTT regularly gathered local customary community organizations (LPMA, or Lembaga Pengembangan Masyarakat Adat) from NTT until 2004. More recently it has slowly disappeared from the scene, since it lost external aid (from Australia) because there were no visible results from its meetings. The national *adat* community alliance, AMAN, remains hopeful that it can be revived. Activities now take place at the district level only.

13. Servas Lawang, an independent member of the provincial assembly in Kupang, comes from Todo. His elder brother, Robert Lawang, studied land disputes in Manggarai as head of a sociology team from the Universitas Indonesia in Jakarta (Lawang 1999).

14. The chairman of the diocesan commission was a close relative of the bupati's wife and a member of the Ruteng bishop's extended family, which was itself involved in a land dispute. The complexity of this intrafamilial dispute came out in Margaret Coffey's "The Bishop and the Bupati," an interview with the commission chairman on the ABC Radio National *Encounter* program, 23 April 2006. The bishop and the bupati worked closely together and would appear at each other's public occasions. There is always a minority of the clergy in each of the four dioceses on Flores who support the people, even when the bishop sides with forestry (or mining) interests.

15. Because administrative buildings, a clinic, and a school were in the vicinity, it was impractical for the people to be located far from their original village.

16. Ten commission members accepted the report, and eleven rejected it. Unofficial leaks suggest that some 500 million rupiahs was needed to fix the vote (personal communication RM, May 2008).

17. In Erb and Jelahut's view, the clearing of the villagers' coffee plantations in this way in the name of ecology was "one of the most disastrous policies ever implemented in the Manggarai Regency" (2008, 223).

18. See A. Mahur (2004); John Atu and Thomas Uran in Suryaalam (2003); and Bachriadi, Bachrioktora, and Safitri (2005, 4–7) for similar cases in west and east Flores.

19. These *nuba* marked the borders of the land being cultivated in a shifting cultivation system, and so would be shifted regularly within the larger *adat* land. The Dutch moved some, but community leaders now intend to replace them.

20. Mainly with *arak* (traditional rice wine) to the local police and a large goat to the subdistrict head.

21. In the army-instigated massacres of March–May 1966, when between 800 and 2,000 people of the district were slaughtered in the capital Maumere, to be called *kafir* was tantamount to being labeled communist (PKI). See Prior (2011). In-depth interviews stored in archives are still too sensitive for publication.

22. The Rajadom of Tana 'Ai was established by the Dutch in 1902 (to balance the influence of the raja of Sikka), but was disbanded by the colonizers in 1929 to centralize power. Today people say that Nai Roa was appointed raja in order to obtain land for Dutch commercial interests.

23. In 2006, use of the plantation was transferred from the Ende archdiocese to the newly established Maumere diocese.

24. A local landowner and "big man," Goban has an "NGO mentality" as well as that of a traditional leader and was elected village head of Utar Wair in 2005. As he married a second time when in Malaysia (and his first wife then took another husband), no Catholic priest would witness his installation. In 2007 he was finally installed after becoming a Muslim. A key figure in the opening phase of the dispute, he lost interest after becoming *kepala desa* in 2005. In 2011 he was serving a prison sentence for corruption.

25. Ben Sareng, the director of PT Diag until 2004, was a Catholic layman and retired head of the Sikka district land office.

26. For a range of examples of the ways in which community mapping has been used to express and defend *adat* claims and as a tool for

community planning, see Peluso (1995), Momberg, Atok, and Sirait (1996), and Warren (2005).

27. Traditionally, certain key elements of the *adat* are jealously safeguarded by the elders. However, mapping in other areas of Sikka regency has not been held up by this taboo, suggesting that the elders felt they could control their rights only through keeping traditional knowledge to themselves.

28. The Tana 'Ai delegation held a so-called long march from Candraditya Research Centre to the district assembly building; it was actually somewhat less than a kilometer! The Centre is run by the Society of the Divine Word (SVD), the cross-cultural mission order of which the author is a member.

29. Only four thousand hectares of Protected Forest are in good condition, and these are in the hands of the local people, whereas the fifteen thousand hectares under the authority of the Forestry Department have been devastated. (Although local people assiduously tend to their own area, they log with abandon in the government's area.) And so the government, the local community, and commercial interests have agreed to a "Multi-Party Forestry Development Program," where the government is facilitator and the local community is acknowledged as both landholder and manager. This program has received a grant from the U.K. Development Fund for International Development (DFID).

30. The congress held in Jakarta in 1999 led to the formation of AMAN, which worked for the acknowledgment that local *adat* communities continue to hold ultimate jurisdiction over their traditional lands (Acciaioli 2001, 90).

31. The Maumere diocese and the SVD (Ledalero Seminary) wish to continue to make use of some of the Nangahale land after 2013. The diocese is extremely busy (re)planting the section of the land that they wish to retain after 2013 with both cash crops and timber.

32. While thirteen of the thirty-member district assembly in Maumere elected in 2004 came from NGO backgrounds, there has been no palpable change of political direction. Virtually all the chairpersons of NGOs in Maumere had put themselves up as candidates in the 2009 general election; a half dozen were elected.

33. Sixty percent of cultivated trees in forest area to be declared government property and cleared; 40 percent to remain in villagers' hands.

34. The church's section, in the end only 40 percent, was distributed among numerous religious communities and institutes. A large number of diocesan employees were also given land for housing and received ownership certificates (*sertifikat hak milik*). Many of these workers

subsequently sold their land to Chinese traders. The rest is now built up with convents, seminaries and the Candraditya Research Centre which obtained six hectares (three plots of two hectares). The various religious orders were allowed up to two hectares each, which can be converted to individual ownership (*hak milik*). The government's 60 percent section was used for public works, including the new district assembly (DPRD) building, and a general hospital, while certain officials, including the then bupati's cronies, got land for private housing. The former coconut plantation is now an integral part of the town of Maumere.

While this ex-HGU land was once customary land belonging to the Koting community (some 10 kilometers inland away from Maumere), no *adat* claims have ever been registered. Whether there will be any in the future remains to be seen.

35. Thus the *sekretaris desa* now owns primary loyalty to the district government, rather than to his village community.

36. Such as the Candraditya Research Centre in Maumere, the van Bekkum-Verheijen Institute in Ruteng, and the Jakarta based Franciscan Commission for Justice, Peace and the Integrity of Creation in Jakarta.

References

Acciaioli, G. 2001. "Grounds of Conflict, Idioms of Harmony: Custom, Religion and Nationalism in Violence Avoidance in the Lindu Plains of Central Sulawesi." *Indonesia* 72:81–114.

Araf, A., and A. Puryadi. 2002. *Perebutan Kuasa Tanah*. Yogyakarta: LAPERA.

Aur, A. 2004. "Dari Babat Kopi ke Babat Nyawa: Narasi Tragedi Petani Kopi Colol." In *Gugat: Darah Petani Kopi Manggarai,* ed. Eman Embu and Robert Mirsel, 102–20. Maumere: Ledalero.

Bachriadi, D., Y. Bachrioktora, and H. Safitri. 2005. *Ketika Penyelengaraan Pemerintahan Menyimpang: Mal Administrasi di Bidang Pertanahan*. Yogyakarta: Lapera Pustaka Utama.

Bagul, A. D. 1998. *Kebudayaan Manggarai Sebagai Salah Satu Khasanah Kebudayaan Nasional*. Surabaya: Ubhara.

Beding, M. 2003. "Keadilan, Menggugat dan Digugat." *Iustitia* 3 (5)(August): 8–10.

Braman, F. 1991. "Mencegah Erosi Melalui Konservasi Tanah dan Air." *Dian* 18 (19): 5, 8.

Cholil, B. 1994. *Teologi Tanah*. Jakarta: Yapika.

Dapangole, Frans, ed. n.d. "Laporan—Rahasia Mengenai Persengketaan Keburea dan Perselisihan Perbatasan Antara-Swapradja Nagekeo dan Swapradja Lio." Official letters and legal documentation from 24 December 1958 to 28 March 1959.

Deno, K. 1994. "Studi Tentang Pengaruh Budaya Terhadap Efektifitas Penerapan Hukum Tanah di Lingkungan Masyarakat Kecamatan Ruteng." Research report, 1994.

Dohu, T. 2001. "Alur Sejarah Perjuangan Masyarakat Adat Wair Kung Tana Ai." Manuscript.

Embu, E. 2004. "Kriminalisasi, Anarki, Tragedi." In *Gugat: Darah Petani Kopi Manggarai,* ed. E. Embu and R. Mirsel, 248–300. Maumere: Ledalero.

Embu, E. J., and R. Mirsel, eds. 2004. *Gugat: Darah Petani Kopi Manggarai.* Maumere: Ledalero.

Erb, M. 1999. *The Manggarians: A Guide to Traditional Lifestyles.* Singapore: Times Editions.

Erb, M., and Y. Jelahut. 2008. "For the People or For the Trees? A Case Study of Violence and Conservation in Ruteng Nature Recreation Park." In *Biodiversity and Human Livelihoods in Protected Areas: Case Studies from the Malay Archipelago,* ed. N. Sodhi, G. Acciaioli, M. Erb, and A. Tan, 222–40. Cambridge: Cambridge University Press.

Fager, J. A. 1993. *Land Tenure and the Biblical Jubilee: Uncovering Hebrew Ethics through the Sociology of Knowledge.* Sheffield: JSOT Press.

Farid, A. 2003. *Terusir dari Tanah Sendiri.* Walhi.

Fauzi, N. 2000. *Otonomi Daerah dan Sengketa Tanah.* Yogyakarta: Lapera Pustaka Utama.

Harsono, B. 1994. *Hukum Agraria Indonesia: Sejarah, Pembentukan Undang-undang Pokok Agraria, Isi, dan Pelaksanaannya.* Rev. ed. Jakarta: Djambatan.

Habel, N. C. 1995. *The Land Is Mine: Six Biblical Land Ideologies.* Minneapolis: Fortress Press.

Hooker, M. B. 1978. *Adat Law in Modern Indonesia.* Kuala Lumpur: Oxford University Press.

Husein, A. S. 1997. *Konflik Pertanahan: Dimensi Keadilan dan Kepentingan Ekonomi.* Jakarta: Sinar Harapan.

Ketentuan Konversi Undang-Undang Pokok Agraria. 1960.

Komisi Kehutanan. 1989. *Instruksi Kementerian No. 417.*

KWI (Konferensi Waligereja Indonesia). 1997. "Keprihatinan dan Harapan." *Surat Gembala Prapaskah.* Jakarta.

———. 2001. "Tekun dan Bertahan dalam Pengharapan: Menata Moralitas Bangsa." *Surat Gembala Paskah.* Jakarta.

———. 2003. "Bangkit Bersama Kristus untuk Mengembangkan Budaya Hidup Bersama." *Surat Gembala Paskah*. Jakarta.

Lawang, Robert. 1999. *Konflik Tanah di Manggarai, Flores Barat: Pendekatan Sosiologik*. Jakarta: Penerbit Universitas Indonesia.

Lewis, D. 1988. *The People of the Source*. Dordrecht: Foris Publications.

Lounela, A., and R. Yando Zakaria, eds. 2003. *Berebut Tanah: Beberapa Kajian Berperspektif Kampus dan Kampung*. Jogyakarta: Insist.

Mahur, A. 2004. "Who Owns Mbondel Land? A Case of Change and Ambiguity Triggering Conflict." In *More Than Just Ownership: Ten Land and Natural Resource Conflict Case Studies from East Java and Flores*, ed. S. Clark, 74–82. Jakarta: World Bank.

Mangunwijaya, Y. B. 1999. *Gereja Diaspora*. Jogyakarta: Kanisius.

Mirsel, R. 2004. "Masyarakat Manggarai: Sejarah, Alam Pemikiran, Tanah dan Hutan." In *Gugat: Darah Petani Kopi Manggarai*, ed. E. Embu and R. Mirsel, 3–53. Maumere: Ledalero.

Momberg, F., K. Atok, and M. Sirait. 1996. *Menggali dan Mengembangkan Pengetahuan Setempat: Sebuah Pandauan Pelatihan Pemetaan oleh Masyarakat: Beberapa Studi Kasus dari Indonesia*. Jakarta: Ford Foundation, YKSPK, WWF.

Muskens, M.P.M. 1979. *Partner in Nation Building: The Catholic Church in Indonesia*. Aachen: Missio Aktuell Verlag.

Parera, V. 2004. "Ekologi versus Ekonomi: Seputar Pembabatan Kopi di Manggarai." In *Gugat: Darah Petani Kopi Manggarai*, ed. E. Embu and R. Mirsel, 123–65. Maumere: Ledalero.

Peluso, N. 1995. "Whose Woods Are These? Counter Mapping Forest Territories in Kalimantan Indonesia." *Antipode* 27:383–406.

Peraturan Daerah Nusa Tenggara Timur No. 8, 1974 tentang Pelaksanaan Penegasan Hak Atas Tanah.

Pontifical Council for Justice and Peace. 1997. *Towards a Better Distribution of Land: The Challenge of Agrarian Reform*. Vatican City.

Prior, J. M. 1988. *Church and Marriage in an Indonesian Village: A Study of Customary and Church Marriage among the Ata Lio of Central Flores Indonesia, as a Paradigm of the Ecclesial Inter-relationship between Village and Institutional Catholicism*. Frankfurt: Peter Lang.

———. 2004. "Dignity and Identity: The Struggle of Indigenous Peoples of Asia to Preserve, Purify and Promote their Cultures." *FABC Papers No. 104*. Hong Kong: FABC.

———. 2011. "The Silent Scream of a Silenced History. Part One: The Maumere Massacre of 1966." *Exchange* 40 (2): 117–43.

———. 2011. "The Silent Scream of a Silenced History. Part Two: Church Responses." *Exchange* 40 (4): 1–11

Ruwiastuti, M. R. 1999a. "Sistem Penguasaan Asli dan Politik Hukum Tanah di Manggarai Tengah." Unpublished manuscript.

———. 1999b. "Sengketa Tanah di Manggarai." Unpublished manuscript.

Silamurti, E. S., and Y. Tasnim, eds. 2001. *Ma Wairkung: Masyarakat Utan Wair Kec. Talibura, Kab. Sikka, NTT. Studi Refleksi Gerakan Pemetaan Partisipatif.* Yogyakarta: Lembaga Nawakamal Jaringan Kerja Pemetaan Partisipatif.

Steenbrink, K. 2007. *Catholics in Indonesia: A Documented History. Vol. II. The Spectacular Growth of a Self-Confident Minority, 1903–1942.* Leiden: KITLV.

Suban Hayon, Y. 2002. "Spiritualitas Tanah dalam Masyarakat Asli Balawelin." *Jurnal Ledalero* 2:48–69.

Subangun, E. 2002. "Laporan Penelitian Kelompok Basis Gerejawi di Regio Jawa." *Sawi* 17:1–92.

———. 2003. *Dekolonisasi Gereja di Indonesia: Suatu Proses Setengah Hati.* Yogyakarta: Kanisius.

Suryaalam, M. R. R., ed. 2003. *Menguak Rahasia di Balik Merebaknya Konflik-Konflik Agraria di Flores dan Timor.* Denpasar: VeCo Indonesia dan Konsorsium Pembaruan Agraria (KPA).

Tim Pemantauan Kasus Manggarai KomnasHAM. 2004. "Hasil Pemantauan Tindak Kekerasan dan Penembakan Petani Manggarai NTT." In *Gugat: Darah Petani Kopi Manggarai,* ed. E. Embu and R. Mirsel, 81–99. Maumere: Ledalero.

Tim Advokasi untuk Rakyat Manggarai (TARM). 2003. "Kronologis Penggusuran dan Pengusiran Petani dan Masyarakat Adat Meler-Kuwus di Kawasan Hutan Adat Meler-Kuwus (RTK 111) Kabupaten Manggarai Nusa Tenggara Timur." Ruteng: Manuscript.

Toda, D. N. 1999. *Manggarai Mencari Pencerahan Historiografi.* Ende: Nusa Indah.

Tule, P. 2004. *Longing for the House of God, Dwelling in the House of the Ancestors: Local Belief, Christianity and Islam among the Keo of Central Flores.* Fribourg: Academic Press.

van Klinken, G. 2002. "Indonesia's New Ethnic Elites." In *Indonesia: In Search of Transition,* ed. S. Nordholt, 67–105. Jogyakarta: Pustaka Pelajar.

van Vollenhoven, C. 1981. *Penemuan Hukum Adat.* Jakarta: Djambatan.

Wahono, B. B. S, ed. 2002. *Kembali ke Akar: Kembali ke Konsep Otonomi Masyarakat Asli.* Jakarta: Forum Pengembangan Partisipasi Masyarakat.

Walhi (Wahana Lingkungan Hidup Indonesia), ed. 2003. *Terusir dari Tanah sendiri. Kertas Posisi.* Jakarta: Walhi.

Warren, C. 2005. "Mapping Common Futures." *Development and Change* 36:49–73.

Woi, A., and J. M. Prior, eds. 2003. *Membaca Tanda Zaman pada Akhir sebuah Zaman: Gereja Nusa Tenggara Mawas Diri.* Maumere: Puslit [Pusat Penelitian] Candraditya.

Zakaria, Y. 1999. "Pengakuan Hak Masyarakat Adat dan Pluralisme Hukum." In *Otonomi Daerah dan Sengketa Tanah,* ed. Noer Fauzi, 44–75. Jogyakarta: Lapera Pustaka Utama.

Newspapers

Flores Pos
Pos Kupang (PK)

Chapter 8

LEGAL CERTAINTY FOR WHOM?

Land Contestation and Value Transformations at Gili Trawangan, Lombok

CAROL WARREN

The conflict over land on the island of Gili Trawangan, Lombok, is one of the many intractable cases inherited from the late New Order. It evolved in the context of rapid value transformations in the local, national, and global economies, as smallholders competed for land with commercial plantations, then resort development, and more recent incursions of the international property market. The case involved repeated government land clearance campaigns, reclaiming actions of local settlers, and emerging social divisions among the island's smallholder farmers and tourism businesses in the ongoing struggle against eviction by a regional government openly allied with big capital. It is a complicated story in which capital accumulation is set against livelihood needs, and value transformations are manipulated to privilege the interests of economic and political elites. But it is also a story of contestation and accommodation as diverse conceptions of equity are pitted against opportunity among local people as well as state actors.

Two Tales of Trawangan — the People and the State

The story of the three-decades-long land conflict at Gili Trawangan, now one of the "jewels" of Indonesia's tourist circuit, very much depends on who tells it, in what social context, and from which perspective on the law. Local settlers recount how Sasak and Bugis fishers had long used the island as a shelter during seasonal stopovers and had begun planting subsistence crops and coconut palm in the early 1970s (interviews, OM and MS, 11 August 2002; SK, 30 May 1999). They recount the difficulties of clearing the land and the satisfactions of building good livelihoods from productive soil once they had transformed the land from its natural state into a smallholder economy. The early pioneers proudly tell also of their role in opening small homestays and food stalls to make Gili Trawangan an international destination before Lombok itself achieved any prominence. But in the embittered rendition of one settler, after all their hard efforts, "When everything was good and beautiful, along come investors without even knocking, trying to take over" (MH, quoted in *Nusa Tenggara,* 29 June 1995).

The regional government (Pemda) account, in contrast, emphasizes its role in fostering the development of the island, in the first instance as an addition to the nation's plantation economy. It has settlers arriving on the island on government invitation to take up land in this "uninhabited mosquito nest" only in 1976 with the plantations' establishment (*Suara Nusa,* 30 September 1991; Pemda Tingkat II 1995, 1). But the plantations soon failed, and after a hiatus of more than a decade, provincial and district governments turned their attention to the more lucrative opportunities of the nascent tourism industry, determined to promote a high value-added resort development on the former leasehold. The state's assertion that ordinary people were incapable of developing a sophisticated and environmentally sound tourism industry provided its rationale for promoting private sector investment over smallholder development.[1] The two accounts differ fundamentally on who cleared and developed the land first and could claim prior right, and how national principles concerning the state's obligations to use land to support the people's welfare should be interpreted and applied.

Origins of Conflict—Corruption, Neglect, and Populist Dreams

Gili Trawangan had been of little interest to government until the 1970s when the national push to expand the country's export base encouraged the opening of new plantations. In 1972 the government divided the island's 338 hectares into three parts. Two companies—PT Generasi Jaya and PT Rinta—obtained one hundred–hectare allocations under commercial use right (HGU) leases on the east and south of the island respectively, while settlers and migrants from Lombok were encouraged to clear the remaining northwestern portion for smallholder farms (DPRD 1995, 4–6). By 1979 there were some 130 households on Gili Trawangan planting coconut trees and dry food crops in smallholdings of one to three hectares, the size depending on the stage of settlement and the capability of each household to clear and work the land under dryland cultivation.[2]

From the outset, the establishment of the PT Generasi Jaya plantation concession had been a blatant example of the patronage and corruption that characterized New Order–style "development." Among the beneficiaries of the concession were the three sons of Governor Wasita Kusuma (typical of the New Order period, a military figure) and a closely connected civil servant. Although planting began in 1974 (Pemda 1995, 1), lease rights were awarded to the four concession holders on the Generasi Jaya plantation only in 1979,[3] and HGU certificates on the leaseholds were not formally issued until 1986,[4] many years after PT Generasi Jaya had ceased actively managing the plantation.

New migrants continued to arrive and along with existing settlers expanded smallholder farms into the abandoned plantation area. PT Rinta, which had ceased operations on the island, officially relinquished its leasehold in 1981. Land in the former PT Rinta plantation was then redistributed to smallholders—mainly new migrants and extended families of those settled on the original smallholder allocation—under the government's Prona titling scheme (AR interview, 27 September 1999).[5] Only the one hundred–hectare PT Generasi Jaya plantation remained officially state land (*tanah negara*), still under HGU (commercial use right) lease, despite the company's abandonment of the plantation soon after establishment.

According to villagers, there had been no oversight of the coconut plantation for years. Those brought to the island to provide plantation labor complain that they were not paid for their work. They received no supplies and had no communication with the company in the years following the initial period of establishment (interviews, RH, 29 August 1999; OM and MS 11 August 2002). They claim there were no complaints by government authorities over the use of land by smallholders until the more lucrative opportunities offered by the tourism industry created new financial prospects for investors, land speculators, and government authorities. "We lived before like worms, eating leaves, eating anything in an unfriendly environment, full of malaria mosquitoes, snakes, and mice. No one paid attention then. But as soon as the jingling sound of the dollar could be heard, they came in droves to push us out" (villager quoted in SMUM 1991, 1). Belated regional government remonstrations to abide by early allotments carried little moral authority with smallholders when impropriety in the award of HGU concessions and subsequent neglect by the leaseholders were set against local needs and industriousness.

Settlers had reason to expect that the same populist redistributive policies that had applied to the canceled PT Rinta lease, and that had been encouraged under provisions of the Basic Agrarian Law, would be extended to the also abandoned Generasi Jaya plantation land. In 1983 they applied for title to the plots they occupied. But despite legislation regarding the state's arguable powers and obligations to resume and redistribute neglected land (*tanah terlantar*),[6] it did not pursue the Generasi Jaya company for abrogating its responsibilities at that stage and refused to support local occupiers' efforts to gain recognition of their conversion of the land to smallholdings, as had occurred with the PT Rinta concession. In the government's view the people had been given fair shares of land on the island: Smallholder farmers had been granted freehold (*hak milik*) rights to the western third in the initial division, and another hundred hectares had been redistributed to new migrants and extended families of existing residents (DPRD 1995, 7) when PT Rinta withdrew.

Not until 1988 did the provincial plantations department begin to take action against the holders of the Generasi Jaya lease for failing to carry out their obligations to manage plantation production and pay requisite royalties to the state (DPRD 1995, 8–9). By this time it had an ulterior motive of furthering the interests of a Jakarta-based company, PT Gili Trawangan Indah, which sought transfer of the lease for a tourism resort development on the former plantation concession.

Value Transformations in the Genealogy of Conflict

The island's economy had begun to take a very different turn by 1981 when the first backpacker tourists arrived. This stimulated transformations in land values much greater than that arising from commercial plantation development, value transformations that drove the conflict between settlers and outside interests for three decades and that complicate resolution to date. On information from Lombok-based relatives of the Gili Trawangan settlers, travel writers had "discovered" the blue coral and exquisite beaches on the east coast of Gili Trawangan and put it on the global backpackers' map. Early visitors stayed in the small homes of local residents, who began adding rooms to their homes and building the stilted thatch and bamboo, rice-barn style bungalows that became characteristic of budget accommodation on the island. Gradually small entrepreneurs among the locals contracted land along this eastern coastal strip from farmers who had by then divided the entire Generasi Jaya plantation area among themselves (interviews, RN, 29 August 1999; AN, 27 September 2009). The 1984 *Lonely Planet Bali and Lombok* travel guide devoted two full pages and much praise to the homestay owned by one of the Gili Trawangan pioneers, who by then had seven small rooms and offered food, snorkeling equipment, and organized transport for his guests (Covernton and Wheeler 1984, 193–94). Five years later, small-scale tourism on the island had grown to eighteen restaurant and accommodation businesses with a total of eighty-two rooms (SMUM 1991, 15).

In 1989 the provincial government declared fifteen tourism zones in Nusa Tenggara Barat Province, including the Gili Indah Islands.[7] This announcement signaled a major shift in land and resource use on Trawangan. The once "useless" part of the plantation leasehold was now priceless beachside property; in the government's view, it was too valuable to be relegated to small-scale tourism facilities run by local people. The locally owned homestay end of the market may have offered more opportunities and better income distribution for Gili Trawangan settlers but represented less of a prospect for significant contributions to regional tax revenue.[8] Although local entrepreneurs did offer to pay Rp 200 million in annual taxes and royalties, equivalent to approximately US$108,000 in 1990 (interview, RN, 29 August 1999), these small-scale enterprises would be unlikely to provide competitive tax revenues without significant capital investment or state support.[9] Perhaps more important from the point of view of rent-seeking officials, locals relying on their own resources could not match the illicit private rewards that had become a significant informal component of major development permit approval processes in late New Order Indonesia and since.

A study was commissioned by the Indonesian Tourism Department to determine appropriate zoning and planning principles for the Gili Indah islands (Gubah Laras 1989). Taking account of the character of the islands that had proved so attractive to tourists, as well as of environmental constraints, particularly the limited availability of freshwater sources and the impact of waste on the surrounding coral reefs, the study recommended against building large-scale tourism facilities, suggesting that these be restricted to sites on the Lombok mainland, leaving the neighboring Gili Indah islands for recreation and short visits (Gubah Laras 1989, §III.01–03, §V.8). It warned of the ecological consequences of significant increases in the population of the islands and specifically recommended against building grand hotels to avoid pollution and protect the traditional atmosphere of the islands. Specific recommendations for Gili Trawangan included that 50 percent of the project land be set aside as a protection zone and that development be limited to thirty hectares with low density accommodation (ten to twenty bungalows per hectare) of light bamboo and thatch construction. It estimated a potential capacity of 400 rooms, but recommended no more than 200 to preserve the character and environmental and social values of the island (Gubah Laras 1989, III.01–14, 18–19, 25; IV.01).

Environmental protection had now become an important rationale for the government's draconian clearance policies, to bring "regulation" and "order" to this unruly outpost (*Bali Post,* 31 August 1992). Ordering actions were "deemed essential to protect the environment of Gili Trawangan as an asset of such great value for tourism in Nusa Tengara Barat Province."[10] Environmental discourse was highly selective, however. While referring to the government-commissioned Gubah Laras report, state authorities completely ignored the inconsistency of the government's own development plans with significant recommendations of the planning document, in particular, the consultants' assessment of the island's limited environmental carrying capacity and emphasis on the inappropriateness of large-scale hotel development.

Gili Trawangan settlers also deployed arguments along environmental lines and were quick to throw back at the government the contradictions between the small is beautiful planning rhetoric and the "megaproject" being promoted for the island. But relatives and acquaintances from Lombok continued to migrate to the island; and over time those successful enough to expand their tourism holdings added rooms beyond the five-room limit stipulated by regional government. Over time, more permanent materials—cement buildings and tile roofs—began to replace the original bamboo and thatch cottages that were vulnerable to fire and so easily cut down by vindictive authorities.

By 1992, the year of the first of three official government eviction campaigns (in 1992, 1993, and 1995), the government team sent to oversee clearance of the disputed land reported 128 bungalows and 12 restaurants operating on the disputed land at Gili Trawangan. According to this report, 83 bungalows and 7 restaurants were pulled down, following unsuccessful "negotiations" and rejection of the government's compensation offer. The remaining small businesses reportedly had been taken down "voluntarily" by their owners after government warnings.[11] The most comprehensive report by the provincial government, issued just before the final clearance campaign in 1995, acknowledges that the conflict emerged with the value transformations wrought by reclassification of Gili Trawangan as a tourism zone, but notably does not credit the role of local smallholders in its development and popularization as a tourist destination, or recognize substantive rights arising from these small entrepreneurs' prior claims (DPRD 1995, 17).

Abuses of Power and the Dissemblance of Law

Portents of impending conflict can be traced back as far as 1983, when smallholders occupying the Generasi Jaya plantation concession applied to the district government to process legal titles to the abandoned company land they now occupied. The Basic Agrarian Law provides that an HGU lease is automatically canceled if it is neglected or abandoned and reverts to state management (BAL/UUPA 5/1960, §34/e). Under land reform legislation, farmers are then eligible to apply for redistribution of that land (PP 224/1961, §1/d).[12] The settlers' application was not processed by the district head, however, on grounds that some of the farmers had already received land in the initial smallholder allocation and subsequent PT Rinta distribution (Pemda 1995, 9). HGU certificates were belatedly issued to the four politically well-connected lessees soon afterward (1986), apparently at this late stage to enable sale of these leases (subsequently judged illegal) by the former governor's relatives.

In 1989, having no response to their requests for regional government to process their applications, the smallholders attempted to seek redress through the courts with legal aid group assistance. They accused the National Land Agency (BPN) and Provincial Plantations Department of neglecting their duty to monitor the plantation, which had been abandoned, and requested that the court require the accused to process smallholder title applications. The litigants appealed to the social function principles of the Basic Agrarian Law (BAL/UUPA 1960, §15), the pursuant obligations of landholders to care for the land, and of the Indonesian state to take account of the needs of those in a weak economic position in land allocation decisions. Most important for their case were provisions for cancellation of rights on neglected plantation land (*tanah terlantar*) under national law.[13]

Official warnings in fact had been issued by the Provincial Plantations Department to the Generasi Jaya leaseholders in 1988, and a further report made to the governor in 1989 indicating that the leasehold was neglected and that royalties owed to the government had not been paid (DPRD 1995, 8–9). This evidence was apparently withheld from the court; at least there is no mention of it in the state court's 1991 decision, which found against the Gili Trawangan plaintiffs, and upheld the validity of the original HGU leases.[14] In its decision, the court argued that the governor's sons had legal rights to the land demonstrated by the HGU certificates presented in evidence; that there was no evidence that the land had been neglected by the lessees; that "legal certainty" would be undermined if it recognized illegal land occupation; that some of the applicant farmers had already received land in earlier allocations; and that some had established tourist homestays on the disputed land that were inconsistent with the land use previously determined—for plantation development, not tourism. Finally the court found the plaintiffs themselves responsible for deterring the accused leaseholders from making a success of their plantation because of their illegal occupation, and awarded court costs against them (Pengadilan Negeri Mataram 1991, 29–35).

In 1993, only two years after the court decision, the HGU plantation leases held by PT Generasi Jaya were canceled by the National Land Agency on grounds of neglect and improper transfer, precisely the arguments that the court had rejected in the smallholders' case.[15] The regional government's submission relied on plantations department reports of neglect, which had apparently been deliberately suppressed during the court case. Since the question of the neglected status of the HGU land had been pivotal in the court's determination of the farmers' case against the plantations department, further legal challenge should have been available to them. Prosecution through the newly established administrative courts (PTUN), however, was not an option because of its strict jurisdictional limitations (Bedner 2011).[16] The corruption of the general court system so evident and the political power of the state having turned to forcible destruction, no further recourse to the judiciary was contemplated.[17]

Request for revocation of the HGU leases came at the behest of the provincial government, by this time in league with the company, PT Gili Trawangan Indah, previously found complicit in an "improper transfer" in 1988 when it attempted to buy the HGU rights to develop the contested Generasi Jaya land for tourism (DPRD 1995, 12–18). The land was then restored to state control, with land use to be revised taking account of the 1989 regional government regulation locating it in a declared tourism zone. Ironically, the development of small-scale tourism operations on land designated for plantations was also a reason the court found against the plaintiff landholders' suit in 1991. Following the court decision against the Gili Trawangan claimants and subsequent cancellation of the original HGU leases, PT GTI obtained location and land use permits for a resort development on the former Generasi Jaya land (DPRD 1995, 13–15, 22–26). Thereafter all the machinery at the disposal of the state was deployed to consolidate its position and clear the land for the GTI development.

Between January 1990 and September 1991, according to the district head's account, he and the government team established to resolve the land dispute over the Generasi Jaya plantation lease had made fifteen trips to the island to "inform" (*penyuluhan*) and "consult" (*musyarawarah*)[18] with local people. Under the "agreement" offered to occupants of the former plantation leasehold, to which GTI obtained land utilization rights (HPL), the eighteen tourism businesses on the site would be given permits at an alternative location outside the disputed site with a maximum limit of five rooms for each business. Compensation would be in the form of a 0.15-hectare plot of land at the new site, as well as the cost of shifting cottages and restaurants and of obtaining certification and business permits. Farmers were to receive Rp 300,000 (US$138) per hectare plus the value of their lost crops and Rp 50,000 (US$23) for relocation and priority if they were prepared to join the transmigration program,[19] or 0.03 hectares for a residence and priority in employment in the new tourism facilities to be developed, if they chose to stay on the island (interview, MH, 28 September 1999; Pemda 1995, 7).

The farmers were incensed and demanded Rp 500,000 (US$227) per *are*[20] (0.01 hectare; Rp 50 million per hectare) in compensation for the land they were cultivating.[21] According to the government, they were illegal squatters on state land. At most, it asserted, given the failure of the plantation company to manage the land as required by law and their subsequent "illegal" colonization of state property, the farmers could claim consolation money (*uang santunan*), but not compensation for land that was not legally theirs.

The blatant inequities of the consultation and compensation process fueled resistance by those who were both absolutely and relatively worse off. But the government's compensation offer had driven a wedge between the farmers and small-scale tourism operators, and among the latter, between those pioneers who had lost larger and more strategically located holdings and those (mostly latecomers) who wound up with slightly more land than what they had originally leased or bought from original settlers. The majority of those rejecting the government offer stood to lose substantial parcels of dry farmland that they had been working for at least a decade. Those who accepted the deal had lost smaller amounts of land or simply lost heart and decided to cut their losses (interviews, AR, 27 September 1999; OM and MS, 11 August 2002).

Farmers who had been working several hectares objected that the three *are* (0.03 hectare) offered to them was completely inadequate for their livelihood needs, and that the additional twelve *are* offered to homestay owners was disproportionate to the size of their original holdings.

> I had two hectares [200 *are*] here. . . . There were some prepared to take the fifteen *are,* especially those [latecomers] that had only three or five *are* to begin with. With fifteen *are* they could build a bungalow or two. But farmers like us who [previously] had two hectares couldn't accept that. . . . This is a question of justice for those who sweated and worked themselves to the bone here. . . . Only three *are!* This is what makes you sick. . . . Three *are* would hold at most five trees. With only three *are* where will I put my children and grandchildren?[22] We agreed to struggle together and that

whoever would support the direct action would get a division of the reclaimed land. We argued, "We too are the Nation! (*Kita juga Negara*)." But they [government and GTI] used force. (interview, MS, 11 August 2002)

The farmers had earlier formed an organization, Petani Pada Maut (Peasants to the Death), when it became apparent regional government was dragging its heels in processing their applications for legal title to the Generasi Jaya concession (interview, MS, 11 September 2000). They were joined by those pioneer homestay and restaurant operators who objected that alternative sites offered for their businesses were too far from the strategic beach area where they had first established their small businesses.

Having failed in the 1990–91 court action, local resistance shifted to political pressure, as student and NGO activists became involved in the case. The resisting landholders went to the district assembly (DPRD) to lobby representatives but were unable to secure any firm commitments. However, they did succeed in recruiting tourists visiting the island to their cause. Sympathetic tourists wrote letters to the editor of the local papers and collected signatures on petitions submitted to government. That positive response from visitors strengthened local determination to resist. "Better to be shot than to live in misery" became the catchcry for locals who suffered intimidation, interrogation, and incarceration, not to mention anxiety about the household livelihoods that depended on their economic base on the island. The group that continued the resistance was accused of PKI sympathies, a threatening accusation in the New Order period, particularly for peasants involved in land conflicts. It intimated that all the power of the state could be brought to bear on its political adversaries and evoked chilling memories of the 1965–66 massacres of alleged Communist party members that brought Suharto to power.

Developers and complicit officials used intimidation tactics to frighten people into agreeing to move from the valuable coastal strip. The family and friends of Daeng Tola, one of the island's founding settlers and resistance leaders, insist that stress caused his death in the tense period leading up to the evictions. According to his daughter, he had been offered land as a bribe to end his resistance, which he refused. But after his death the islanders split into two factions, "those that gave in and those that didn't.... The group that continued to resist was labelled PKI. We couldn't meet together here freely until Suharto was ousted" (interview, RN, 29 August 1999).

In 1991 three of the homestay owners still holding out were arrested, taken to court, and sentenced to forty-five days in prison "for opening a business without a permit" (*Suara Nusa,* 30 September 1991).[23] The district head ordered these cottages sealed off and initiated an inventory of accommodations then operating on Gili Trawangan, which showed a doubling of local tourist facilities between 1988 and 1991 in contravention of the regional government's ban on expansion.

News that the villagers had again opened homestays to receive tourists and the circulation of a petition in English by tourists against the regional government's development plans for Gili Trawangan seem to have aroused the ire of regional government beyond containment. The governor instructed the district head to carry through its "ordering" operation "to the finish" in coordination with the regional government task force, Muspida.[24] The district head himself directed the eviction (*Suara Nusa,* 30 November 1991; interview, MH, 28 September 1999).

1992–95 *Ordering and Eviction*

"*Setiap ada penataan, ada pergusuran.*"
—Anonymous interviewee, 2002[25]

The series of brutal expulsions and reoccupations in 1992, 1993, and 1995 gave the Gili Trawangan case national exposure. "Thirty labourers wielding chain saws levelled the cottages on stilts, some with tourists still in them, as security forces looked on. Bungalows that the people had saved for years to build were cut down indiscriminately" (*Surya,* 26 August 1992). Constructed of woven bamboo and thatch on stilts, each bungalow which fell victim to the government's clearance campaign represented a substantial investment by Gili Trawangan's small entrepreneurs (SMUM 1991, 9). The government's action was described in the press as "killing the small enterprises that had been slowly nurtured, and sowing enmity among the people toward the government." Several residents described the action as "more cruel than anything they had experienced under colonialism" (*Surya,* 26 August 1992).[26] Student activists put out a press release decrying the forcible expulsion "gifted to the *rakyat* of Gili Trawangan only days after celebrating the 47th anniversary of Indonesian Independence that had been fought in the name of ideals of justice and prosperity for the people."[27]

An American student who arrived the day following the most drastic clearance in April 1995,[28] described the forced removal of the thirty-one families who had rebuilt on the disputed site since the 1992 and 1993 evictions. "Three hundred Indonesian soldiers—many of them veterans of the conflict in East Timor—converged upon the island with another two hundred police and various hired laborers, and . . . destroyed every house and business on the disputed land" (Gross 1996, 3–4).

One month before the final effort to force the occupying villagers off the contested land, the national Human Rights Commission (KomnasHAM) sent representatives to Gili Trawangan in response to the villagers' appeal for an investigation.[29] The outcome, however, was a great disappointment. After a brief visit, the commission concluded that there had been no human rights violations since the regional government had "conferred repeatedly" with residents. It advised the resisting group to accept the government's terms (*Nusa Tenggara,* 29 June 1995).

After the 1995 eviction, the government agreed to recommend additional allocations of twelve *are* to be excised from the original lease (SK Bupati Lombar 684/1996), so that farmers would obtain compensation equivalent to other claimants. But a small core of resisters continued to hold out, refusing to accept the compensation offer, and rebuilt once again on the GTI concession. "We came right back after each of the expulsions. I used a tent to sleep at the mosque. I never gave in or moved. After the first expulsion, we just pulled up the flattened bamboo buildings and set them up again." (Interview, RN, 29 August 99).

1998 Reoccupation—Possession, Equity, and the Law

The balance of power and expectation changed dramatically in 1998, when the Suharto regime fell from power. Ibu Rona described her role in the resistance and her elation at the collapse of the Suharto regime when it finally came in 1998.

> In 1998, I went to Jakarta with the students to demonstrate. We carried a banner "The Government Colludes with Investors." I shouted, "Down with Suharto! We here are—the people." When we came back from Jakarta, inspired by Cimacan, we straightaway began to divide up the land. We tore down the fence around the sixty-five hectares put there by PT GTI and threw it into the sea. Soldiers came six or eight at a time, but we realised that if we stood together, they wouldn't dare to do anything. Actually they were scared to go out at night. (Interview, RN, 29 August 1999).

As in many of these land conflict cases, women played a prominent role in the resistance. They often fronted direct actions to reduce the risk of violence by security forces and to "shame" authority figures[30] (interview, LJ, 29 August 1999). The leader of the resisting farmers' organization commented, "When it comes to solidarity, it is the women that we count on to be tough. If the women come out, Pemda will run. The men can't do that, they would all wind up in jail" (interview, MH, 28 September 1999).

In the aftermath of the spectacular and unanticipated collapse of the Suharto regime in 1998, a new sense of confidence in direct actions and people's justice took hold. As Rona's statement suggests, there was a certain triumphal assurance that now history was on their side and that the people's rights of prior possession and use would again become some part of the law. But a decade after the fall of Suharto and the final land occupation, promises of reform have yet to produce resolution of their legal status. A delegation of twenty people from Gili Trawangan to the national parliament (DPR) in 1998 returned with a letter of support from parliamentary representatives that they took as a "green light" validating their reoccupation. They were promised resolution "within a month." Later they were assured that as soon as regional autonomy was in effect, the district would take action to resolve the situation. In 2002, officers from the district land office of the National Land Agency (BPN), again surveying the land, suggested that certificates were imminent. In 2009, villagers awaited elections for the newly established North Lombok District with more promises that their rights would finally be recognized (interviews, MH, 29 August 1999; TF, 9 August 2002; ZN, 19 August 2009).

Nonetheless, since 2006, villagers have been summoned to the district police station on several occasions following GTI complaints that squatters were preventing them from carrying out their obligations to develop the land. To date resisting landholders have managed to rely on old solidarities, and in response to the most recent police summons, refused to attend unless all supporters were called in together. So far reclaiming landholders' insistence on collective response (and doubtless the much greater tourist presence and media risk compared to the early 1990s) has succeeded in forestalling another clearance campaign. Rumors are rife that GTI has plans to subdivide the land with the intention of selling the lease to other investors. Many locals believe that the government has been dragging its heels in the expectation that activist support for the landholders would dissipate and internal factionalism would ultimately break the back of local resistance (interviews, RJ, 3 March 2008 and 1 November 2008).

Maintaining internal solidarity and support for a cause with such indefinite prospects has been a serious problem throughout the conflict. Within the community tensions were exacerbated by the inequitable compensation scheme offered to occupying landholders by the government. Those who had been offered more land than they held originally had an incentive to settle, weakening the position of the remaining dissidents. When the reoccupation of the GTI concession was organized in 1998, the question of how the land should be allocated was a complex and contentious issue. How much consideration should be given to the size of previous holdings, second-generation family needs and those of later migrants, or to roles in the resistance movement? All these issues inevitably complicated the distributive equity question. Could original settlers with numerous descendants legitimately lay claim to new resources on the basis of expanding need? And what then of those newer migrants who couldn't make the original claims to land of the initial pioneers on the island but had supported the people's struggle and risked their safety in doing so?

In the end it was determined that pioneers in the struggle would have larger beachside shares. Rona's family, for example, received three plots (0.34 hectares) in the reclaimed area for her immediate family and another two for an uncle and sibling. She justified the differential land allocations: "We worked the land, and opened it for [others]. . . . Let them come and ask me. I fought. I lost my mother and father over this. The rest we divided among all those who were prepared to support us, three *are* (0.03 hectares) each. The ones in front [on the beach] were for the original people who worked the land. I want a secure life after all those years of uncertainty. I'm fed up struggling for nothing" (interview, RN, 6 September 2002). Not all agreed that the outcome was fair. A late migrant, also active in the resistance, regarded the allocation of land shares as nepotistic (interview, NJ, 8 September 2002).

Value Transformations and the Question of Equity

But inequities in the division of lots after reoccupation hardly compare with the structural inequities generated by the property regimes tied to international circulations of capital. Rona's own entrepreneurial engagements reflect the realities of a globalizing market exchange model that is difficult to reconcile with concepts of fairness or distributive justice that underpin debates about land use and land rights. The situation also raises questions about the concept of legal certainty in a speculative regime that depends for its profits on extreme structural asymmetries across time and space.

Having struggled for more than a decade, building and rebuilding their small bungalows each time they were pulled down, Rona was now tapping foreign capital in her family's search for economic security. "Last year I tried an internet and travel service. No one came. I quickly turned the office into two rooms that are now always full at Rp 50,000 a night (US$6)" (interview, RN, 6 September 2002). She estimated she could pay off the cost of renovation in two years. She also "joined" with Australians to build a homestay on her portion of reoccupied land. The partners have no certificate on the disputed land, but they have an agreement witnessed by the heads of the hamlet and the village committing to provide all necessary capital to develop it—Rona guessed some Rp 200 million. "When would I ever have the capital to do that?" she asked. In return for these rights to develop one of her lots on the contested land, she will receive 20 percent of profits from the foreign partners. Another foreign national had signed an annual contract worth Rp fifty million with a landholder in the contested area to build a dive shop; and numerous other contracted arrangements for space along the high value coastline were already in place in 2002 (interview, RN, 6 September 2002). By 2009, tourism was booming and the number of substantial foreign interests in Gili Trawangan properties and businesses was approaching the hundred mark; at least a dozen of these were in the contested area and included upmarket accommodation, restaurants, and other businesses (interview, NJ, 19 August 2009).

But entry into global capitalist circuits through luxury tourism and real estate development presages another route to marginalization and displacement for the local community on Gili Trawangan. Over forty years the commercial value of land on the island rose from virtually nothing to per hectare values that would support an ordinary household in Lombok for decades, largely in consequence of Gili Trawangan's growing international reputation as a "hot" travel destination and the island's corollary entry into the international property market catering to the lifestyle desires of metropolitan holders of capital.[31]

The original settlers did not buy the fields that they cleared in the 1970s, because "then it was empty, so you didn't have to buy or sell" (interview, RN, 29 August 1999). When they moved to the beach to take advantage of the first backpacker tourists, small local entrepreneurs paid token compensation (*ganti rugi*) to those farmers whose land extended to this formerly unproductive area. At this stage, relatively small amounts of money changed hands among neighbors for what was regarded from a farmer's point of view as worthless wasteland. Those granted plots in the defunct PT Rinta concession paid Rp 75,000 (US$117) per hectare in the government-mediated compensation arrangements in the mid-1980s (interview, AR, 27 September 1999). As capital investment took off with the deregulation of the banking industry in 1988 and accelerated with relaxation of investment rules in 1993, a binge of speculative land acquisitions for megaresort and real estate developments ousted farmers from their sources of livelihood across Indonesia.[32] Deregulation policies also established mechanisms for circumventing the still unchanged provisions of the Basic Agrarian Law prohibiting foreign ownership of land.

The value transformations currently taking place augur displacement of the meaning and value of land and community to which the Basic Agrarian Law and the original peasant farmer/fishers of Gili Trawangan aspired. A long-time NGO activist involved in the case said, "It would be good if they would put into the village regulations (*awiq-awiq*) a rule against buying and selling land. But no one seems to want to talk about that, or the fact that further down the track, many will have sold their land" (interview, DS, 14 August 2002). Despite the clear prohibition of land ownership by foreign nationals, a global real estate industry is now established in Gili Trawangan. Land for which farmers were offered token sympathy money of Rp 300,000 per hectare in the early 1990s was in 2008 being sold to foreign interests up to Rp 100 million per *are* (0.01 hectare). Even depressed by the impact of the terrorist bombings in Indonesia and the early stages of a world economic recession, the front page of the *Bali Advertiser* (2–16 July 2008) offered Gili Trawangan beachfront property on the less favored western side of the island, under either freehold or use right,[33] for US$4,000 per *are* (equivalent to roughly Rp 39 million), almost eighteen times (in adjusted terms) the value smallholder farmers had demanded in compensation from the government in 1995.

Although some of the ongoing development of the island's tourism industry remains in local hands, this is largely a consequence of the survival of elements of legal constraint on foreign ownership that necessitates partnership with locals for legal security. Generally, the experience of small-scale tourism is that it moves out of local hands and marginalizes the poorest as the capital-intensive end of the industry becomes dominant. The property market component of the tourism development trajectory only accelerates this process and remains an underrecognized and underresearched dimension of the political economy of this "Cinderella" industry.[34]

Legal Certainty for Whom?

Those Gili Trawangan claimants who resisted had no more formal status on the disputed land fifteen years after the Reform Era began than they had throughout the years of conflict under the New Order. In the early heady days of the reform movement, the sense that Trawangan locals needed outside protection had dissipated. They clearly believed local arrangements were what mattered, and so did a significant number of small foreign investors who had taken the risk of negotiating arrangements with landholders on the disputed part of the island. Other aspects of the "development" of the island also proceeded through these informal processes.

One Western joint venturer commented on the vagueness of the legal arrangements under which his fifteen-room boutique hotel was being built. He had gone ahead with construction without requisite permits on the advice of the village head and other local leaders,[35] though he admitted the arrangements were confusing. He said he was advised by an Indonesian business consultant that his company "owns" the land—indefinitely as he understood it—but technically, as HPL use-right rather than freehold, requiring renewal every thirty years. "The business consultant explained the whole arrangement: Three kinds of PT [company] ownership . . . something like that. Anyway. I leave it all to them. The PT is 95 percent in my name and 5 percent in the name of a local, which I give to him when I sell it. He found the land, and he has the land ownership certificate" (interview, LC, 12 August 2002). The consultant who facilitated this arrangement said that most foreigners who "buy" property through a complex process colloquially described as "borrowing the name" of an Indonesian citizen as silent partner to circumvent restrictions on foreign land ownership, often do so through highly informal arrangements and little knowledge of Indonesian law or local language and culture (interview, LS, 14 August 2002). Not least surprising is the preparedness of these Western partners to invest with relatively little formal legal certainty—something they presume that money (bribery) can buy. As an Indonesian outside observer of the Gili Trawangan case commented, "If you speak of legal certainty, that may exist for the elites; but for ordinary people, the law is never straight" (interview, WG, 11 August 2002).[36]

Insofar as pan-Indonesian normative principles underlie popular understandings of land use and tenure rights,[37] they rely on a range of time-honored popular assumptions that recognize legitimate rights to land as primarily derived from originally opening the land, continuing to work it, and maintaining good social relations with the community that validates those claims. They are socially embedded use-value concepts, now increasingly challenged by the various forms of exchange value that multiple economic transformations have wrought to the place of land in smallholder farming and small-scale tourism, on the one hand, set against the commercial plantation and resort/real estate sectors, on the other. These alternative values are tied to particular economic regimes with at least partly distinct moral and political economies.

Qualified use-value concepts of land rights have operated at local level more or less effectively across Indonesia in the absence of formal processes of registration and transfer. Where the government pursued formalization of land law, local people relied on normative practices of negotiation (*musyawarah*), compensation for loss (*ganti rugi*), and various forms of reciprocal obligation in land use and tenure transfer that continue to have salience in local practice.[38] For the people of Gili Trawangan, it is precedence and the raw, hard work of opening fields and small businesses, alongside the shared endurance of adversity, that continue to legitimate land rights. These claims have been preempted by the state on the basis of political sovereignty and eminent domain, rationalized by its ostensible role as proxy for a wider, national construction of the people's interest.

Both the Gili Trawangan farmers' and the state's positions share underlying customary concepts embedded in the Basic Agrarian Law and pursuant land reform legislation. The focus on productive use and the restrictions this legislation places on land transactions—limiting the accumulation of landholdings, providing for the resumption of neglected land, and prohibiting foreign ownership—have philosophical roots in this traditional emphasis on precedence and use right.[39] Although Trawangan landholders were not claiming explicit *adat*-based rights to their land or any type of communal property, they nonetheless share certain notions of right and responsibility with respect to land access and use, that in their view ought to inform interpretations of formal law.

Customary foundations in the architecture of Indonesian land law are important to understanding local popular responses in the Gili Trawangan case. In the state's argument, it represents the wider "community" of the national "*rakyat*" and has the obligation to manage state land to serve the public good. The little people of Gili Trawangan argue precedence of their moral and legal right to the land as first and ongoing users, and as the real "*rakyat*" whose well-being the Indonesian state is responsible to ensure. Arguably, the extent to which local smallholders succeeded in applying these shared principles is not always consistent, although certainly, on evidence of the Gili Trawangan case, it has been no less so than state practice has proved.

We might speculate on whether state and local claims could have accommodated mutual objectives at Gili Trawangan:

- if the "national interest" clause in the BAL had not been hijacked in the service of politico-business elites in the initial land and license allocation process;

- if there had been genuine negotiations that took account of local conceptions of fairness, and incorporated the needs of different land users and future generations in forward planning;

- if the state had not played off one sector of the community against another in its effort to bring the dissenting claimants to heel;

- if the Gili Trawangan community for its part had been able to organize, negotiate, and maintain a fair and sustainable distribution of land and income opportunities across the smallholder sector in the early years of land pioneering, and if the community had been able to respond collectively to the value transformations that Gili Trawangan subsequently experienced;
- if the state had committed its energies to supporting and upgrading the small-scale tourism ventures that had been pioneered by Gili Trawangan settlers, and supporting the integration of local farmers and fishers into the developing tourism economy;
- if the extreme value transformations of different land uses were fairly adjusted through progressive taxation and redistribution mechanisms for both local and wider community benefit.

Then perhaps a resolution of the conflict could have been found that would have been to the benefit of "the people" as construed in both national and local narratives.

One of the leaders of the dissident farmers' group at Gili Trawangan framed his interpretation of land law and justice in a manner that draws local normative models and the formal law of the state together into a populist moral economy framework. His focus is on local people's rights and responsibilities based on use value, provenance, and reciprocity,[40] and on the state's loss of moral authority for want of evenhanded justice. For him local customary principles were compatible with the social function principles of formal law regarding limits to accumulation, and popular rights of access to land and compensation. Those same principles might have been adapted to curb accumulation by local people as well,[41] he suggests, if the state itself had not transgressed its common good obligations and misused its authority.

> Now if the government were to say, "Pak M has already received his share of land," that's fine. But [emphatically] why is it that government, wants to devour our land? For what? Have they worked the land or not? And what should be the case according to law? If someone takes too much land, then we also have [a right] to take it back. Fundamentally, you have a right to own land if you use it. Yes

or no? If someone doesn't work the land, if they acquire it because of corruption, then we have to resist—"give it back!" ... [The company] was given the lease on that land for thirty years. After four years it was abandoned. So we were forced to take it. And because the land was never compensated—we only received compensation for the trees on the land—so we took it back. . . . That's why the students were prepared to help us, because the government was greedy. (Interview, MH, 29 August 1999)

The fact is that the interests of government officials, both as private actors and public officials, remain with large-scale developments rather than the "people's economy" of national rhetoric; to turn alternative development options into serious propositions would necessitate more active involvement and less easy reward.

Postscript

The establishment of the North Lombok District and election of a new bupati have to 2012 done nothing to secure the position of the occupying landholders at Gili Trawangan, now numbering some 470 households. Since 2009 some of these have been paying land and building tax, which however does not guarantee legal recognition of their tenure status. While PT GTI's claim appears for the time being to be dormant, part of the disputed former plantation land that had been transferred under mysterious circumstances to another company (PT WAH), and similarly neglected, is now the site of new pressure on occupying households. Its owner is connected with the same party as the new bupati of North Lombok. Since 2010 gangs (*preman*) hired by the company, assisted by a police Brimob brigade, have been intimidating those occupying this section of the former plantation lands. Twenty-four local people have been charged and found guilty of occupying land illegally, one of whom was jailed in February 2012. Others have been offered inducements to sign documents admitting "illegal" occupation. Meanwhile, domestic and foreign investors vie for access, offering amounts up to Rp 100 million per *are* for land whose legal status remains clouded. The Lombok branch of the SPI farmer's union, now involved in this and other cases, anticipates that with the opening of the new airport in Lombok, land conflicts across the island will inevitably intensify (WP, personal communication, 12 February 2012; and interviews conducted by Agung Wardana with RN, JN, IS 17 February 2012, and with SPI activists 18 February 2012).

Notes

This research was initiated at the request of student activists from the University of Mataram through Catur Kukuh who met with Anton Lucas following the first eviction at Gili Trawangan in 1992. Subsequent field research was undertaken by the author during visits to the island in the period 1999–2002 and again in 2009. Documentation was made available from the archives of Yayasan Koslata and Senat Mahasiswa Universitas Mataram. I wish in particular to thank Dwi Sudharsono, Rujito Martowiyono, Wayan Gandera, Denik Puriati, and Agung Wardana for research assistance over these years. Adriaan Bedner, Widodo Putro, and Agung Wardana gave invaluable advice on legal dimensions of the case. Except where otherwise indicated, interviews were conducted and translated by the author, who remains solely responsible for the interpretation placed on the information presented. Names and initials of informants have been changed for their protection.

1. "The government intended to protect Gili Trawangan from ruin [*kerusakan*] . . . to raise the income of the people and facilitate development" (West Lombok District Head in *Bali Post*, 2 September 2000). Officials regarded local facilities as dirty and unkempt, and claimed locals didn't consider the environment because they were solely oriented to their businesses (*Bali Post*, 31 August 1992; Pemda 1995, 30).

2. From the 1989 land office (BPN) map it appears that the larger blocks of around three hectares were held by founding settler families and a few well-connected individuals from outside the island.

3. The initial application in the company's name was rejected by the home affairs minister for reasons that are not clear (DPRD 1995, 3), but it probably had to do with limits to regional government rights to allocate plantation concessions up to twenty-five hectares.

4. Sertifikat HGU/Pemenang Barat No. 1:28/1/86 and Nos. 2–4:21/8/86.

5. PRONA was the government's group land-titling scheme, which was intended to make certification of land affordable for ordinary Indonesians.

6. See Harsono (2007) for provisions concerning maximum limits on landholdings, as well as cancellation of private rights due to neglect, abandonment, or absentee ownership under the Basic Agrarian Law (BAL/UUPA 5/1960: §27a3; §34e and §40e). UU 56/1960 §8 tasks the government with working toward achieving a minimum viable holding of two hectares for smallholders to raise the standard of living of the peasant population. While UU 51/1961 prohibits unauthorized use of public or private land, article 5 nonetheless makes special provision for occupied plantation and forest lands to be resolved by the Minister of Agrarian Affairs, taking account of the interests of both the people using the land and official land-title holders. See Fitzpatrick (1997, 179ff.) on the ambiguities of the legislation on "unlawful occupation" in contrast to customary practices, which allow for acquisition of rights through uninterrupted adverse possession.

7. Peraturan Daerah (Perda) No. 9/ 1989 tentang Penetapan 15 Kawasan Pariwisata di Nusa Tenggara Barat.

8. Multiplier effects for local tourism in general tend to be inversely correlated with the scale of development (Wall 1997). The difference in price between budget and luxury accommodation at Gili Trawangan ranged from US$10 to US$500 per night in 2009.

9. It should be noted, however, that while local small entrepreneurs did pay taxes on their businesses (one reported paying as much as Rp 2 million in one year), PT Generasi Jaya had paid no royalties. Royalties alleged to have been negotiated by its successor PT GTI were 20 million per annum, with a 5 percent increase after each five-year period (RN 9 August 1999).

10. Bupati Lombok Barat, Laporan Lanjutan Pelaksanaan Penertiban Gili Trawangan [Report on Law and Order Implementation at Gili Trawangan], No. 593/3713, 11 September 1992, 4.

11. Laporan Khusus mengenai pelaksanaan penertiban bangunan untuk usaha pariwisata tanpa ijin di Pulau Trawangan, 2 September 1992.

12. See note 6 above for sources on competing legal interpretations.

13. Their deposition to the court refers to BAL/UUPA 5/1960, §§6, 10, 15, 28, and SK Menteri Pertanian 510/1983. See Pengadilan Negeri Mataram 1991.

14. Pengadilan Negeri Mataram 1991, 33.

15. The evidence accepted by the land office was based on the above-mentioned plantations department reports of 7 November 1989 and 15 August 1990 verifying that the land in question was not properly managed by the concession holders and was classified as *"terlantar"* (DPRD 1995, 8–11).

16. Recent proposals would significantly expand the jurisdiction of the administrative courts over all cases of unlawful acts by government, but

have yet to be enacted into law. Bedner (2011, 226) regards the emergence of yet another set of specialized courts to deal with both civil and administrative land cases as the most likely outcome of the present inadequacies of both the general and administrative court systems.

17. Avoidance of the legal system is part of popular wisdom, as implied in the proverb "*yang menang akan menjadi arang; yang kalah akan menjadi abu*" (The winners become charcoal; the losers become ash).

18. What the government called "consultation," the people described as "ultimatum."

19. The press later reported (*Merdeka,* 12 June 1993) that land on Lombok supposedly set aside for relocation of these farmers was already owned or occupied by others.

20. One *are* is equivalent to 0.01 hectare or 100 square meters. Currency equivalents of rupiah to US dollars are calculated at the rate current for the different periods referred to in the text, and change drastically after the economic crisis of 1997–98.

21. In the early 1990s, land was being forcibly resumed for similar developments in Bali at Serangan Island and Tanah Lot against strong landholder opposition. There compensation of Rp 2.5 million per *are* (0.01 hectare) for recognized land titles was deemed inadequate. Even at this rate, payments to landholders were well below market values by a factor of at least ten (see Warren 1998).

22. Villagers also pointed to parcels that had been allocated to officials, including police, lawyers, and bureaucrats who had never settled on the island but had acted in support of the government's actions. That sixteen among those listed to receive three *are* allocations were not farmers at all, is acknowledged in the provincial government's own report (DPRD 1995, 20).

23. The fact that the lack of building permits (IMB) was used to legitimate their incarceration and the subsequent clearance of bungalows suggests uncertainty about the strength of government claims of "unlawful occupation." See Bupati Lombok Barat, Laporan, 11 September 2011, 3 (full reference note 10).

24. Muspida is the regional security advisory group consisting of heads of all district-level civil and military authorities.

25. "With every ordering, comes eviction" (interview, NJ, 10 August 2002).

26. Press coverage, however, was not entirely sympathetic to the "little people" who lost their livelihoods in these government clearance campaigns. The violation of permit requirements and environmental guidelines, repeated government "consultations" and warnings, and allusions to instigation by parties with antigovernment sentiments were among the

justifications for eviction cited in some of the press reports (*Kompas,* 29 August 1992; *Merdeka,* 12 June 1993).

27. "Our witness on behalf of the oppressed people of Gili Trawangan," press release by Mataram Students' Communications Forum, 27 August 1992.

28. The ferry to the island was shut down for several days. Gross took a fishing boat to Gili Trawangan, staying on the island for the next two and a half months.

29. The 1995 compilation of documents and summary accounts by district and provincial government authorities (Pemda 1995 and DPRD 1995) of January and March were prepared in advance of the Human Rights Commission visit and in anticipation of the final forced removal. No mention of the previous clearance campaigns is made in these submissions, which focus primarily on the respective parties' positions, government "consultations," and the resisting group's rejection of compensation offers. The district head's deposition, however, refers to authority given under Law 51/1960 to "empty by force" land occupied illegally (Pemda 1995, 8).

30. In an acutely sensitive act of defiance "the women opened their blouses to [shame] the bupati. 'If you have sympathy for our women, don't take our island. . . . If you want money to go to Mecca don't sell my land'" (interview, RN, 29 August 1999).

31. High-end beachfront property can sell for US$10,000 per *are,* or US$1 million per hectare, according to real estate industry sources (interview, DH, 12 November 2008), several thousand times the "compensation" offered to Gili Trawangan landholders in 1995. Because of foreign exchange and labor value asymmetries, foreigners of even modest means are tempted by the prospect of owning a small piece of "paradise" with low living costs and cheap domestic labor. Land values and exchange rates throughout this chapter are converted at prevailing rates in the year indicated. The Indonesian rupiah was severely devalued from Rp 1,643 to the US dollar in 1990 to Rp 10,000 to the US dollar in 2009 due to steady devaluations and a precipitous fall in the Asian economic crisis of 1997–98.

32. See Warren (1998) for discussions of the impact of the development boom in Bali during this period.

33. Interestingly in Western property advertisements, there is little or no distinction in the value of property listed as "freehold" (*hak milik*) or "use right" (*hak pakai*). Only Indonesian citizens can technically acquire "freehold" title under the BAL. Several real estate agency websites summarize the options under liberalized regulations for circumventing this principle. See, for example, http://www.lombok-global.com/property

_law.htm and http://ppbali.com/indonesian-law-guide.php, Accessed 27 September 2011.

34. Some farmers did benefit or at least broke even as a consequence of these value asymmetries between the subsistence and global property markets. One Gili Trawangan farmer was able to sell twelve of the fifteen *are* offered in compensation for the loss of his two hectare piece of farmland to investors for Rp 170 million (US$17,486). He bought two hectares of farmland on the Lombok mainland for Rp 100 million and remains resident on the remaining three *are* at Gili Trawangan, where he works as a laborer. Few farmers have been successful in converting their settlement award into small business enterprises, however (interview, AS, 27 September 1999).

35. The hotel was being built on a forty-*are* block that had been part of the second round of compensation settlements to three claimants at the northeast end of the island. It remained state land with HPL rights only, not freehold, as the Westerner seems to assume in his reference to "owning" the land. One of the village elders said, "They were going crazy trying to get permits, etcetera. I told the local partner to just go ahead and build. We will back him if there's any trouble. What good would a permit be anyway if we didn't approve?" (Interview, RK, 11 September 2000) See Fitzpatrick (1997, 179, 206) on customary mechanisms by which outsiders gain rights of use in return for recognition money, the customary equivalent of BAL principles on foreign access to land use rights.

36. Nonetheless, real estate agents and lawyers admitted that in cases where such contractual land agreements between Indonesian nationals and foreigners are challenged, the latter's rights are rarely upheld in court.

37. The Dutch scholar of *adat* law, Van Vollenhoven, was convinced of the existence of underlying *adat* principles applied to land use and rights of allocation across Indonesia. For different perspectives on the sources and implications of this premise, see Van Vollenhoven in Holleman 1981 and Burns 1999.

38. According to the provincial land office (BPN) only 30 percent of the registrable land in the province of Nusa Tenggara Barat had been issued with certificates of title since 1960 (*Bali Post,* 26 March 2008).

39. The Basic Agrarian Law states, "Every person and legal body that holds a right in agricultural land is fundamentally obliged to actively work that land themselves, and to prevent exploitation" (BAL/UUPA 1960, §10/1).

40. See Verdery and Humphrey (2004, 139ff.) on the reciprocal obligations implicit in property rights. See also Benda Beckmann, Benda Beckmann, and Wiber (2006).

41. The 1988 district investigation team reported that only twenty of the seventy-seven occupants of the Generasi Jaya leasehold were directly working the land; the other fifty-seven having turned over land use to others (Bapparda Tingkat II "Kesimpulan/Kesepakatan pertemuan antara pemerintah daerah dengan pemilik usaha pariwisata di Gili Trawangan, Gili Meno dan Gili Air," 9 January 1990).

References

Bedner, A. 2011. "'Shopping Forums': Indonesia's Administrative Courts." In *New Courts in Asia,* ed. A. Harding and P. Nicholson, 209–31. London: Routledge.

Benda Beckmann, F. von, K. von Benda Beckmann, and M. Wiber. 2006. *Changing Properties of Property.* New York: Berghahn.

Burns, P. J. 1999. *The Leiden Legacy: Concepts of Law in Indonesia.* Jakarta: Pradnya Paramita.

DPRD. 1995. Laporan Hasil Kerja Tim Assistensi DPRD Propinsi Daerah NTB tentang Penataan Tanah Hak Pengelolahan (HPL).

Covernton, M., and T. Wheeler. 1984. *Bali and Lombok: A Traveller's Survival Kit.* South Yarra, Australia: Lonely Planet Publications.

Fitzpatrick, D. 1997. "Disputes and Pluralism in Modern Indonesian Land Law." *Yale Journal of International Law* 22 (1): 171–212.

———. 1999. "Beyond Dualism: Land Acquisition and Law in Indonesia." In *Indonesia: Law and Society,* ed. T. Lindsey. Melbourne: Federation Press.

Gross, S. 1996. "Trouble in Paradise: A Study of Tourism, Oppression and Opposition on a Small Island in Eastern Indonesia." BA honors thesis. Department of Anthropology, Wesleyan University.

Gubah Laras. 1989. Studi Rencana Tata Ruang dan Pedoman Perancangan Teknis Kawasan Pariwisata Gili Meno dan Gili Trawangan. Laporan Sementara, Departemen Pariwisata, Pos dan Telekomunikasi, Direktorat Jenderal Pariwisata, Proyek Pengembangan Pariwisata Nusa Tenggara Barat.

Harsono, B. 2007. *Hukum Agraria Indonesia: Himpunan Peraturan-Peraturan Hukum Tanah.* 11th rev. ed. Jakarta: Penerbit Djambatan.

Holleman, F. D., ed. 1981. *Van Vollenhoven on Indonesian Adat Law.* The Hague: Martinus Nijhoff.

Pemda [West Lombok District]. 1995. [Including deposition of the Lombok Barat District Head, Lombok Barat, 29 March 1995.] "Penjelasan tentang Kasus Gili Trawangan dan Upaya Penyelesaiannya," 29 March 1995, Pemda Tingkat II Lombok Barat.

Pengadilan Negeri Mataram. 1991. Putusan Perkara No. 088/PDT/G/1990 /PN. MTR, 22 April.

SMUM. 1991. "Gili Trawangan—Antara Pembangunan dan Penghancuran, Suatu Pembelaan Kritis: Mahasiswa Masyarakat Gili Trawangan." Unpublished ms. Mataram: Senat Mahasiswa Universitas Mataram (SMUM), Komisi Advokasi dan Solidaritas.

Verdery, K., and C. Humphrey. 2004. *Property in Question: Value Transformation in the Global Economy.* Oxford: Berg.

Wall, G. 1997. "Scale Effects on Tourism Multipliers." *Annals of Tourism Research* 24 (2): 446–50.

Warren, C. 1998. "Tanah Lot: The Political Economy of Resort Development in Bali." In *The Politics of Environment in Southeast Asia: Resources and Resistance,* ed. P. Hirsch and C. Warren, 229–61. London: Routledge.

Newspapers

Bali Advertiser
Bali Post
Kompas
Merdeka
Nusa Tenggara
Suara Nusa
Surya

Chapter 9

DEALING WITH THE URBAN POOR

Changing Law and Practice of Commercial Land Clearance in Post–New Order Bandung

GUSTAAF REERINK

During the New Order, a considerable number of land disputes in Indonesia were related to the clearance of urban kampong[1] land for commercial development. This was particularly the case after the 1980s, when the Suharto regime undertook a series of deregulation measures to stimulate oil-independent economic growth, which resulted in commercial land development becoming one of Indonesia's prime investment sectors. The urban poor residing in kampongs were often pressured by developers—who could generally rely on the government's support—to give up their land for low compensation rates. As far as the urban poor dared to resist, such resistance had little success. These practices made clear the weakness of the rule of law in Indonesia.

After 1998, Indonesia embarked on an ambitious reform program. Reforms included four constitutional amendments, of which the second amendment resulted in the inclusion in the 1945 Constitution of an extensive catalogue of human rights.[2] Furthermore, Indonesia acceded to various international human rights treaties, one of which was the International Covenant on Economic, Social and Cultural Rights (ICESC).

Both the Amended 1945 Constitution and the ICESC refer to the right to adequate housing.[3] According to the UN Committee on Economic, Social and Cultural Rights, this right requires a degree of tenure security that guarantees legal protection against forced eviction, harassment, and other threats irrespective of tenure status.[4] Indonesia's reform program also involved regional autonomy, various measures against corruption, and, albeit on a limited scale, land law reform.[5] Ideally, these reforms would strengthen the rule of law, bring an end to New Order commercial land clearance practices and make the right to adequate housing a reality.

This chapter discusses the law and practice of commercial land clearance during the New Order and, after considering post–New Order reforms, takes a closer look at urban commercial land clearance practices in Bandung, Indonesia's fourth largest city and the capital of West Java Province. Bandung has been confronted with a process of rapid land commoditization, resulting in increased risks for the urban poor faced with developers who want their land. To illustrate how they deal with this problem, this chapter examines the Paskal Hyper Square case, which involved the clearance of kampong land for the realization of a commercial development project. It looks into this case from both a legal-administrative and a sociopolitical perspective, paying attention to six steps in the land clearance process: the administrative procedure preceding the land clearance process, the nature of the negotiation process and the level of compensation offered, the composition of popular resistance, the argumentation and strategies used in resistance, the role of legal norms and institutions, and the effect of resistance. This analysis gives insight into change and continuity in commercial land clearance policy in post–New Order Bandung and, more generally, the rule of law at the local level in Indonesia.

Law and Practice of Commercial Land Clearance under the New Order

In the first decades after independence, commercial land clearance remained unregulated in Indonesia. It was simply a matter between private parties, without interference by the state.[6] This changed in the 1970s. Following the New Order's "developmentalist" shift to state-led industrialization and large-scale exploitation of natural resources, the Indonesian Parliament enacted two laws on foreign and domestic investment in 1967 and 1968.[7] In 1974 the minister of Home Affairs subsequently enacted an implementing regulation on the disposal of land for commercial interest, with particular reference to housing and industrial estates.[8] The regulation's aim was to enhance economic growth by meeting developers' need for land.[9] To that purpose the regulation created a permit mechanism, which theoretically at least took account of spatial planning law and the "social function" provisions of the BAL.

It is clear that the 1974 regulation was not primarily meant to protect landholders, although it contained some provisions that could contribute to this.[10] Soon after the promulgation of the regulation the Indonesian government enabled developers to call on the assistance of the authorities in commercial land clearance. A 1976 Minister of Home Affairs regulation declared the procedures on land clearance in the public interest applicable to commercial land clearance if this was determined to be in the interest of the state. In this procedure the so-called Land Release Committee, consisting of at least eight different government officials, supervised the land clearance process and determined the level of compensation.[11] The regulation resulted in an unclear distinction between public interest and commercial land clearance.

Although the legal basis for commercial land clearance changed constantly, the permit mechanism remained pivotal.[12] A permit that played a central role was the location permit (*izin lokasi*), which allowed a developer to start negotiations with landholders in a designated area on the basis of traditional deliberation (*musyawarah*) processes for the clearance of land for a specific purpose. This procedure had to be followed with regard to all types of landholders, including squatters, and under the supervision of the authorities that had issued the permit, for instance on the basis of reports and site visits.[13]

From the late 1980s, two developments took place in commercial land clearance law. First, in an effort to increase oil-independent economic growth, the Indonesian government introduced a series of deregulation measures, enacting separate regulations on commercial land clearance for housing development and the development of industrial areas in 1987 and 1989 respectively.[14] In 1992, the 1974 regulation was finally replaced by a new regulation, which was to improve and speed up the permit granting process for commercial land clearance by simplifying procedures.[15] In 1993, the 1992 regulation was replaced by yet another regulation, which centralized the authority to issue location permits from the provincial governor to the National Land Agency (Badan Pertanahan Nasional, hereafter BPN).[16]

The deregulation policies significantly contributed to commercial land development becoming one of the country's prime investment sectors. It not only became easier for developers to obtain the permits required for land clearances, the banking sector and thus the credit market for housing also expanded. After a dip in the early 1990s, further deregulation policies ensured that land development was again booming by 1993 (Winarso and Firman 2002, 488–91).

Deregulation policies resulted in more landholders being affected by commercial land clearance and led to land clearance practices coming under increasing public scrutiny. A second development, part of a general policy of "openness" as a response to increasing criticism of the New Order regime, involved legal reforms that potentially supported the interests of landholders. So in 1990, the head of the National Land Agency sent a circular letter to its provincial offices, requesting that they establish separate Supervision and Control Teams for Commercial Land Clearance (Tim Pengawasan dan Pengendalian Pembebasan Tanah untuk Keperluan Swasta, also called Tim Wadal) at the municipal/district level. Consisting of government officials only, the teams had the task of supervising and controlling the land clearance process.[17] In 1991, the regime established administrative courts (Pengadilan Tata Usaha Negara, or PTUN), allowing landholders to subject decisions about government permit issuing to judicial review.[18] Finally, in 1993 it replaced the 1975 regulation on land clearance in the public interest with a new regulation that no longer allowed developers to apply the procedure for land clearance in the public interest for commercial purposes.[19]

Though containing some safeguards to protect landholders, legislation pertaining to commercial land clearance could hardly contribute to this. The mechanism to supervise commercial land clearance was ineffective, because authorities could only issue warnings if a developer harmed the interests of landholders.[20] There was however nothing to prevent the government, having issued several warnings, from refusing extension of or even withdrawing a permit.

Insofar as commercial land clearance law could theoretically protect landholders, this was not the case in practice. Knowing that land speculators—officials (or others who had been informed by them) who knew about a development plan—were active and that once a location permit had been issued land prices would rise anyway, some developers started to acquire land before obtaining a permit. To speed up the process, they often employed their own front men (*calo*) (Leaf 1991, 153–54). Developers also continued to acquire land after the term of their permit had already expired. Others simply never took the trouble to obtain a permit. It was rarely in authorities' interest to apply the rules strictly. They frequently issued permits that were not in accordance with spatial plans.[21]

Holding a location permit or not, developers commonly pressured landholders to give up their land for very low compensation rates. A location permit facilitated this process. Landholders were often made to believe that the permit formed a right to claim the land (Sumardjono 1999, 16). Some developers limited residents' access to land by building walls around plots of those who refused to sell their land, or they deliberately disturbed them by construction activities (Suyanto 1996, 47).

Although it was common knowledge that landholders were pressured to give up their land rights, authorities did little to prevent this. According to Firman (1996, 1041), many authorities regarded the permit procedure as a way to collect fees rather than a system to control commercial land clearance. In fact, authorities often assisted developers by lending their coercive power. Developers could deploy officials or even security forces to intimidate landholders. In combination with the large number of permits that were issued and the continuous extension of such permits, many landholders thus had to live in uncertainty for a long time. Authorities also assisted developers in commercial land clearance by applying alternative procedures to get people off their land. Developers generally preferred to follow the procedure for land clearance in the public interest (Struyk, Hoffman, and Katsura 1990, 137–40), and municipal governments often applied this procedure for commercial land clearance even after 1993, when legally this was no longer possible. They abused the concept of "public interest," extending it to include such items as golf courses (see chapter 4). In order to clear squatter-occupied land, municipal governments proved willing to apply the procedure set out in a 1960 law on the use of land without permission of the rights holder.[22] UU 51/1960 forbids such use and even makes it a criminal offense.[23] It also grants regional government authorities discretionary power to evict "unlawful occupants," after taking account of zoning and land use plans, and provision of compensation in the form of "assistance/sympathy money" (*uang santunan*).[24] In other instances authorities reverted to municipal building regulations, on the basis of which they could demolish buildings erected without a building permit, again without the obligation to compensate. Though constituting a clear abuse of power, some municipal governments justified the use of these regulations by the fact that they had not yet enacted implementing regulations regarding commercial land clearance (Struyk, Hoffman, and Katsura 1990, 136).

The aforementioned conditions resulted in landholders accepting inadequate compensation. Not knowing that there was a plan to develop the land commercially, they accepted offers from speculators and front men that, had there been no development plan, sometimes seemed reasonable. The urban poor, always short on cash and often knowing little about market prices, were all the more inclined to do so. Many seemed unaware of the negative consequences of having to move to another place in the long term. As soon as it had become common knowledge that a developer held a location permit, the value of the land tended to rise. Yet landholders could not benefit from this, because the developer holding the location permit had an exclusive right to develop the area (Ferguson and Hoffman 1993, 62–63). A survey in the late 1990s on land conversion on the fringes of Bandung showed that two thirds of the landholders had sold their land for the purpose of commercial development, despite low compensation offers, primarily because they believed they had no choice but to release it (Firman 2000, 15). Compensation was particularly low if alternative procedures were applied to acquire the land, such as the procedure for land clearance in the public interest. Squatters who were evicted on the basis of the 1960 law on the use of land without permission of the right holder often received no compensation at all.

Though repression was strong, some landholders dared to resist the above practices, particularly after 1989, when the period of "openness" set in (Lucas 1997, 243). From then on, rights-oriented nongovernmental organizations (NGOs), which were already active in land disputes, were joined by the student movement (Lucas 1992, 90). However, NGOs and the student movement tended to concentrate their attention on land clearance that affected peasants, rather than the urban poor. For one thing, massive infrastructure projects in rural areas sometimes displaced thousands or tens of thousands, whereas urban cases typically involved smaller projects, affecting fewer people in each case. Ideologically, the activists were influenced by "structural" theories that prioritized the working class and peasants as potentially strategic political forces, not the informal sector or the urban poor.[25] Insofar as urban land disputes drew the attention of NGOs and the student movement, they generally focused on cases of land clearance in which the state played a significant role. This provided the opportunity to directly criticize the New Order regime. Where legal activists had an interest in a case, they often became important mediators in translating land claims into legal and political action, particularly through litigation against land clearance and the level of compensation. Commonly they would commence proceedings in a district court (Pengadilan Negeri) or, from 1991, an administrative court.

Combined with NGO-coordinated litigation, student activists "lived in" in communities, mobilized, and organized protests (Aspinall 2005, 116–25). Such campaigns did not always immediately present firm demands. Only after dialogue with developers, officials, or politicians proved fruitless would activists organize demonstrations. Physical confrontations with security forces, the destruction of property, and the arrest and prosecution of demonstrators were common (Aspinall 1996, 41–44; see also chapters 4, 5, 7, 8 in this book).

The results of resistance by landholders were generally disappointing. Litigation rarely succeeded. The urban poor generally had weak legal claims, and the few protective provisions contained in legislation were easily subjugated to the overriding principle of "development" (Fitzpatrick 1997, 199). Judges were susceptible to bribes from the well-to-do and equally susceptible to executive interference. When rulings did favor the claimants, they were rarely implemented (Nusantara and Tanuredjo 1997; Butt 1999). The notorious reputation of the courts weakened their authority in society.[26] Political action also failed. To my knowledge there is not a single account of a case in which commercial land clearance was prevented. Compensation was almost invariably inadequate. Commercial land clearance not only resulted in a loss of land but also a loss of livelihood opportunities, particularly for the urban poor, who often depended on the strategic location of residence for income generation and lacked the means to commute. In this way, as Struyk, Hoffman, and Katsura (1990, 139) conclude, small landholders partially subsidized the cost of urban development during the New Order.

Post–New Order Legal Reforms

Just a month after Suharto's fall, there already were indications that the government wanted to bring an end to the past practices of commercial land clearance. As discussed above, developers commonly continued to acquire land after the term of their permit had already expired. In June 1998 the head of the BPN sent a circular letter to the agency's provincial offices, asking them to remind permit holders whose location permits were no longer extendable, that these permits were null and void and could no longer be used for land clearance. Henceforth, permits to acquire remaining land would only be issued to those who were "really serious and acted in good faith."[27] A few days later, the head of the BPN sent another circular letter, in which he referred to deviations in past commercial land clearance practices and required provincial offices of the BPN to include several new provisions in allocated location permits: namely, that the location permit did not reduce the rights of landowners (note that the letter explicitly refers to landowners, not landholders generally) in the area for which the permit had been issued; that it would be forbidden to limit access of people in the area; that the permit holder had the obligation to protect the wider public interest as well as that of local people; and that s/he was obliged to create an enclave or consolidate land for those landowners who did not want to give up their rights. Representatives of landowners would now have to be involved in the permit-granting procedure through the organization of a coordination meeting. In case of field monitoring, officials of the BPN should identify the occurrence of (unlawful) land occupation by people as well as examine the willingness of landowners to give up their rights. Finally, the municipal/district land office should still provide services to those landowners who had not yet given up their rights.[28]

The above letters suggest a new stance of the government toward commercial land clearance. They did not, however, ultimately lead to better protection of landholders confronted with developers wishing to acquire their land. This was mainly due to the enactment of a new regulation in 1999, supplementing the 1993 regulation.[29] In accordance with the spirit of regional autonomy, the regulation transfers the authority to issue location permits from the head of the BPN to mayors/district heads.[30] With regard to the interests of landholders, the regulation is ambiguous.

To start with the positive changes, landholders are now consulted before a location permit is issued.[31] To avoid any misunderstanding about the rights attached to the permit, the regulation clarifies that as long as a developer has not reached agreement with a rights holder regarding the transfer of the land, the latter's rights and interests regarding the land are maintained, including the right to obtain a land certificate, to use the land in accordance with the General Spatial Plan, and to transfer the land to third parties.[32] Yet again the regulation does not refer to any sanctions that can be imposed on developers who fail to respect the interests of landholders. Worse still, it fails to refer to any concrete form of supervision, for instance by the previously discussed supervision and control teams for commercial land clearance. Obviously, this renders enforcement more difficult.

The regulation contains some other bad news for landholders. Many landholders cannot benefit from any of the above, potentially protective, provisions, as the 1999 regulation refers to an extensive list of cases in which no location permit is required for commercial land clearance. This exemption, for instance, applies to land needed for nonagricultural investment of less than 10,000 square meters (one hectare); a size most urban development projects will not pass.[33] A developer is only required to inform the BPN about his plan, after which he can directly start acquiring the land. This does not mean that the developer needs no permits at all to realize his project. Projects require other permits, such as the land allocation and use permit and building permit, which can only be obtained if in accordance with spatial plans.[34] Further details on the location permit procedure should be regulated by the mayor/district head.[35]

On the basis of the 1999 regional autonomy laws, part of the authority over the land sector was transferred from the central government to the municipalities and districts. Their authority to issue site permits, as granted by Regulation of the Head of the NLA 2/1999, was thus reconfirmed. It must be noted, however, that mayors and district heads felt free to depart from the regulation's intent. Though referring to the regulation, the implementing decree in Bandung makes no reference to the consultation procedure. So, contrary to what the regulation requires, the mayor can issue a location permit without the prior involvement of landholders.[36]

In relation to commercial land clearance, legal reforms remained limited to the above legislation. Legislation permitting forcible commercial land clearance, such as the previously discussed 1960 law on the use of land without permission of the rights holder, remains in force, despite the fact that it is inconsistent with the right to adequate housing enshrined in the Amended 1945 Constitution and the ICESC.

Now that we have gained an insight into recent legal reforms, the question arises how the practices of commercial land clearance have changed and, more generally, what it says about the rule of law at the local level in Reform Era Indonesia. In order to shed light on these questions, the following section presents a case study, involving commercial clearance of land affecting a low-income urban kampong community in West Bandung.

Practice of Commercial Land Clearance in Post–New Order Bandung

In the first years of *reformasi,* clearance of urban kampong land for commercial purposes was limited. Indonesia's economic crisis affected the urban economy, in particular the manufacturing and property sectors. As a result, land development activities slowed down. Business, offices, and condominium construction projects came to a standstill and land that was acquired for commercial development remained unutilized (Firman 2002, 234–36). As happened on plantation land across Indonesia, some land on the fringes of large cities was reoccupied by people who had earlier given it up (Firman 2000, 17–18).

The period of economic decline did not last long; within two years Indonesia's economy showed signs of recovery. In Bandung this was evidenced by the initiation of a considerable number of commercial development projects. Malls, factory outlets, upper-class real-estate complexes, and luxury hotels are being built, particularly since the opening in 2005 of the Cipularang toll road between Jakarta and Bandung and the connecting Pasupati flyover, which leads to an increasingly functional relationship between the two cities. To realize these projects, there is again a great appetite for land. This appetite has actually increased compared to the New Order years.

Land that has proved attractive for developers includes that situated alongside railway tracks. This land is centrally located, flat, and therefore easy to build on, and most important, it is state land (*tanah negara*) managed by the state-owned Indonesian Railway Company

(PT Kereta Api Indonesia, or PT KAI). The land is mostly occupied by urban poor who have no (or no longer have) formal claim to the land, making it relatively easy and cheap to acquire.

PT KAI itself is interested in developing railway land, as it is in need of new revenue streams. In 1997 the World Bank launched the Railway Efficiency Project, which led to the reorganization of PT KAI. This included the establishment of a property division, which should result in higher financial returns on the company's assets. In 2004 it started documenting the houses that had been built on its land as a first step toward making this asset commercially productive.[37] In 2007 a law was enacted that requires the government to stop subsidizing PT KAI and to give private companies access to the railway network.[38] Finally, the revenues from ticketing have decreased significantly in recent years, particularly as a result of the previously mentioned opening of the toll road between Jakarta and Bandung, making it quicker to go by car than by rail between the two cities.

To meet its financial needs, PT KAI now undertakes public-private partnerships (Kerjasama Operasi, hereafter PPP) with developers for a period of thirty-four years; that is, four years for the development of the project and thirty years for its exploitation. PT KAI argues that this not only serves the company itself and developers, but also the common good. It can continue providing public transport, which the exploitation of its assets cross-subsidizes. Besides, the project supports the municipal government in spatial management as well as attracting investors.[39] Developers who conclude a PPP agreement with PT KAI are required to clear the land themselves. "I therefore look for strong developers, who are able to get this done," the head of the property division clarified in an interview.[40]

The Paskal Hyper Square Project

The first project involving the development of railway land in Bandung on the basis of a PPP, forming a model for the many projects on PT KAI land to come, is the Paskal Hyper Square project, for which PT KAI signed an agreement with PT Citra Buana Prasida

(PT CBP) on 25 April 2003.[41] PT CBP would develop Bandung's biggest business center, consisting of shop-front houses, a trade center, shopping mall, serviced apartments, and a five-star hotel, involving an investment of Rp 350 billion (about US$35 million).[42] The project was to be realized on a plot of about 16.5 hectares in Kelurahan Kebunjeruk and Ciroyom, Kecamatan Andir, West Bandung.

The plot on which the project was to be realized was not vacant. Over several decades migrants occupied and subdivided the land and built houses. Most residents had moved in after 1975, but the oldest residents had been living there for more than fifty years. The majority were squatters. Some "bought" or "leased" the land from so-called *oknum* (rogue employees of PT KAI or shady dealers) who passed themselves off as employees of PT KAI and kept these revenues for themselves.[43] Since the 1980s, most residents signed short-term contracts with PT KAI granting them official lease rights (*hak sewa*). The contracts contained a provision requiring the residents to unconditionally clear and transfer the land in case the company needed it. If the residents refused to meet this obligation, they would be evicted by force. However, after the late 1990s the contracts were no longer renewed.[44] At the start of the project almost 1,500 houses and up to 10,000 people resided on the land.[45] Residents generally worked in the informal sector as street hawkers, trading goods, or offering small services in the city center. The central location of their kampong was thus important for their livelihood.

PT CBP was exempted from the requirement to obtain a location permit, since PT KAI already owned the land and PT CBP implemented the investment plan of PT KAI. PT CBP did require a land allocation and use permit as well as a building permit. In November 2002, the mayor therefore issued a land use agreement (*persetujuaan pemanfaatan ruang*).[46] This "permit in principle" (*izin prinsip*) forms a first step to obtain these other permits and allowed PT CBP to start clearing the land.[47] The permit did contain a provision requiring PT CBP to pay residents proper compensation for buildings, as well as a clause stating that in the event PT CBP did not fulfill prevailing legal requirements, the agreement could be canceled. The "permit in principle" was extended in June 2004, a few months after a new General Spatial Plan had been enacted, which actually stipulated that in West Bandung, development of housing, trade, and services should be limited.[48]

Land Clearance in Kebonjeruk

In order to facilitate the land clearance process, PT KAI and PT CBP formed a land clearance team, which consisted of employees of both companies.[49] In May 2003 this team "socialized" their plan among local officials and community leaders. It underlined that residents were under contractual obligation to give up the land. They should actually be grateful that they could have resided on the land for such a long time at such low cost and were certainly not entitled to any compensation. Yet "out of humanity" the developer offered a nonnegotiable sum of "assistance/sympathy money" of Rp 60,000/square meter for nonpermanent buildings, Rp 110,000/square meter for semipermanent buildings, and Rp 210,000/square meter for permanent buildings (about US$6–21/square meter).[50]

Although residents felt under pressure to accept the developers' offer, most immediately rejected it. They did not want to give up the land on which some people had been residing for more than fifty years, let alone "for the realization of a commercial project that only benefited the elite."[51] Besides, residents were generally of the opinion that the offer was too low as it did not allow them to buy a comparable dwelling.[52] They were also afraid to lose their source of income. Some of the residents were willing to move, provided that they received real compensation instead of nominal "assistance/sympathy money." This could come in the form of cash or new accommodation. Those who wanted money asked for compensation many times higher than the "assistance/sympathy money" offered, namely Rp 1–1.5 million/ square meter (about US$100–150/square meter).[53]

To enforce their claims, the residents established a community association called the People's Aspiration Team (Tim Aspirasi Masyarakat), consisting of a large group of formal and informal community leaders. The team soon started to organize street protests, which were initially aimed at convincing the developer to cancel the project altogether. When this proved unfeasible, the team organized street protests to get support from the municipal council, provincial assembly, and, through the media, the wider public. At this stage the residents proved sufficiently unified to organize as a group. They did not look for assistance from NGOs or the student movement. Nor did the latter offer assistance.

The team felt that litigation was no option, although there were grounds for this.[54] As a former neighborhood head argued: "People do not have ownership rights. They know if it becomes a legal process they will lose. Then the judge will ask: 'Where is your certificate?'"[55] In their protests, residents also avoided legal discourse. So, instead of referring to a right to compensation, the residents legitimated their demands by pointing to the hardship they would have to cope with if the developer did not offer real compensation.

The protests were widely covered by the media but did not provoke the public response residents were hoping for. Several members of the municipal council did call upon the municipal government not to issue the permits required for construction activities until the negotiations had ended and offered to support residents in the negotiations. Residents were skeptical about their intentions, though. The municipal government ultimately did nothing beyond making false promises.[56] The mayor said he would construct tenement buildings for the residents, but this proposal never materialized. He also did not respond to the call of the members of the municipal council to postpone the issuance of permits.

In May 2004 the CEO of the PT CBP, Soeparman Natajuda, said he wanted to finish the land clearance process in Kebonjeruk within a month and in Ciroyom within six months.[57] In order to avoid any further delays, the developer adopted a new strategy. First, it was decided to clear the land in successive stages. The first stage involved land clearance in Kebonjeruk for the construction of the shop-front houses (first zone); the second and third stages involved land clearance in Ciroyom for the construction of the apartments (second zone) and hotel (third zone), respectively.

Next, PT CBP subjected the residents of Kebonjeruk to divide-and-rule and intimidation practices. The developer sidelined the People's Aspiration Team by secretly commencing direct negotiations with individual residents. It particularly focused on influential residents, who were offered high compensation and also cash, a motorcycle, and even a house if they convinced other residents to give up their land.[58] Residents were harassed, typically at night, by people visiting them and telling them in an intimidating manner that they should give up their land, but they were not physically harmed. Several residents claimed they faced demands to sign a blank paper, which they had refused.[59] Employees of PT CBP and their "thug" front men (*preman*), including members of the organization Joint Initiative of the Sons of Siliwangi (Gabungan Inisiatif Barisan Anak Siliwangi, or GIBAS), were said to be responsible for these practices.[60]

The developer's approach proved successful. Various influential residents were co-opted, and over time more residents were willing to negotiate, even members of the People's Aspiration Team started to back PT CBP. Several residents claimed that the members had been bribed by the developer.[61] Under these conditions, community unity was replaced by an atmosphere of suspicion. By September 2004 land clearance in Kebonjeruk was accomplished, three months later than planned. To celebrate this, the CEO of PT KAI organized a special ceremony, at which occasion he thanked PT CBP for clearing the land and turning the area "into a more representative location."[62]

Despite—or as PT CBP argued, as a result of—the residents' resistance, compensation remained low. "Ordinary" residents were offered sympathy/assistance money and, depending on their cooperativeness, a so-called bonus of about 30 percent of that sum, and some other minor fees.[63] Residents who needed time to move received part of the money and the rest as soon as their building had been demolished. The residents could choose to demolish their house themselves or leave this to PT CBP. In any event, they were under the contractual obligation to leave within two weeks after the sympathy/assistance money had been paid.[64]

Obviously, the compensation was insufficient to buy another house at a similar location. Most people moved away to the outskirts of the city, such as Buah Batu, or out of Bandung to their place of origin, such as Banjaran, Padalarang, Cipatat, Soreang, Cicalengka, and Garut, where they could afford to live. Only a few households found accommodation in the vicinity, usually a rented house.[65] Not surprisingly, all interviewed residents of Kebonjeruk felt victimized, as they lost their home and often also their livelihood, without receiving sufficient compensation to replace all this.

Land Clearance in Ciroyom, Second Zone

In February 2005 PT CBP initiated the second stage of land clearance in Ciroyom. Initially, the process unfolded just as it had in Kebonjeruk. The developer held on to its offer to pay Rp 60,000/square meter for temporary buildings, Rp 110,000/square meter for semipermanent and Rp 210,000/square meter for permanent buildings (about US$6–21/square meter).

Like the residents of Kebonjeruk, the residents of Ciroyom (again) rejected the offer. No longer having confidence in the People's Aspiration Team, they established a new organization, the Kebonjeruk-Ciroyom Reject Eviction Forum (Forum TPKC) and organized new street protests. Despite the forum's name, the residents realized it would be hard to prevent eviction. The main concern was now to obtain real compensation.

The street protests had some effect. Hearing about the negotiations in Ciroyom, the municipal council installed after the 2004 general elections asked the municipal government not to issue the required permits for construction activities before the negotiations between PT CBP and the residents had ended. One member of the municipal council, Aat Safaat Hodijat (Golkar Party), argued that although the residents were not the owners of the land, they should be protected. "Their compensation should not be too low, leaving people in misery," he stated.[66] The municipal government ignored this call, however.

Residents still refrained from litigation and avoided legal discourse. They acknowledged that legally they were in a weak position but asked PT CBP to act on the basis of humanitarian considerations.

The residents hoped they would have a better fate than those of Kebonjeruk, who were now living in further distress. All they wanted were sufficient means to afford a similar place to live.[67]

Meanwhile PT CBP took up its divide-and-rule and intimidation practices again and with success. This time the role of *preman* was limited, likely because their assistance in clearing the first zone had proved ineffective. As in Kebonjeruk, the developer found it easier to co-opt influential residents, including members of the forum. Many people in consequence gave up their land, and by December 2005 only forty-seven households in the second zone, occupying in total 6,877 square meters of land, still refused to accept the offer of PT CBP.[68]

The last residents did not give up easily. As a replacement of the co-opted forum, they established the smaller People's Rescue Team (Tim Penyelamat Warga), consisting of a handful of (new) neighborhood heads.[69] It was formally registered as an association to avoid being accused of provocation. The team also consisted of a "militia" that was to cope with the police, military, and *preman* (if any). It tried to negotiate a compensation rate of Rp 800,000 (about US$80/square meter) for all residents, irrespective of the quality of buildings or number of floors.[70]

When PT CBP failed to acquire the last plots of land, PT KAI requested the assistance of the chief prosecutor (*Jaksa Tinggi*) of West Java, Holius Hosen, to "mediate" in the dispute.[71] He was willing to do so—some residents suspected, because he had been bribed by the developer—and ordered family heads to discuss the matter.[72] The order obviously worried the residents, who felt intimidated by involvement of this new party. Still, about ten residents dared to reply to the letter with a refusal to attend.[73] Other residents did attend, at which occasion they handed the chief prosecutor a letter stating their willingness to give up the land, provided that they received proper compensation. If no such compensation would be offered, they wanted to stay and lease the land from PT KAI or the developer for the price that they used to pay.[74] The chief prosecutor was not accommodating, however.

Meanwhile, the residents continued with street protests. In March 2006, they gained support from members of the provincial assembly, who sent a letter to the chief prosecutor, questioning the land clearance process. A month later the chief prosecutor replied that "the demand of residents for compensation could not be agreed to, as there was no legal basis for it and there was no report of any transfer of right."[75] Apparently the members of the provincial assembly were satisfied with this answer; they undertook no further action.

Basically the chief prosecutor's "mediation" effort failed. PT CBP thereupon began to report residents to the police for unlawful land occupation, embezzlement/swindle, and slander. The developer also started civil proceedings against some residents, requesting a court order to demolish their houses. Some residents received a warning and an announcement that their houses would be demolished.

Faced with this new challenge, the residents started to look for support from legal aid organizations. As they were convinced that the dispute ultimately could be won only by political means, however, they deliberately looked for party-affiliated legal aid organizations.[76] The first organization that assisted the residents was the legal aid organization of the PKB, the National Awakening Party.[77] Later, the representative of PKB's legal aid organization was believed to be too close with the developer and was replaced by a commercial lawyer, who four months later was in turn replaced for the same reason by a legal aid organization that has connections with the Indonesian Democratic Party-Struggle (Partai Demokrat Indonesia-Perjuangan, or PDI-P).

The legal aid organizations could not protect residents from prosecution. In July 2006, a resident of Ciroyom was fined Rp 25,000 (about US$2.50) and sentenced to five days imprisonment for unlawful occupation.[78] Next, although the ruling was not yet final and conclusive, the local police, PT CBP, and members of GIBAS demolished his buildings, including a building that later turned out to be someone else's. The action provoked fierce protests from residents, and the perpetrators were reported to the regional police, to no avail.[79] In September 2006, the house of another resident was demolished, based on a court order in a civil proceeding of a year before.[80]

The prosecutions still did not silence resisting residents. In 2007 they asked for support from the Islamic Youth Movement (Gerakan

Pemuda Islam, or GPI), some of whose members were part of the kampong community.[81] With their support, residents organized new street protests, which were joined by as many as three hundred residents.[82] For months the negotiations were in a deadlock. The resisting residents of the second zone finally came to an agreement with PT CBP in August 2007. They received the compensation they had demanded of Rp 800,000/square meter (about US$80/square meter).[83] In terms of compensation, the residents' prolonged resistance—with the support of the Islamic Youth Movement—thus proved to pay off.

Despite the agreement, as of mid-2008 PT CBP had not managed to clear all land in the second zone. One of the residents refused to demolish his house because he had received only the original sympathy/assistance money offered and not the bonus the parties had finally negotiated. PT CBP reported the resident to the police, after which he was arrested, taken into pretrial detention, and prosecuted for embezzlement and/or swindling.[84] The prosecutor demanded a sentence of one-year imprisonment minus pretrial detention. The court concluded that the case was not of a criminal law, but of a private law nature, but that there was no contractual breach on the part of the resident, and therefore acquitted him.[85] Some residents believe that the political connections of the legal aid organization contributed to this result, which its associates obviously deny.

Land Clearance in Ciroyom, Third Zone

Before completing land clearance in the first and second zones, PT CBP had already been acquiring some land in the third zone. Nonetheless, to the end of 2007 many of the 183 households, or about 1,600 people, had not given up their land. With the support of GPI, the remaining residents continued with street protests, although solidarity remained fragile. Suspected of being too close to the developer, several members of the People's Rescue Team were removed from the team.[86]

With the elections coming up in 2008, residents adopted a new strategy. In April 2008, the residents announced they would lodge blank votes in the West Java governor elections. They blamed the candidates for having no moral commitment to their fate.[87] The threat had little effect. One of the candidates promised to visit the community but did not keep his promise. Later it turned out that the boycott action was not supported by all residents; a majority actually did vote for a candidate.[88]

In August 2008 the remaining residents of Ciroyom threatened to lodge blank votes in the mayoral elections. At the municipal level, the candidates took the residents' threat seriously. Two of the three candidates visited the community, including the incumbent candidate, Dada Rosada. Notably, his partner candidate for vice-mayor was Ayi Vivananda, one of the founders of the legal aid organization that supported the community. On that occasion Dada Rosada finally promised not to issue permits required for construction activities to PT CBP in both the second and third zones until the negotiation process would be settled.[89]

As of the last stage of fieldwork in 2009, the latest strategy of the residents of Ciroyom finally seemed successful. PT CBP has realized the first stage of the Paskal Hyper Square project in the first zone, where it has built a shopping mall and shop-front houses. Most shop-front houses, 60–105 square meters, have been sold at Rp 1–1,815 billion (about US$100,000–181,500) each, which is a price per square meter of up to 288 times the "sympathy/assistance money" some residents were offered and still twenty-one times the compensation some resisting residents received.[90] At the time of writing, construction activities in the second zone had yet to begin. Land clearance in the third zone continued for several months but stopped during 2009. It seemed that Dada Rosada, who won the mayoral elections, had kept his word not to issue the required permits until agreement has been reached over compensation. Furthermore, it was rumored that business partners of PT CBP have been scared off by the long, difficult, and relatively costly land clearance process. It also appeared, in view of the sobering experiences in this "model" project, that developers may have lost interest in initiating other projects on railway land in the near future. As of 2013, however, all land for the development of the Pascal Hyper Square project, including the third zone, had been cleared. While residents managed to delay the project, and negotiate higher compensation, in the end none of the residents or their allies would prevent eviction.

Commercial Land Clearance and the Rule of Law

What can we learn from the Paskal Hyper Square case? On the surface it suggests that post–New Order reforms have benefited urban poor who are confronted with developers wishing to clear land for commercial development. At the same time the case exposes some clear weaknesses of the rule of law at the local level and raises questions about the Indonesian government's commitment to its obligations regarding the right to adequate housing.

Apparently it is still common for developers to pressure the urban poor to give up their land, while offering low compensation. Aside from using divide-and-rule tactics, residents were victims of intimidation from militias and youth gangs, "civil society" organizations that do not act with much civility. Since the fall of Suharto, new groups have emerged in Bandung. Some are affiliated with political parties, others with whosoever is willing to pay. GIBAS, with a notorious reputation, is but one of the many *preman* organizations in Bandung that are now involved in land clearance (Honna 2006, 87–88). In some respects, since these groups operate outside the law, it is harder to hold them accountable than official entities such as the military.

Authorities do not protect the urban poor against the above practices. Even when residents started to organize street protests and the media began to report the developer's tactics pressuring residents to give up their land, the municipal government refused to offer support, although it could have canceled its "permit in principle," because PT CBP did not fulfill prevailing legal requirements, such as paying residents proper compensation for buildings.

The military is no longer (directly) involved in land clearance, but the police, the public prosecutor (*jaksa*), and even the chief prosecutor (*Jaksa Tinggi*) proved willing to lend their coercive powers to developers. Residents were intimidated by warnings, threats, and orders to report. Some became victims of arrest, prosecution, and destruction of property. Reports of unlawful acts by the developer and the police were ignored.

Authorities' willingness to assist developers in commercial land clearance can be explained by the fact that they have vested interests in the success of development projects, particularly since the implementation of regional autonomy.[91] By using its new permit granting authority, the municipal government can redevelop kampongs that it classifies as slums, an ambition expressed in Bandung's latest Spatial Plan.[92] More important, because of the new fiscal relations between Jakarta and the regions, the municipal government gains extra local revenue (*Pendapatan Asli Daerah,* or PAD) from commercial land development by issuing permits. Furthermore, commercial land development increases the value of land, which in turn yields increased government tax income. It also results in extra PAD revenue through advertising, parking, hotel, and restaurant levies. The effects of administrative decentralization and new fiscal relations between Jakarta and the regions, therefore, are not necessarily positive. If democratic control fails, financial return is easily prioritized over social issues. Corruption apparently continues to play a major role too. Issuing permits likely brings in extralegal fees, which end up in the pockets of the municipal leaders, politicians, and officials.[93] The involvement of the prosecutor general in the Bandung case also raises questions.

The above practices are made possible by weaknesses in commercial land clearance law. The law still imposes no sanctions against authorities who fail to follow the location permit procedure. The mechanism in the 1999 regulation on location permits for supervising commercial land clearance is indeed not effective. Furthermore, the interpretation of the regulation remains constrained by the 1960 law on the use of land without permission of the right holder, which, despite the fact that it is outmoded, is still used by authorities to evict people. On a positive note, in 2007 a new spatial management law (UU 26/2007) was enacted, under which officials issuing permits that are not in accordance with spatial plans can be sentenced to up to five years' imprisonment or fined up to Rp 500 billion (about US$50 million) besides being dishonorably discharged.[94] But considering the pervasiveness of such violations, it can be doubted whether this stipulation will lead to a structural change in their behavior.

Indonesia's new local democracy—also fostered by political decentralization—partly compensates for the previously discussed conditions. The urban poor now dare to resist commercial land clearance. Residents organized street protests and used their right to vote to put political pressure on the executive. These acts were covered by the media, albeit only in the initial stage of the protests and not extensively. The municipal council and provincial assembly gave some support. In an interview, several members of the municipal council said that they often handled commercial land clearance cases they considered "inhumane." Their support is what one member of the municipal council called "legal protection by political means."[95] However, some residents were suspicious about their intentions, which, considering the numerous media reports on legislative corruption, does not come as a surprise. In any event, the influence of the municipal council and the provincial assembly was limited vis-à-vis the executive. The mayor was willing to act only when he risked losing votes.

The student movement remained absent, as initially did (rights-oriented) NGOs. In this case, a religious youth organization (GPI) served as champions protecting the little people (*rakyat kecil*). Rights-oriented NGOs became involved only after the residents asked for support. Notably, these legal aid organizations were party-affiliated. Subsequent resistance was more successful, but it remains unclear to what extent their political connections have contributed to this.

The residents did not initially opt for a litigation strategy. Instead, they presented their demand for better compensation as a moral claim. By formulating their demands as a moral claim, residents put themselves in a vulnerable position, depending ultimately on political favoritism. Residents' choice of this approach is understandable, particularly given the level of reputed corruption in the judicial system. There are indications that they were unaware of the full extent of their rights. But the deliberate choice to ally with NGOs that had political connections indicates that residents had little trust in the law and legal institutions.

The residents' lack of trust in legal institutions was confirmed as soon as the courts began to play a role. They continued to apply outmoded laws on the use of land without permission of the rights holder. As a result, several people were sentenced to fines and imprisonment.

Because of the previously discussed failures in the process of rule of law formation at the local level, the right to adequate housing exists only on paper. The authorities failed to protect residents against forced eviction; they were actually responsible for it, with no substantive public interest justification. There were no public consultations or efforts to seek alternatives, and legal remedies or procedural protections were limited. Some residents could negotiate higher compensation than initially offered, but this compensation remained inadequate. Finally, the people's right to alternative accommodation under international convention was not fulfilled.

A Need for Further Reforms

This chapter has discussed changing law and practice in commercial land clearance in post–New Order Bandung. During the New Order, commercial land development was one of Indonesia's prime investment sectors, particularly after the 1980s, when the New Order regime introduced a series of deregulation policies to stimulate oil-independent economic growth. These developments affected the urban poor residing on valuable land in inner city kampongs. Despite protective legislative measures, they were forced by developers, who could generally rely on the government's support, to give up their land for low compensation.

Post-1998 reforms should have brought an end to unfair New Order land clearance practices. Our Bandung case study shows that the reforms have been of some benefit to the urban poor who are confronted with developers wishing to clear land for commercial development but that there are also some clear failures in the rule of law at the local level. Developers continue to pressure the urban poor to give up their land at low compensation levels. Instead of protecting these people against such practices, the authorities actually assist developers. Because of regional autonomy and corruption they have a clear interest in the success of development projects. These practices are made possible by weaknesses in the law. The case shows that there is little to expect from the courts. Indonesia's new local democracy partly compensates for these conditions, but it proves hard for the urban poor to organize effectively to exert effective political pressure. For the time being, the right to adequate housing thus exists only on paper.

There is clearly a need for further reforms. The right to adequate housing to which the Amended 1945 Constitution and the ICESC refer should form the point of departure for such an effort. Furthermore, reform of land tenure legislation must be combined with more general anticorruption measures and court reforms. Beyond institutional reforms, legal empowerment of vulnerable groups like the urban poor must be addressed, so they can stand up for their rights, including the right to adequate housing.

Notes

The research conducted for this chapter was part of a PhD project on land tenure security for Indonesia's urban poor for the Van Vollenhoven Institute, Leiden University. I acknowledge the help of Ivan Rahadian, who assisted me in acquiring the case study data discussed in this chapter. During fieldwork, I was a visiting scholar at the Faculty of Law of the Parhayangan Catholic University in Bandung. I am much indebted to former Dean Ismadi Bekti, fellow researcher Tristam Moeliono, and other staff for their hospitality and the excellent research environment they provided. Finally, I am grateful to the Dutch Royal Academy of Sciences, the Society for the Advancement of Research in the Tropics (Treub-Maatschappij), the Netherlands Organization for Scientific Research (NWO), the Adat Law Foundation (Adatrecht Stichting) and the Leiden University Fund (LUF), which gave financial support for the fieldwork in Bandung.

1. *Kampong* means community, village, or rural settlement. In the urban context it refers to low-income settlements within municipalities.
2. The second amendment was passed on 18 August 2000.
3. §28H(1) Amended 1945 Constitution; §11(1) ICESC.
4. See §11(1) and General Comment by the UN Committee on Economic, Social and Cultural Rights, §3 on the Nature of State Parties'

Obligations, §4 on the Right to Adequate Housing, and §7 on Forced Evictions. The ICESC took effect in Indonesia in 2006.

5. Regional autonomy was introduced with UU 22/1999 and UU 25/1999, revised with UU 32/2004 and 33/2004. Measures against corruption included UU 28/1999 and UU 31/1999.

6. Commercial land clearance was regulated in the colonial period as far as it involved *adat* land. In order to protect the Indonesian population, colonial land law prohibited the sale of such land to non-Indonesians (cf. 1870 Agrarian Decision and the 1875 Ordinance on the Alienation of Individual Adat Rights on Land of Natives to Non-Natives). These pieces of legislation were nullified in 1960 by the enactment of the Basic Agrarian Law (UUPA 5/1960, henceforth BAL) (Harsono 2005, 134–35).

7. UU 1/1967 on Foreign Investment; UU 6/1968 on Domestic Investment. These laws were slightly revised by UU 11/1970 on the Revision and Extension of UU 1/1967 on Foreign Investment and UU 12/1970 on the Revision and Extension of UU 12/1967 on Domestic Investment, respectively.

8. Regulation of the Minister of Home Affairs 5/1974 on Provisions for the Disposal and Delivery of Land for Business Interests.

9. BAL/UUPA 5/1960, General Consideration (c).

10. See, for instance, Regulation of the Minister of Home Affairs 5/1974, §11(3 and 5), which stipulates that the mayor may mediate in cases where problems arise in the negotiating process and that he may even cancel a permit where the land clearance process is not implemented appropriately or within a certain time limit.

11. See Regulation of the Minister of Home Affairs 2/1976, on the Use of the Procedure for Land Clearance in the Government's Interest for Land Clearance by Private Parties, §1, in conjunction with Regulation 15/1975 on Provisions regarding the Procedure for Land Clearance. Regulation 15/1975, §11(2).

12. See Regulation of the Minister of Home Affairs 3/1987 on the Allocation and Granting of a Right on Land for the Need of Housing Development Companies; Presidential Decision 53/1989 on Industrial Areas; Regulation of the Head of the BPN 3/1992 on the Procedure for a Company to Acquire Land Reservation, Location Permit, Granting, Extension, and Renewal of the Right of Land and the Issuance of a Certificate; Regulation of the Head of the BPN 2/1993 on the Procedure to Obtain a Location Permit and the Right to Land for a Company for Capital Investment as elaborated by Decision of the Head of the BPN 22/1993 on Operational Directives for the Granting of a Location Permit for the Implementation of Head of the BPN Regulation 2/1993; Decision of the

Head of BPN 21/1994 on the Procedure to Obtain Land for Companies in the Framework of Investment.

13. Compare Regulation of the Minister of Home Affairs 5/1974, §11(3) and Decision of the Head of the BPN 22/1993, Annex B. Notably, the annex only requires the developer to state his willingness to pay compensation or offer an alternative site to titleholders, not to others, such as squatters. See, however, §6(9), which requires a developer wishing to obtain a land right on state land to first clear it of *garapan* (squatting) and other forms of occupation.

14. Regulation of the Minister of Home Affairs 3/1987. For a discussion of the main provisions of this regulation, see Struyk, Hoffman, and Katsura 1990, 129–34; Presidential Decision 53/1989.

15. Regulation of the Head of the BPN 3/1992. The regulation implemented Presidential Decision 33/1992 on the Procedure for Investment.

16. Regulation of the Head of the BPN 2/1993, §3 and Annex D. The regulation was elaborated by Decision of the Head of the BPN 22/1993 on Operational Directives on the Granting of a Location Permit for the Implementation of State Minister of Agrarian Affairs/Head of the BPN Regulation 2/1993; Decision of the Head of BPN 21/1994 on the Procedure to Obtain Land for Companies in the Framework of Investment.

17. Circular Letter of the Head of the BPN 580.2-5568.D.III, dated 6 December 1990. See also Regulation of the Head of the BPN 1/1994, §47, and Circular Letter of the Head of the BPN 500-1988, 29 June 1994, section 5. The teams were called Supervision and Control Teams for Land Preparation (Tim Pengawasan dan Pengendalian Pengadaan Tanah). The establishment of these teams should have been (re-)regulated by a decision of the head of the BPN, but such a decision was never enacted. Consequently, the establishment of the teams remained based on the earlier discussed Circular Letter of the Head of the BPN 580.2-5568.D.III, 6 December 1990.

18. See UU 5/1986 on Administrative Justice, §1(3 and 4), §47(1), §53.

19. Presidential Decision 55/1993 on Land Preparation for Development Activities in the Public Interest. Presidential Decision 55/1993 annulled Minister of Home Affairs Regulations 15/1975 and 2/1976 (§24).

20. Compare Circular Letter of the Head of the BPN 580.2-5568.D.III; Decision of the Head of the BPN 22/1993, Annex E, and Circular Letter of the Head of the BPN 460-572-DII, 21 February 1995. See also Sumardjono 1999, 22–24.

21. See Firman and Dharmapatni 1994.

22. UU 51/1960.

23. UU 51/1960, §2, 6(1), under a.

24. UU 51/1960, §§3–4.

25. Thus, in urban areas, rights-oriented NGOs like the Legal Aid Institute (Lembaga Bantuan Hukum or LBH) were mostly concerned with the status of informal sector small traders, labor rights, wages, and conditions (Eldridge 1995, 101).

26. For a discussion of some of the few cases that did end up in administrative courts, see Bedner (2001, 158–61).

27. Letter of the Head of the BPN 462-2033, dated 26 June 1998.

28. Letter of the Head of the BPN 462-2083, 30 June 1998.

29. Regulation of the Head of the BPN 2/1999 on Location Permits. The regulation does not annul the earlier discussed Regulation of the Head of the BPN 2/1993 and 22/1993, which means that formally these regulations are still applicable. See also Letter of the Head of the BPN 110-424, which explains the aims of the regulation.

30. The BPN's role is now limited to collecting all required documents and preparing a coordination meeting with related bodies.

31. Regulation of the Head of the BPN 2/1999, §6. In the explanatory letter, the head of the BPN explains that this form of public participation should lead to people supporting the land clearance process (Letter of the Head of the BPN 110-424, §7).

32. The head of the BPN explains that this provision is needed because of past misconceptions (Letter of the Head of the BPN 110-424, §1 and 4).

33. Under Regulation of the Head of the BPN 2/1999, §2(2).

34. See Bylaw of Bandung Municipality, No. 4/2002, on the Land Use Permit §7(1) and permit Bylaw of Bandung Municipality 14/1998 on Buildings in the Municipal Region Level II Bandung, §41(1).

35. Since no such regulation has been implemented, the 1993 regulation remains in force (Regulation of the Head of the BPN 2/1999, §7).

36. Decree of the Mayor of Bandung 170/1999 on the Procedure for the Granting of Location Permits, implementing Head of the BPN Regulation 2/1999 on Location Permits.

37. *Pikiran Rakyat*, 7 June 2004.

38. UU 23/2007 on the railways.

39. Article from website of PT KAI, 16 April 2004; *Pikiran Rakyat*, 15 May 2004.

40. Interview, the head of the Property Division of the Indonesian Railway Company, 9 January 2005.

41. See Decision of the CEO of PT KAI U/A.35/KL401/KA-2003 and the PPP agreement, both dated 25 April 2003. The Minister of State Companies had approved the plan for a PPP by Letter S-560/M/MBY/2002, dated 28 August 2002.

42. Article from website of PT KAI, 23 September 2004; *Business Indonesia,* 27 May 2004.
43. Interviews, two residents of Ciroyom, 11 August 2008 and 14 August 2008 respectively.
44. *Republika,* 17 April 2004.
45. The media reported that Kebonjeruk consisted of 393–434 houses and Ciroyom 1,042–1,200 houses. See *Kompas,* 18 May 2004; *Kompas,* 17 May 2004; *Pikiran Rakyat,* 28 May 2004. It is hard to estimate the exact number of people that resided on the land because some residents had not formally registered at the *kelurahan* office and/or were circular migrants. The number mentioned here was derived from media reports. See *DeTik,* 14 May 2004; *Jakarta Post,* 15 May 2004; *Pikiran Rakyat,* 15 May 2004; *DeTik,* 24 January 2007.
46. Letter of the Mayor of Bandung 340/252.7-Bappeda, dated 12 November 2002.
47. *Kompas,* 4 June 2004.
48. Letter of the Mayor of Bandung 593/1766-Bappeda, dated 28 June 2004; Bylaw of Bandung Municipality 2/2004 §14(2)c.
49. *Tim Terpadu Pengosongan Lahan Ex. Emplasemen Stasiun Bandung Gudang,* PT KAI, 16/Apr/2004; *Republika,* 17 April 2004.
50. *Pikiran Rakyat,* 14 April 2004; Article from website of PT KAI, 16 April 2004; *Pikiran Rakyat,* 29 May 2004.
51. *Pikiran Rakyat,* 15 May 2004; *Kompas,* 18 May 2004; *Pikiran Rakyat,* 4 June 2004.
52. *Pikiran Rakyat,* 15 May 2004.
53. *Republika,* 17 April 2004.
54. There are rumors that PT KAI has never taken the trouble to obtain an official state management right (*hak pengelolaan*) on the land concerned, on which the colonial "Staatsspoorwegen" used to have European land rights. Presidential Decree 32/1979 sets a time limit for the registration of former European rights; all of those should have been registered before 1980. If not, the land reverts back to state domain. Kampong dwellers occupying such state land have in principle a priority right over third parties to request a (new) land right. As far as PT KAI does hold an official state management right on the land, it arguably forms neglected land (*tanah terlantar*). According to PP 36/1998, replaced in 2010 by PP 11/2010, land is neglected land if it is not used in accordance with the right to which it is subject or is not well taken care of. A BPN declaration that land is neglected may lead to forfeiture of rights, after which the land again reverts to the state and kampong dwellers occupying such land have a priority right over third parties to request a (new) land right.

55. Interview, former neighborhood head, 11 August 2008.
56. *Kompas,* 4 June 2004.
57. *Business Indonesia,* 27 May 2004.
58. Interviews, a resident of Kebonjeruk, 17 July 2006; a local official, 24 July 2006; and another resident of Kebonjeruk, 26 July 2006.
59. *Pelita,* 25 October 2009. See also Ruling of the Bandung General Court of First Instance 424/PID/B/2008/PN.BDG discussed below.
60. Interviews, a resident of Ciroyom, 19 July 2006; another resident of Ciroyom, 10 August 2008; a member of the People's Protection Team, 14 August 2008.
61. Interview, a former member of the forum, 19 July 2006. The former forum member acknowledged that he had received higher compensation than ordinary residents.
62. Article from the website of PT KAI, 23 September 2004.
63. Interviews, a resident of Ciroyom, 11 July 2006; a resident of Kebonjeruk, 26 July 2006; an associate of a legal aid organization, 19 August 2008.
64. Interviews, a resident of Kebonjeruk, 17 July 2006; and a former community leader, 11 August 2008.
65. Interviews, a resident of Ciroyom, 11 July 2006; and a resident of Kebonjeruk, 26 July 2006.
66. *Pikiran Rakyat,* 22 February 2005.
67. *Pikiran Rakyat,* 21 February 2005; *Pikiran Rakyat,* 22 February 2005.
68. *Pikiran Rakyat,* 14 December 2005.
69. Referring to the number of neighborhood heads of which the team was composed, it was also called Team of Five (Tim Lima).
70. Interview, member of the People's Protection Team, 14 August 2008.
71. See Letter of the CEO of PT KAI HK-214/XII/2/KK-2005.
72. Interview, member of the People's Protection Team, 14 August 2008.
73. *Galamedia,* 24 March 2006.
74. *Pikiran Rakyat,* 14 December 2005.
75. See Letter of the West-Java Prosecutor-General B-1336/O.2/Gph/04/2006.
76. Interview, member of the People's Protection Team, 14 August 2008.
77. *Lembaga Hukum dan HAM Partai Kebangkitan Bangsa* or Lakum HAM PKB.
78. Ruling of the Bandung General Court of First Instance 282/CR/PID/2006/PN.BDG. The resident was condemned on the basis of UU 51/1960, §6(1)b.
79. *Seputar Indonesia,* 15 May 2006; interviews, associates of GPI, 11 August 2008; member of the People's Protection Team, 14 August 2008.

80. The demolition was covered by Metro TV, a national news channel. See www.metrotvnews.com, checked on 9 January 2009.

81. The Islamic Youth Movement has a long history as a militant religious organization. Its predecessor was the Indonesian Islamic Youth Movement (Gerakan Pemuda Islam Indonesia), an organization established by key members of the Masyumi party just after the Proclamation of Independence, to fight for religious freedom and independence by means of the establishment of an Islamic state. Following two attacks on President Sukarno, in which the Indonesian Islamic Youth Movement was believed to be involved, the organization was disbanded in 1963. Soon a new organization was established, the Youth of the Islamic Community Union (Pemuda Persatuan Ummat Islam). In 1969, this organization was renamed the Islamic Youth Movement. In recent years the movement has been associated with all kinds of anti-Western activities, ranging from participating in anti-American demonstrations, attacking nightclubs and bars, to recruiting students for foreign *jihad*.

82. *DeTik*, 24 January 2007.

83. Interviews, associates of GPI, 11 August 2008; member of the People's Protection Team, 14 August 2008.

84. §372 and §378 of the Penal Code.

85. Ruling of the Bandung General Court of First Instance 424/PID/B/2008/PN.BDG. The public prosecutor filed an appeal before the Supreme Court, thus bypassing the Court of Appeal. At the time of writing, a ruling is still awaited.

86. Interviews, two members of the People's Protection Team, 14 August 2008.

87. *Tribun Jabar*, 11 April 2008; *DeTik*, 11 April 2008; *Tribun Jabar*, 12 April 2008.

88. *DeTik*, 13 April 2008.

89. Interviews, two members of the People's Protection Team, 14 August 2008.

90. Data derived from developer's brochure, on file with the author.

91. See also Reerink (2009).

92. See By-law of Bandung Municipality 2/2004 on the General Spatial Plan of Bandung Municipality, §14(2c). See also Reerink (2009).

93. See also Pemerintah Kota Bandung 2004, a recent joint research project of the Municipal Research and Development Office and a consultancy firm in which the problem of corruption in relation to permits is explicitly acknowledged.

94. UU 26/2007 on Spatial Management, §73.

95. Interviews, members of the Bandung Municipal Council, 20 December 2004.

References

Aspinall, E. 1996. "Students and the Military: Regime Friction and Civilian Dissent in the Late Suharto Period." *Indonesia* 59:21–44.

———. 2005. *Opposing Suharto, Compromise, Resistance, and Regime Change in Indonesia*. Stanford: Stanford University Press.

Bedner, A. W. 2001. *Administrative Courts in Indonesia, A Socio-Legal Study*. Leiden: Kluwer International.

Butt, S. 1999. "The *Eksekusi* of the *Negara Hukum:* Implementing Judicial Decisions in Indonesia." In *Indonesia, Law and Society,* ed. T. Lindsey, 247–57. Sydney: Federation Press.

Eldridge, P. J. 1995. *Non-government Organizations and Democratic Participation in Indonesia*. New York: Oxford University Press.

Ferguson, B. W., and M. L. Hoffman. 1993. "Land Markets and the Effect of Regulation on Formal-Sector Development in Urban Indonesia." *Review of Urban and Regional Studies* 5 (1): 51–73.

Firman, T. 1996. "Land Conversion and Urban Development in the Northern Region of West Java, Indonesia." *Urban Studies* 34 (7): 1027–46.

———. 2000. "Rural to Urban Land Conversion in Indonesia during Boom and Bust Periods." *Land Use Policy* 17 (1): 13–20.

———. 2002. "Urban Development in Indonesia, 1990–2001: From the Boom to the Early Reform Era through the Crisis." *Habitat International* 26 (2): 229–49.

Firman, T., and I. A. I. Dharmapatni. 1994. "The Challenges to Sustainable Development in Jakarta Metropolitan Development." *Habitat International* 18 (3): 79–94.

Fitzpatrick, D. 1997. "Disputes and Pluralism in Modern Indonesian Land Law." *Yale Journal of International Law* 22 (1): 171–212.

Harsono, B. 2005. *Hukum Agraria Indonesia, Sejarah Pembentukan Undang-Undang Pokok Agraria, Isi, dan Pelaksanaannya*. Jakarta: Penerbit Djambatan.

Honna, J. 2006. "Local Civil-Military Relations during the First Phase of Democratic Transition, 1999–2004: A Comparison of West, Central, and East Java." *Indonesia* 82:75–96.

Leaf, M. 1991. *Land Regulation and Housing Development in Jakarta, Indonesia, From "Big Village" to "Modern City."* PhD diss. Berkeley: University of California.

Lucas, A. E. 1992. "Land Disputes in Indonesia: Some Current Perspectives." *Indonesia* 53:79–92.

———. 1997. "Land Disputes, the Bureaucracy, and Local Resistance in Indonesia." In *Imagining Indonesia, Cultural Politics, and Political*

Culture, ed. J. Schiller and B. Martin-Schiller, 229–60. Athens: Ohio University Press.

Nusantara, A. H. G., and B. Tanuredjo. 1997. *Duo Kado Hakim Agung Buat Kedung Ombo: Tinjauan Putusan-Putusan Mahkamah Agung tentang Kasus Kedung Ombo.* Jakarta: Lembaga Studi dan Advokasi Masyarakat.

Pemerintah Kota Bandung. 2004. *Kajian Sistem Perijinan di Kota Bandung.* Bandung: Kantor Litbang and PT HEGARDAYA.

Reerink, G. O. 2009. "When Money Rules over Voice: Regional Autonomy and Spatial Planning in Bandung Benefits the Elite." In *Inside Indonesia* (98).

Struyk, R. J., M. L. Hoffman, and H. M. Katsura. 1990. *The Market for Shelter in Indonesian Cities.* Washington, DC: Urban Institute Press.

Sumardjono, M. S. W. 1999. "Land Policy and the Law: The Implication of the Policy on the Granting of a Location Permit for Real Estate Development." In *Current Developments of Laws in Indonesia,* ed. K. Hardjasoemantri and N. Sakumoto, 9–31. Tokyo: Institute of Developing Economies.

Suyanto, B. 1996. "Pembangunan Kota dan Sengketa Tanah, Kasus Kotamadya Surabaya." *Prisma* 25 (9): 37–49.

Winarso, H., and T. Firman. 2002. "Residential Land Development in Jabotabek, Indonesia: Triggering Economic Crisis?" *Habitat International* 26 (4): 487–506.

Newspapers

Business Indonesia
DeTik
Galamedia
Jakarta Post
Kompas
Pelita
Pikiran Rakyat
Republika
Seputar Indonesia
Tribun Jabar

Chapter 10

THE AGRARIAN MOVEMENT, CIVIL SOCIETY, AND EMERGING POLITICAL CONSTELLATIONS

DIANTO BACHRIADI, ANTON LUCAS, AND CAROL WARREN

When Suharto was finally forced to step down in May 1998, in the face of an intractable economic crisis, Indonesia's political constellation altered suddenly and dramatically. The crisis period was characterized by the emergence of ad hoc alignments of activist students, NGOs, and newly formed or revived community groups, which began to take on the mantle of long-repressed civil society. Government departments and international agencies now found themselves in round-table discussions with groups they formerly ignored or treated with suspicion.

NGO and Popular Alliances in Emerging Civil Society

The role of nongovernment organizations and student activist groups in supporting resistance to compulsory expropriation of peasants' land had become increasingly important in the latter years of the Suharto regime, playing strategic roles in the Cimacan, Nagari Kinali, Flores, and Gili Trawangan cases described in this book.[1] NGOs acted as supporters and sometimes coordinators of protest actions, often in conjunction with student groups, out of which many of these organizations had emerged. NGO involvement in grassroots struggles also influenced the form protest actions took, tying them to broader political agendas for democratization and clean government, as well as linking local groups to international environment and human rights movements. Broad social movement discourses became part of the framework within which local struggles were being articulated and facilitated the attraction of substantial support from international donor agencies that underwrote large congresses, bringing together mass organizations from far-flung provinces. Although the language of the movement for "civil society" may have seemed little more than jargon for some peasant and indigenous organizations, many local groups had actively joined in the students' struggle for political reform in Jakarta in early 1998 and incorporated a number of the idioms associated with global movements into their platforms.[2]

Grassroots organizations sprang up everywhere, linking with existing networks and forming new ones. *Adat*-based groups, representing some of the people most disadvantaged by the politics of development during the New Order, joined together in 1999 to establish the Alliance of Indigenous (Adat) Peoples of the Archipelago (AMAN) in an effort to overcome the long history of marginalization experienced by "indigenous"[3] minorities under the Indonesian state (Davidson and Henley 2009). The systematic confiscation of land and resources and the displacement and denigration of minority cultures sowed the seeds of separatist movements and interethnic and resource conflicts from Irian Jaya to Aceh. The formation of AMAN at a national congress in March 1999 marked a significant turning point for indigenous minorities with far-reaching political potential. The congress was attended by 208 delegates from 121 minority *adat* groups in twenty-three provinces, and was facilitated by thirteen environmental and human rights NGO networks (AMAN 1999; IWGIA 1999).

The position statement produced at the 1999 AMAN congress accuses the Indonesian state of "systematic destruction" of *adat* communities (*masyarakat adat*) through legislation that negated *adat* resource rights, and through lack of respect for community beliefs and values in government policy. The AMAN conference statement called for the repeal or revision of all legislation in which the concept of national control over resources was used to disenfranchise *adat* communities and for a new law guaranteeing full recognition of the sovereignty of *adat* peoples. Finally, the declaration called on the Indonesian government to become a signatory to International Labour Organization Convention No. 169 and to the Draft UN Declaration on Indigenous Peoples (AMAN 1999, 3–5, 25–30). Indonesia joined 143 other nations in finally ratifying the UN Declaration in September 2007, but continues to resist becoming a signatory to ILO Convention 169, according to Bedner and van Huis (2008, 169) because the wording of the ILO Convention would provide a stronger basis in international law for self-determination and resource rights for Indonesia's estimated fifty to seventy million "*adat* peoples."

In the same period, steps toward the revival of an independent national peasant farmers' movement were taken, when the national Federation of Indonesian Peasants' Unions (FSPI) began to take up more overtly political issues associated with agrarian reform. The 2001 Cibubur National Conference on Agrarian Reform brought together peasant groups that had been actively engaged in resistance to expropriation cases and others that had not been politicized so directly. The event was regarded as a major achievement along the road to broadening the popular organizational base needed to assert the interests of this increasingly marginalized sector of the nation's economy. Attended by 110 representatives of more than thirty farmers' unions, including the previously New Order–controlled official farmers' union (HKTI), and forty activists from nongovernment organizations, the congress produced a Declaration of Peasants' Rights (*Deklarasi Hak Hak Petani*), extending human rights claims beyond the conventional focus on political and civil rights to include social, cultural, and economic rights.

The declaration states that peasants had been betrayed by the New Order government's failure to implement reforms prescribed by the Basic Agrarian Law. Appealing to the rubric of international human rights, the declaration claims peasants' rights to livelihood, access to land and other natural resources, as well as rights to organize and to free expression.[4] The conference also passed resolutions calling for a serious commitment from the government to the priority of agrarian reform as mandated under the International Covenant on Economic, Social and Cultural Rights of the United Nations.[5] In pursuit of this goal, it resolved to pressure the People's Consultative Assembly (MPR) to formulate a parliamentary policy directive (TapMPR) as the basis for revived legislation on agrarian reform.

Both congresses represented major steps toward integrating and strengthening the agrarian movement in Indonesia. Land conflicts under the New Order had precipitated the formation of numerous local organizations in the 1990s. But these had been largely informal and lacked extensive networks as a result of the long history of repression of all forms of local political activity since the obliteration of the Communist Party in 1965–66. Many of the peasants' organizations formed in the course of struggle to occupy or reclaim land did not have the opportunity to develop a long-term set of principles toward broader reform of agrarian polices. They tended to read "land reform" as limited to recognition of their rights of occupation and ownership. These farmers' organizations reflect rural people's immediate concerns—namely their need for land, infrastructure, input subsidies, and price supports. The long period in which state policies prevented organization and political activism at the grassroots level has resulted in a tendency toward short-term, nonstructural perspectives on the land and resource problem that, compounded by class and cultural differences, sometimes place these grassroots groups at odds with the NGO and student activists campaigning for their cause. These factors have inhibited the consolidation of a national political party representing peasant farmers' interests in the Reform Era (Lucas and Warren 2003; Peluso, Afiff, and Fauzi Rachman 2008).

NGOs have had a complex and sometimes contentious place in the popular agrarian movement as locally active, but also metropolitan-oriented, organizations with middle-class, highly educated, urban leaderships, often coming from outside the regions in which they operate. They are dependent on external sources of funding, which require that their activities be compatible with human rights, governance, and sustainability criteria set by donors located in global metropolitan capitals. In this way, discourses on human rights, indigenous people, gender, and environmental protection became part of the framework within which local struggles are being acted out and inflect the documents produced by these peoples' organizations, if not always without challenge.[6] Although NGOs have been actively engaged in coordinating the organization and funding of these newly institutionalized people's forums, and certainly have influenced the framing of their platforms, they could not be said to have driven popular actions. As Bachriadi, then a member of the Consortium for Agrarian Reform (KPA) executive,[7] commented, "Local groups are springing up everywhere—and not at the behest of NGOs. In fact we have the opposite problem compared to the situation before [*reformasi*]—how to keep up with the explosion of these groups and keep them working together so they don't dissipate their efforts or lose momentum."[8]

Reformasi Setengah Hati (Half-Hearted Reform)? Civil Society and Agrarian Reform in the Post-Suharto Era

Since 1998, NGO and grassroots activists' struggles to get legal reform on agrarian issues onto the national policy agenda have met with qualified success. Political parties have been reluctant to commit themselves on this issue other than in the most vague and rhetorical of terms.[9] In the immediate aftermath of the New Order's demise, a number of initiatives signaled potentially significant changes in policy direction on land and resources.[10] Both a presidential decree (KepPres 48/1999) establishing a study team to review land reform policy and law and a ministerial regulation (PerMenagraria 5/1999) setting out guidelines for resolving the problem of the territorial rights (*hak ulayat*) of *adat* communities explicitly recognize that implementation of the Basic Agrarian Law had, in the words of the presidential decree, "not been consistent with popular values and the norms of social justice."[11]

Political struggles between 1999 and 2001 left virtually all urgent policy issues in limbo.[12] Nonetheless, the media coverage given to the most high profile land cases, and pressure mounted by repeated demonstrations involving farmers' groups, students, and NGOs, could not help but exert some influence on the political parties, which now had to compete seriously for the first time at the ballot box. Through this period of political infighting, NGOs concentrated their efforts on getting the People's Consultative Assembly (MPR)[13] to pass a policy directive ("TapMPR") on agrarian reform. The vagaries of political action and the complexity of the negotiation processes in which they became enmeshed are indicators of the practical difficulties activists face in pushing forward significant reforms on resource issues in the ongoing "Transitional" Era (as NGOs began to label the period) and the absolute prerequisite for organized and broadly based alliances between grassroots organizations, NGOs, and the media to insist that parliamentary institutions become responsive to the needs of ordinary people. The experience of activist groups also points to the heavy weight of persisting practices of corruption and intimidation inherited from the previous regime and the pervasive emphasis on rhetoric in lieu of serious commitment to effective implementation of policy and law.

Initial efforts to put agrarian reform on the MPR's policy agenda at the 1999 and 2000 annual sessions were unsuccessful. The Consortium for Agrarian Reform (KPA) had been working with student and farmers' groups in organizing mass protest actions at regional assemblies across the country. It also initiated a "Million Signatures for Agrarian Reform" campaign addressed to political parties and the national parliamentary secretariat in Jakarta. Despite initially responsive gestures, the MPR committee responsible for drafting policy directives dropped agrarian reform from the list of items to be dealt with in 1999, claiming that it was "not very important and unrealistic to implement."[14] While activists blame lobbying and inducements from plantation and mining company associations, KPA leaders also admitted in retrospect that there had not been enough groundwork done with members of the parliamentary committee.

After this early failure, KPA joined a coalition of influential academics and NGOs, forming the Agrarian Reform Study Group (KSPA)[15] in an effort to impress upon the MPR and BPN[16] the urgency of dealing with the agrarian reform issue. The NGO-academic alliance this time succeeded in prompting parliamentary action. The MPR committee appointed two working parties with joint responsibility for drawing up a draft policy directive on natural resource management and agrarian reform that the committee could then submit to the annual MPR assembly.[17]

The KSPA coalition then recruited representatives of another group of NGOs concerned with environmental and natural resource management issues, PSDA, with the intent of integrating both sustainable resource management and agrarian reform within what KSPA insisted should be a single policy directive.[18] This was an issue within the NGO coalition as well as between it and the parliamentary working parties. The KSPA/KPA position emphasized a structural approach to agrarian reform, with primary attention to the needs of the mass of rural peasant-farmers, whereas the environmental NGO groups (PSDA) were concerned with the sustainable management of resources, which some among them felt might be compromised if the proposed MPR directive subordinated sustainability to agrarian rights. The environmental NGOs eventually agreed to support a single policy directive to avoid the kind of "sectoral" separation between natural resources and land law that would represent a continuation of New Order exploitative practices. Although ultimately persuaded to commit to one MPR directive (TapMPR), KSPA and PSDA remained two differently oriented groups, in somewhat uneasy alliance.[19] Nevertheless, an effective working relationship made it possible for the groups to formulate a draft MPR directive that combined aspirations of the environmental NGOs (PSDA) and the agrarian reform (KSPA) group.[20]

The joint advocacy team they formed then had to contend with the two parliamentary working parties on agrarian reform and natural resources management, where the issue of separate policy directives on land and environment arose for a different reason: forestry, mining, and plantation industry lobbies wanted continuation of distinct sectoral legislation to assure their interests in resource access. The chair of the working party on natural resources is said to have objected strongly to the input of "external [NGO] forces" in the Tap drafting process, and attempted to sabotage the Bandung conference organized to discuss agrarian reform issues in the lead-up to the MPR session. In the end, a compromise outcome—"two substances in one Tap"—prevailed in the final 2001 MPR document. The separate section on natural resources, promoting "optimal exploitation" (§5/2b), however, is expressed in much more developmentalist language than the agrarian reform section and raises questions about continued contradictions between proposed reform in the two spheres.

Combined with pressure mounted by an increasingly organized and articulate farmers' movement, the deliberate strategy to broaden the base of the campaign by bringing in environmental NGOs and to channel much of the debate through academic forums paid off. A single policy directive, now with support from within the MPR committee itself, notably from the Muslim party (PPP) and special interest group members who had NGO backgrounds, finally made its way to the 2001 MPR general session.

Not to be underrated in the strategy for reviving parliamentary interest in agrarian affairs was the political pressure mounted by organized peasant groups during the course of these parliamentary discussions. Thousands of farmers from the Aliansi Petani Indonesia (API),[21] prevented by security forces from entering the city of Bandung to carry their protest to the Pre-MPR Bandung Conference, succeeded in stopping traffic along the main thoroughfare and forcing five of the parliamentary working party participants to leave the conference to engage in a dialogue on the outskirts of the city.[22] MPR members met the farmers' representatives, led by the popular secretary general of the Sundanese Peasant Union (SPP),[23] Agustiana, who demanded that the proposed TapMPR incorporate seven principles: (1) implement the spirit of the Basic Agrarian Law (UUPA), and persuade the government to revive land reform, particularly on state land; (2) resolve land dispute cases in a humanitarian and just way; (3) revise existing resource laws and regulations so there is no conflict with the BAL/UUPA; (4) end the use of force and the criminalization of peasant-farmers in their struggles for rights to land; (5) stop giving state-owned enterprises a monopoly over natural resources via commercial use rights leases (HGU); (6) review, revoke, and return to the people all plantation (HGU) and forest (HPH) concessions obtained by companies through KKN (collusion, corruption, or nepotism); (7) ensure that agrarian development is based on principles of sustainability, democracy, and justice (interview with Agustiana, at Garut, West Java, 26 April 2001).

Agustiana asserted that the large-scale demonstration that choked traffic into Bandung for much of the day was necessary because to that point no attention had been paid to peasant farmer protests. During that heated dialogue,[24] the chair of the MPR committee admitted that the land problem was a fundamental question of justice. He committed himself to "battle" to satisfy the farmers' demands, promising that he would resign from his position as committee head if he failed.[25] The combined peasant unions' protest action appears to have been decisive in shifting the position of the Bandung conference participants, which, in the view of NGOs had initially been stacked in favor of mining and plantation interests.

After meeting with the protesting peasant farmers, MPR committee members attending the crucial Bandung conference in the lead-up to the MPR session produced a statement "defending the interests of Indonesian peasant-farmers." Its language, in a spirit of reform that could have been written by the farmers and NGOs themselves, argues that the oppression of Indonesia's peasants should be of concern to all. Parliamentary committee participants had apparently been startled at the extent of peasant support demonstrated at the protest and agreed to the SPP/API demands presented to them (interview with Agustiana, at Garut, West Java, 26 April 2001). Their statement promised to support the peasants' struggle for justice and welfare through the new MPR policy directive.[26] Despite preferences for rhetoric over political action and spectacular reversals of policy positions by political representatives in the *Era Transisi,* the persistence of the loose alliance of peasants, academics, and NGOs, for all their differences, influenced the outcome of committee deliberations. Certainly the statement issued by parliamentary members of the MPR committee was a significant departure from earlier assertions that agrarian reform was "neither necessary nor realistic."

In the event, the new Parliamentary Directive (TapMPR IX/2001)[27] on Agrarian Reform and Management of Natural Resources was passed on 9 November 2001. It recognizes that the management of natural and agricultural resources has caused poverty, structural inequalities, social conflict, and environmental degradation. It explicitly confronts the two critical issues associated with land conflicts in the New Order period, customary *adat* rights and the stalled land reform program. Article 4(j) sets out the principle of "recognition, respect and protection of the rights of *adat* law communities, and the relationship between cultural diversity and agrarian/natural resources." Article 5(1b) resuscitates land reform, stipulating a restructuring of land tenure and use that promises justice through revived commitment to a "land for the people" policy. It requires review of former acts and regulations, thoroughgoing inventory and registration of landownership and use, the implementation of land reform, and action toward resolution of land disputes.

NGOs were satisfied that the fundamental reform issues they had fought to bring back into the legislative domain were included in the final MPR policy directive. Many were troubled, however, that the compromise split between agrarian and natural resource management reform within the text would prove a weakness that would haunt policy reform. Certainly the prominent reiteration that natural resources represent "national wealth" that must be "optimized"[28] and the obligatory primacy given to national integrity and unity (§4/a) were cause for concern. These phrases conjure once again the state-centrist developmentalism that had subsumed earlier populist and socialist commitments of the Indonesian Constitution and Basic Agrarian Law.

As serious for the future of the agrarian reform movement and its implications for democracy and equity in the post-Suharto era, are divisions that emerged within the peasant farmers' movement and between it and their NGO supporters over symbolic issues in TapMPR IX. Agustiana's[29] SPP and API were very much in support of TapMPR IX, believing that now peasant organizations had legitimacy and a legal basis for negotiating their claims with local governments.[30] But other peasants' groups, most vocally the FSPI and SPJB (The West Java Peasants' Union), did not support the MPR policy directive. Excluded from the consultation process that produced the NGO drafts, FSPI had submitted its own draft Tap directly to the MPR committee. They believe that TapMPR IX threatens the existence of the Basic Agrarian Law—which the MPR policy directive does not even mention[31] and which they see as central to the protection of their rights.[32] They were particularly concerned that the new policy directive could displace the symbolic and legal centrality of the BAL/UUPA and its commitment to the nation's peasant farmers, as well as opening the door to a thoroughgoing neoliberal approach to agrarian policy. Given the ambiguities in the final document and its circumvention of the symbolic capital that the BAL/UUPA represents, critics regarded this studied avoidance of reference to the Basic Agrarian Law as a serious miscalculation by the activist groups who had campaigned for this legislative route to reform.

To Revise or Not the Basic Agrarian Law (UUPA)? Of Strategies and Symbols

Significant sectors of the reform movement were disturbed by the outcome of the long deliberations leading up to the passage of TapMPR IX/2001 and by its failure to address the question of the Basic Agrarian Law (UUPA). In a piece published in the national newspaper, *Kompas,* Idham Samudra Bey, executive secretary of the Centre for Agricultural Policy Studies (CAPS),[33] points to the significance of the ideological relationship between UUPA, with its popular-socialist grounding, and Indonesia's "peasant" class who were the quintessential *"rakyat"* (people),[34] the pivotal focus of policy and law in the period from the revolution to 1965. He insists that TapMPR IX shows no signs of "fulfilling the hopes and dreams of Indonesia's farming people" (*Kompas*, 10 January 2002). However satisfying the flowery language of human rights and sustainability liberally peppering the document, he asserts, it does not position peasant-farmers or "the people" at the center of state policy in the unequivocal way that the Basic Agrarian Law (BAL/UUPA) has done. Concerns expressed in Idham's letter—that the policy directive would become the wedge with which to overturn the UUPA—are echoed in the response of the West Java Peasants' Union (SPJB) statement rejecting the MPR policy directive. Theirs is an explicitly class-situated argument.

> The passage of TapMPR No IX . . . will severely hurt the peasant class. . . . [It] restricts the meaning of the concept *agraria* to the matter of land, which opens the door as widely as possible for the entry of big capital in the exploitation of natural resources. We have to remember that the politics and economy of Indonesia continue to be piloted by and dependent on the IMF that is patently capitalist. In all likelihood, the outcome of the TapMPR on Agrarian Reform and Natural Resource Management will be laws and regulations coming from the legislature (DPR) that will pave the way for the entry of foreign capital. We all know that the composition and interests of the DPR members in no way reflect the interests of the people. The agrarian problems faced by the people are already great. The birth of this policy directive will cause only more irregularity in the law on agrarian matters, stir up existing conflicts, and provoke new ones. Until now, UUPA No. 5 1960 has been the basis of agrarian law. . . . The vision contained in the new policy directive is fundamentally different. (Candrawiguna 2002)

There was no consideration of the need to strengthen farmers' organizations in the policy directive. Nor was the proposal from the previous KPA congress incorporated, to establish an agrarian court including representatives of peasant groups as well as legal specialists to settle disputes and implement land reform. None of the agrarian reform principles in TapMPR IX suggest this level of direct participation in the legal process for Indonesia's marginalized peasant farmers. For critics, TapMPR IX offers nothing that was not already promised by UUPA but risked mortgaging all its symbolic capital (SPJB press release, 15 February 2002).

Circumvention of the Basic Agrarian Law was more than a technical legal question for these critics. Its historical context and symbolism carry great weight, despite the contradictory implications it eventually had for the "people" it was supposed to protect. In his stinging critique, Idham argued that replacement of the Basic Agrarian Law would prove the final nail in the coffin for the people's interests it once represented, interests which were "castrated" by New Order policy and the resource legislation it spawned. TapMPR IX prepared the way for liberalization toward the market-friendly land policies advocated by the World Bank and National Land Agency (BPN), inevitably spawning new conflict between resource developers' and peasant farmers' interests. In Idham's words the Tap "strikes the death knell for the Basic Agrarian Law" and "signifies the return of dark clouds over the future of Indonesia's farming people" (*Kompas,* 10 January 2002).

In a response to these criticisms, Dianto Bachriadi (2002), representing the Consortium on Agrarian Reform (KPA), argued that the agrarian situation inherited from the New Order regime had so evidently departed from any commitment to the needs of the popular majority expressed in the Basic Agrarian Law, that the MPR directive imposing a mandate from the people on the new government was an urgent political necessity, compromises notwithstanding.

> The heart of Idham's concern . . . regarding the effect of TapMPR IX on the fate of the country's peasants lies in its failure to invoke or to clarify the position of [BAL] UUPA 1960, and the lack of any clear instrument that would be used to carry out the land reform mentioned in the MPR directive. One point that must be clearly situated in relation to this disagreement is that the MPR directive was the optimal result from the political process that could be achieved, with the greatest potential to bring about change that we have at the

moment. If we take account of all the [polarized] potential of these changes—the evidence of people's and peasant-farmers' organization, the strength of middle-class ideology represented by NGOs, the weak attention and commitment from intellectuals and academics, the constellation of the political parties and parliament, the system of constitutional law, the pressure of international interests, alongside the changes in the political conjunctures within Indonesia itself, then the promulgation of MPR Directive No. IX/MPR/2001 must be welcomed.... If we look at the process of change that must take place in this country from a transitional perspective, that is, leaving behind all the political, economic, and cultural practices of the past in order to begin life as a people and a nation that is based on new principles, then this directive can become an instrument to push the transitional process along political and legal lines.[35]

In practice, Bachriadi argued, the Basic Agrarian Law had already been dwarfed and disabled. He pointed to the Land Reform Law (UU 56/1961) based on UUPA, which, while never revoked, has contributed little to the lives of Indonesia's rural population since the New Order came to power. The "national interest" proviso in UUPA had been the grounds for legitimizing plantation leases and timber concessions that were the source of most of the land conflicts now plaguing the country. For the *adat* communities of outer island Indonesia, there was never the positive association with land redistribution that the Basic Agrarian Law originally conveyed to inner island Indonesian peasants, only the experience of land expropriation for resource and transmigration programs. The exclusion of forests and other resources from the effective jurisdiction of the Basic Agrarian Law under New Order sectoral laws in any case made the revision of all land and resource legislation urgent. If necessary, KPA was prepared to jettison the Basic Agrarian Law, its contribution to the people's welfare ambiguous at best. "If political calculation dictates that a better outcome would result from a new law that was comprehensive—at least as comprehensive as UUPA 1960—but isn't named 'UUPA,' in the framework of translating the mandate to progress agrarian reform, there need be no tears shed if UUPA 1960 has to be displaced."[36]

The Indonesian scholar Gunawan Wiradi acknowledged that the MPR directive leaves open the possibility that other laws, even the UUPA, may be revised in a manner that would weaken rather than strengthen its core policy objectives. But he took the view that the passage of TapMPR IX had its own strategic and symbolic significance. "It is no longer possible for farmers to be accused of communist actions since land reform is back on the national agenda. Before by just talking about land you could be accused of being communist" (Gunawan Wiradi, pers. comm., 29 April 2002). In general, NGO and academics' viewed TapMPR IX as renewing the mandate for land reform, but only a first step.

For the optimists, the question was then how to put teeth into TapMPR IX.[37] They pressed the government to undertake a review and revoke all laws in conflict with the policy directive and to establish an autonomous and independent body to carry out this task, as well as a special Agrarian Disputes Board as proposed by the National Human Rights Commission (KomnasHAM). Neither body was set up: the latter halted when President Yudhoyono issued a letter stating that a new commission was not required, since conflicts could be resolved by existing institutions such as KomnasHAM itself, the National Land Agency, and the administrative courts (PTUN).[38] In fact a National Commission for Agrarian Conflict Resolution (KNuPKA) had been proposed because the administrative courts cannot legally process appeals beyond ninety days after the policies have been promulgated. As a consequence, decisions to extend forest concessions and plantation leases from the 1980s and 1990s cannot be effectively challenged. This was the situation with respect to government agency misconduct in the Lombok case study (chapter 8) where documents subsequently revealed evidence of misrepresentation by government departments. Nor would the important question of the large land concentrations speculatively acquired for plantation, timber concessions, resort, real estate, and golf course megadevelopments be subject to serious scrutiny.

Meanwhile, Ministry of Environment plans for a new Sustainable Resource Management Law (with which environmental NGOs had been engaging despite commitment to a single piece of agrarian legislation to cover all natural resources) stalled, evidently because of resistance from mining, plantation, and forestry departments. BPN's proposal for revising the Basic Agrarian Law (BPN Team Penyelaras 2004) also failed to gain interdepartmental approval because it attempted to resolve the overlapping jurisdictions of the same three departments, while they competed to retain their "sectoral power" over these resource domains. KPA dropped discussions with BPN on the establishment of a national agrarian reform committee (KNPA) when it shifted its strategy to support President Yudhoyono's agrarian program.

The exigencies of an inherited governmental framework and the need to achieve concrete outcomes appear to be driving ambiguous strategies among NGO coalition groups, who retain their in-principle commitment to integrate the agrarian legal regime in the long term.[39] The effect of the schizophrenic formula for dealing with resource and agrarian reform issues and the exclusion of any reference to the Basic Agrarian Law in TapMPR IX was to leave many of the concerns that originally motivated the drive for passage of the MPR directive unanswered. The different orientations of the two sections on agrarian reform and natural resource management in the directive derive ultimately from two preceding bodies of legislation. They are creatures of two regimes with two different conceptions of how social justice for Indonesia's people is to be achieved. More than a decade into the Reform or Transitional Era, the fundamental questions affecting resource security for Indonesia's subaltern classes remain unanswered.

Ultimately the devil had been left to the detail. The MPR policy directive was partly able to placate competing interests by deferring substantive reform issues to subsequent legislation yet to be enacted by the Indonesian legislature (DPR). Big questions remain to be answered: Would the Basic Agrarian Law, particularly its emphasis on the social function of land and the state's right of control, be revised or jettisoned? Would long-standing claims of occupants on "state lands" be recognized through official transfer of title, and would plantation timber and mining concessions imposed over the customary territories of *adat* communities be rescinded or renegotiated? Would restrictions on land speculation and land concentration for large development projects be imposed? Would the BAL provisions against foreign ownership of land be further eroded? And would genuinely effective mechanisms for enforcing old and new agrarian reform legislation be established? Little in the directive indicated how the promise of justice for the Indonesian people it reiterated would finally be achieved, and nothing that has happened in the years since it was issued by the MPR has clarified the situation. The day before the policy directive was passed through the MPR, seven hundred farmers representing SPP, AMAN, API, and FSPI demonstrated at the Parliament building against the failure of the TapMPR to mandate the rescinding of all existing legislation that adversely affects their livelihoods, and to require cancellation of permits and leases to forest, mining, tourist, and agribusiness ventures on land stolen from them. To their protest that the policy directive showed no serious intent to eliminate the causes of the suffering of rural farmers, a delegation from the MPR committee responded with an inauspiciously vacuous statement: "For a full year we have traveled throughout Indonesia and have taken in all the aspirations that have been coming forth from the people."[40]

Genuine reform will depend ultimately on the popular reformists' capacity to mobilize political pressure to ensure forward movement. The fragility of the alliances among and between NGO and peasant farmers' groups and the failure to maintain the backing of significant factions among the very subjects of the agrarian reform movement or to involve them at critical points in the negotiation process—all threatened to derail the momentum that surrounded the TapMPR struggle.[41] Although NGO groups generally regarded the resuscitation of land reform in the parliamentary directive as a victory, they nevertheless expressed concern at the "half-hearted" commitment to integration of land and resource matters in the Tap and its failure to address past grievances with concrete steps toward resolution (*Kompas*, 2 November 2001).

Insofar as NGOs claimed success in their efforts to get the policy directive on agrarian reform through the MPR, it has been as much on grounds of building process as outcome. Despite differences of position within the NGO movement and between NGOs and the local groups they attempt to represent, despite general disappointment with governance practices carried over from the Suharto regime, and despite the continued efforts of bureaucratic and business interests to frustrate reform efforts, debate, and negotiation—despite all these, strategic alliances and political pressure achieved what some activists regarded as a reasonably accommodating foothold upon which to mount the next stage of their struggle. NGOs took the passage of TapMPR IX as a sign of political commitment and an instrument that could be used to achieve concrete change.

The fragility of that foothold has been evident in the failure to convert TapMPR IX into a clear framework of law, policy, and practice that could resolve disputes and drive transformative change. The deployment of populist rhetoric in lieu of political action remains a hallmark of post-Suharto party politics, which, except for the important effects of widening the political playground to other participants in the "democracy festival," has not produced serious practical attempts to address structural inequalities affecting Indonesia's landless and land-poor. Regrettably, during the Habibie, Wahid, Megawati, and Yudhoyono presidencies that followed one another in rapid succession after the fall of Suharto, the call for agrarian reform has been drowned out by power politics and a one-sided focus on investment liberalization as the route to recovery in the wake of the 1997–98 financial crisis. Successive governments in post–New Order elections continued to relegate the land issue to the "too hard" basket.

Political Positions on National Land Policy in the Era Transisi

In 1998–99 the interim administration of President Habibie initiated far-reaching changes in governance with promulgation of the 1999 laws on regional autonomy, which has had mixed implications for land rights and conservation policy (see Warren and McCarthy 2009). Proclaimed to be the basis for sweeping changes in the relationship between the state and the people, the Regional Government and Revenue Allocation Acts (UU 22/1999 and UU 25/1999) offered to the regions the prospect of more local autonomy and a larger share of the income from resources previously appropriated by central government. But decentralization has been a fractious process, introducing new resourcing needs and rent-seeking opportunities at the local level. The expectation that democratically elected regional governments would be more sympathetic to their constituents' claims has only in a few instances been matched by better outcomes, as case studies in this volume have demonstrated.

Policy initiatives dealing directly with the fraught issue of agrarian reform proved subject to elite-capture or political subversion from the outset. When Abdurrachman Wahid became president, he expressed the view that plantation company shares should also be owned by local communities and announced his intention to redistribute 40 percent of land controlled by state-owned plantations that had been occupied and cultivated by peasant farmers. Wahid took the position that control of land by large companies was excessive and had created "land-hungry" peasants (*Surya,* 24 May 2000) However, these plans were not implemented before he was removed from office by the parliament on hotly contested corruption charges. Whatever Wahid's political failings, the fact remains that since the founding fathers of the republic, Hatta (1946) and Sukarno (1960), called for land reform and agrarian justice, no other Reform Era president has challenged the concentration of landholdings as a significant cause of economic exploitation in rural Indonesia.

In 2000 Wahid established the National Ombudsman Commission (KON) to deal with the high level of complaints in three priority areas—corruption in the judiciary, performance of the police, and agrarian issues.[42] With respect to land policy reforms, the ombudsman made several recommendations,[43] spelling out the need for integration of legislation to resolve the issue of sectoralism in agrarian and natural resources law, introduction of standard operating procedures for obtaining rights to land, and establishment of a mechanism for transparent monitoring of land administration (Bachriadi, Bachrioktora, and Safitri 2002, 169–71). Only the second recommendation was acted upon when BPN, with World Bank support, initiated programs to improve administrative procedures, making it easier for the public to obtain land certificates.

During Megawati's presidency (2001–4), some consideration was given to the problems of land speculation, illegal under the Basic Agrarian Law, and primarily responsible for the large areas of land left out of production. Expressions of concern with this "sleeping land" problem and the low levels of officially titled land were the Megawati administration's main response to widespread land disputes.[44] However, no practical program to resolve these two serious issues was instituted. Instead, the Megawati government handed over responsibility for resolving land issues to the Minister for Economic Affairs (*Kompas,* 27 May 2003), with the intent of changing the Basic Agrarian Law and signaling an investment-friendly direction for a new national agrarian legal framework. The previous minister in Wahid's cabinet had been reluctant to take on such a task because of its sensitivity (see Bachriadi 2006).

The long-awaited presidential decree concerning national policy on land matters, KepPres 34 2003,[45] pursuant to the MPR policy directive, was issued by Megawati on 23 May 2003, promising the completion of a draft law "refining" the Basic Agrarian Law and related legislation. This was doubtless meant to appeal to rural voters in the lead-up to the impending election; the implied retention of BAL/UUPA apparently intended to placate some of the peasant groups alienated by TapMPR IX. The presidential decree does mention implementation of land reform, but only in the context of the "development of a land management and information system" aimed at extending the survey and registration of landholdings through resumption of the World Bank–funded Land Administration Project (LAP). Also controversial has been the devolution of administrative authority for implementing specified aspects of land policy to the district level. The most important of these regional government responsibilities now include issuing location and development permits and processing land procurement for these projects, resolving land disputes and compensation settlements, determining what land is available and who is eligible for land redistribution, and dealing with the issue of "neglected" lands under commercial use right leases (HGU), which had been left undeveloped and should under BAL/UUPA have reverted to public ownership, potentially available for redistribution. However, BPN still maintains centralized authority over important aspects of land regulation and the power to issue large-scale HGU licenses: the jurisdiction of district-level land administration remains unclear and capacity is weak.

There were a variety of views on what the impact of the presidential decree would be. KPA was concerned that KepPres 34/2003 diverged from the intent of TapMPR IX/2001; by this time, some were having misgivings about their earlier support for the compromise MPR policy directive. First, the mandated review of the Basic Agrarian Law continued to exclude mining, forest, and coastal areas from the provisions of land law. Second, it promoted land reform in the context of land registration, which KPA has consistently opposed, at least where it is oriented toward privatizing land tenure and relies on market mechanisms for redistribution.[46] Finally, the relegation of land conflict resolution to the district level would not be of much advantage to peasant farmers in the vast majority of districts that do not have well-coordinated farmers' organizations or local NGOs to provide advocacy for peasant farmers in land disputes, to no avail as it turned out in the Lombok case (chapter 8).[47] Nevertheless, this provision placed resolution of conflicts closer to the source.[48] SPP leader Agustiana's view represents the position of many farmers' organizations: "KepPres is the moment we have been waiting for to sit down and talk with district government about agrarian issues."[49]

Whatever influence the agrarian reform movement might have had on legal formulations and political rhetoric, the governments elected since the fall of the New Order have generally been reluctant to deal with agrarian issues beyond gesture, treading carefully to avoid alienating monied power brokers and attracted to market-based "solutions" that do not confront resource concentration. There remains an abyss between what little lip service is granted to the need for agrarian reform and the prevailing pragmatic accommodation of vested interests that fund political campaigns and patronize party leaderships (interview with Nissa Wargadipura, director of Yapemas, Garut, 7 September 2007).

Reform Era governments continue to pass regulations facilitating resource control that are in direct conflict with provisions of the Basic Agrarian Law, such as the 2004 Plantation Law (UU 18/ 2004) and the amended Foreign Investment Law (UU 25/2007) discussed below. As Afiff et al. (2005) and Peluso, Afiff, and Fauzi Rachman (2008) point out, we should not forget that the government itself is the biggest landlord in Indonesia because of the inherited colonial plantation system and its appropriation of vast forestlands. It is therefore not surprising that an investigation of agrarian problems by the national parliamentary ombudsman, carried out together with the Consortium for Agrarian Reform (KPA) in 2002, found that 46 percent of the government bureaucracy with land administration authority had acted illegally in issuing permits and concessions.[50] This investigation also found that 67 percent of land expropriations for commercial investment had broken various laws and regulations on land allocation and transfer processes. Sixty-four percent of land "clearances" were for private purposes, technically illegal, in many cases carried out by henchmen with tacit support of the state apparatus. The remaining 36 percent were for public purposes (see Bachriadi, Bachrioktora, and Safitri 2002).

Hijacking "Reform"

On the legal front, it has been the sectoral interests allied with government resource departments and neoliberal "reformists" that have succeeded in using MPR Directive IX/2001 to push through new sectoral legislation under the banner of "law reform." This has been driven by promarket forces, aiming to reduce the role of government in economic affairs and furthering the privatization agenda. The passing of the new Plantation Law (UU 18/2004), for example, strengthened commercial use rights on plantation land and explicitly criminalized plantation occupations, providing harsh penalties of five years' imprisonment and fines of Rp 5 billion for occupation or damage to plantation property. This legislation replaced the more ambiguous 1960 Law Prohibiting the Use of Plantation or Forestland without Permit

(UU 51/1960) which imposed comparatively lighter penalties of three months in jail and/or Rp 5,000 fines for violations. Furthermore the earlier legislation sympathetically instructed the agrarian minister to take account of the people's interests in resolving occupation cases (UU51/1960, §6).

The new plantation law reflected the success of the plantation lobby's efforts to strengthen their control over state land, and marked a retreat from the principle of the people's rights to land and natural resources, which was a constitutional principle and a key element of the Reform Era campaigns. This trend was also reflected in the passing of the Water Resources Management Law (UU 7/2004), which opened the way for private companies to monopolize water distribution, while UU19/2004[51] gave mining companies access to protection forests. The revised Oil and Natural Gas Law (UU 22/2001), followed by Yudhoyono government changes in investment legislation (UU 25/2007) and the Mineral and Coalmine Act (UU 4/2009), liberalized foreign ownership and investment rules related to natural resources. A constitutional court judicial review did reject the investment law provision extending foreign commercial lease rights (HGU) to ninety-five years (see Mahkamah Konstitusi 2007) on grounds that it was in conflict with the spirit of the Basic Agrarian Law and the Constitution. But it did not declare the entire law unconstitutional, as the appellants had hoped.[52] Provisions of the BAL aimed at reducing land concentration were entirely ignored in policy discussions on Indonesia's natural resources sector.

Besides resistance from supporters of the 1960 Basic Agrarian Law, proposals for revising the BAL failed to get support from other government agencies that did not want to risk losing control over their forest, plantation, and mining fiefdoms through new amendments (Fauzi 2009a, Peluso, Afiff, and Fauzi Rachman 2008). In 2007, the BPN finally decided to discontinue its effort to produce a new law to replace the 1960 Basic Agrarian Law. Instead, with Asian Development Bank funding, it began to formulate new complementary legislation, to accommodate complaints from private enterprise concerning the complicated and costly process of land transfer in Indonesia (see Asian Development Bank 2007).[53] At the same time, the planning authority,

Bappenas, reversed its policy supporting replacement of BAL/UUPA, which has been the World Bank's position, to one opposing significant change (Bappenas 2006). In the face of agrarian scholar-activists' criticism of the draft National Land Policy framework at a Bappenas workshop,[54] on grounds that it transgressed the social function of land principle and the nationalist view on public ownership of natural resources, as well as populist land reform, Bappenas moved away from its earlier position that the Basic Agrarian Law should be totally revised. The National Land Policy framework draft was modified to state that "the spirit of the UUPA No. 5/1960 should remain in place as one of the basic principles of land policy" (Bappenas 2006, 6).

PPAN: Yudhoyono's New Format "Reformasi Agraria"

One more volley in the somersault politics that has been producing ambiguous and contradictory effects for the reform agenda began in January 2007, when the Yudhoyono government, which succeeded Megawati in the 2004 elections, launched the National Agrarian Reform Program (PPAN), which purportedly would redistribute some 9.25 million hectares of land.[55] Although implementation of land redistribution was a fundamental concern of the rural poor and agrarian reform proponents, PPAN immediately sparked controversy among activists. Some saw the program as an opportunity to influence the BPN and realize implementation of the populist ideas of agrarian reform (Setiawan 2007; Tjondronegoro 2007b). Others argued the program was only a maneuver to gain support in the 2009 election and that it surreptitiously incorporated in a new format privatized land distribution as part of a program bundle that would cement the hold of neoliberal land policies over Indonesia (see Bachriadi and Juliantara 2007).

The appearance of PPAN was nonetheless an outcome of intensive efforts of agrarian reform proponents to put the issue back onto the national policy agenda. Yudhoyono had been lobbied by NGOs and scholar-activists[56] in the lead-up to the first direct presidential elections in 2004. As a result, his draft "Vision, Mission and Program" statement was revised to include two paragraphs concerning implementation of agrarian reform if he were to win the election (see Yudhoyono and Kalla 2004, 55–69). But through most of his first five-year term in office, it was unclear whether or how these commitments would be honored. Social movement groups organized several protests to demand that Yudhoyono keep his campaign promise (*Kompas,* 23 March 2005; *Sinar Harapan,* 17 May 2006). Finally in 2007, with the second term election in view, PPAN appeared as the response. On Peasants' Day 2007 the head of the BPN, Joyo Winoto, acknowledged the injustices of the concentration of power and ownership over land as the "ultimate issue" since the Basic Agrarian Law had been enacted forty-seven years earlier: "The peoples' access to land as the source of their livelihoods is still weak. Short-term perspectives and immediate interests and hegemony have always disguised that injustice." The government promised to "overcome the concentration of assets . . . [and] imbalances in control over land by allocating state land through agrarian reform" (*Republika,* 24 September 2007). The state land that was slated for redistribution would be drawn from 1.1 million hectares designated for distribution under the old land reform regulation (PP 224/1961)[57] and 8.15 million hectares from production or conversion forest (*Media Indonesia,* 22 May 2007; *Republika,* 23 May 2007; *Pikiran Rakyat,* 28 May 2007). Which farmers would become the subjects of this land distribution, how distribution would be implemented, or what kind of land rights and support the beneficiaries would receive were unspecified.

Once again it appeared the agrarian reform concept was being deployed to gain short-term political support from the rural sector, rather than representing a long-term commitment to agrarian justice. It seemed highly unlikely that the PPAN land redistribution program would include the wider socioeconomic support commitments that reformists sought from government, given the policies that the Yudhoyono government had already implemented, such as raising the price of fuel, reducing agricultural subsidies, allowing cheaper agricultural imports,[58] privatizing some health and education services, and allowing the market to take control of other social services. Government support for neoliberal economic policies, including the position on free trade and investment of the World Trade Organization and the land policies promoted by the World Bank would have to be significantly revised if equitable and sustainable agrarian reform were to be implemented in Indonesia.

The PPAN land redistribution program was evidently not designed to resolve the agrarian conflicts or land occupations that have festered in Indonesia for decades (*Kompas*, 23 May 2007; *Media Indonesia Online*, 22 May 2007). Not only was there no mention made in Yudhoyono's announcement of intent to curb the size of individual and corporate landholdings, but a substantial portion (2.15 million hectares, roughly 25 percent) of the land redistributed under PPAN was to be allocated to business interests as part of this "comprehensive model of agrarian reform" (Sutarto 2006).

Yudhoyono's agrarian reform program has to be considered in the context of large-scale land appropriation policies for biofuel, aquaculture, and for the "revitalization" of the plantation sector, all of which have the potential for creating new forms of land concentration. Ironically, the 2009 campaign advertisement, promoting his government's land reform credentials, indicates HGU commercial agricultural leases increased during his first period of government by 1.47 million hectares, compared to credit taken for people's land redistributions of a much smaller figure of 717,000 hectares.[59] There are also indications that the current government's agrarian reform program may be a newly packaged attempt to strengthen the role of big plantations employing small farmers in such schemes as contract farming and the *"inti-plasma"* (core-satellite) plantation model.[60] The National Land Agency head stated that agrarian reform is only a "complementary program" to revitalize the agriculture, plantation,[61] fisheries, and forestry sectors.[62] The concept of partnerships (*kemitraan*) between big plantations and small farmers using the core-satellite model is an old idea that has generally failed to empower small farmers (see chapters 5 and 6 in this volume on palm oil plantation developments in Sumatra and Kalimantan).[63] The Cisarua Petition, written by several agrarian experts and activists (Poniman et al. 2005; Bachriadi and Juliantara

2007), insisted that whoever came to power in Indonesia after the 2004 election should not treat agrarian reform as an ancillary program to a "revitalization" of agriculture that depended on capital-intensive investment to exploit local potential.

Many land occupations of plantation estates and state forest were nearly complete when Yudhoyono's minister for Land Affairs (head of BPN), Joyo Winoto, began promoting PPAN and seeking support from peasant-farmer groups. These groups, consolidated in SPP and the Bengkulu Peasants' Union (STaB) among others, understandably supported PPAN initially, because their land occupations lacked legal security, and they expected that PPAN would at least mean legal recognition. But by the end of 2008, PPAN's very existence was in doubt; the president had not signed legislation to implement the program that had been a flagship of his first term.[64] A new design for land redistribution now referred to by BPN as "land reform plus asset reform" was mooted that would combine land distribution to farmers with commercial interests and manage postdistribution production activities.[65]

The tension between BPN and the Ministry of Forestry unquestionably contributed to the impediments affecting implementation of PPAN. The National Land Agency's intent to carry out redistribution of state forestland was challenged by the Minister of Forestry, arguing that its own redistribution program would give local people access to state forest through a community forestry program (PHBM, *Pengelolaan Hutan Bersama Masyarakat*) (*Warta FKKM* 2006). If PPAN was to be implemented in forest areas, the Ministry of Forestry demanded to manage this redistribution program directly, not via BPN. Because of conflicts of interest between departments[66] and the likelihood of conflict between large-scale plantation owners and local people, local authorities and farmers' organizations were not convinced that the program could be implemented (interview with secretary general of STaB, 26 February 2007; *Pikiran Rakyat*, 26, 28, and 30 May 2007; *Kompas*, 6 June 2007).[67]

The failure to deliver the promised resolution of land conflicts has led to disappointment and distrust among peasant groups. "We don't know what has happened with all the data compiled on occupied land that we sent to BPN" (interview with Marhendi, 26 February 2006). This STaB leader publicly condemned Joyo Winoto, the head of BPN, in an open letter sent to various civil society organizations in Indonesia.[68] In a focus group discussion in Central Java, some leaders of social movement groups and peasant organizations that earlier had pinned their hopes on Yudhoyono's *"reformasi agraria"* program now concluded that PPAN had the potential to destroy the consolidation of peasant movements in Indonesia.[69] An activist who was involved in the Batang Peasants' Advocacy Forum (FPBB) stated that in the end "PPAN became a bad thing, causing infighting among ourselves. PPAN is weakening our struggle" (interview with HD, 6 June 2007). FSPI and SPI concluded the PPAN had become a broken promise, without commitment to real action.[70] SPP, in contrast, remains one peasant organization that still believes PPAN cannot be abandoned. One of its organizers argued, "SPP's struggle needs small victories. Because our chance of winning the struggle for land is very small, we have to use it.... SPP has to think about the interests of thousands of people, who have never had as good an opportunity as provided by PPAN [to gain land]. It is hard for SPP to ignore this program" (interview with SPP organizer, 6 June 2007). Agustiana, secretary general of SPP, believes the pro-agrarian reform activists can use PPAN to strengthen existing peasant organizations and to form new ones. He also expected PPAN could be used to halt, or at least reduce, further expansion of large-scale plantation activities (interview Tasikmalaya, 23 December 2008).

At the same time PPAN was being proffered as a solution to land conflicts, the government unveiled its master plan (M3PEI) for an ambitious acceleration of Indonesian economic growth, announcing plans for megadevelopment and infrastructure projects that it claimed would take Indonesia from its current annual per capita income level of US$3,000 to US$18,000 and status as a high-income country by 2025.[71] With the backing of the master plan investors told the government that without a law to facilitate land acquisition, they "won't invest in Indonesia."[72] Thus there is an expectation of the business community that the new land acquisition law would provide the cheaper land that they claim is needed for investment. But NGO activists argue that development of important infrastructure won't happen while speculators drive up the price of land for important projects; the Jakarta Banjir Kanal flood control project (where compensation was twice as high as the cost of project works), the Trans Java Tollway along the north coast, and the Trans Java Southern Bypass—all stalled in part because of compensation issues. From the critics' perspective, reform of the law must deal with speculative acquisition, even from the perspective of developers' interests.

The promulgation of the new law on land acquisition initiated another round of controversy regarding the reformist intentions of this Indonesian government. The Law on Land Acquisition for Development and the Public Interest (UU 2/2011) was finally passed by the DPR on 16 December 2011.[73] According to the deputy chair of the parliamentary special committee responsible for the bill, outstanding issues still under discussion before the bill was passed were the role of private enterprise in public infrastructure projects, legal protection of landowners, and dispute settlement before the courts, including for those whose land is not covered by land certificates. Land valuation to determine compensation was another difficult issue (*Jakarta Post*, 12 December 2011). Valuations (based on market rates not taxation valuations) are carried out by an independent appraisal team in areas where infrastructure development is a priority.[74] Although the law states that land acquisition has to reflect a balance between the interests of development and the interests of the community (§10) and acknowledges the issue of compensation for land cultivators/landholders without legal ownership rights, it struggles to define *"kepentingan umum"* as both public interest and public good.[75] It also fails to connect with relevant articles of the UUPA and subsequent legislation, in particular UU 20/1961 on revocation of land rights, which protects both owners and occupiers of land and dwellings on land being resumed.[76] Compensation should be paid not only to those holding land rights but also to those residents and cultivators who lose livelihoods and homes and need resettlement (UU 20/1961, General Elucidation §5 [2]). Another weakness is that there is no indication of how the new land acquisition law will address the problem of speculation, although the issue is mentioned in passing several times.

Both Government Regulation 11/2010 on Neglected Lands and to a much lesser degree Law 2/2012 on Land Acquisition for Development in the Public Interest attempt to resolve problems that have existed since the Basic Agrarian Law was passed in 1960—the processes involved in resumption of abandoned or neglected land and of compensation for land resumed for public-interest development projects. The regulation on neglected lands gives investors three warnings and three months before BPN can formally declare the land to be neglected *tanah terlantar* and subject to resumption by the state. Land thus declared is then automatically eligible for the Yudhoyono land reform program. It recognizes the reality that much of Indonesia's neglected land is already being cultivated by landless communities. Once the head of the National Land Agency has declared land to be *tanah terlantar,* leasehold rights are automatically revoked without compensation. But the regulation exempts land controlled by state-owned companies and authorities, including the Forest Department. It also leaves BPN in a position to use and withdraw the threat of neglect (*terlantar*) declarations in order to obtain bribes (I. Nurdin, pers. comm., 20 March 2012).

The new Law on Land Acquisition (UU 2 /2012), having the status of a "law," in theory should be more able to protect landholders' rights than previous government regulations or presidential decrees that have a "lower" and therefore weaker legal status. Although land acquisition by the state is supposed to be in the public interest, it nevertheless allows compulsory acquisition of land for private energy and infrastructure projects. Furthermore, the drawn-out process of lodging an objection to state resumption leaves dispossessed landholders in a weak position to defend their rights. Nor does the legislation address the issue of land speculation (I Nurdin, pers. comm., 20 March 2012).

It appears that the natural resource legislation agenda of pro-market investors and policy analysts is being rapidly consolidated by the Indonesian government. This does not mean that the era of reform brought only defeat for pro-agrarian reform activists. Unquestionably, political change from an authoritarian to a more democratic regime has opened up space for social movements at the village level to carry out collective action toward legal recognition of land rights (see Afiff et al. 2005; Peluso, Afiff, and Fauzi Rachman 2008). Our own and other case studies, however, indicate that these local successes are often thwarted by vested political and economic interests, internal factionalism, and elite capture.

Peasant/NGO Responses—"Land Reform by Leverage"

Using land occupations in their "land reform by leverage" strategy,[77] farmers in West Java and Sumatra who are members of SPP and STaB collectively organized against large plantation interests, while also taking the land occupation movement beyond the immediate livelihood needs of their constituents. In Bengkulu, with political confidence built on efforts to consolidate bases in local elections, StaB—together with a number of other Indonesian reformist forces—launched an alternative political party, the PPR (People's Confederation Party) (Simpul Bengkulu 2006, 339). Inaugurated in 2005, PPR put forward a platform based on populist agrarian reform and national industrialization. It has articulated a clear position against the implementation of free market principles in the socioeconomic development of Indonesian society (PPR 2007, 121–30).[78] The agrarian reform program of the People's Confederation Party seeks "to change the ownership, control and use of agrarian resources in the interests of farmers, farm labourers, and the poor" (PPR 2007b). To ameliorate the main causes of poverty, land redistribution must be accompanied by providing credit, agricultural inputs, and marketing facilities to improve farmers' returns. By agrarian reform, PPR means not only land redistribution for the development of agriculture, but a complete reorganization of the system of management and control of all natural resources, including forestry, plantations, mining, fisheries, and other coastal resources to create a genuine people's basis for industrialization.[79] But the official

PPR platform does not spell out its position on the knotty issues of which land should be redistributed, what ceiling there would be on legal holdings, what kinds of title would be available, whether resale of redistributed land would be prohibited, and how subdivision of redistributed land in the next generation would be dealt with (Simpul Bengkulu 2006, 339).

Unfortunately, even though PPR succeeded in consolidating social movement activists across the country through rural grassroots organizing, establishing a political network in twenty provinces and hundreds of districts, this attempt failed to meet the administrative requirements that would have enabled the new political party to stand in the 2009 election. In April 2008, the Department of Legal Affairs and Human Rights decided the PPR failed to qualify for the next stage selection processes administered by the electoral commission (KPU).[80]

Although the transition to democracy that has occurred in Indonesia since 1998 influenced both social movements and popular politics at the local level, these political changes have yet to provide a real breakthrough in the dynamics driving rural social change, or for that matter Indonesia's political economy at large. The political changes to date have yielded only formal or minimalist democratization rather than the more fundamental transformations that were expected (Harriss, Stokke, and Törnquist 2004; Prasetyo et al. 2003). None of the conditions that would enable systematic resolution of the deep-seated structural issues that underpin agrarian conflicts has materialized.

Political changes since the Reform Era have reduced the intensity of state repression of land occupations, although these still take place. Efforts to prevent people's direct actions by state forces or by the private militias in the employ of companies persist, and may be on the increase (Wilson 2006). Nonetheless, a more open political system since 1998 has enabled groups of farmers who have occupied land to strengthen their networks and in some cases to gain traction with wider political forces at the regional and national levels. In a few cases reformists have been able to gain control of village-level institutions in order to defend their land occupations and to shift political alignments, as occurred to some effect in the Cimacan case (chapter 4), but so far without clear resolution in the Gili Trawangan case (chapter 8).

In addition to building political networks to protect their reclaiming actions, peasant organizations have also adopted social and cultural strategies to avoid the political stigma attached to the "communist" label previously associated with the peasant movement and 1960s occupations. The Sundanese Peasant Union (SPP), for instance, has developed an "Islamic missionary corps" that formulated the rationale for the SPP's occupations from an Islamic perspective. Other sociocultural and economic approaches include the establishment of agricultural cooperatives, marketing centers, political education programs, education for women, and schools for peasant farmers' children, as well as various religious activities, which are not exclusively for SPP and STaB members but also provide for the wider community. These developments suggest an increased social cohesiveness at the village level and stronger social ties, as well as the development of widening social consciousness among members of the two peasant organizations.

Despite the difficulties in gaining recognition for the PPR as a formal political party to represent farmers' interests, it would not be an exaggeration to say that the collective actions by peasant organizations such as SPP and STaB have brought reformist-minded people into government, who are committed to developing pro-poor policies. SPP and STaB have actively supported their cadres to become village heads, members of village councils, and district representative assemblies—BPD[81] and DPRD. In the future they may yet gain sufficient political agency to influence general elections and policy at the national level. These peasant action groups have become the focal point for grassroots interests and must be considered by politicians seeking to gain or maintain power. This means that social movement organizations with a mass base will need to collaborate with other political forces, including parties and individuals with authority, without losing sight of their core commitments or becoming co-opted by elite interests. This effort to widen their political influence, building on collective action gains, is now dominating the agenda of mainly village-based social movement groups.

Since the declaration of its formation in 2001, SPP has been active in lobbying BPN and district governments to legalize land occupied by its members.[82] In Ciamis District, for example, SPP successfully pushed the local government to form an official team for land conflict resolution in 2005. In October 2007, the Ciamis Land Office released 493 certificates of ownership on parcels of land formerly held as HGU by PT Mulya Sari that expired in December 2005.[83] The beneficiaries were 368 people—almost all of them members of SPP—who had originally leased land from the plantation company. Having applied for land certificates since 2000 without success, they joined SPP in 2002 to fight for legal title. There were no conditions attached to these landownership certificates, which have private (*hak milik*) title. This is a significant departure from land certificates issued during the 1960s land reform program, which made clear that redistributed land could not be transferred for at least fifteen years and must be cultivated productively during that period by the beneficiaries.

To date, of the 8,660 hectares of land occupied by SPP members in Ciamis District, (4,377 hectares of state forestland and 4,283 of plantation land), only 57.76 hectares of ex-HGU from PT Mulya Sari have been officially allocated to members of SPP. Contrary to claims made in the media, this was not carried out through Yudhoyono's PPAN but through the old PRONA land titling program.[84] However, the legal status of the remaining land occupied by SPP members in Ciamis, Tasikmalaya, and Garut districts of West Java, and in most of the case studies reported in this volume, remains uncertain, despite claims of the Yudhoyono administration to have tackled the land problem with a massive redistribution program under PPAN (see Fauzi 2009a).

As troubling as the long legal hiatus has been for the sustainability of the movement itself is the short-term interest of some of its supporters. Some SPP members who obtained certificates of landownership through recent distributions no longer support SPP activities. It seems that "once they achieved their landownership certificate, they lost their enthusiasm for further involvement in the SPP struggle" (interview with SPP organizer, Ciamis, 13 July 2008). There is some reason to consider whether granting outright *hak milik* individual titles will have the effect of defusing the collective action commitment of recipients.

Agrarian Reform: "Far from Where It Should Be"[85]

Was the optimism among many social movement activists that the agrarian reform ideas of the scholar-activists would be implemented through PPAN well founded? From one perspective, political and economic realities—whether global, national, or regional—have actually narrowed the space for implementing the genuine agrarian reform ideas of the 1960s, ideas that were revived by agrarian reformists in the 1990s but languished in the face of global ideological shifts surrendering social policy to free market mechanisms. The co-optation of "agrarian reform" by the Yudhoyono regime via PPAN will make it more difficult to radicalize the agrarian reform concept at the local level. In practice, PPAN will offer only partial land reform, because the program will not resolve the more sensitive and difficult long-term questions of how to provide land for the people on a long-term sustainable and equitable basis. Indonesians will end up with a land certification program that activists have systematically rejected. This focus on certification was reinforced with the announcement of the Service to the People for Land Registration (LARASITA) program in 2008, minus any vision of structural reform of the existing unequal land distribution or agrarian conflict resolution mechanisms (Nurdin 2008; Fauzi 2009b). The program's objective of improving services would speed up certification but without any framework for delivering distributive justice. It is at the same time true that this certification approach suits the aspirations of many of Indonesia's peasant farmers, since obtaining land certificates would theoretically give greater legal certainty of their rights over land, including rights to sell or mortgage, despite the associated specter of alienation.

Beyond the accomplishments of SPP and STaB organizers, there is anxiety that land gained via land occupations will ultimately be lost.[86] A salutary example was the outcome of the Sagara case in Garut, West

Java, where State Forest Corporation land was found by the National Land Office (BPN) to be subject to land reform, as a result of which villagers were able to obtain private tenure.[87] But within three years of the hard-fought settlement, activists were disillusioned to find that most of the 580 hectares, redistributed to villagers in one of the few successful land occupation campaigns to gain formal legal recognition, had been sold (Afiff et al. 2005, 4; Peluso, Afiff, and Fauzi Rachman 2008, 30). In many cases, such as at Gili Trawangan (chapter 8), land was already changing hands with and without the legal assurance of certified title. In contrast, Safitri found in her study in Lampung, Sumatra, that forestland that was not subject to private certification changed hands more frequently than nonforestland or forestland where use rights were formally recognized (2009, 568–69).

Can these social movement organizations influence the long-term vision and restrain the short-term aspirations of those members who choose to sell land obtained by long struggle? This was considered the most difficult problem faced by organizers of the agrarian movement groups at the village level in Bengkulu and Priangan, where Bachriadi (2010) carried out field research. The question crucially affects the sustainability of land reform programs, since alienation through the market could simply reproduce a landless class without resources in future generations. Furthermore, the sustainability of the organizational solidarities that underpin reform by leverage is jeopardized where success weakens the consolidation of the peasant farmers' movement, making it difficult to push the agrarian reform agenda forward. The compromised character of Reform Era politics (Komisi Hukum Nasional 2002; Harriss, Stokke, and Törnquist 2004; Robison and Hadiz 2004; Schulte Nordholt and van Klinken 2007; Aspinall and Mietzner 2010) has also hampered the consolidation of the agrarian reform movement in Indonesia. It is true that *reformasi* opened up many opportunities for popular direct action land occupations in regional areas, and several of the groups involved have gone on to become politically strong. But this has not led to genuine and systematic reform, which many hoped would be the basis of a new, more equitable Indonesian society.

The strengths and weaknesses of civil society organizations have been a significant factor accounting for the mixed results we have seen in the agrarian struggle since the Reform Era. Where organized alliances of local peasant farmers' groups and NGOs are able to stay the course and coordinate engagement with government departments and policy makers, creative possibilities have emerged. In Cieceng village, described by Affif et al. (2005), where the powerful SPP-KPA, peasant-NGO alliance turned its attention to the district level, taking advantage of the competition between regional and central government politicians as well as between sectoral agencies (in this case, the Ministry of Forestry and the National Land Agency), it proved possible to reconfigure power relationships. External links forged with the district government and NGOs gave invaluable legal information to support the Cieceng occupation of contested State Forest Corporation lands. Villagers learned that the forest plantation that had appropriated their lands in the colonial period had expanded illegally, to double the official allocation under its HGU lease, which by 1997 had expired. Here NGO and peasant groups engaging in "land reform by leverage" were able to legitimate direct action occupations, combining the pro-people's language of the Constitution and 1960s agrarian legislation with the political potential of organized peasant groups in the democratizing atmosphere of *reformasi* (Affif et al. 2005).

Yet the Cieceng case reveals some of the ideological and practical conundrums of the agrarian reform movement also evident in the studies in this volume. In the Cieceng case, there were heavily constrained efforts to confront the distributive and sustainability dilemmas that plagued so many land occupations where political and personal factors resulted in uneven division of occupied land. When SPP joined forces with local activists, their efforts were compromised by popular expectations and diverse conceptions of equity, similar to those expressed by Gili Trawangan villagers in chapter 8. Each local SPP chapter had its own regulations on how to distribute occupied land, but as a general rule local SPP chapter leaders got more land than other members, justified by their risks and contribution to the struggle.[88] SPP saw no point in pressing for "true egalitarian principles," when most of their membership sought individual property rights on the land they occupied. Attempts to assert "collective" rights in terms of land control and ownership have been unsuccessful in the SPP case, despite the organization's strength (Bachriadi 2010, 317). Ultimately 0.25 to 0.5 hectare were distributed to all those over fifteen years of age, with the exception of leaders, who received up to 1.5 hectares. In total, 600 hectares were divided among 800 occupying landholders, including eventually several of the plantation overseers (*mandor*) who had changed sides in the course of the confrontation.

The SPP-KPA alliance was able to turn the uncertain short-term gains achieved through the occupation into political action with potential for longer-term outcomes. One of the local leaders of the peasant action was elected as hamlet head and eventually as village head. Cieceng has since achieved recognition as a "model" village, actively involved in regional development programs and noted for the high level of public commitment of villagers, who pride themselves on their capacity for collective action, and whose economic position has palpably improved as a result (Affif et al. 2005, 19–26).[89]

The local SPP chapter in Cieceng developed the rules that subsequently became a model for others in the area.[90] In principle, the occupying holders cannot transfer land without permission from the Cieceng SPP chapter; otherwise there are sanctions under which the local chapter takes over control of the land, which then becomes an SPP asset. However, members can transfer their land to other members and/or nonmember families, who are then required to join SPP in order to access the land.[91] Existing or joining SPP members should pay for transferred "cultivation rights' (*uang ganti garap*) to previous holders of occupied land through SPP; in some cases a fee will be charged, the amount depending on agreement between the three parties. The Cieceng SPP chapter holds no formal records of the price of transfer payments, or the size of fees paid to the local chapter. In 2009, seven years after the Cieceng occupation actions took place, around sixty-three hectares of occupied land had been transferred from more than 120 previous holders to only fourteen SPP members, mostly local middlemen (*bandar*). Some of these *bandar* are also leaders of the local Cieceng SPP organization.

Although SPP and NGOs provided technical assistance to improve local organization in Cieceng by setting up cooperative-based production and distribution units, agricultural extension support, and training in mixed farming of cash and food crops to increase the economic viability and sustainability of smallholder farming (Afiff 2005, 22–24), the results have not been as expected. Some members and leaders in local SPP chapters including Cieceng have been able to manage their economic interests as *bandar*, for example, to compete with cooperative units, and finally gain control of local farming activities, particularly related to the distribution of harvested produce.

There is a real tension between the need to recognize differential personal risks in the land occupations and principled commitment to a common cause. The inequitable division and the unviable size of some of the land parcels distributed—as little as 0.25 hectare—constitute a feature of these distributions that has to be considered in assessing the effectiveness of this aspect of land reform strategy, although the social security function of small amounts of land, if only for residential and household gardens, cannot be ignored either (Safitri 2009, 569). Research remains to be done on the reasons for and extent of on-selling and elite capture, which undermine the sustainability of land distribution solutions to rural poverty problems.

The uncertain legal basis of the occupied landholdings of SPP members and the individual economic interests of SPP members have led this largest and to date most effective of Indonesia's peasant movement organizations to compromise with President Yudhoyono's PPAN and other market-friendly certification approaches, which remain the bulwark of neoliberal land policies. Fauzi (2009a) notes that Hernando de Soto (who advocated land titling as the key to releasing the economic potential of poor rural populations) was invited to Indonesia, where he has had a significant influence on the PPAN agenda. His approach resonates with demands of local farmers for private title, although more directly in Java than in the case of many outer island *adat* communities. The global hegemony of neoliberal ideology has unquestionably had a serious impact on the range of possibilities that appear plausible to struggling peasant farmers. Of course, the peasant class cannot be expected to bear the burden of social reform on its own, and the politics of the possible has to be set against the ideological commitments of the activist and the theoretical imaginings of the academic in assessing the "progressive" aspects of these programs and processes.[92]

But the confluence of current world political, economic, and environmental crises will ultimately need to shift the overwhelmingly private interest context within which the agrarian reform movement has had to struggle since the Indonesian revolution. The unequivocal neoliberal convictions of the last decades have been shaken with the largely unanticipated and acute political, economic, and environmental crises of the new millennium. At the same time, however, various attempts at capital reconsolidation to deal with the current global economic crisis are pressing for new patterns of land concentration. Land grabs for the establishment of new plantation estates for agro-fuel industries, for example, have appeared in Indonesia and other parts of the world (see for instance chapters 5 and 6 in this volume; Colchester et al. 2006, Marti 2008; Potter 2008; Borras and Franco 2012). Private business interests are also using the formation of new soft global environmental policies such as REDD (deforestation reduction) and other schemes (Casson, Tacconi, and Deddy 2007; Nesadurai 2009), as well as infrastructure developments such as construction of privately managed tollways and municipal water supplies, to further their control of land and other natural resources in Indonesia. The final chapter considers the Indonesian case in the context of these sweeping changes in the global context.

Notes

1. See chapters 4, 5, 7, and 8. NGOs with international links were less prominent in more remote locations in the early period and in cases involving the urban poor for reasons Reerink sets out in chapter 9. In remote areas NGO support was more difficult to obtain and erratic.

2. Demonstrations on *Hari Tani* (Peasants' Day) 2001 directly linked local agrarian issues to the worldwide antiglobalization campaign. In West Java, Surabaya, Yogyakarta, and Palu protesters carried "stop

WTO" placards and called for a halt to importation of agricultural commodities and to the introduction of genetically modified crops, alongside demands for the return of stolen lands (*Kompas,* 25 September 2001; *Koran Tempo,* 25 September 2001). Campaigns against neoliberal agrarian policies underpinned the Konsortium Pembaruan Agraria (KPA)'s agrarian platforms since its formation in 1995. The opposition of the NGO-farmers' alliance to globalizing capitalist land and agrarian policies was reinforced when the Federation of Indonesian Peasants' Unions (FSPI) joined the international organization Via Campesina. See Peluso, Afiff, and Fauzi Rachman (2008) for a discussion of its influence on the agrarian movement in Indonesia.

3. The use of the term "indigenous" is another example of the influence of international movements. The term was regarded as unacceptable by the Indonesian government because of its political implications in international law (Bedner and van Huis 2008) and because all but the small percentage of mainly ethnic Chinese Indonesians could be regarded as "indigenous." "Indigenous minorities" is nevertheless an appropriate means of distinguishing marginalized ethnic groups from the Javanese ethnic majority that has dominated Indonesia's politics and cultural policy since independence. As indigenous rights became a global human rights issue, this discursive framework was imported and increasingly began to influence representations of Indonesia's cultural minorities. Today the term *masyarakat adat* ("*adat* communities/peoples"), often glossed as "indigenous peoples," has become the preferred usage of NGOs referring to non-Javanese ethnic minorities.

4. Conference resolutions called for support for agrarian courts, an end to arbitrary arrests of farmers, opposition to liberalization of trade in agricultural products and genetic engineering, and revision of the Basic Agrarian Law proposed by the BPN. The full text of the 2001 Cibubur "Declaration on Peasants' Rights' is published in KSPA, Pokja PSDA, and KPA 2001, 42–53 and Wahono 2002.

5. In 2006 Indonesia acceded with the reservation that the "right of self determination does not apply to a section of people within a sovereign independent State." Article 11 (2) of the covenant obliges implementation of agrarian reform. http://treaties.un.org/Pages/ViewDetails.aspx?src=TREATY&mtdsg_no=IV-3&chapter=4&lang=en#EndDec. Accessed 25 January 2010. The resolutions of the Agrarian Reform Conference are published in KSPA, Pokja PSDA, and KPA (2001, 54–56).

6. See the IWGIA (1999, 209–19) report on the AMAN Congress, which suggests NGO influence over the agenda and outcome of the congress on at least two fronts that were contested by some of the delegates:

First, by channeling the separatist sentiments that were openly expressed by some of the groups represented, in favor of a more politically acceptable demand for local autonomy and full recognition of the precedence of *adat* rights; second, its focus on gender issues confronted not only the disenfranchisement of women through state policy but also some of the customary practices of indigenous minority cultures themselves. Women's issues were among the key parts of the program of action AMAN set for itself, and a male and female representative from each province were to make up its steering council (AMAN 1999, 21). Similar tensions were observed by Warren at the KPA (1998) and INFID congresses (1999).

7. From the outset of this research project in 1998, Bachriadi made a key contribution both in his role as a member of KPA and as an independent researcher. We have distinguished between his earlier activist/informant role and that of academic coauthor in this chapter with separate reference to personal communications with the other coauthors in the period prior to undertaking doctoral studies at Flinders University in 2007.

8. Bachriadi, pers. comm., 15 September 1999. The number of organizations attending KPA national congresses rose from 66 in 1995, to 165 in 2009 (KPA data), despite some groups hiving off into new peak bodies such as AMAN over that period. Nine KPA member organizations are also members of the AMAN network. That KPA was one of the driving forces for the establishment of AMAN is an indication of the success of the agrarian reform movement in maintaining a united front on what could otherwise have been a debilitating conflict over the claims of indigenous minorities to traditional territories and those of other poor peasant farmers, including transmigrants, concerned with land reform and redistribution.

9. See the summaries of political party platforms published in Suryakusuma et al. (1999); and Setiawan and Nainggolan (2004).

10. On forest utilization, PP 6/1999 granted communities the right to take forest products for their daily needs within concession areas. Also, under KepMen 677/Kpts-II/1998, communities could gain rights to harvest timber and utilize traditional forest management systems as long as they do not negatively affect "forest sustainability." Community-based cooperatives could apply for "community forestry leases" over production and protection forests as well as in specific conservation zones (*Suara Pembaruan*, 3 and 14 November 1998).

11. KepPres 48/1999 Menimbang:b.

12. Abdurrachman Wahid was elected president as a compromise candidate, replacing interim President Habibie following the 1999 general election, but Wahid was forced to step down only a year later,

when Megawati Sukarnoputri took over the presidency. The daughter of founding nationalist President Sukarno, Megawati was not sympathetic with the implications of decentralization for the authority of the nation-state and initiated changes in the regional autonomy law. The revised law (UU 32/2004) restored some of the authority of the provinces, and reduced the degree of legislative control over executive decision-making at both district and village levels.

13. The MPR, Majelis Permusyawaratan Rakyat (People's Consultative Assembly), had been an upper house appointed from social groups and the military, which met to produce the policy outline (GBHN), the basis of Indonesia's five-year plans, and to elect the president under the New Order. Constitutional amendments during the *reformasi* period abolished military seats in the parliament, and created a new upper house (DPD—Dewan Pemerintah Daerah) consisting of two elected members from each of Indonesia's provinces. This new body, together with the Representative Assembly DPR, will henceforth constitute the MPR.

14. D. Bachriadi, pers. comm., 3 March 2000. Throughout this period, Dianto Bachriadi and Noer Fauzi were members of the KPA executive, directly involved in the negotiations described in this chapter.

15. KSPA members included Sediono Tjondronegoro (University of Indonesia), Gunawan Wiradi (Institute Pertanian Bogor), Ifdhal Kasim (ELSAM), Sandra Moniaga and Dandang Juliantara (LAPERA), Noer Fauzi and Dianto Bachriadi (KPA).

16. The National Land Agency (BPN) is responsible for issuing land titles and location permits. It acquired a reputation as one of the most corrupt and ineffective arms of the bureaucracy and was under serious threat from reformists. Hasan Basri Durin, however, proved to be an active agrarian minister in Habibie's transitional cabinet and, as head of BPN, was responsible for the new regulation promising practical recognition of *adat* land rights (PerMenagraria 5/1999). One of the more accessible figures in the transitional administration, he circulated a number of draft revisions to the Basic Agrarian Law and accepted invitations to attend NGO symposiums to debate government proposals. Although the BPN had been slated by President Wahid for abolition in 1999 because land matters were to be managed by the districts (*kabupaten*) under the 1999 regional autonomy laws, BPN officials mounted a campaign with the theme "Land for the People," promoting the need for agrarian reform. NGOs were uncertain whether this radical change in BPN discourse reflected a genuine change in attitude within the agency. In any event, the BPN survived but now comes under the Ministry of Home Affairs.

17. Six drafts were in circulation before submission of the final document to the 2001 sitting of the MPR. These were produced by KPA, KSPA, Professor Tjondronegoro, two drafts produced by MPR working parties separately treating agrarian reform and natural resource management, and one produced by the FSPI. The first five versions were combined into one draft policy directive, before submission, while the Peasants' Federation draft was submitted separately to the MPR committee for reasons explained below. These were published in Semiloka (2001b) and KSPA, Pokja PSDA, and KPA (2001, 35–119).

18. See Lucas and Warren (2003, 108) for a full list of NGOs involved in the PSDA and KSPA working groups, as well as more detailed discussion of the intra-NGO politics that emerged in these negotiations.

19. Interview with Wiwiek Awiati, director of the Indonesian Centre for Environmental Law, 26 September 2002; Dianto Bachriadi, pers. comm. 26 August 2001 and 24 September 2001. See also Peluso, Afiff, and Fauzi Rachman (2008) on the relation between the two movements.

20. The combined draft submitted by the KSPA-PSDA team to the MPR committee argues that agrarian reform and sustainable and just management of natural resources are inseparable. Implementation of agrarian reform depends on resolving conflicts and reforming unequal agrarian social structures and unsustainable natural resource management practices (see Semiloka 2001b and KSPA, Pokja PSDA, and KPA 2001, 26–32).

21. The Indonesian Peasants' Alliance (API) is a breakaway group of the Federation of Indonesian Peasants' Unions (FSPI), covering thirty-one local farmers' organizations from Java, Sumatra, Bali, NTB, NTT, and Central Sulawesi. API was formed in response to the restrictive membership of FSPI, which recognized only large provincial and/or interdistrict-level farmers' organizations, as members (API general secretary, interview, 22 April 2005). The Bengkulu Peasants' Union (STaB) and the Sundanese Peasants' Union (SPP) were the only local farmers' organizations under the API alliance that had been represented in FSPI, but both had withdrawn by 2007. Most API members have strong links with Bina Desa, an old Indonesian NGO focused on rural development and capacity building, making it easier for them to consolidate a new national coalition (vice-director of Bina Desa, interview, 21 April 2005). All these organizations prefer to translate *petani* as peasant, except for the New Order HKTI (Himpunan Kerukunan Tani Indonesia) which translates *petani* with the less politically charged term "farmers."

22. *Metro*, 15 September 2001.

23. SPP, with a membership of some 20,000 Sundanese farming households, is the largest of the original peasant organizations that were

founding members of the FSPI. In 2007, SPP resigned from FSPI when the federation, now SPI, underwent organizational restructuring and implemented a regulation to restrict SPI members from membership in other national coalitions. In 2009, SPP decided not to continue its involvement in any national coalition, because of tendencies to involve political interests (statement of SPP general secretary, Bandung, 27 August 2009). See Peluso, Afiff, and Fauzi Rachman (2008) and Bachriadi (2009, 11–16; 2011, 294–303) for discussions of SPP's role in land occupations in West Java, and the eventual falling-out among the national coalitions of peasant movements over issues such as leadership, membership, political manipulation, and autonomy of local peasant-farmers' organizations.

24. A farmer from Garut demanded an end to extensions of plantation leases, and granting of titles to local people for *adat* land taken from them for plantations. Otherwise, he threatened, the cocoa and rubber trees planted on the land would "be razed to the ground" (*Pikiran Rakyat*, 15 September 2001).

25. *Republika*, 15 September 2001; *Kompas*. 15 September 2001; *Forum Keadilan*, 7 October 2001. See Sudibyo (2001, 173–94) on media representations.

26. Statement in Support of Indonesia's Peasant Farmers, Bandung, 14 September 2001, signed by nineteen members of the MPR working Group.

27. *Ketetapan Majelis Permusyawaratan Rakyat Republik Indonesia Nomor IX/MPR/2001 tentang Pembaruan Agraria dan Pengelolaan Sumber Daya Alam*, 9 November 2001. Hereafter referred to as TapMPR IX/2001.

28. The NGO drafting team proposed replacing "optimal" with "*lestari*" (conserve) to emphasize preserving rather than maximizing exploitation of resources. It also attempted unsuccessfully to reword reference to natural resources as "entrusted" (*titip*) rather than "bestowed" (*rahmat*) by God on the Indonesian nation. Although there are several references in TapMPR IX to sustainability and protection of resources for future generations, environmental NGOs expressed concern that there is no recognition of the need to limit exploitation, or to revise policies that have caused ecosystem degradation. KPSDA letter to MPR working party, 19 October 2001.

29. Agustiana has close ties with KPA. He has been a member of the KPA council for some years, and he has served as its chair.

30. An SPP member commented: "Before Tap IX we were considered to be an irregular organization. Now our existence is recognized from the grassroots level to the bupati. . . . Every local peasants' group has a brochure about the Tap, and we also gave it to local government" (interview with the southern region coordinator of Ciamis SPP branch, Garut, 26 April 2002). Another SPP activist said that thanks to TapMPR IX,

there is now less suppression of SPP activities by local officials, whereas previously members were accused of being ex-communists and "looters" (*penjarah*) (interview with AA, Garut, 21 April 2002). SPP members and their supporters—claiming to be 400,000 strong—have taken control of 36,000 hectares of forest estate and plantation land in Garut, Tasikmalaya, and Ciamis since *reformasi* began in 1998.

31. The KSPA-PSDA and MPR committee working party drafts reaffirmed the basic BAL/UUPA principle that agrarian law has a primarily "social function," stressing the integrity of land and resources and the people's right to them; but significantly they do not mention the Basic Agrarian Law explicitly. Only the submissions by Professor Tjondronegoro and the Peasants' Union refer directly to BAL/UUPA in their proposed versions of the policy directive. Tjondronegoro's draft emphasized the need for restructuring of the agrarian system to assist in the transformation from an agrarian to an industrial society, guaranteeing justice and equality of access to natural resources, and reactivating the Basic Agrarian Law to bring natural resource legislation again under its jurisdiction. The Indonesian Peasants' Union draft insists that implementation of agrarian reform must be based on UUPA, but that parliament must rectify misuse of the much abused state right of control and national interest provisions of the UUPA. They also include the radical demand to identify officials and businessmen who have caused agrarian conflict and bring them to a human rights court. See KSPA, Pokja PSDA, and KPA 2001, 119–23, where the FSPI draft is published along with the five other draft submissions.

32. Under Indonesian constitutional law, TapMPR had an ambiguous standing. Although these upper house (MPR) policy directives set out principles that should eventually be represented in lower house (DPR) legislation as well as presidential decrees, their implementation was not regarded as binding on either. Acts promulgated by the DPR refer to the Constitution, not to TapMPR, for their legal authority. Nevertheless, TapMPR IX/2001 remains a legal precedent, despite subsequent changes to the MPR's role and processes. Although new Tap are no longer enacted, those of the previous parliaments remain valid until the legislative policy mandates they set out has been implemented (Bedner and van Huis 2008, 187).

33. CAPS was not a member of KSPA or PSDA. Idham Samudra Bey, a lecturer at Muhammadiyah University in Solo, walked out at the first Bandung conference in August 2001, expressing concern at the use of "natural resources management" and "sustainable development" rhetoric to justify exploitation of people and resources. Idham was a student of Sritua Arief, a prominent left-wing economist, who was one of the first Indonesian social scientists to introduce dependency theory.

34. See chapter 1, note 5 on the different connotations associated with the English terms "peasant" and "farmer" for the Indonesian "petani"/"tani" that have both ideological and socioeconomic implications.

35. See also the statement by Noer Fauzi, director of KPA, arguing that the TapMPR will be "an additional tool in the efforts to pressure for the realization of national commitments to respect, protect, and fulfill the human rights of the nation's farmers" (*Wacana HAM* 2001).

36. Bachriadi elaborated on his views in an earlier personal communication (21 April 2001): "Few people today in Indonesia have seen any concrete results of UUPA. . . . We have to throw out the bath water, fully aware that we might also be throwing out the baby. If we only accept the symbolic significance of UUPA, then we are in danger of romanticizing it."

37. Noer Fauzi, pers. comm., 23 April 2002. See also *Forum*, 26 November 2001.

38. *Menteri Sekretaris Negara atas nama President Soesilo Bambang Yudhoyono* no B-708/MenSekneg/10/2005, 25 October 2005.

39. Interview with Wiwiek Awiati, ICEL/PSDA, Perth, 26 September 2002. The agrarian reform groups remained concerned that government departments would continue to pursue independent regulations relating to natural resources exploitation, antagonistic to peasant interests. As at other pivotal points in the struggle for agrarian law reform, differences among NGO orientations and between them and peasant farmers' groups appear to have dissipated the limited time and resources of the reform coalition (Gunawan Wiradi, pers. comm. 22 July 2002).

40. Aisyah Amini, quoted in *Kompas*, 7 November 2001.

41. Significantly, in the light of the subsequent opposition to TapMPR IX from most of the peasant farmers' groups, there was no farmers' organization representative on the KPA/KPSA advocacy team, which later rationalized that farmers' organizations needed to exert independent influence through rallies and demonstrations. Neglect of the FSPI viewpoint expressed in their alternative draft TapMPR may have been the unintentional result of Bandung-based KPA's proximity and closer relationships with West Java farmers groups (API and SPP) and their leaders, as well as the NGOs' focus on negotiating differences among themselves (Gunawan Wiradi, pers. comm., 22 July 2002).

42. The National Ombudsman Commission invited KPA to conduct joint research into land issues. Bachriadi, a member of KPA's advisory council at the time, was involved in this research.

43. At the time, the National Ombudsman Commission did not have the power to instigate prosecutions on behalf of complainants because

KON was established by presidential decree. Under the recent National Ombudsman Law (UU 37/2008) its powers have since been strengthened to enable it to conduct independent investigations and initiate prosecutions.

44. This perspective on the protracted land conflicts had been promoted by the World Bank in Indonesia since the early 1990s when it funded the Indonesian Land Administration Project. See World Bank 1994, and chapter 3 in this volume.

45. KepPres 34/2003 on national policy in land matters.

46. The KPA position on land redistribution is that all parties must refer to existing laws (BAL/UUPA 5/1960, UU 56/1960 and PP 224/1961; see also chapters 1 and 2). Priority must be given to landless peasants, small peasant landholders, and agricultural workers. The government must recognize the priority of customary law claims. With respect to rights to buy and sell land redistributed as part of a land reform program, KPA supports existing law, which does not permit farmers to sell distributed land for fifteen years. KPA has not yet begun to discuss dividing land among heirs, but in principle supports communal forms of tenure (to reduce the likelihood of alienation). KPA argues that land courts and local committees involving farmers' organizations are critical to processes based on social justice (Fauzi 2009a).

47. Even in West Java, SPP has a strong presence in only three districts, namely Ciamis, Tasikmalaya, and Garut.

48. Under the presidential decree, districts (*kabupaten*) were able to set up their own agrarian reform and dispute resolution committees. Noer Fauzi (a founder and former executive chairman of KPA) proposed that the latter committees adopt a number of strategic approaches to dealing with the agrarian issues at local level: mapping the scale and type of land disputes, establishing a neutral process of hearing complaints and settling disputes, implementing mechanisms for clarification and proof, monitoring and public accountability. Committees should include NGOs and peasant groups as well as representatives from central government bodies, the National Land Agency, and the Department of Forestry (Fauzi 2003b).

49. Interview with Agustiana in Ciamis, 10 July 2003. In his view the fact that districts have to deal with land disputes and their resolution via local BPN offices should enable the central BPN to collect more accurate data on land cases. As an example of existing deficiencies, the central BPN office in Jakarta has data on only one HGU commercial lease case in Ciamis, while SPP has recorded fourteen HGU disputes in that district.

50. Illegalities included issuance of multiple certificates of title, issuance of HGU commercial lease rights on land that already belongs to local

people, and permitting operation of large-scale plantations without formal lease rights. See Bachriadi, Bachrioktora, and Safitri (2002). In October 2005, the Riau Province Plantation Authority reported that 21 percent of 161 existing large-scale plantations operated without HGU permits (*Riau Online*, 19 March 2004).

51. For a list of land legislation during the *reformasi* and Yudhoyono eras see the KPA webpage http://www.kpa.or.id/?page_id=408. Accessed 14 March 2012.

52. See articles III and IV of the transitional provisions chapter of the BAL/UUPA 1960.

53. Complaints to the government were expressed during the 2005 Infrastructure Summit in Jakarta to which the newly elected Yudhoyono government formally responded through Presidential Regulation Kep-Pres 36/2005 concerning land allocation for development projects, replacing the previous KepPres 55/1993. Critics considered this new regulation to favor business, because it facilitates land eviction for "development projects" rather than legalizing land already occupied by people for their livelihood needs. Because of the wave of protests against this regulation, it was revised by KepPres 65/2006. But according to Sumardjono, an agrarian law expert from Gadjah Mada University, the new regulation was not a significant improvement on the one it replaced (Sumardjono 2006).

54. Gunawan Wiradi and Dianto Bachriadi attended the Bappenas workshop conducted in Jakarta on 6 November 2006.

55. The program described as *"reforma agraria"* in Yudhoyono's speech is based on: (1) limited redistribution of land, mostly degraded forestland already slated for conversion to agriculture, and (2) land certification (Yudhoyono 2007, 10).

56. Sediono MP Tjondronegoro and Gunawan Wiradi, two prominent Bogor-based agrarian scholars, played a key role in formulating the *Petisi Cisarua* (Poniman et al. 2005), which called for agrarian reform implementation by the newly elected national government in 2004. At the same time KPA activists lobbied Yudhoyono through his other army-led election team.

57. There are four kinds of land that may become the object of land reform according to Indonesian law: excess private land above the maximum ceiling; private absentee land; state land formally controlled by autonomous local authorities (*swapraja*); and other state-controlled land (including ex-HGU land already occupied by peasant farmers). See PP 224/1961 §1.

58. See McCulloch and Timmer (2008) for discussion of the extensive debates on the mixed impacts of these policies on Indonesia's poorest

income sectors, some of which were aimed at price stabilization during the economic and food security crises. Fane and Warr (2008, 134) argue that democratization since 1998 has "increased the political influence of farmers and agricultural processors," contributing to increased protection in the period since 2000. Our case studies suggest this has proved far less the case than might have been expected. See chapter 4, which suggests various reasons for lack of political representation of farmers in village and district elections. The lack of support by formal political organizations for their land claims, contrary to Fane and Warr, suggests that they have relatively little political influence. Candidates in local elections avoid talking about agrarian reform because of the complex conflicts of interest involved, and the strength of money politics means that candidates who win elections are usually from the village political or religious elite.

59. Titled "Land for the People: Not Just Empty Words," the advertisement pictures Yudhoyono as a world leader committed to agrarian reform. See Fauzi 2009a, which reproduces the poster, and KPA 2009 for a critical discussion of misleading data used in this political advertisement.

60. In the core-satellite model, small growers are consolidated to produce certain agricultural products under the management of a big enterprise. The enterprise controls all the production processes of small growers through provision of seeds, technology, and processing on credit. Through these rent-facilities they can control and monopolize the price and quality of harvested products. See Wilson (1986); Wiradi (1991); and White (1997). See also McCarthy, Gillespie, and Zen (2012) on the liberalization of restrictions on the required proportion of smallholder allocations under new oil palm plantation regulations.

61. See Departemen Pertanian (2007). Direktorat Jenderal Perkebunan *Program Revitalisasi Perkebunan,* Jakarta: Direktorat Jenderal Perkebunan Departemen Pertanian RI.

62. *Tempo Interaktif,* 28 September 2006. Local banks, which have prepared credit schemes to support new agricultural production on redistributed land, prefer a contract farming model in which small cultivators produce plantation commodities such as palm oil, cocoa, and rubber. However, these credit schemes cannot be implemented before PPAN redistribution takes place (interview with Bengkulu provincial plantation authority officer, Bengkulu, 24 December 2007).

63. Although the government describes the *inti-plasma* model applied in the Indonesian context as a "partnership," in reality it is little more than turning farmers into cheap labor on their own land (Wiradi 1991; Bachriadi 1995; Gunawan, Thamrin, and Grijns 1995; and White 1997). Stoler (1985) and Mubyarto (1992) conclude that the large plantation

system does not support rural development, but exploits rural productivity potential for the interests of outside capital.

64. To the end of his first term as president, Yudhoyono had not revised or signed the draft regulation that would replace PP224/1961 and put PPAN into effect. This sixth draft was apparently rejected by other government departments, namely Finance (because it was too expensive to implement), Forestry and Mining (which wanted to keep their own sectoral laws), and Agriculture (which wanted coordination between departments under its control).

65. This new design appeared in the sixth draft government regulation on PPAN (2007). UU 56/1960, §2 and PP 224/1961, §§1–5 already give the state the legal right to take excess land (over the maximum ceiling) and redistribute it to qualified beneficiaries, no reference to which was included in the last PPAN draft regulations.

66. The Forestry, Land Administration, and Agriculture ministers come from different parties, not all of which are in official alliance with Yudhoyono's own party. Bargaining for ministerial positions in cabinet begins after the national election results are announced. There is no connection between the pre-election campaigns and subsequent postelection cabinet appointments.

67. President Yudhoyono's PPAN, promised at the beginning of his first term of office, but unimplemented, has now been resurrected in the wake of the newly passed land acquisition law (Undang Undang Pengadaan Tanah [see below]). The president promised the PPAN draft implementation decree (Peraturan Pemerintah Tentang Reforma Agraria) early in 2012.

68. Serikat Tani Bengkulu, 2007, "Surat Terbuka STaB" [open letter from STaB].

69. Focus group discussions (FGD) were carried out on 6 June 2007 in Magelang together with "democracy consolidation" activities by the Kelompok Kerja Jaring Demokrasi (KKJD) Jawa Tengah on 5–7 June 2007.

70. FSPI/SPI statement, 27 February 2008, available at http://www.spi.or.id. Accessed 19 January 2012.

71. http://www.ekon.go.id/news/2011/05/27/siaran-pers-masterplan-percepatan-dan-perluasan-pembangunan-ekonomi-indonesia-m3pei. Accessed 19 January 2012.

72. Interviews in Yogyakarta, 14 and 15 December 2011.

73. After much debate the original Law on Land Acquisition for Development had the words "in the Public Interest" added to the title to enable its passage by parliament. See the KPA website for an account of the politics surrounding passage of the law at http://www.kpa.or.id/?p=571. Accessed 3 March 2012.

74. Landowners can appeal to the courts if they disagree with the valuations. Apart from cash payments, compensation can be in the form of resettlement or land swaps or a combination of both (§40)

75. See "11 Sesat Pikir dalam RUU Pengadaan Tanah Untuk Pembangunan" posted 10 March 2011 by the People's Coalition against Land Grabbing (Koalisi Rakyat Tolak Perampasan Tanah (KARAM Tanah), a coalition of forty-one nongovernment organizations and peasant and workers' unions, which includes KPA, WALHI, AMAN, SPI, JKPP, Bina Desa, LBH. For the full text of this critique of the land acquisition law by KARAM Tanah, and a list of the signatories, see http://www.kpa.or.id/?p=537. Accessed 4 March 2012. See also the Civil Society Petition "Stop the Land Grab Bill" to the Members of the House of Representatives, also organized by KARAM Tanah, at http://apmdd.org/news/52-civil-society-petition-stop-the-landgrab-bill (26 September 2011) on the Jubilee South Asia Pacific Movement on Debt and Development website. Accessed 7 March 2012.

76. Compensation would be based on the "the real/actual value" not on the common price (*harga umum*) which can be the speculators' price (*harga "catut"*) (General Elucidation 5). Land rights will be revoked for private sector projects only in "exceptional circumstances' (General Elucidation, 4b) (Harsono 1996, 678, 680).

77. See Powelson and Stock 1987 for discussion of the original concept; see also Hardiyanto 1996; Wiradi 1997; and Bachriadi 2009 for discussion in the Indonesian context.

78. PRD (People's Democratic Party) was the only other party that incorporated similar positions on agrarian reform and national industrialization in its party platform for the 1999 general election.

79. "Tentang Reforma Agraria," *Partai Perserikatan Rakyat,* 21 April 2007.

80. There has been no clarification from Dephukham on why registration was refused, despite three letters from PPR requesting explanation. Local corruption also played a big role in the failure of PPR's electoral attempt. Under electoral law, PPR had to obtain local approval to establish branches in 60 percent of Indonesian provinces and districts and 75 percent of subdistricts. At every level of government from subdistrict through district and province, officials asked for illegal payments of Rp 100,000 to 5 million to sign the required letters of domicile (SKD). In the province of Jakarta, the asking "price" for the SKD was Rp 2 billion, later reduced to Rp 1 billion. To bypass Dephukham's administrative selection procedures, officials illegally asked PPR to pay Rp 5 billion (interview with PPR chairperson, Jakarta, 17 March 2009).

81. See chapter 4 on the role of BPD (Badan Perwakilan Desa) in resolving the Cimacan dispute, and how this changed after the revised

regional autonomy law (UU32/2004) weakened village councils by undermining their authority and democratic selection processes.

82. See *Pikiran Rakyat*, 11 July 2002 and 27 May 2007; *Radar Garut*, 2 December 2005 and 25 May 2007; *Kompas*, 23 March 2005.

83. Ciamis District Land Office SK No. 07/520.1–10.19/PRONA/2007, 25 May 2007.

84. See *Priangan Post*, 26–28 May 2007; and Kantor Pertanahan Kabupaten Garut 2007.

85. From the Indonesian expression *api yang semakin jauh dari panggang*—literally "a fire receding from its hearth."

86. For a comparative overview of the literature on different approaches to land reform—namely, the "state-instigated," "peasant-led," "state/society-driven," and "market-led" approaches adopted in countries such as Zimbabwe, Brazil, the Philippines, Columbia and South Africa—see Rosset (2002); Borras (2001); Deininger (2003); Franco and Boras (2005); Moyo and Yeros (2005).

87. See also Lukmanurdin (2002) for a detailed account of the land-reclaiming action in the Sagara case.

88. Based on fieldwork in West Java in 2002–3 and 2007 in several SPP local chapters in the districts of Garut, Tasikmalaya, and Ciamis (including Cieceng), Bachriadi found that peasant groups organized by SPP typically distributed land according to the following principles. Occupying landholders were classified into two types according to degrees of active commitment to the struggle: "Regular members" actively involved in the occupation actions received 0.5 hectares, and those who only became followers received 0.25 hectares of land. "Leaders" who became the core group during the actions obtained 1.0 hectare, and "leaders" who masterminded the occupation and took command during the actions received 1.5 hectares of occupied land. All those who joined the organization after the occupation actions received 0.25 hectares of remaining unallocated occupied land (Bachriadi 2010, 316).

89. Further details on the Cieceng land occupation can be found in "*Berjuang untuk Tanah*" (2003), cassette nos. 27–28; Mismuri and Prasetyohadi (2008); and Bachriadi (2010, 315–19).

90. SPP has more than fifty local chapters, but it has not developed consistent principles or regulations on redistribution of occupied lands, although local SPP chapters have their own regulations, which must be approved by the SPP secretary general.

91. Technically, sale of occupied land is forbidden by central SPP rules, and of course has no validity in formal law. Mobility due to marriage or job-seeking, raising emergency funds for health care or school fees, as well as

lack of capital to improve farming productivity, and plots that are dispersed or unviable in size are the common reasons SPP members gave for needing to transfer their occupied land to others. Instead of "transfer," SPP refers to "safekeeping" of land (*nitip lahan garapan*). Although the original cultivators remain registered with the Cieceng SPP as occupying landholders, in practice use rights do change hands. The central SPP leadership turns a blind eye to the practice of "safekeeping" transfers in order to retain peasant support. The term "safekeeping" was also useful to SPP as it implied to outsiders that the occupied land was not being bought and sold. Although SPP does not specify the kind of land tenure that its members should ultimately be seeking, it accepts individual tenure as long as it is not more that five hectares (SPP adheres to UU56/1960 on this issue), although members apparently may still control more than five hectares of occupied land if they already held land elsewhere (in which case, possibly transgressing the prohibition on absentee landholding in the BAL UUPA) before joining the Cieceng occupation actions. As a social movement organization, SPP does not want to oppose members' desire to have control of occupied land on a "free individual" basis, in part due to SPP's need to keep members involved in the organization (see Bachriadi 2010, 317n40, 318n41).

92. Indonesian NGOs, however, remain convinced that unqualified private title certification is not agrarian reform and will not deliver social justice to Indonesia's marginalized rural farmers. In a press release on 3 July 2009, KPA's secretary general argued: "Land title certification . . . without agrarian reform, is a systematic tool that forces farmers to sell their land more quickly, and fall to big capital, so that the existing unequal land distribution becomes even worse. That's why farmland is now increasingly owned by urban nonfarming groups, while poor farmers become farm laborers" (quoted in Fauzi 2009a).

References

Acciaioli, G. 2001. "Grounds of Conflict, Idioms of Harmony: Custom, Religion, and Nationalism in Violence Avoidance at the Lindu Plain, Central Sulawesi." *Indonesia* 72:81–114.

Affif, S., N. Fauzi, G. Hart, L. Ntsebeza, and N. Peluso. 2005. *Redefining Agrarian Power: Resurgent Agrarian Movements in West Java, Indonesia.* Center for Southeast Asian Studies Working Paper No. 2-05, University of California at Berkeley. Available at http://respositories.cdlib.org/cseas/CSEASWP2-05.

Alisjahbana, A., and C. Manning. 2006. "Labour Market Dimensions of Poverty in Indonesia." *Bulletin of Indonesian Economic Studies,* 42 (2): 235–61.

AMAN. 1999. *Menggugat Posisi Masyarakat Adat terhadap Negara.* Jakarta: Kongres Masyarakat Adat Nusantara and Lembaga Studi Pers and Pembangunan.

———. 2003. Hasil Keputusan Kongres Masyarakat Adat Nusantara II, Tanjung-Lombok Barat, NTB. 21–25 September 2003.

Asian Development Bank. 2007. *Republic Indonesia: Enhancing the Legal and Administrative Framework for Land Project.* ADB Technical Assistance Report Project No. 37304.

Aspinall, E., and M. Mietzner. 2010. *Problems of Democratisation in Indonesia.* Singapore: ISEAS.

Bachriadi, D. 1995. *Ketergantungan Petani dan Penetrasi Kapital: Lima Kasus Intensifikasi Pertanian dengan Pola Contract Farming.* Bandung: Akatiga.

———. 1999. *From Liberalism to Neoliberalism: Big Plantations, Small Plantations, and Plantation Workers Conditions in Indonesia.* Research Report for the International Union of Food and Agriculture Workers (IUF) and Konsorsium Pembaruan Agraria (KPA).

———. 2002. "Lonceng Kematian atau Tembakan Tanda Start? Kontroversi seputar Ketetapan MPR RI No. IX/MPR/2001. Komentar untuk Idham Samudra Bey." *Kompas,* 11 January.

———. 2006. *Invasions to the Last (Law) Fortress of Populist Land Reform: Neoliberalism and Land/Agrarian Reform in Current Indonesia.* Paper to International Conference on "Land, Poverty, Social Justice and Development: Social Movements Perspectives." 12–14 January. The Hague: Institute of Social Studies (ISS).

———. 2009. *Land, Rural Social Movements and Democratisation in Indonesia.* Transnational Institute Working Paper on Agrarian Justice. Amsterdam: Transnational Institute. Available at http://www.tni.org/archives/bachriadi-indonesia.

———. 2010. "Between Discourse and Action: Agrarian Reform and Rural Social Movements in Indonesia post-1965." Flinders University PhD dissertation, available at http://theses.flinders.edu.au/public/adt-SFU20110222.150002/index.html.

Bachriadi, D., Y. Bachrioktora, and H. Safitri. 2002. "Ketika Penyelenggaraan Pemerintahan Menyimpang: Maladministrasi di Bidang Pertanahan." Laporan Penelitian Kerjasama Komisi Ombudsman Nasional dan Konsorsium Pembarhuhan Agrarian. Jakarta. (Republished in 2005 by LAPERA Pustaka Utama).

Bachriadi, D., E. Faryadi, and B. Setiawan, eds. 1997. *Reformasi Agraria: Perubahan Politik, Sengketa, dan Agenda Pembaruan Agraria di Indonesia.* Jakarta: Penerbit Fakultas Ekonomi Universitas Indonesia.

Bachriadi, D., and D. Juliantara. 2007. "Demi Keadilan Agraria: Keharusan Menjalankan Pembaruan Agraria secara Menyeluruh untuk Keadilan Sosial di Indonesia (Sekali Lagi: Pandangan dan Usulan kepada Presiden RI): Pokok-pokok Pikiran Kelompok Studi Pembaruan Agraria (KSPA) tentang Pembaruan Agraria (Reforma Agraria) dan Program Pembaruan Agraria Nasional (PPAN)." Unpublished document of the Kelompok Studi Pembaruan Agraria (KSPA) delivered to the President of Indonesia, 20 January 2007.

Bappenas. 2006. *Rumusan Sementara Lokakarya Nasional Finalisasi KKPN,* 6 November 2006.

Bedner, A., and S. van Huis. 2008. "The Return of the Native in Indonesian Law." *Bijdragen tot de taal-land-en volkenkunde* 164 (2/3): 165–93.

Bey, I. S. 2002. "Lonceng Kematian UUPA 1960 Berdentang Kembali— Menyoal TapMPR No. IX/MPR/2001." *Kompas,* 10 January.

"*Berjuang untuk Tanah, Penghidupan, dan Kebebasan*" (Struggle for Land, Livelihood, and Freedom). 2003. Cassette-recorded voices of peasant leaders in Cieceng. Interviewed by Dianto Bachriadi and Hilma Safitri for "CLARA oral history project of the oppressed people in Indonesia." Cassettes no. 27–28. Collection of the Agrarian Resource Centre, Bandung.

Borras, S. 2001. "State-Society Relations in Land Reform Implementation in the Philippines." *Development and Change* 32 (3): 545–75.

———. 2003. "Questioning Market-Led Agrarian Reform: Experiences from Brazil, Colombia and South Africa." *Journal of Agrarian Change* 3 (30): 367–94.

Borras, S., and M. Franco. 2012. "Global Land Grabbing and Trajectories of Agrarian Change: A Preliminary Analysis." *Journal of Agrarian Change* 12 (1): 34–59.

BPN. 2007a. *Petunjuk Pelaksanaan Koordinasi Lintas Sektoral Penanganan PPAN.* Internal document. Badan Pertanahan Nasional.

———. 2007b. *Petunjuk Tenis Pelaksanaan Fasilitasi Pembentukan dan Peningkatan Partisipasi Kelompok Masyarakat Tertib Pertanahan (Pokmasdartibnah) dalam PPAN.* Internal document. Badan Pertanahan Nasional.

———. 2007c. *Petunjuk Pelaksanaan Penyuluhan dalam PPAN.* Internal document. Badan Pertanahan Nasional.

BPN (Team Penyeleras). 2004. "Naskah Rancangan UU Sumberdaya Agraria (sebagai hasil penyempurnaan UU No 5 Tahun 1960 tentang Peraturan Dasar Pokok-pokok Agraria oleh BPN)." Unpublished

BPN document, Public Consultation Forum, National Land Agency, Jakarta, 23 April.

Byres, T. J. 2005. "Neoliberalism and Primitive Accumulation in Less Developed Countries." In *Neoliberalism: A Critical Reader,* ed. A. Saad-Filho, 83–90. London: Pluto Press.

Candrawiguna, K. 2002. "Serikat Petani Jawa Barat Menolak Tap IX/MPRRI/2001 mengenai Pembaruan Agraria dan Pengelolaan Sumber Daya Alam." Press release. 15 February.

Casson, A., L. Tacconi, and K. Deddy. 2007. *Strategies to Reduce Carbon Emissions from the Oil Palm Sector in Indonesia.* Paper prepared for the Indonesian Forest Climate Alliance, Jakarta.

Christodolou, D. 1990. *The Unpromised Land: Agrarian Reform and Conflict Worldwide.* London: Zed Books.

Colchester, M., N. Jiwan, Andiko, M. Sirait, A. Y. Firdaus, A. Surambo, and H. Pane. 2006. *Promised Land: Palm Oil and Land Acquisition in Indonesia—Implications for Local Communities and Indigenous Peoples.* Bogor: Forest Peoples Programme, Sawit Watch, HuMA and ICRAF.

Davidson, J., and D. Henley, eds. 2009. *The Revival of Tradition in Indonesian Politics.* London: Routledge.

Deininger, K. 2003. *Land Policies for Growth and Poverty Reduction.* World Bank Policy Research Report. Oxford: Oxford University Press.

Departemen Pertanian. 2007. Direktorat Jenderal Perkebunan *Program Revitalisasi Perkebunan,* Jakarta: Direktorat Jenderal Perkebunan Departemen Pertanian RI.

Eckholm, E. 1979. *The Dispossessed of the Earth: Land Reform and Sustainable Development.* Worldwatch Paper no. 30.

Evers, P. J. 1995. "Preliminary Policy and Legal Questions about Recognizing Traditional Land in Indonesia." *Ekonesia: A Journal of Indonesian Human Ecology* 3:1–24.

Fane, G., and P. Warr. 2008. "Agricultural Protection in Indonesia." *Bulletin of Indonesian Economic Studies* 44 (2): 133–50.

FAO. 1981. *Peasant Charter.* Rome: UN-FAO.

Fauzi, N. 1998. *Sesat Pikir Undang-undang Pertanahan Nasional: Pandangan KPA atas draft UU Pertanahan Nasional yang Disusun oleh BPN.* Paper presented to DPR-RI, Jakarta, March.

———. 2001a. "Sesat Pikir yang dapat melanggengkan ketidakadilan agraria kritik terhadap naskah revisi UUPA versi BPN" "[Background Papers for] Seminar dan Lokakarya, "Arah Kebijakan Nasional mengenai Tanah dan Sumberdaya Alam Lainnya." Bandung, 20–23 August.

———. 2001b. "Berbagai versi alasan merevisi UPA" [Background Papers for] Seminar dan Lokakarya, "Arah Kebijakan Nasional mengenai Tanah dan Sumberdaya Alam Lainnya," Bandung, 20-23 August.

———. 2003a. *The New Sundanese Peasants' Union: Peasant Movements, Changes in Land Control, and Agrarian Questions in Garut, West Java.* Paper prepared for Crossing Borders' Workshop on New and Resurgent Agrarian Questions in Indonesia and South Africa, Center for Southeast Asia Studies and Center for African Studies. University of California at Berkeley, 24 October.

———. 2003b. "Penyelesaian sengketa agraria di kabupaten: usulan awal pembentukan badan penyelesaian sengketa." Paper presented at a discussion on Keputusan Presiden No 34/2003 tentang Kebijakan Nasional di Bidang Pertanahan. Ciamis, July 10.

———. 2009a. "Land Titles Do Not Equal Agrarian Reform." *Inside Indonesia* 98, available at http://insideindonesia.org/content/view/1250 / 176/.

———. 2009b. *Gunawan Wiradi: Reforma Agraria Perjalanan yang Belum Berakhir.* 2nd ed. Bogor: KPA, Sayogyo Institute, and Akatiga.

Fauzi, N., and R. Y. Zakaria. 2000. "Men-siasat-I Politik Otonomi Daerah Demi Pembaruan Agraria: Masuk dari Pintu yang Tersedia, Keluar dari Pintu yang Baru." Paper presented in the KEDAI (Study Group on Indonesia, *Adat*) discussion series I. Cisarua, 26-28 May 2008. Bogor: ICRAF.

Franco, J., and S. Borras, eds. 2005. *On Just Grounds: Struggling for Agrarian Justice and Citizenship Rights in the Rural Philippines.* Quezon City: Institute for Popular Democracy; and Amsterdam: Transnational Institute.

Gunawan, R., J. Thamrin, and M. Grijns. 1995. *Dilema Petani Plasma: Pengalaman PIR-Bun Jawa Barat.* Bandung: Akatiga.

Hardiyanto, A. 1996. *Land Reform by Leverage in Indonesia.* KPA Position Paper No. 001/1996. Bandung: Konsorsium Pembaruan Agraria.

Harman, B. K. ,P. Irianto, N. Fauzi, B. Fidro, and S. Pranawa. 1995. *Pluralisme Hukum Pertanahan dan Kumpulan Kasus Tanah.* Jakarta: Yayasan Lembaga Bantuan Hukum Indonesia.

Harriss, J., K. Stokke, and O. Törnquist, eds. 2004. *Politicising Democracy: the New Local Politics of Democratisation.* Hampshire, Eng.: Palgrave Macmillan.

Harsono, B. 1996, 2000, and 2007a (13th, 14th, and 18th rev. ed.) *Hukum Agraria Indonesia: Himpunan Peraturan-Peraturan Hukum Tanah.* Jakarta: Penerbit Djambatan.

———. 2002. *Menuju Penyempurnaan Hukum Tanah Nasional.* Jakarta: Pernerbit Universitas Triskati.

Hatta, M. 1992. *Beberapa Pokok Pikiran.* S. Swasono dan F. Ridjal, ed. Jakarta: UI-Press.

Ho, P., and Max Spoor. 2006. "Whose Land? The Political Economy of Land Titling in Transition Economics." *Land Use Policy* 23 (4): 580–87.

IWGIA. 1999. *The Indigenous World, 1998–1999.* Copenhagen: International Work Group on Indigenous Affairs (IWGIA).

Kantor Pertanahan Kabupaten Garut. 2007. "Berita Acara Penyerahan Sertifikat Hak Milik atas Tanah Obyek Landreform Melalui Kegiatan Pembaruan Agraria Nasional T.A. 2007. Desa Padaawas, Kecamatan Pasirwangi, Kabupaten Garut." Document Garut Land Office.

Kartodihardjo, H., et al. 2005. *Di Bawah Satu Payung: Pengelolaan Sumber Daya Agraria.* Jakarta: Suara Bebas.

Kay, C. 2000. "Latin America's Agrarian Transformation: Peasantisation and Proletarianisation." In *Disappearing Peasantries? Rural Labour in Africa, Asia and Latin America,* ed. D. Brycesson, C. Kay, and J. Mooij, 123–38. London: ITDG Press.

Koalisi Rakyat Tolak Perpres 36/2005. 2005. *Cabut Segera Perpres 36/2005 dan Usut Tindakan Represif Aparata Kepolisian terhadap Petani!!* Statement of Koalisi Rakyat Tolak Perpres 36/2005. Unpublished document KPA.

Komisi Hukum Nasional. 2002. *Peta Reformasi Hukum di Indonesia, 1999–2001: Transisi di Bawah Bayang-bayang Negara,* Jakarta: Komisi Hukum Nasional Indonesia.

KPA. 1998. *Deklarasi Pembaruan Agraria,* 1998. Bandung, Konsorsium Pembaruan Agraria.

———. 2001. "Strategi Advokasi untuk Implementasi TapMPR-RI No. IX/MPR/2001 tentang Pembaruan Agraria dan Pengelolaan Sumberdaya Alam." Unpublished dokumen, KPA.

———. 2007. *Hentikan Kriminalisasi Petani!,* Siaran pers KPA tentang Kesepakatan antara NPN dengan Polri tentang Penanganan Masalah Pertanahan, 29 August.

———. 2009. *Keliru Jika SBY Dianggap Telah Melakukan Pembaruan Agraria.* KPA press release No. 047/Sekretariat/KPA/VII/2009.

KRHN and KPA. 1998. *Usulan Revisi Undang-Undang Pokok Agraria: Menuju Penegakan Hak-Hak Rakyat Atas Sumber-Sumber Agraria.* Jakarta: KRHN (Konsorsium Reformasi Hukum Nasional) and KPA.

KSPA. 2001. "Ketetapan MPR RI tentang Pembaruan Agraria sebagai Komitmen Negara Menggerakkan Perubahan menuju Indonesia yang Lebih Baik: Masukan Pemikiran dar Kelompok Studi Pembaruan Agraria." Working paper submitted to Panitia Ad Hoc II Badan Pekerja MPR-RI, 21 May.

KSPA [Kelompok Studi Pembaruan Agraria], Pokja PSDA and KPA. 2001. *Meneguhkan Komitmen Mendorong Perubahan: Argumen-argumen dan Usulan Ketetapan MPR-RI tentang Pelaksanaan Pembaruan Agraria dan Pengelolaan Sumberdaya Alam yang Adil dan Berkelanjutan.* Bandung: KSPA, Pokja PSDA, KPA.

Li, T. M. 2000. "Articulating Indigenous Identity in Indonesia: Resource Politics and the Tribal Slot." *Comparative Studies in Society and History* 42 (1): 149–79.

Lucas, A., and C. Warren. 2003. "The State, the People and Their Mediators: The Struggle over Agrarian Law Reform in Post–New Order Indonesia." *Indonesia* 76:87–126.

Lukmanurdin. 2002. "Menolak Klaim Perhutani atas Tanah Rakyat Sagara." In *Memecahkan Ketakutan Menjadi Kekuatan: Kisah-kisah Advokasi di Indonesia,* by Sapei, et. al., 305–348. Yogyakarta: Insist Press.

MacAndrews, C. 1986. *Land Policy in Modern Indonesia: A Study of Land Issues in the New Order Period.* Boston: Oelgeschlager, Gunn and Hain, and Lincoln Institute of Land Policy.

Mahkamah Konstitusi. 2007. *Putusan Mahkamah Konstitusi No. 21–22/PUU-V/2007.* Constitutional Court decision on review of the Law No. 25/2007 concerning investment. http://www.mahkamahkonstitusi.go.id/putusan /putusan_sidang_Putusan%2021-22%20PUU%20V%202007%20Baca %2025%20Maret%202008_ASLI2.pdf. Accessed 16 January 12.

Marti, S. 2008. *Losing Ground: The Human Rights Impacts of Oil Palm Plantation Expansion in Indonesia.* Bogor: Life Mosaic, Sawit Watch Indonesia, and Friends of the Earth.

McCarthy, J., Gillespie, P., and Zen, Z. 2012. "Swimming Upstream: Local Indonesian Production Networks in 'Globalized' Palm Oil Production." *World Development* 40 (3): 555–69.

McCulloch, N., and C. P. Timmer. 2008. "Rice Policy in Indonesia: A Special Issue." *Bulletin of Indonesian Economic Studies* 44 (1): 33–44.

Mismuri, H., and Prasetyohadi. 2008. *Gerakan Petani Dusun Cieceng di Tasikmalaya,* available at http://sppasundan.multiply.com/tag/kebun.

Moyo, S., and Yeros, P. 2005. *Reclaiming the Land: The Resurgence of Rural Movements in Africa, Asia and Latin America.* London: Zed Books.

Mubyarto. 1992. *Tanah dan Tenaga Kerja Perkebunan: Kajian Sosial Ekonomi.* Yogyakarta: Aditya Media.

Nesadurai, H. E. S. 2009. *Land Rights, Global Soft Law Regimes and Land Conflicts: An Exploratory Study of the Impact of REDD and RSPO on Land Conflicts Using Sarawak as a Case Study.* Paper presented at the 2008/2009 East Asian Development Network Annual Forum. Bangkok, 21–22 May.

Nurdin. 2008. *Tentang Peresmian Program Layanan Rakyat untuk Sertifikasi Tanah (LARSITA) BPN-RI.* Unpublished document, Bandung: KPA.

Parlindungan, A. P. 1991. *Undang-undang Bagi Hasil di Indonesia: Suatu Studi Komparatif.* Bandung: Mandar Maju.

Peluso, N. L., S. Afiff, and N. Fauzi Rachman. 2008. "Claiming the Grounds for Reform: Agrarian and Environmental Movements in Indonesia." *Journal of Agrarian Change* 8 (2–3): 377–407.

Poniman, A., S. M. P. Tjondronegoro, G. Wiradi, D. Bachriadi, S. Bahari, U. Setiawan, N. Fauzi, D. Juliantara, Agustiana, and M. Nurudin. 2005. *Petisi Cisarua: Rekomendasi untuk Presiden Republik Indonesia Periode 2004–2009, "Reforma Agraria dalam Rangka Pelaksanaan Visi, Misi dan Program Pemerintah Baru."* Bandung: Pergerakan.

Potter, L. 2008. *Dayak Resistance to Oil Palm Plantation in West Kalimantan, Indonesia.* Paper presented to the 17th Biennial Conference of the Asian Studies Association of Australia in Melbourne, 1–3 July.

Powelson, J., and R. Stock. 1987. *The Peasant Betrayed: Agriculture and Land Reform in the Third World.* Boston: Oelgeschlager, Gunn and Hain.

PPR. 2007a. *Mengapa Kita Berpartai: Panduan Membangun dan Mengelola Partai Perserikatan Rakyat (PPR).* Jakarta: Partai Perserikatan Rakyat.

———. 2007b. *Tentang Reforma Agraria.* Internal document. Partai Perserikatan Rakyat. 21 April.

Prasetyo, S. A., et al. 2003. *Indonesia's Post-Soeharto Democracy Movement.* Jakarta: Demos.

Prosterman, R. L., M. N. Temple, and T. M. Hanstad, eds. 1990. *Agrarian Reform and Grassroots Development: Ten Case Studies.* Boulder. CO: Lynne Rienner.

Rianto, G. 1995. "Kasus Gunung Badega-Garut." In *Pluralisme Hukum Pertanahan dan Kumpulan Kasus Tanah,* ed. B. K. Harman, P. Irianto, N. Fauzi, B. Fidro, and S. Pranawa, 139–48. Jakarta: Yayasan Lembaga Bantuan Hukum Indonesia.

Robison, R., and V. R. Hadiz. 2004. *Reorganizing Power in Indonesia: The Politics of Oligarchy in an Age of Markets.* London: Routledge.

Rosset, P. 2002. *The Good, the Bad, and the Ugly: World Bank Land Policies.* Paper presented to the seminar "The Negative Impacts of the World Bank's Policies on Market-Based Land Reform," George Washington University, Washington, DC. 15–17 April.

Ruwiastuti, M. R. 2000. *Sesat Pikir Politik Hukum Agraria: Membongkar Alas Penguasaan Negara atas Hak-hak Adat.* Yogyakarta: Insist Press-KPA-Pustaka Pelajar.

Ruwiastuti, M. R., N. Fauzi, and D. Bachriadi. 1998. *Penghancuran Hak Masyarakat Adat atas Tanah: Sistem Penguasaan Tanah Masyarakat Adat dan Hukum Agraria.* Bandung: KPA.

Safitri, M. A. 2009. "The Mystery of Formalising Informal Land Tenure: The Case of Langkawana Lampung Indonesia." In *Legalising Land Rights,* ed. J. M. Ubink, A. J. Hoekema, and W. J. Assis. Leiden: Leiden University Press, 549–74.

Schulte Nordholt, H., and G. van Klinken. 2007. *Renegotiating Boundaries: Local Politics in Post-Suharto Indonesia*. Leiden: KITLV Press.
Semiloka (Seminar dan Lokakarya). 2001a. "Arah Kebijakan Nasional Mengenai Tanah dan Sumberdaya Alam Lainnya." Laporan Kegiatan. Bandung: KSPA, Pokja PSDA, and KPA.
―――. 2001b. "Usulan Rancangan Ketetapan Majelis Permusyawaratan Rakyat Republik Indonesia tentang Pelakasanaan Pembaruan Agraria dan Pengelolaan Sumberdaya Alam yang Adil dan Berkelanjutan." Unpublished papers. Bandung, September.
Setiakawan. 1991. "Badega: Solidarity Is Strength" and "Chronology of the Badega Land Dispute." *Setiakawan* 6:34–37.
Setiawan, B., and B. Nainggolan, eds. 2004. *Partai-partai Politik Indonesia: Ideologi dan Program, 2004-2009*. Jakarta: Penerbit Buku Kompas.
Setiawan, U. 2007. "Momentum Baru Reforma Agraria." *Kompas*, 23 February.
Simatupang, P., and C. P. Timmer. 2008. "Indonesian Rice Production: Policies and Realities." *Bulletin of Indonesian Economic Studies*. 44 (1): 65–80.
Simpul Bengkulu. 2006. "Dari Penonton Menjadi Pemain: Konsolidasi Gerakan Politik Kerayatan di Bengkulu." In *Negara adalah Kita: Pengalaman Rakyat Melawan Penindasan*, ed. Eko Bambang Subiyantoro, Andi Wilson, K. Yuwono, and A. Bunyamin, 337–61. Jakarta: FBB Prakarsa Rakyat dan Perkumpulan Praxis.
Sitorus, F., and G. Wiradi, eds. 1999. *Sediono M.P Tjondronegoro: Sosiologi Agraria Kumpulan Tulisan Terpilih*. Bandung: Yayasan AKATIGA.
Sodiki, A. 2004. *Pandangan Kritis terhadap Rancangan Undang-undang Sumberdaya Agraria Konsep Badan Pertanahan Nasional*. Paper presented to Working Group for BAL 1960 Amendment, Jakarta: 20 May.
Soekarno. 1960. *Laksana Malaekat Jang Menjerbu dari Langit!: Djalannya Revolusi Kita*. Speech of Presiden Republik Indonesia pada HUT RI ke-15, 17 August. Jakarta: Departemen Penerangan.
―――. 1962. *Saja Tjinta BTI*, amanat P.J.M. Presiden Soekarno pada Kongres Nasional ke IV BTI di Jakarta, 23 July. Jakarta: Dewan Pimpinan Pusat Barisan Tani Indonesia.
SPP. 2006. *Daftar Rekapitulasi Kasus-kasus Tanah Wilayah SPP*. Internal document. Serikat Petani Pasundan.
STaB. 2006. *Data Pendudukan Tanah oleh Anggota-anggota STaB 2006*. Internal document. Serikat Tani Bengkulu.
Stoler, A. 1985. *Capitalism and Confrontation in Sumatra's Plantation Belt, 1870–1979*. New Haven: Yale University Press.
Sudibyo, A. 2001. *Politik Media dan Pertarungan Wacana*. Yogyakarta: LKIS.
Sumardjono, M. 2004. "Naskah Rancangan UU Sumberdaya Agraria (sebagai hasil penyempurnaan UU No 5 Tahun 1960 tentang Peraturan Dasar Pokok-pokok Agraria oleh BPN)." Unpublished BPN

document, Public Consultation Forum, National Land Agency, Jakarta, 23 April.

———. 2006. "Perpres No 65/2006, Apa yang Berubah?" *Kompas*, 21 June.

Suryakusuma, J. I., et al. 1999. *Almanak Parpol Indonesia*. Jakarta: Yayasan API.

Sutarto, Endriatmo. 2006. *Perlunya Konsensus Mengenai Reforma Agraria ala Indonesia*, pidato sambutan Ketua STPN dalam Lokakarya Perumusan Hasil-hasil Simposium Agraria Nasional. Yogyakarta, 17–18 Desember.

Tauchid, M. (1951) 2009. *Masalah Agraria sebagai Masalah Penghidupan dan Kemakmuran Rakjat Indonesia*. Vol. 1. Jakarta: Penerbit Tjakrawala.

Tjondronegoro, S. M. P., G. Wiradi, D. Bachriadi, U. Setiawan, E. Raryadi, and N. Fauzi. 2004. "Kritik terhadap Naskah Rancangan Undang-undang tentang Sumberdaya Agraria." Paper prepared for the National Public Consultation of the BAL 1960, revisions conducted by BPN. Jakarta, 27 April.

———. 2007a. "A Brief Quarter Century Overview of Indonesia's Agrarian Policies." Paper presented at the Seminar Nasional "Land and Households Economy 1979–2005: Changing Roads for Poverty Reduction," ICASEPS and UNESCAP-CAPSA. Bogor. 25 June.

———. 2007b. *Strategi Implementasi PPAN*, available at www.kpa.or.id.

van Klinken, G., and E. Aspinall, eds. 2010. *The State and Illegality in Indonesia*. Leiden: KITLV Press.

Wacana HAM. 2001. "Pembaruan Agraria dan Hak Asasi Petani." No. 4/Tahun II: 14 November.

Wahono, F. 2002. *Hak-hak Petani dan Proses Perumusannya*. Yogyakarta: Yayasan Cindelaras.

Wallace, J., and I. Williamson. 2006. "Building Land Markets." *Land Use Policy* 23 (2): 123–35.

Warren, C., and J. F. McCarthy, eds. 2009. *Community, Environment and Local Governance in Indonesia*. London: Routledge.

Warta FKKM. "Reforma Agraria ala Kehutanan." 2006. Available at http://www.fkkm.org/Warta/index2.php.

White, B. 1990. "Agroindustri, Industrialisasi Pedesaan dan Transformasi Pedesaan." In *Industrialisasi Pedesaan*, ed. Sayogyo and M. Tambunan, 199–250. Jakarta: Sekindo Eka Jaya.

———. 1997. "Agroindustry and Contract Farmers in Upland West Java." *Journal of Peasant Studies* 24 (2): 100–136.

Wijardjo, B. 1994. "Insiden Nipah: Pengunjuk Rasa Ditembaki." In *Demokrasi, Antara Represi dan Resistensi: Catatan Keadaan Hak Asasi Manusia di Indonesia 1993*, ed. Mulyana W. Kusumah et al., 178–83. Jakarta: YLBHI.

Wilson, I. 2006. "Continuity and Change: The Changing Contours of Organized Violence in Post-New Order Indonesia." *Critical Asian Studies* 38 (2): 265–97.

Wilson, J. 1986. "The Political Economy of Contract Farming." *Review of Radical Political Economy* 18 (4): 47–70.

Wiradi, G. 1991. *Industri Gula di Jawa dalam Perspektif Model "Inti-Satelit": Kasus di Kabupaten Cirebon, Jawa Barat.* Working paper PSP-IPB. Vol. A-31. Bogor: PSP-IPB.

———. 1997. "Pembaruan Agraria: Masalah yang Timbul Tenggelam." In *Reformasi Agraria: Perubahan Politik, Sengketa, dan Agenda Perubahan Agraria di Indonesia,* ed. Dianto Bachriadi, Erpan Faryadi, and Bonnie Setiawan, 39–43. Jakarta: Lembaga Penerbit Fakultas Ekonomi UI dan KPA.

———. 2000. *Reforma Agraria: Perjalanan yang Belum Berakhir.* Yogyakarta: Insist Press-KPA-Pustaka Pelajar.

World Bank. 1994. *Staff Appraisal Report: Indonesia Land Administration Project.* Unpublished World Bank Report No. 12820-IND.

———. 2004. *Project Appraisal Document for a Land Management and Policy Development Project.* Unpublished World Bank Report No. 28178-IND. Jakarta, 31 March.

Yudhoyono, S. B. 2007. *Pidato Presiden Republik Indonesia DR H. Susilo Bambang Yudhoyono pada awal tahun 2007.* Jakarta, 31 January.

Yudhoyono, S. B., and J. Kalla. 2004. *Membangun Indonesia yang Aman, Adil, dan Sejahtera: Visi, Misi, dan Program Susilo Bambang Yudhoyono dan M. Jusuf Kalla.* Program statement for the 2004 presidential election.

Yudhoyono, S. B., and Boediono. 2009. *Membangun Indonesia yang Sejahtera, Demokratis, dan Berkeadilan: Visi, Misi dan Program Aksi.* Program statement for the 2009 presidential election.

Newspapers

Jakarta Post
Kompas
Koran Tempo
Media Indonesia
Metro
Pikiran Rakyat
Priangan Post
Radar Garut
Republika
Riau Online
Surya

Chapter 11

AGRARIAN RESOURCES AND CONFLICT IN THE TWENTY-FIRST CENTURY

CAROL WARREN AND ANTON LUCAS

Lain tapi sama saja?
—Indonesian saying[1]

The symbolic relation between land and Indonesian identity, captured in the evocative aphorism *"Tanah Air"*—literally, meaning "land water," and standing for the nation—remains closely tied to popular images of the "little people" (*rakyat*) for and by whom the Indonesian revolution was fought and in whose name the state claims its raison d'être.[2] For all that modern, capitalist, and developmentalist visions of the future came to dominate policy and the lifestyles of the emerging middle classes during the Suharto period, the shirtless farmer remains the iconic source of a popular subaltern narrative in political rhetoric and the Indonesian media. Forty-one percent of the Indonesian workforce earns income from primary production in agriculture, forestry, and fisheries. But only 15 percent of Indonesia's GDP is attributed to this important sector of the economy,[3] indicating the parlous market value placed on the production of the most basic and universal of livelihood supports.

The shock of the Asian economic crisis of 1997–98 stimulated a new appreciation of the links between Indonesia's agricultural base and the social security of its large population. The world economic and environmental crises looming a decade later produced a series of threats barely anticipated even a few years before: bankrupted capital and credit markets; rising prices for oil and agricultural inputs; the impacts of climate change on agricultural production; rapidly escalating demand for biofuels to provide "green energy"; and the rising price and declining availability of arable land for food production[4]—all of which combined to produce a global food crisis in 2008. Rising food prices[5] and food security threats caused riots in countries around the globe, precipitating the introduction of export controls and revival of subsidies and trade restrictions in some countries. In an effort to tackle this food security problem, the Yudhoyono government issued the Protection of Agricultural Land for Food Sustainability law (UU 41/2009). The law is aimed at stemming the tide of land alienation, which saw half a million hectares of riceland removed from production in the decade between 1991 and 2001 (Simatupang and Timmer 2008, 72), as part of Indonesia's speculative developmentalist boom.[6]

Paradoxically, the long hiatus in which land law was given little official notice by New Order authorities—a situation of legal ambiguity and political contradiction that continues into the reform period—has had as much to do with perceived dangers of tampering with a body of principles that continue to hold much importance for ordinary Indonesians as it has with contrary official perceptions of the outdatedness of agrarian issues in relation to new development objectives.[7] The Asian economic crisis, which precipitated Indonesia's political upheavals, demonstrated the importance of revisiting the place of the agrarian sector,[8] on which all others are ultimately predicated, in the wider scheme of national development policy and political reform. Protection of Indonesia's agricultural base and the welfare of its farming population require a reconsideration of tax regimes, subsidies, commodity price floors, and insurance against crop failures.[9]

One legacy of the Basic Agrarian Law has been that it kept alive a recognition of the relation between citizenship and resource rights.

BAL/UUPA implicitly treated equitable access to land and resources for livelihood security as a civil right and the ultimate raison d'être of the nation-state. Real reform requires a reconciliation of rhetoric, policy, and practice. Only the sustained engagement of organized activist local groups and nongovernment organizations with the media and the parliamentary process could ultimately accomplish this.[10] Much depends on local forces joining with wider social currents to achieve the necessary tipping points, if the combined implications of ecological[11] and economic crises are to produce a radical realignment of the relationship between institutions and ideologies from local through national and global scales. To date the Parliamentary Policy Directive (TapMPR IX) and the political process generally have failed to deliver that reconciliation. Core concerns of the Basic Agrarian Law remain pivotal questions in the "Land for the People" movement; and the relation between the market and social function of land represents the fundamental point of tension in agrarian policy.

That land is an increasingly critical resource is indicated by the astronomical prices it is capable of commanding in the upper circuits of the global economy and the massive focus on speculative accumulation in the "land-grabbing" phenomenon of recent years (Borras et al. 2011). Large-scale land acquisitions for future food, biofuel, and other resources are estimated to have involved some twenty to forty-five million hectares globally between 2005 and 2008 (Borras et al. 2011, 209). In barely half of these global acquisitions have the proposed agricultural developments materialized (Deininger and Byerlee 2011, 51).[12] In the Indonesian case, we have seen (in chapters 1 and 2) that huge areas of forest reserve, amounting to 70 percent of the nation's land mass, were theoretically excluded from smallholder agriculture under the New Order and that business interests have been steadily acquiring expanded exploitation rights both within and outside that forest estate since. The food crisis in Indonesia forced the issue of "sleeping," or neglected, lands and the broader questions of accumulation and control of capital back on the policy agenda, although the state has largely ignored this key feature of the Basic Agrarian Law.[13]

The pressure of global population increments and the rapid growth of middle-class consumption in the powering economies of Asia, combined with the end of cheap energy and the need to protect heavily pressured environmental services through biodiversity and carbon sequestration programs, are separately and together contributing to a land accumulation drive in the most remote parts of the earth. Much of this land grabbing, as McCarthy, Vel, and Affif (2012) point out, is "virtual,"[14] aimed at securing vested interest claims for future indefinite benefit through commitment to whichever among these competing needs might deliver high profits.[15] But those economic values are increasingly contested and more overtly pitted against other social, cultural, and ecological claims by civil society forces, with outcomes likely to be dependent on the extent to which these alternative claims on the commonweal can be converted into a practical and convincing political and economic program.

Also concerning to those for whom agrarian resource security and poverty alleviation drive the land tenure struggle is the problem of alienation. The high rate of turnover of landholdings under occupation (and even in the few cases where settlement has been achieved), along with the relatively poor income advantage smallholders receive relative to off-farm incomes (chapter 2), appears to undercut some of the assumptions regarding the poverty reduction potential for redistribution underpinning the land reform movement. Lack of viability (because of small size, poor productivity, or low prices) and insecurity of holdings offer part of the explanation for the disappointingly high proportion of land transfers by peasant farmers involved in conflict cases described in this book (see chapters 2, 4, and 8). There are paradoxes to be explained with respect to those factors contributing to land concentration and the decapitalization of rural classes. The complexity of the data has challenged assumptions on both sides of the land tenure formalization and market liberalization debate. On the one hand, there is substantial evidence that under conditions of greater security and supports toward achieving adequate income potential, land transfers decline; on the other hand, there tends to be relatively less opportunity for income improvement in the smallholder agricultural sector than in the nonagricultural sector under free market conditions, at least in the boom cycle.[16] At heart, in the debates over the positive or negative role of markets in resolving the dilemmas of the rural peasant class, is the question of social security versus economic opportunity values. Apparent anomalies in the decisions of smallholder peasant farmers are well explained by the relative perception of economic risks against socioeconomic benefits tied to landholding and primary production. Changing dynamics of the global economy, as well as interventions specifically aimed at leveling the playing field for rural agriculturalists, could shift the balance in rural prosperity and decision making.[17]

The World Bank–funded study of the sudden surge in large-scale investments in agriculture (Deininger and Byerlee 2011, 68–81) following the food-security scare sets out the complex constellation of factors affecting potential opportunities for boosting employment, technology, market access, and tax generation posed by international agro-investment and land transfers over recent years. These are set against a repertoire of risks (Deininger and Byerlee 2011, 55, 63–66, 71), including superficial consultation processes, inadequate legal redress, neglect of environmental and social safeguards, discretionary approval processes, lack of transparency, monitoring, and enforcement—the same intractable failures of governance that have dogged land and resource conflicts in Indonesia into the present. These institutional weaknesses mean that "instead of generating sustainable benefits, [large-scale investment projects] contributed to asset loss and left local people worse off than they would have been without the investment." Ensuring access and benefits to local people "will depend on the capacity, cohesiveness and entrepreneurial aspirations of local communities as well as the level of economic activity, public goods available and capacity of local governments" (Deininger and Byerlee 2011, 71). Proposed principles for responsible agro-investment involve a combination of local capacity building, good governance, and standard setting.[18] This could be effective only if mandatory and if accompanied by levels of intervention and regulation of market processes that conflict with the free market philosophy so fundamental to the global capital expansion of recent decades.

Borras et al. (2011, 212-13) argue in a special issue of the *Journal of Peasant Studies* devoted to the land-grabbing phenomenon that wage-work and contract farming in the agribusiness sector need not be impoverishing. "Why should they be, if labor and farmers are well organized and their rights, claims and contracts are actively promoted and protected by government and the legal system?" But any introduction to political economy will tell us that disproportionate power comes with disproportionate capital accumulation. The unfettered global concentration of land and capital, justified by arguments for technological improvement and economies of scale,[19] inherently works against the social equity and environmental sustainability goals of triple bottom line accounting that are often held to fetter accumulation.

Using the World Bank Report's own data, Li (2011) demonstrates the real implications of the large-scale agricultural investment it advocates for rural smallholders. With only ten to four hundred jobs per thousand hectares, depending on the commodity produced, and heavy investments of between US$50,000 and US$200,000 required per job created, there is meager employment potential and little long-term prospect of good returns to either labor or land from this strategy. World Bank data showing much larger income to smallholders than to agricultural wage labor led Li to conclude that parceling up large plantations into smallholdings would be the way to go if poverty reduction were the real aim of agrarian policy. Suppression of labor and land prices in favor of returns to capital is the inevitable outcome of intensified large-scale investment in agriculture in the absence of solid redistributive policies (Li 2011, 282-83).

In the Indonesian context, research on the booming oil palm sector indicates that returns to smallholders can be substantial. Where advantages for smallholders are protected by government policy, companies are forced to pay wages and rent sufficient to guarantee the needed labor force and production. The critical factor is whether smallholder farmers are able to maintain autonomy to organize their own production. In this regard, Indonesian central and regional governments, competing for investment in the sector, have engaged in a race to the bottom at the expense of ordinary farmers. In "liberalizing" conditions for establishment of core-satellite plantation regimes under Agriculture Ministry Regulation 26/2007, the state has drastically reduced the minimum proportion of project land required to be reserved for smallholders, leaving many—especially those in remote areas with few alternative development options—to face deteriorating terms for their land and labor (McCarthy, Gillespie, and Zen 2012, 560–65).

What is perhaps most disturbing about the cases described in this volume has been the ineffectiveness of the reform movement in dealing with issues that affect such a significant sector of the population and the national economy. This is so despite a revolutionary heritage that placed popular welfare at the core of the state's claims to legitimacy, a decade of sweeping political changes that brought about previously unparalleled freedom of organization and expression, and a major redistribution of power and resources between the center and the regions. It was to be expected that this political transformation should have given the long-standing populist agrarian cause more than a rhetorical place in the nation's reformist policy agenda.[20]

The studies in this book have shown that the law has not only proved unable to fulfill its obligations to ordinary citizens, but in some cases has been actively hostile to the interests of the *rakyat* whose welfare it is charged to protect. The failures of local peoples' legal claims in the Cimacan golf course dispute (chapter 4), of the *adat* land claims against plantations in West Sumatra (chapter 5) and Flores (chapter 7), of the Gili Trawangan dispute over abandoned plantation land (chapter 8), and the efforts to protect the urban poor residents of Bandung from land clearance for a private development (chapter 9)—all have been attributed to combinations of bribery, elite political connections, and perverse interpretations of the law by the courts. Rather than having their grievances redressed, litigants often found themselves convicted instead of illegal occupation and damage to property (chapters 2, 4, 7 and 8). Indeed, investment-oriented policies throughout the Asian region have been focused on enclosure of vast territorial areas at the expense of local people (see, for an overview, Hall, Hirsch, and Li 2011).[21]

Yet there are signs that slowly the wheels of democratic politics are having some impact in Indonesia as a result of the new political constellations accompanying democratization and decentralization after the demise of the New Order. Both Government Regulation 11/2010 on Neglected Lands and Law 2/2012 on Land Acquisition for Development in the Public Interest address long-standing issues of forcible resumption by the state, distribution to landless cultivators of neglected lands, and compensation to landholders for state expropriation of land in the public interest, but with significant limitations. The proliferation of new legislation may offer little comfort to those who hoped for greater gains in government commitment to the people's interests, but the regular turnover of elected parties and constant revision of legislation makes evident that the balance of forces is such that no authority or interest can expect uncontested implementation of its policies and practices. The move to resolve land conflicts through the establishment of a parliamentary Special Committee on Agrarian Conflict Resolution (*Kompas*, 11 January 2012) may represent a serious effort to resolve issues, or just more of the same stalling tactics that have marked so many aspects of Reform Era politics (D. Bachriadi, pers. comm., 17 March 2012; I. Nurdin, pers. comm., 18 March 2012).[22]

The aims of the former director of the National Land College (STPN), which trains bureaucrats responsible for land management, including registration, certification, and implementation of the PPAN land distribution program, may be an indication of more positive directions in government policy and practice. A student of the scholar-activist Sajogyo's, Endriatmo has proposed substantial reform of the STPN curriculum to promote "the people's welfare, social justice, harmony and prevent conflict" (Endriatmo, interview, 12 December 2011). Inspired by the long scholar-activist tradition pressing for agrarian reform, STPN has forged a research and publication alliance with the Sajogyo Institute that aims to focus on "the structural problems which maintain and reinforce rural poverty and . . . correct the unequal agrarian structures bequeathed by colonialism and developmentalism of the neoliberal era" (Ahmad Nashih Luthfi 2011, ii).[23]

In the forested areas of Indonesia, legal changes also suggest positive shifts in the bargaining status of local communities. A constitutional court decision (KepMK 21 February 2012) and Forestry Department circular (SE 01/Menhut II/2012) require the resolution of conflicts with customary communities before confirmation of forest status. This potentially will give participatory community mapping programs that have been carried out with NGO support in the years leading up to and since *reformasi* an important role in the definition and disposition of forestland in the future (*Kompas,* 21 March 2012).

The Leiden "Legalizing Land Rights" project analyzes a range of adaptive "third" paths already emerging in response to the inadequacies of free market–friendly private versus inalienable communal tenure regimes, preferred by polarized interests of global financial institutions and social movement groups (Otto and Hoekema 2011). These involve formal government recognition of community-based tenure, in which a range of possibilities for individual, secondary, and communal use rights gain external validation based on prevailing practice and/or locally negotiated arrangements. Experiments with community forest rights described by Safitri (2010) also suggest ways of improving the resource security of forest communities.

To date, however, for large numbers of the peasant farmer and poor urban landless class, the more things change in post-Suharto Indonesia, the more they remain the same. The specter of land and food insecurity remains a potent reminder of the failures of the Indonesian commitment to the people's welfare. Food security was the overt rationale for the socially and environmentally disastrous million hectare peat project under the Suharto regime described in chapter 6. Land conflicts continue to dominate reported human rights abuses, accounting for the largest number of cases filed (738 out of 4,502) in 2011 at the National Commission on Human Rights. The Centre for Strategic and International Studies attributes the accompanying violence to the failure of the state to address long-standing grievances (*Jakarta Globe,* 16 January 2012).

Pramoedya Ananta Toer, Indonesia's most prominent literary figure, quoted in the introduction to this book, spoke optimistically of the fundamental changes taking place in rural areas across Indonesia since *reformasi*—a remarkable activism among some of those most brutally silenced under the New Order. Whether Pramoedya's remarks regarding the grassroots activism of the last decade prove prophetic or merely the wishful thinking of a social conscience from a bygone era will depend on the extent to which these mass social movements are able to find genuine institutional expression through Indonesia's reform politics; or whether, losing sight of common cause through a combination of competing private interests and factionalism, in the face of official corruption and the resurgence of the use of force by unaccountable power,[24] Indonesia's peasant farmers will once again be "robbed of their voices." Their capacity to articulate their common interests with other subaltern groups will define the peasant farmers' place in a national and global regime that can no longer afford to continue business as usual or ignore the plight of rural peasant farmers and poor urban workers. Li concludes that standards, regulation, and titling reforms have no traction except as the result of "hard-fought struggles that settle the matter on the terrain of politics, where social groups with different interests confront each other" (2011, 292). But this cannot happen in a vacuum separate from the fate of other social movements aimed at equity and sustainability, or from the currents articulating local with national and global struggles toward these ends. The history of the labor and farmers' movements in the already industrialized economies at the turn of the millennium show how rapidly those gains can recede. We have no choice but to move to the international scale of politics and the expansion of formal regulation in the global domain if these movements are to achieve something of the level playing field that could make the outcomes of those struggles promising.

There is every likelihood that the contradictions in Indonesian government policy, practice, and law will remain—as they have in the international arena—until social reform groups consolidate and/or until further grave crises force the issue. Meanwhile, skirmishes in which different local outcomes result from differing constellations of political forces and actors will doubtless produce a repertoire of accommodations and compromises. We can only aim to build upon those that offer ways forward toward a still diversely conceptualized and elusive common good.

Notes

1. "Different, but just the same," the Indonesian equivalent of "the more things change, the more they stay the same."

2. The previously mentioned (chapter 10 and frontispiece) "Land for the People" campaign poster is subtitled with a phrase from the national anthem: "Indonesia, my nation, land where I spilled my blood." These words draw on historical and cultural associations between land and popular identity in the Indonesian context. They refer to the people's sacrifice for the good of the nation and the general welfare, which the nurturing relationship between land and national identity is meant to provide.

3. BPS statistics for workforces engaged in agriculture, forestry, hunting, and fishing as of February 2009 are found at: http://dds.bps.go.id/eng/tab_sub/view.php?tabel=1&daftar=1&id_subyek=06&notab=2. GDP by Industry for 2007–9 may be found at http://dds.bps.go.id/eng/brs_file/eng-pdb-10feb10. Accessed 15 December 2012. Only in the crisis years of 1998 and 1999 did agricultural growth exceed that of other economic sectors; in those two years by factors of ten and three respectively (ADB 2004 Key Indicators of Developing Asian and Pacific Countries). Bachriadi's data (pers. comm., 17 March 2012) collected from the BPS showed that the contribution of agriculture, livestock, forestry, and fisheries sectors to GDP was 14.3 percent (2004); 13.1 percent (2005); 13.0 percent (2006); 13.7 percent (2007); 14.5 percent (2008); 15.3 percent (2009). Agricultural employment increased in the years following the 1997/98 crisis (Alisjahbana and Manning 2006, 241) and again in 2008/09, reversing pre-crisis trends. The head of the government body responsible for overseeing commodity trading [Bappeti] in Indonesia's Department of Industry and Trade, bemoaned the fact that farmers receive only 24 to 34 percent of the value of agricultural production (*Bali Post,* 26 February 2005).

4. Aside from speculative acquisition, five to ten million hectares of land are estimated lost to agriculture through degradation (IFAD 2008, cited in de Schutter 2011, 257). Additional pressure on land resources arises from population growth, urbanization, energy, and animal feed crop production, which require an estimated nine to twenty-six million additional hectares annually (de Schutter 2011, 257),

5. Food prices in many countries rose 30 to 50 percent due to a combination of fuel and fertilizer price increases, crop failures, and the conversion of land from food crops to biofuel and animal fodder to satisfy the tastes and energy demands of consumers in developed economies and the rapidly growing middle classes in China and India. In 2008, rice prices rose 80 to 300 percent, and staple crops doubled in price on world

markets, although farmers did not reap the benefits, since most of this increase has gone to higher prices for inputs and transport (Reuters 3 May 2008). The domestic price of rice in Indonesia rose 94 percent between 2004 and 2008 (McCulloch and Timmer 2008, 34).

6. The 2009 legislation does tackle the development permit system, which has been a primary source of corruption, providing windfalls to rent-seeking officials for large-scale project approvals and fostering the displacement of agricultural land to other uses. Whether the Rp 500 million (US$50,000) fine and one- to five-year jail sentences for violations will be enforced, or prove sufficient to deter approval of massive land consuming projects remains to be seen. The "public interest" (§44) exception has also to be tested against the backdrop of decades of distortions of this concept under the New Order. How restricted the designation of land to be zoned for "sustainable food production" will prove to be, and whether existing zoning for forestry, commercial plantation development, industry, tourism, and real estate development will mean land that falls within these broadly mapped zones is excluded from the protection of this legislation, will determine the significance of these seeming shifts in agrarian policy.

7. Despite declining incomes for agricultural produce, and the acceleration in industrial production since the mid-1980s, the total number of households in Indonesia dependent on agriculture rose marginally between the 1983 and 1993 agricultural censuses, while the amount of land in agriculture dropped from eleven million to ten million hectares (see chapter 2).

8. As a caller to Bali's popular regional radio talk-back program *Warung Global* (Global Café) commented: "From long ago Indonesia was known as an agrarian country. It seems our government has forgotten the peanut for its shell" (*Bali Post*, 26 August 2005).

9. In addition to legal security for landowners, tax regimes and economic frameworks that encourage sustainable practices and ensure fair and stable prices have to be placed on the national and international drawing boards. Current Indonesian tax policy uses the market value of land as the basis for the land and building tax (PBB) to which farmers are subject. Those living in peri-urban, tourism, or industrial areas face land taxes that bear little relation to the incomes provided by agricultural products. Provisions for tax relief (§37) and establishment of a publicly funded bank for farmers (§63(f)) in the new legislation on agricultural lands and food sustainability (UU 41/2009) are steps in this direction. Not least is the need to encourage the development of farmers' organizations both as political and economic forces. The role of cooperatives—which have always been asserted as the

cornerstone of Indonesia's "people's economy"—as a means of enhancing farmers' bargaining power must also be taken seriously.

10. Among the antidemocratic developments in the Reform Era has been the extension of corruption and money politics to the most routine activities within two of the institutions vital to the democratization process. Not only are parliamentarians' votes routinely bought either directly through illegal payments or indirectly through campaign contributions, but the press is similarly afflicted by the power of money inducements to determine what is and is not published. In one case, dispossessed Balinese landholders' representatives, pursuing a case of illegal land expropriation to the DPR committee responsible for land conflict issues, were faced with the demand from the head of that committee for several million rupiah, allegedly to pay journalists to cover the hearing (interviews, September 2001, October 2002).

11. Although national ideologies and mainstream academic theory before the twenty-first century had grappled with questions of equity and distribution, they generally did not confront the implications of environmental limits. The BAL is based on a nationalist, socialist, and populist worldview that has yet to come to terms with the question of environmental degradation. In this regard, it is imperative that environmental activists continue to engage with those concerned with people's resource rights to find genuinely sustainable approaches to the agrarian question.

12. For Indonesia this figure was 16.7 percent at the end of the New Order (see table 1.4, in chapter 1 of this volume).

13. The Basic Agrarian Law stipulated that land, whether under leasehold or freehold title, had to be worked productively in order to satisfy its social function. In the face of economic crisis, food riots, and land occupations, the government issued new regulations requiring leaseholders to grow food crops on undeveloped, or "sleeping," land. Under new regulations, if landholders leave agricultural land unutilized, local authorities may allow other parties to work that so-called sleeping land. At the height of the crisis, the government moved to require the immediate utilization of such land. Two months before stepping down, Suharto signed Regulation 36/1998 on the ordering and use of neglected (*terlantar*) land; this was followed a month after he left office by a Ministerial Regulation (PerMenAg 3/1998) on the use of empty land (*tanah kosong*) for food crops. That these regulations bracket the last days of the New Order regime and the first days of the caretaker Habibie government is indicative of the critical political and economic issue the land and food crisis had become. Both regulations reiterated the "social function" of land. But as of 2008, the National Land Agency inventory still showed 7 million

hectares classified as neglected or abandoned, of which 1.7 million was state land under commercial use leases. Actual figures for neglected lands are undoubtedly much higher (Setiawan 2010, 347). Although a recent regulation (PP 10/2010) controlling empty lands may for the first time offer some protection to landholders from companies that seek leasehold land only to obtain bank credit, past experience gives reason to doubt that the law on compulsorily acquired land (UU 2/2012) will provide either the protection or compensation that the government asserts.

14. In a pattern similar to that described in the West Sumatra case study in chapter 5, the land grab in West Papua is anything but "virtual." Under the umbrella of MIFEE (Merauke Intergrated Food and Energy Estate) the national government has granted location permits to forty-six companies covering 2.2 million hectares in Papua province for plantation projects, production forests, and large-scale agriculture (rice, soybeans, and sugarcane). HGU and HTI leases were obtained supposedly with the authorization of local *adat* leaders and the local government bureaucracy. Thousands of hectares of old-growth tropical hardwood forests have been cleared by Medco Group and South Korean energy companies to make wood pellets as replacement for coal in electricity generators in South Korea and Japan. Fierce opposition from local groups and Walhi's publicity on conflicts in nine of the fifteen districts has highlighted unfair compensation, lack of cooperation with local communities, conflicts between clans over areas and boundaries of leased land (no maps were attached to original agreements), and compensation paid to the wrong families (resulting in compensation having to be paid twice). Work has ceased on logging in some areas, which means promised community facilities remain unbuilt. Companies complain that the holdup is due to the as yet unimplemented government regulation PP 2/2011 on special economic areas, which is supposed to provide special infrastructure, technical, and financial support to companies with location permits in the Merauke region (*Tempo*, 2–8 April 2012).

15. These land grabs are "virtual" in another sense, in that the land they have leased might not exist. As Hall, Hirsch, and Li (2011, 204) note, these so-called empty lands grabbed by agro-business are often "hard to find" on maps, when plantation companies cannot locate the large blocks for which they thought they had obtained concession rights.

16. Safitri (2009, 568–72) found land markets to be more active in forest areas where there is no legal possibility of long-term security of tenure, compared to nonforest areas where tenure is potentially secured through certification. Household incomes among the Lampung agro-forest farmers she surveyed (2009, 556) show a remarkably similar pattern of farm and

nonfarm income relative to size of forest gardens, to that which we saw in the national statistics analyzed by Bachriadi and Wiradi in chapter 2.

17. Safitri (2009, 563–64) reports that one action research intervention, which focused on a capacity-building forest governance initiative, resulted in increased incomes for agro-forest dependent communities and achieved better forest protection outcomes.

18. FAO, IFAD, UNCTAD, and World Bank, discussion note on "Principles for Agricultural Investment that Respects Rights, Livelihoods and Resources," 25 January 2010. http://siteresources.worldbank.org/INTARD/214574-1111138388661/22453321/Principles_Extended.pdf. Accessed 3 February 2012.

19. Industrial-scale agriculture is arguably more productive than sustainable smallholdings but also more environmentally damaging. It is more likely to feed animals or cars than people in a world where capacity to pay is skewed by the intensifying economic models promoted by international finance institutions. Other evidence supports an inverse correlation between farm scale and productivity (Borras, cited in de Schutter 2011, 258).

20. Aspinall (2012) makes an analogous point, in a review of the place of the political left in contemporary Indonesia. He notes the irony of the persistence of leftist ideology across broad sectors of the Indonesian populace, while the social movements that have kept this ideology alive have been conspicuously impotent. Weak organization, attributed to the fragmented NGO model that dominates activism in Indonesia, in his view, accounts for the failure to convert ideas into political power, with the consequence that a nation that has become a model of democratization remains dominated by oligarchy and patronage. Nonetheless, Aspinall acknowledges gradual political shifts are taking place, pointing to the new prominence of health care and social security in public policy as a result of electoral pressure. Not to be ignored is the fact that the "continuing influence of a general leftist sensibility" defending the interests of the poor has worked "to provide space for a social justice agenda." Paradoxically, "ideals of social justice, of state intervention to assist the poor, and even of redistribution are deeply embedded in the contemporary political culture," while the political movements that promote those ideals "remain marginal and splintered" (Aspinall 2012).

21. This important study shows how exclusion of local people from land across Southeast Asia is brought about through a combination of market and state power: through land legislation and titling programs, and through resuming land for large hydroelectricity dams, shrimp farming, palm oil, and coffee plantation developments, conservation and environmental programs, and peri-urbanization or conversion of agricultural land

to nonagricultural uses. More recent are the large-scale exclusions through "land grabs" by international agro-business companies noted above.

22. Another team was formed to investigate violations of existing laws and government regulations, while a parliamentary working committee has been established with authority to call government agencies to the DPR to cooperate in finding solutions to problems (such as the BPN in the case of land disputes) (I. Nurdin, pers. comm., 19 March 2012).

23. Endriatmo describes himself as a member of the Bogor School of critical agrarian studies, founded by Sajogyo and Wiradi. In a recent introduction to an anthology on agrarian issues Indonesia, Endriatmo says STPN needs to listen to "the silent voice" (English original) that speaks about the realities of the poor in Indonesia who can no longer find livelihoods from the land (Saluang 2010, vi).

24. Now thugs (*preman*) and private "security" forces serve vested interests, often with tacit collusion of the state apparatus (van Klinken and Aspinall 2010; Wilson 2012). Not long after the PPAN program was announced, the National Land Agency (BPN) signed a joint cooperative agreement (*Kesepakatan Kerjasama Bersama*) with the Indonesian police to deal with the problem of land conflicts, with "illegal" land occupations to be treated as criminal acts (Joint Agreement No. 3/SKB/BPN/2007 and No. B/576/III/2007, 14 March 2007, concerning the handling of land problems). In December 2008 the media reported one child killed, several villagers injured, and a hundred houses burned when police and civilian guards drove out hundreds of people occupying contested forestland that had been leased to a pulp supplier in Riau. It was one among many post-*reformasi* cases demonstrating the continuity of state authority privileging Big Capital at the expense of the Little People (*Riau Terkini,* 20 December 2008). See also reports of a shooting at Bulukumba and Takalar in South Sulawesi, over demands for the return of customary lands (*tanah ulayat*) (*Kompas,* 18 October 2008). Sixteen farmers were reported injured, one killed, and twenty-five others arrested in Bulukumba; and seventeen farmers were reported shot at and wounded, forty others injured through beatings, and one killed in Takalar. For other reports of violence by hired *preman* in land conflict cases, see *Kompas,* 4 July 2009. Thirty-two villagers are reported to have been killed in Lampung (Sumatra) since 2008, the most recent incident in November 2011 as a result of a dispute between locals and plantation companies (*Jakarta Post,* 9 January 2012). Police were reportedly involved in that incident as well as in an incident in Bima where local protesters against an Australian goldmining company were killed and injured (*Jakarta Post,* 13 January 2012; Reuters, 24 December 2011. http://af.reuters.com/article/commoditiesNews/idAFL3E7NO02N20111224.

References

ADB. 2004. *Key Indicators for Asia and the Pacific.* Manila: Asian Development Bank.

Alisjahbana, A., and C. Manning. 2006. "Labour Market Dimensions of Poverty in Indonesia." *Bulletin of Indonesian Economic Studies* 42 (2): 235–61.

Aspinall, E. 2012. "Still an Age of Activism. *Inside Indonesia,* special issue "Where Is the Left?" 107 (January–March 2012). http://www.insideindonesia.org/feature/still-an-age-of-activism-22012883. Accessed 5 March 2012.

Bachriadi, D. 2009. *Land, Rural Social Movements and Democratisation in Indonesia.* Transnational Institute Working Paper on Agrarian Justice. Amsterdam: Transnational Institute. Available at http://www.tni.org/archives/bachriadi-indonesia.

Borras, S., R. Hall, I. Scoones, B. White, and W. Wolford. 2011. "Towards a Better Understanding of Global Land Grabbing: An Editorial Introduction." *Journal of Peasant Studies* 38:209–16.

Deininger, K., and D. Byerlee, with J. Lindsay, A. Norton, H. Selod, and M. Stickler. 2011. *Rising Global Interest in Farmland: Can It Yield Sustainable and Equitable Benefits?* Washington: World Bank.

De Schutter, O. 2011. "How Not to Think of Land Grabbing: Three Critiques of Large-scale Investments in Farmland." *Journal of Peasant Studies* 38 (3): 249–79.

Hall, D., P. Hirsch, and T. M. Li. 2011. *Powers of Exclusion: Land Dilemmas in Southeast Asia.* Singapore: National University of Singapore.

Li, T. M. 2011. "Centering Labor in the Land Grab Debate." *Journal of Peasant Studies* 38:281–98.

Luthfi, Ahmad Nashih. 2011. *Melacak Sejarah Pemikiran Agraria: Sumbangan Pikiran Mazhab Bogor.* Yogyakarta: STPN Press, Pustaka Ifada, and the Sajogyo Institute.

McCarthy, J., P. Gillespie, and Z. Zen. 2012. "Swimming Upstream: Local Indonesian Production Networks in 'Globalized' Palm Oil Production." *World Development* 40 (3): 555–69.

McCarthy, J., J. Vel, and S. Affif. 2012. "Trajectories of Land Acquisition and Enclosure: Development Schemes, Virtual Land Grabs and Green Acquisitions in Indonesia's Outer Islands." *Journal of Peasant Studies* 39 (2): 521–49.

McCulloch, N., and C. P. Timmer. 2008. "Rice Policy in Indonesia: A Special Issue." *Bulletin of Indonesian Economic Studies* 44 (1): 33–44.

Otto, J. M., and A. Hoekema. 2011. *Fair Land Governance: How to Legalise Land Rights for Rural Development.* Leiden: Leiden University Press.

Safitri, M. 2009. "The Mystery of Formalising Informal Land Tenure in the Forest Frontier: The case of Langkawana, Lampung, Indonesia." In *Legalizing Land Rights,* ed. J. Ubink, A. Hoekema, and W. Assies. Leiden: Leiden University Press.

———. 2010. "Forest Tenure in Indonesia: The Socio-legal Challenges of Securing Communities' Rights." PhD diss., Leiden University.

Saluang, S., ed . 2010. *Antologi Puisi Agraria Indonesia.* Yogyakarta: STNP Press.

Setiawan, U. 2010. *Kembali ke Agraria.* Yogyakarta: STNP Press.

Simatupang, P., and C. P. Timmer. 2008. "Indonesian Rice Production: Policies and Realities." *Bulletin of Indonesian Economic Studies* 44 (1): 65–79.

van Klinken, G., and E. Aspinall, eds. 2010. *The State and Illegality in Indonesia.* Leiden: KITLV Press.

Wilson, I. 2012. *The Politics of Protection Rackets in Post-New Order Indonesia.* London: Routledge.

Newspapers

Bali Post
Jakarta Globe
Jakarta Post
Kompas
Riau Terkini

Index

A page number in italic type indicates an illustration on that page. A word or phrase in italic type is in a foreign language as used in the text. The letter *n* following a page number indicates an endnote on that page. The number(s) following the *n* indicate(s) the note number(s).

abandoned (neglected) land. See *tanah terlantar* (neglected, abandoned land)
absentee landholding, 69–70, 73, 80n54, 99, 107n11, 268n6, 361n91
Abulrachman Wahid, 122, 203, 326, 349n12
"active doing" defined, 207
adat: Alliance of Indigenous Peoples of the Archipelago (AMAN) and, 108, 228, 235n12, 237n30, 309–10, 348n3; certification and, 100–102, 104, 105; communal land/domains and, 6–8, 100–102, 104–5, 107–8, 150, 155–60, 173–74, 187–89, 220–27, 233–34, 309–10, 321–23; community mapping and, 108n15, 227, 236n26, 237n27, 355n48, 380; Council of the Alliance of Indigenous Peoples of the Archipelago Region (AMAN NTT) and, 220, 235; customary law community organizations (LPMA) and, 225; defined, 6–7; elders and, 237n27; Land Administration Project (LAP) and, 96, 100–102; leaders and, 158–59, 176n14, 234n2, 234n4, 385n14; "Legalizing Land Rights" project and, 380; positive law and, 229–30, 233; revival and, 225; socially embedded use-value concepts and, 263; uses in Central Kalimantan and, 187, 189–90, 194–95

Administrative Court (PTUN). See court cases
Advocacy and Research Institute (LRA), 177n25
Afiff, 329, 344–46, 375
Agency for the Conservation of Natural Resources (BKSDA), 219
Agrarian Act of 1870, 27n12
Agrarian Reform Study Group (KSPA), 72
agricultural censuses, 20–21; 1963, 42; 1963 to 2003, 43; 1973, 49; 1983, 49; 1993, 50–51; 1999 regulation and, 282–83; 2003, 55
Agricultural Development Council, 4
agricultural productivity, 43–44
Agriculture Ministry Regulation 26 of 2007, 378
Agro Economy Survey Foundation (SAE), 52
Agustiana, 315–16, 328, 352n29, 355n49
Aliansi Petani Indonesia (API), 315
Alliance of Indigenous Peoples of the Archipelago (AMAN), 108, 228, 235n12, 237n30, 309–10, 348n3
Amended 1945 Constitution. See Constitution of 1945
Amir, 131–32, 139n10, 143n44
Arief, S., 51
Asian Development Bank, 330
Aspinall, E., 386n20
Atma Jaya Research Team, 101–2

Aurora company, 16
AusAID, 205

Babatan, 16
Bachriadi, Dianto, 4–5, 105, 343, 350n14, 354n36; on TapMPR IX of 2001, 320–21
Bagul, Antony Dagur, 218, 220
BAL, 75n9
Bala, John, 225
Bali, 18
Bali Advertiser, 261
"Ballad of the Evicted," 139n13
Bandung, 22–23
Bappenas, 331
Barisan Tani Indonesia (BTI), 4
Barraclough, S. L., 98, 107n10
Basic Agrarian Law (BAL/UUPA 5/60), 2–3, 19–20, 40, 187, 268n6, 271n39; adequate housing and, 275; ambiguities and contradictions in, 7–8, 28n14; available land and, 3–4; case studies and, 20–23; citizenship, resource rights and, 373–74; commercialization of agriculture and, 5; commodification and, 43–44; environmental protection and, 384n11; foreign ownership and, 41, 261; forms of title and, 28n15; globalizing market exchange model and, 259–60; HGU leases and, 31n33, 250–51; land concentration and, 330; land distribution and, 4–5, 75n9; land productivity and, 384n13; land reform and, 106; "national interest" provision and, 321; plantation land and, 12; popular values, norms of social justice and, 313; principles of, 41; private commercial interests and, 13–14; social function of land and, 3–5, 6–9, 76n11; socially embedded use-value concepts and, 263; subsequent implementing regulations and, 3–4, 26n4; Suharto and, 8–9; Sukarno and, 3–4; TapMPR IX of 2001 and, 318–20; tourism, real estate development and, 259–60; underlying customary concepts and, 264–66

Basic Forestry Law of 1967, 8–9, 77n16, 187
Batang district, 18
Batang Peasants' Advocacy Forum (FPBB), 335
Bedner, A., 310
Bekasi District BPN, 69
Bengkulu Peasants' Union (STaB), 334–35
bera land, 80n52
Bey, Idham Samudra, 318–19, 320–23, 353n33
Bina Desa, 351n21
"Bishop and the Bupati, The" (Coffey), 235n14
Booth, Anne, 52, 58, 60
Borneo Orangutan Survival Foundation (BOS), 204–5
Borras, S., 376
BPN. *See* National Land Agency (BPN)

Campbell, J., 8
Catholic Church, 22
Central Kalimantan, 22, 192–93; *adat* uses in, 187, 189–90, 194–95; canal system and, 197; corruption and, 197–98, 200; dynamics of transformative processes in, 186–87; ethnic conflicts in, 201–2; as frontier area, 184–88; industrial logging and, 186, 202–3; Kapet and, 203; "Million hectare" Peat Land Development Project (PLG) and, 184–85, 192–93, 209n8; New Order policy and, 186–87; Ngaju Dayak and, 188–89; oil palm, timber estates and, 187, 203–4; peatland fires and, 198; peat swamp forests in, 188–89, 193–94, 195; PLG project and, 196–97; sequestered carbon and, 206–7; spatial planning and, 194; timber concession system (HPH) and, 187–88, 190; timber extraction and, 198–200; transformative processes in, 208; transmigration programs and, 186, 190–91, 195, 201–2, 209n7, 210n11; "vacuum of indecision" and, 203, 204

Central Kalimantan province, 22
Centre for Agricultural Policy Studies (CAPS), 353n33
Centre for Strategic and International Studies, 380
Chalid, 98
Cianjur district, 5
Cibodas Golf Course Resort and Villas, 114–15
Cibubur National Conference on Agrarian Reform, 310
Cieceng village case, 344–45
Cimacan, 18, 21, 114–16, 126; elected BPD in, 136–37; farmers and, 137–38; headman elections in, 136, 143n37; village government and, 142n34; wages for officials and, 144n46
Cimacan land dispute, 378; BPD and, 124–25, 126; Bupati Cianjur Decision of 2000, 141n28; compensation for loss of livelihood and, 126, 127–29, 132–33; compensation payments and, 129–34; dissatisfactions, conflict and, 126–27; district-level money politics and, 127–28; land swap and, 133–34; missing village land and, 134; plantations and, 140n22; rental of land and, 140n21; students and NGOs in, 129–32; use rights and, 141n24. See also Cibodas Golf Course Resort and Villas
Ciroyom: clearance by zone and, 289–90; compensation payments and, 290; election strategies and, 293–94; First Zone (see Kebonjeruk [First Zone]); Islamic Youth Movement (GPI) and, 292–93; Kebonjeruk-Ciroyom Reject Eviction Forum (Forum TPKC) and, 290; legal aid and, 292; mediation and, 291, 292; National Awakening Party and, 292; People's Rescue Team and, 291; prosecutions and, 292, 293; residents and, 290–91; Second Zone and, 290–93; street protests and, 291–92; Third Zone and, 293–98
Cisarua Petition, 333–34

civil society organizations, strengths and weaknesses of, 344–45
Collier, W. L., 69–70
Colol village: money politics and, 222; violence and, 221–22
commercial use leases (HGUs), 12–15, 19, 48, 153–57, 176n12, 223–29, 231–32, 245–46, 250–53, 356n57
Communist Party. See Partai Komunis Indonesia (Indonesian Communist Party, PKI)
Community Alliance for Justice (AMUK), 121, 143n41; local BPD and, 129
companies. See under PT
compensation, 9, 14–18, 115–20, 125–29, 132–37, 158–67, 170–73, 256–66, 274–81, 286–98. See also specific cases
Consortium for Agrarian Reform (KPA), 312, 314, 348n2, 349n8; alliance with SPP and, 345; KepPres 34 2003, 328; land conflicts inventory and, 10, 68–69; land redistribution and, 355n46; LAP evaluation and, 97, 105–6; "Million Signatures for Agrarian Reform" campaign and, 313
Constitution of 1945, 75n4, 104, 274–75, 283–84, 317–18, 330; pro-people's language in, 344; TapMPR IX of 2001 and, 353
corruption, 14–18, 23, 158–59, 197–98, 236n24, 296–99, 350n16, 383–84; Gili Trawangan (Lombok) and, 269n22; money politics and, 12–13, 115, 120, 143n38, 157, 384n10. See also case studies
court cases, 31n33, 99, 119–24, 128–32, 158–59, 164–67, 219–22, 230–31, 251–54, 281; Administrative Courts (PTUN), 10, 17, 26, 34n61, 251, 277, 302n26, 322; Constitutional Court, 330; Land Reform (agrarian) courts, 27n8, 29n19, 41, 44, 319, 348n4, 355n46

Datuak BBS, 157–58, 159, 162–63, 177n24
Dede Dachroni, 126–27, 136, 145n54

Index   393

de Soto, Hernando, 95, 102–5, 106n2, 346; *Mystery of Capital, The,* 95
Djuanda, R. D., 119
Djuhari, A., 66
Durin, Hasan Basri, 350n16
Dutch colonial regime, 190, 217; 1870 Agrarian Act and, 27n12; Catholic Church and, 222–23; land holdings and, 56; landowner bias and, 53; land policy and law and, 6–9, 11–12, 18–20, 189–90, 208, 223, 256, 300n6, 303n54; plantations and forest land and, 12, 28n13, 329, 344

Eckholm, E., 71
Emergency Law 8/1954, 30n27
Endriatmo Sutato, 379, 387n23
England, enclosure in, 207–8
Era Reformasi, 14–19; legal title, compensation and, 18; reclaiming actions and, 18. See also *reformasi agraria*
Era Transisi, 325
Erb, M., 236n17

Fane, G., 356n57
Fauzi, Noer, 346, 350n14
Federation of Indonesian Peasants (FSPI), 310, 348n2
Firman, T., 278
Fitzpatrick, Daniel, 7, 104
Flores, 22, 215–16, 378; *adat* and, 233, 234n2, 234n4, 237n27; *adat* law, positive law and, 229–30; Catholic Church and, 232–33; Colol village and, 219–21; court system, weakness of and, 230–31; ecology of, 218; economy of, 218, 230; ethnic elite politics in, 228; massacres of 1966 and, 236n21; Multi-Party Forestry Development Program and, 237n29; NGOs in, 232; reforestation project and, 218–20; summary of land conflicts in, 233–34
Ford Foundation, 4
forestland, 249n10; agro-forestry and, 217n8, 222; community forest and, 237n29, 334, 349, 380; conglomerates and, 77n18; legal changes and, 379–80; loss of, 68–69; sacred forests and, 218, 223

Forestry Department Circular of 2012, 379–80
forestry police, 235n9
Franke, R., 76n15
frontiers, conflict and, 183–84

Ganie-Rochman, M., 108n14
Garut district, 5, 352n24
Gili Trawangan (Lombok), 18, 22, 378; abandoned plantations and, 268n15; backpacker tourism and, 247; community tensions and, 258–59; corruption and, 269n22; environmental protection and, 249, 269n22; fall of Suharto and, 257; foreign ownership and, 262–63, 271n35, 271n36; globalizing market exchange model and, 259–60; government eviction campaign of 1992, 1993, 1995, 249, 255–56; government objectives and, 267n1; Indonesian Tourism Department study and, 248; land conflicts, origins of, 243–44, 250; landholding in, 267n2; legal certainty and, 262, 271n35; marginalization of local communities and, 260; Muspida and, 269n24; occupying landholders and, 266–67; Peasants to the Death (Petani Pada Maut) and, 254; plantation leases on, 245–46; press coverage and, 269n26; PRONA titling scheme and, 245, 267n5; property values in, 261, 270n31, 270n33; resistance to compensation offers and, 254–55, 256; smallholder sector and, 245–46, 250; socially embedded use-value concepts and, 263–66; state and local claims and, 264–66; tourism and, 247–48, 261–62, 268n8; unlawful occupation and, 269n23; value transformations and, 243, 271n34; women in the resistance and, 257, 270n30
Gini ratios: 1963 to 2003, *43*; definition of, 42; equal landholding structure and, 70; farm households and landholdings, 1973 to 2003, *50, 52*; landless tenants and, 65
Goban, Josef Lewor, 225, 226, 236n24

golf courses, 32n39. *See* also Cibodas
  Golf Course Resort and Villas
Government Regulation on Land
  Registration of 1997, 100
Government Regulation on Neglected
  Lands of 2010, 337
Green Revolution, 62, 76n15, 93;
  economic growth and, 191–92;
  failure of, 74

Habibie regime, 200, 325; "sleeping"
  land and, 384n13
hak guna usaha (HGU). *See* commercial
  use leases (HGUs)
Hakim, Lukmanul, 143n39
hak milik, 27n11; BAL and, 94;
  credit need and, 96; definitions of,
  7; financial impacts of, 96; land
  abandonment and, 54; plantation
  projects and, 35. See also under *adat*
hak ulayat, 7, 27n11. See also under *adat*
Hall, D., 385n15, 386n21
Hardjono, Joan, 96–97, 103, 107n9
Hari Tani, 3, 347n2
Harsono, Boedi, xxi, 26n4, 268n6
Harsono, Soni, 109n19
Hatta, Mohammad, 76n12, 326
Haverfield, R., 28n13, 101
HGU. *See* commercial use leases
  (HGUs)
Hirsch, P., 385n15, 386n21
Hoffman, M. L., 281
Holius Hosen, 291
Home Affairs Ministry decree no 64,
  123
Hutchison, J., 108n13

Idham Samudra Bey. *See* Bey, Idham
  Samudra
Indonesia, 383n6; administrative
  courts and, 268n16; Asian
  economic crisis of 1997 to 1998,
  373; commercial land clearance in,
  275; court system, weakness of in,
  230–31, 251–52, 269n17, 281, 297–98;
  decapitalization of rural classes
  in, 375–76; democratic politics in,
  378–79; economic crisis, civil society
  and, 308; food shortages and, 192,

373; GDP and, 139n12; households
  in, 77nn28–31; land and currency
  equivalents in, 269n20; land and
  food shortage fears in, 380, 382n5;
  livelihoods, GDP and, 372, 382n3,
  383n7; NGOs in, 178n25; oil palm
  sector and, 152–56, 377–78; police
  in, 387n24; political left and, 386n20;
  rakyat welfare in, 378; socially
  embedded use-value concepts
  and, 263–66; social security *versus*
  economic opportunity in, 376; state-
  centric developmentalism and, 317;
  transition to democracy and, 339–40
Indonesian Peasants Union (BTI),
  29n19
Indonesian Railway Company (PT
  KAI), 284–85
Indro Cahyono, 130–31
International Covenant on Economic,
  Social and Cultural Rights (ICESC)
International Labour Organization,
  310
inti-plasma model, 357n63
Islamic Youth Movement (GPI),
  292–93

Jabodetabek, 48
Jakarta Administrative Court, land
  disputes and
Jakarta Legal Aid Institute (YLBHI), 120
Jamal, E., 66
Japan, 56–57
Java: absenteeism, 69–70; BAL/UUPA
  and, 6; hamlet heads in, 144n51; land
  clearances in, 11; large-scale projects
  and, 66; rice production in, 66
Jember, 32n43
Jenggawah, 15, 17–18
Journal of Peasant Studies, 377
Joyo Winoto, 17, 105, 332, 334, 335

kampongs, 274–75, 284, 286, 296, 298,
  299n1, 303; landrights and, 303n54
Kano, H., 49, 52
Katsura, H. M., 281
kebun plasma, 150, 153, 157, 161–62,
  168–69, 171–72, 174, 179n29;
  development, use of and, 178n27

Index 395

Keponjeruk (First Zone): divide-and-rule and intimidation and, 289; land clearing process and, 288; population of, 303n45. *See also under* Ciroyom
KepPres 34/2003, 327–28, 355n48, 356n53; KPA and, 328
Kompas, 318
Konsorsium Pembaruan Agraria (KPA) Database on Agrarian Conflicts, 29nn23–24
KSPA. *See* Agrarian Reform Study Group (KSPA)

Ladejinsky, Wolf, 4, 27n7, 42, 44, 72–73
Land Administration Project (LAP), 21, 327; *adat* and, 100–102, 104, 108n16; Atma Jaya Research Team and, 101–2; bureaucracy, legal system and, 99–100; capital access and, 103; credit need and, 96; funding of, 94; gender impacts of, 96–97; Government Regulation on Land Registration of 1997 and, 100; implementation of, 97–98; land concentration, distribution and, 98–99; land poor, landless and, 106; land transfers and, 104; liberalizing market model and, 98; migrant populations and, 100; NGOs and, 105–6; objectives of, 94–95; openness and, 280; permit mechanism and, 276, 281–82; Project Preparation Report, 107n111; public interest and, 279; Regional Autonomy Law of 1999 and, 283–84; regional studies and, 107n7; regulation of 1974 and, 276; urban dwellers and, 109n20
land clearance, 10–11, 31n32, 198, 203, 218, 232, 249, 255–58, 270n29, 293–98; commercial land clearance law and, 300n6; compensation and, 279–81; deregulation measures and, 277; Land Release Committee and, 276; legal protection by political means and, 297; National Land Agency (BPN) and, 276–77, 281–82; NGOs, student movements and, 280–81; "openness" and, 280; permit mechanism and, 276, 281–82; Phase I (1994 to 1999), 96; protection of landholders and, 278–79, 281, 282–83; "public interest" and, 279; Regional Autonomy Law of 1999 and, 283–84; spatial management law of 2007, 296; Supervision and Control Teams for Commercial Land Clearance, 277. *See also specific cases*
land conflicts, 2, 10; absenteeism and, 69; cases of, 31n36; landgrabbing and, 234; large corporations and, 73; New Order policy and, 317; North Sumatra and, 34n63; plantations, timber concessions and, 321; PPAN and, 335; promised resolution of, 334; regional distribution of, 11; Special Committee on Agrarian Conflict Resolution of 2012 and, 379; titling and, 94, 105; violence and, 387n24; World Bank and, 355n44. *See also specific cases*
land control, patterns of, *43*
land conversion: large-scale projects and, 66, 80n49, 109n18; population growth and, *65*
land distribution, 4–5, 75n9; development options and, 266; genuine reform and, 324; globalizing market exchange model and, 259–60; Land Reform Committees and, 75n7; land reform implementation and, 75n9; peasant landholders and, 63; PPAN and, 332–33; socially embedded use-value concepts and, 263; tourism, real estate development and, 259–60
Land for the People campaign, 2, 360n92, 374, 382n2; calendar and, v, 11
land grabs, 183, 228, 234, 347, 359n75, 374–77, 385n14, 387n21
landlessness, 60–61; categories of, *64*; definitions of, 75n8; deforestation, erosion and, 71; Gini ratios and, *65*, 78n35, 78n37; increase of, 62, 63–64, 68; national economy and, 71; social and political instability and, 70

Land Management and Policy Development Project (LMPDP), 105
land reform, 69–70; agrarian power structures and, 72; alienation and, 375; certification and, 94; compensation and, 140n20; credit need and, 74; data on land availability and, 73; development and, 71–72; different approaches to, 360n86; land degradation and, 382n4; National Ombudsman Commission (KON) and, 326; need for supporting programs and, 72; objects of, 73; politics and, 328; population growth and, 72–73; post-1965 policies, politics and, 74; poverty and, 375, 377; productivity and, 386n19; requirements for, 324, 383n9; resource control and, 329; risks of agroinvestments and, 376; smallholder sector and, 74; speculative accumulation and, 374–75, 376; TapMPR IX of 2001 and, 324; types of land and, 356n57
Land Reform Committees, 41, 44, 75n7
Land Reform Courts, 41, 44
land registration, 108n15
land tenure and access issues, 2–3
land titling, 93–94, 103, 109n21; de Soto and, 346; land transfers and, 95; legal certainty and, 95; PRONA and, 94, 106n1, 341. *See also* Land Administration Project (LAP); Land Management and Policy Development Project (LMPDP)
land utilization, 1963 to 2000, 67; trends of, 68–69
Late New Order (1988-1998) land disputes, 9–11
Lawang, Servas, 220–21, 235n13
Law Faculty of the University of Nusa Cendana, 233
Law on Land Acquisition for Development and the Public Interest of 2011, 336
Legal Aid Foundation (YLBHI), 15, 24; land conflicts and, 10–11, 18–19, 24; *reformasi* and, 16
legal cases. *See* court cases

"Legalizing Land Rights" project, 380
Li, T. M., 356n57, 377, 385n15, 386n21
Local Government Act of 2004, 135; Village Representative Councils (BPDs) and, 135–36
Lombok. *See* Gili Trawangan (Lombok); North Lombok District
Lonely Planet Bali and Lombok, 247
Lucas, Anton, 4–5

M3PEI economic master plan, 335–36
Manggarai, 216; District Court of, 230; Dutch colonial regime and, 217; forest categories and, 216–17; Forestry Use Rights (HPKH) in, 217–18
Manggarai University Students Alliance Forum, 220
Mangkoedilaga, Benjamin, 120
Marx, Karl, 102
Mawas National Park, 205
McCarthy, J., 375
media, 15, 166–67, 288, 295, 297, 383n10; biased statistics and, 29n23; Nagari Kinali agrarian protests and, 166–67, 174–75; NGOs and, 231; political leverage and, 313, 374
Megawati government, 48; decentalization and, 349n12; land speculation and 327, 48
"million hectare" Peat Land Development Project (PLG), 21–22; aftereffects of, 200–201; corporate beneficiaries of, 198; corruption, misuse of funds and, 197–98; Habibie and, 200–201; high modernist planning and, 196; summary of, 208–9; transmigration programs and, 201; World Bank and, 196
Minangkabau society, 150
Mineral and Coalmine Act of 2009, 330
mining projects, land for, 47–48; concessions and, 77n19
Ministry of Forestry: planning categories and, 194; plantation land and, 12–13; PPAN and, 334; REDD+ and, 205–6; sectoral agencies and, 344

Index   397

Mintoro, A., 51
Moa, Paulus, 228
Mohammad Hatta, 44
money politics: Colol village and, 221; district level and, 127–28; parliament, the press and, 383n10; political, religious elites and, 356n58; Village Representative Councils (BPD) and, 123–24; zoning regulations and, 138
Morad, A. A., 42, 72
Mortimer, R., 3
MPR Directive IX of 2001, 329
MPR. *See* People's Consultative Assembly (MPR)
Munggorro, D. W., 98
Mystery of Capital, The (de Soto), 95

Nagari Adat Councils (KAN), 150
nagari defined, 150
Nagari Kinali, 21, 149–50; ABMA and, 164–65; Adat Council of (KAN), 155, 156, 157; communal land and, 151–52, 160–61, 175n3, 175n13, 180n43; community protests and, 159–60, 162–63, *164*, 167, 173; Community Rights Advocacy Team and, 158, 167, 177nn123–24, 178n27; companies and, 167; compensation payments and, 160–61; government role and, 170; Kinali Subdistrict and, 159; land transfers and, 154–56; lobbying letters and, 177n23; media and, 166–67, 174–75; Padang district court and, 165; Pasaman District and, 163; population of, 175n2; protest methods and, 163–65, 178n26, 179n28, 179n33, 179nn128–29; *reformasi* and, 165–66, 174; role of the state and, 174; smallholder sector and, 161, 168, 170; state bureaucracy and, 180n38; swampy areas, usage of, 175n7; West Pasaman District and, 159. *See also* oil palm sector; plantations
Nai Roa, 224
Nasoetion, L. I., 66
National Agrarian Reform Program (PPAN), 331, 358n67; certification and, 342; core-satellite model and, 333, 357n60, 378; landholding sizes and, 333; land redistribution and, 358n65; local banks and, 357n62; Yudhoyono and, 358n64
National Awakening Party, 292
National Human Rights Commission (Komnas HAM), 10, 222, 256, 270n29, 322, 380
National Land Agency (BPN), 9–10, 66, 350n16; 1999 regulation and, 282–83; administrative procedures and, 326–27; land cases and, 17; land clearances and, 276–77, 281–82; location permits and, 13, 30n31; Ministry of Forestry and, 334; permit mechanism and, 276–77; role in land clearance and, 302n30
National Land College (STPN), 379
National Ombudsman Commission (KON), 326, 354n43
neglected land. See *tanah terlantar* (neglected, abandoned land)
New Order. *See* Suharto (New Order) regime
Noer Fauzi, 350n14, 350n15, 354n37
nongovernment organizations (NGOs), 11, 132; Flores and, 231–33; importance of, 308–9, 312; LPMAs and, 229; media and, 231; title certification and, 360n92; urban areas and, 302n25. *See also specific cases and organizations*
North Lombok District, 266
North Sumatra, 15
NTT Islands Indigenous Adat Community Movement's Network (JAGAD-NTT), 220
Nucleus Estate and Smallholder (NES) model, 153–54
Nusamba Group, 198
Nusra Tenggara Legal Aid Society, 226, 227

Oil and Natural Gas Law of 2001, 330
oil palm sector: Central Kalimantan and, 187; company leases and, 155–56, 163; government and, 187, 203; Indonesia and, 152–53; local government revenues and, 172, 174; Nagali Kinali and, 149; New Order

policy and, 152–54; Nucleus Estate and Smallholder (NES) model and, 149, 154, 161, 173; plantations and, 12, 21; smallholders and, 151, 153, 377–78; transmigration programs and, 209n7; Yudhoyono and, 204. *See also* Nagari Kinali

Old Order. *See* Sukarno (Old Order) regime

Partai Komunis Indonesia (Indonesian Communist Party): PKI, 3–4; accusations/labelling and, 115, 236n21, 254–55; growth of, 5, 9; land reform and, 3–5, 27n5; suppression of, 8, 29n19

Participatory Mapping Work Network (JKPP), 227

Pasaman District, 171, 173

Paskal Hyper Square Project, 23, 285–86, 288; authorities, developers and, 296; commercial land clearance law and, 296, 298–99; corruption and, 296; divide-and-rule and intimidation and, 295; land clearing process and, 287; litigation strategy and, 297; municipal government and, 296–97; NGOs, student movements and, 297; People's Aspiration Team protests and, 287–88; permit mechanism and, 286–87; regional autonomy and, 296; residents lack of trust in legal institutions and, 297–98; squatters and, 286; summary of, 295–96

patok defined, 139n14

Payment for Environmental Services, 206

peasants: global economy and, 376, 381; income sources and, 57, 59–60; land-grabbing and, 377; political networks and, 338–40; social and cultural strategies and, 340; *tani* defined, 27n5. *See also* agricultural productivity; poverty

people-based agriculture, land for, 50

People's Coalition against Land Grabbing, 358n75

People's Confederation Party (PPR): agrarian reform and, 338–39;

disqualification and, 339, 359n80; formation of, 338

People's Consultative Assembly (MPR), 311, 313, 350n13, 351n17, 351n20; agrarian reform and, 316–17; Bandung conference and, 315–16; Parliamentary Directive on Agrarian Reform and Management of Natural Resources of 2001, 317

Perum Perhutani, 16

petani, 78n27

PKI. *See* Partai Komunis Indonesia (Indonesian Communist Party): PKI

Plantation Law of 2004, 329–30

plantations, 12–13, 173; commercial use leases (HGUs) and, 12–15, 19, 76n12, 153–57, 174, 176n12, 223–29, 245–46, 250–53; companies, community leaders and, 159; investors, the state and, 153; land for, 48; New Order and, 30n29; Nucleus Estate and Smallholder (NES) model and, 153–54; smallholder sector and, 161–63; speculation and, 13; statistics on, 12–13; UU 51/1960 and, 29–30n26. *See also* oil palm sector

PN VI, 174, 178n27

poverty: land clearances and, 281; land-grabbing and, 377; landholding and, 51, 58; landlessness and, 21, 50–53, 60–63, 70, 79n39; land reform and, 375, 377

PPAN. *See* National Agrarian Reform Program (PPAN)

Pramoedya Ananta Toer, 1

preman, 15, 121, 143, 219, 222–24, 266, 289, 291, 295, 387n24; land speculation and, 383n6

Protection of Agricultural Land for Food Sustainability law of 2009, 373

PT AMP, 168, 178n26

PT Argo Pantas, 121, 142n29

PT BAM (Bandung Asri Mulya), 116, 117; civil action against Cimacan farmers and, 119; compensation and, 143n42; eviction of Cimacan farmers from golf course, 121

PT Bukit Asri Padang Golf, 121–22; compensation payments and, 129–30, 133

Index 399

PT Citra Buana Prasida (PT CBP), 285–86; "assistance/sympathy money" and, 287, 289–90
PT Diag (Archdiocese of Ende), 224
PT Generasi Jaya, 244–45, 251, 267n3, 268n9, 272n41; abandonment of, 246–47
PT Gili Trawangan Indah (GTI), 266; compensation offer of, 252–53; resort development and, 252; smallholder sector and, 253–54; squatters and, 258
PT Inhutani III, 199
PT Jayanti Group, 190
PT KAI. *See* Indonesian Railway Company (PT KAI)
PT Lintas Inter Nusa, 168; credit need and, 169
PT Mengkatip, 190
PT Perkebunan Nusantara VI, 154
PT PMJ, 168
PT Rente Mario, 199
PT Rinta, 246; granted plots and, 261; patronage, corruption and, 245
PT Sumatera Timur, 192
PT TSG, 164–65, 168, 169, 170, 174, 178n26
PTUN. *See* Administrative Courts

Rachman, Fauzi. *See* Noer Fauzi
Rajuddin Nuh, 154
Raptor Conservation Society, 138
reclaimed lands, 34–35n66
redistribution, land availability for, 42
Reducing Emissions from Deforestation and Degradation (REDD+), 205–6
Reerink, Gustaaf, 103–4, 107
reformasi agraria, 8, 13, 33–34, 337–38, 343; Cimacan land dispute and, 121–22; decentralization of government and, 150–51; economic decline and recovery and, 284; local government financing and, 172; Nagari Kinali and, 165–66; rule of law and, 284, 329; transition to democracy and, 339–40. *See also* National Agrarian Reform Program (PPAN); Yudohyono regime

Regional Autonomy Law of 1999, 232–33, 300n5; BPDs and, 125; district level autonomy and, 135; land clearances and, 283–84; *sekretaris desa* and, 238n35
Regional Government and Revenue Allocation Acts of 1999, 123, 325–26
registration of land. *See* land registration
released and unreleased land, 25
release of title procedures, 13–14
residential, tourist, industrial projects, land for, 48–49
resource control, BAL and rice production. *See under* agricultural productivity
Rona, Ibu, 257, 259–60
Rotok, Christian, 222
Rudini, 119, 140n20

Safitri, H., 343, 385n16, 386n117
Sagara case (Garut, West Java), 342–43
Sajogyo Institute, 379
Saleh, C., 51
Salim, Sacono, 142n29
Salim conglomerate, 12–13
Sambu Group, 192
Sareng, Ben, 236n25
Schmink, M., 183
Scott, J. C., 195–96
Serangan Island, 269n21
Servas Lawang, 220–21
Service to the People for Land Registration (LARASITA) of 2008, 342
Share Cropping Act of 1960, 41
SKEPHI, 46, 121, 129–32
"sleeping lands" *(tanah tidur)*, 13, 32n40, 66, 100, 103, 107n9, 204, 327, 374, 384n13. *See also tanah terlantar* (neglected, abandoned land)
Socially Concerned University Students Forum, 220
Soeparman Natajuda, 288
Sofandi, Haji, 136, 145n55
Soge people, 223–24
Special Committee on Agrarian Conflict Resolution of 2012, 379
State land. *See tanah negara* (state land)

statistical data, 79nn39–40
Struyk, R. J., 281
Suharto (New Order) regime, 1–2, 8–9, 281; as agent of development, 191–92; BAL/UUPA and, 8–9; Central Kalimantan and, 186–87; collapse of, 14; commodification of land and, 43–46; land policy, disputes and, 43–46, 274; land reform and, 62, 93; "million hectare" Peat Land Development Project (PLG) and, 184–85, 380; oil palm and, 152–56; peasant agriculture and, 53, *54*; PKI and, 29n19; rice production and, 191–92; "sleeping" land and, 384n13; transmigration programs and, 45, 56; village government and, 122, 150. *See also* Green Revolution; transmigration programs
Sukarno (Old Order) regime, 1–2, 3, 6, 326; Islamic Youth Movement and, 305n81; land reform and, 29, 56, 70, 326; "Progress of Our Revolution," 40–41; rice farming and, 76n15; *tani* and, 20, 27
Sundanese Peasant Union (SPP), 315–16, 328, 334, 351n23; alliance with KPA and, 345; effectiveness of, 341–42, 346; grassroots interests and, 340; Islamic missionary corps and, 340; land distribution and, 360n88, 360n90; land reform by leverage and, 338, 344; PPAN and, 335; sale of occupied land and, 360n91; seven principles of, 315–16; sustainability and, 341–42

Tana 'Ai rajadom, 223, 236n22, 237n28
tanah ganjaran, 33n56
Tanah Lot, 269n21
tanah negara (state land), 5, 9, 28n13
tanah terlantar (neglected, abandoned land), 66, 246, 251, 337
tani (petani) defined, 27n5
TapMPR IX of 2001, 317–18, 352n30, 374; agrarian reform *versus* natural resource management and, 323; constitutional law and, 353n32; drafts of, 353n31; genuine reform and, 324; KPA/KPSA and, 354n41; NGOs and, 352n24; shortcomings of, 319–20, 325; unanswered questions and, 323–24
Tempo magazine, 120
TGHK (Tata Guna Hutan Kesepakatan), 80n51
Thailand, 99–100
Tjondronegoro, Sediono MP, 350n15, 351n17, 353n31, 356n56
TK.ZB, 156–57, 158
transmigration programs, 5, 7, 44, 45–46, 56, 76n14, 93; Central Kalimantan and, 186, 190–91, 195; families, redistributed land and, *45*; indigenous people and, 46
TR Company, 161
TSG Company, 160, 161–62

Ujar, 144n51
United Nations: Draft Declaration on Indigenous People, 310; International Covenant on Economic, Social and Cultural Rights, 311
University of Indonesia, 233
Uray, Burhan, 190
USAID, 98
Utan Wair village, 222–23, 224–25; clearing of diocesan plantation land and, 226

van Huis, S., 310
Vel, J., 375
Village Government Law of 1979, 122–23,
Village Representative Councils (BPDs), 123; Local Government Act of 2004 and, 135; money politics and, 123–24; Village Consultation Councils (BMDs) and, 142n31
virtual land grabs, 375, 385n15. *See also* land grabs

Walhi, 385n14
Warr, P., 356n57
Warsito Rasman, 192
Water Resources Management Law of 2004, 330

Weber, Max, 102
West Java, 17; reasons for land cases in, 114
West Java Peasants Union (SPJB), 114; TapMPR IX of 2001 and, 319
West Papua land grab, 385n14
West Pasaman District, 151–52
West Sumatran University Students Communication Forum (FKMS), 177n25
West Sumatra Provincial Government Regulation of 2000, 151
Wetlands International, 204
White, B., 51–52
Wiradi, G., 322, 356n56
Wiranto, G., 5
women: land ownership and, 96–97, 107nn6–7; politics and, 143n37; resistance and, 257, 270n30

Wood, C. H., 183
World Bank, 21, 106; administrative procedures and, 326–27; land policies of, 333; LAP evaluation and, 94, 96, 98; perspective on land conflicts and, 354n44; PLG project and, 196; Railway Efficiency Project and, 285; study of agricultural investments and, 376, 377
World Trade Organization (WTO), 333

Yayasan Petak Danum (YPD), 204
Yudohyono regime, 105, 202–3, 322; agrarian reform and, 331–32; land reform and, 109n22; ministers' political parties and, 358n66; PPAN and, 358n64; *reforma agraria* and, 356n55

Contributors

AFRIZAL lectures in the Department of Sociology, Faculty of Social and Political Science, Andalas University in Padang, West Sumatra. He works with a number of nongovernment organizations and has published on agrarian conflict and agrarian movements, including the regulation and the resolution of agrarian conflict in Indonesia. His publications include *Sosiologi Konflik Agraria: Protes-Protes Agraria dalam Masyarakat Indonesia Kontemporer* (2006); *The Nagari Community, Business and the State: The Origin and the Process of Contemporary Agrarian Protest in West Sumatra* (2007); *Pembangunan dan Konflik: Hasil Penelitian Para Dosen Ilmu-Ilmu Sosial Universitas Andalas* (2010). His current research interests include the use of mediation in agrarian conflict resolution.

DIANTO BACHRIADI is a scholar-activist and researcher at the Agrarian Resource Center (ARC) in Bandung and a member of the Advisory Board of the Consortium for Agrarian Reform (KPA). His research interests include land conflicts, agrarian transformation, and rural social movements. His publications include *Ketergantungan Petani dan Penetrasi Kapital* (1995); *Merana di Tengah Kelimpahan* (1998); *Enam Dekade Ketimpangan: Masalah Penguasaan Tanah di Indonesia* (2011, coauthored with Gunawan Wiradi); and *Land, Rural Social Movements and Democratisation in Indonesia* (2009). He can be contacted at dianto.bachriadi@gmail.com.

ANTON LUCAS is an adjunct associate professor in the School of International Studies at Flinders University. His publications include *One Soul One Struggle: Region and Revolution in Indonesia* (1991);

One Soul One Struggle: Peristiwa Tiga Daerah (2004); *Merampas Tanah Rakyat: Kasus Tapos dan Cimacan* (2001, coauthored with Dianto Bachriadi); and *Radikalisme Lokal: Oposisi dan Perlawanan terhadap Pendudukan Jepang di Jawa* (1942–45) (2012, editor). His current research interests include decentralization and reform, the politics of natural resources conflicts and agrarian change in post-Suharto Indonesia.

JOHN MCCARTHY lectures in the Australian National University's Crawford School. He researches issues concerning agrarian change, land tenure, environmental governance, and natural resource policy. He has carried out various assignments with agencies in Australia and Indonesia, including AusAID and the Centre for International Forestry Research (CIFOR). His publications include *A Political Ecology of Sumatra's Rainforest Frontier* (2006), and *Community, Environment and Local Governance in Indonesia: Locating the Commonweal* (2009, coedited with Carol Warren), as well as recent publications in *World Development* and *The Journal of Peasant Studies*.

JOHN MANSFORD PRIOR teaches at St. Paul's Institute of Philosophy Ledalero, in the Maumere district of Flores in Nusa Tenggara Timur, where he has lived since 1973. His interests include issues of faith and culture among the marginalized in rapidly changing indigenous societies. Recent publications include "Researching Mission: Rooted Locally, Engaged Globally," *Verbum SVD* (2011); "Antara Monarki dan Demokrasi: Melacak Jejak Laku Hirarki Gereja 40 Tahun Terakhir," in *Allah Menggugat, Allah Menyembuhkan*, edited by Paul Budi Kleden, Otto Gusti Madang, and Anselm Meo (2012), and *"Timor," Religion Past and Present* (2012). John is senior researcher at Candraditya Research Centre, Maumere, and an Honorary Researcher at MCD University of Divinity in Melbourne, Australia.

GUSTAAF REERINK is a former PhD researcher of the Van Vollenhoven Institute for Law, Governance and Development at Leiden University. He completed, defended, and published his dissertation *Tenure Security for Indonesia's Urban Poor: A Social-Legal Study on*

Land, Decentralisation and the Rule of Law in Bandung (Leiden University Press) in 2011. Currently, he works as an attorney-at-law in Jakarta.

CAROL WARREN is a Fellow of the Asia Research Centre at Murdoch University. She teaches sociology and anthropology and has published widely on customary law, social change, and environmental politics in Indonesia and Malaysia. Her publications include *Adat and Dinas: Balinese Communities in the Indonesian State* (1993), *The Politics of Environment in Southeast Asia* (1998, coedited with Philip Hirsch), and *Community, Environment and Local Governance in Indonesia: Locating the Commonweal* (2009, coedited with John McCarthy). Her current research interests include sustainable community development, indigenous rights, and cultural heritage policy.

GUNAWAN WIRADI is a member of the Advisory Board of the Consortium for Agrarian Reform (KPA). He is a senior rural sociologist in Indonesia, and a mentor for many Indonesian agrarian reform scholar-activists. He has published widely on agrarian reform and rural transformation in Indonesia, including *Reforma Agraria: Perjalanan Yang Belum Berakhir* (2000); *Good Times and Bad Times in Rural Java* (2002, coauthored with Jan Breman); *Enam Dekade Ketimpangan: Masalah Penguasaan Tanah di Indonesia Six* (2011, coauthored with Dianto Bachriadi). He received an honorary doctorate in Rural Sociology (Agrarian Studies) from the Bogor Institute of Agriculture (IPB) in 2009.

RICHARD ROBINSON
OF COUNTERSETT
1628 – 1693

AND

THE QUAKERS
OF WENSLEYDALE

Front Cover   *Countersett Hall, the home of Richard and Margaret Robinson and their descendants from 1650 to 1794. A truly vernacular house standing virtually unchanged, as solid as the Crag behind it.*
Photograph by J. C. Moore, Harrogate, 1968.

Back Cover   *The trefoil headed fire window chosen by Richard and Margaret Robinson for a bedroom at Countersett Hall.*
Photograph by J. C. Moore, Harrogate, 1968.

Richard Robinson's personal seal drawn from an original impression surviving in the Philip Swale manuscripts.